HISTORIC PHOTOS OF
ERNEST HEMINGWAY

TEXT AND CAPTIONS BY JAMES PLATH

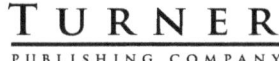

TURNER
PUBLISHING COMPANY

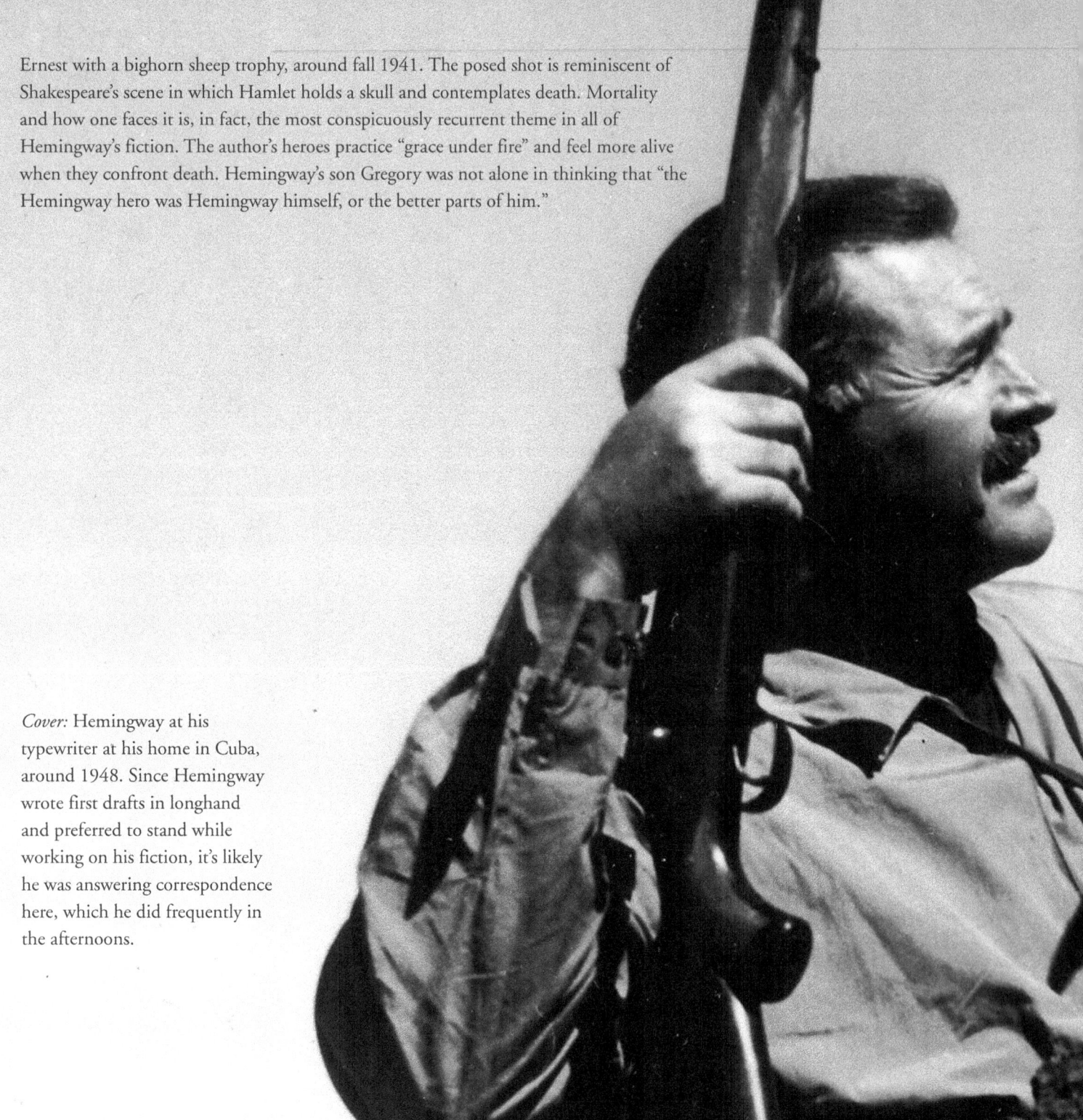

Ernest with a bighorn sheep trophy, around fall 1941. The posed shot is reminiscent of Shakespeare's scene in which Hamlet holds a skull and contemplates death. Mortality and how one faces it is, in fact, the most conspicuously recurrent theme in all of Hemingway's fiction. The author's heroes practice "grace under fire" and feel more alive when they confront death. Hemingway's son Gregory was not alone in thinking that "the Hemingway hero was Hemingway himself, or the better parts of him."

Cover: Hemingway at his typewriter at his home in Cuba, around 1948. Since Hemingway wrote first drafts in longhand and preferred to stand while working on his fiction, it's likely he was answering correspondence here, which he did frequently in the afternoons.

HISTORIC PHOTOS OF
ERNEST HEMINGWAY

Turner Publishing Company
www.turnerpublishing.com

Historic Photos of Ernest Hemingway

Copyright © 2009 Turner Publishing Company

Library of Congress Control Number: 2008938802

ISBN-13: 978-1-59652-516-0

Printed in the United States of America

ISBN 978-1-68442-041-4 (hc)

CONTENTS

ACKNOWLEDGMENTS...VII

PREFACE VIII

FROM OAK PARK TO PARIS
    (1899–1925) 1

WRITING AND OTHER ADVENTURES
    (1926–1938) 57

ONE HUNDRED PERCENT PAPA
    (1939–1951) 115

LIFE TAKES ITS TOLL
    (1952–1961) 153

NOTES ON THE PHOTOGRAPHS 202

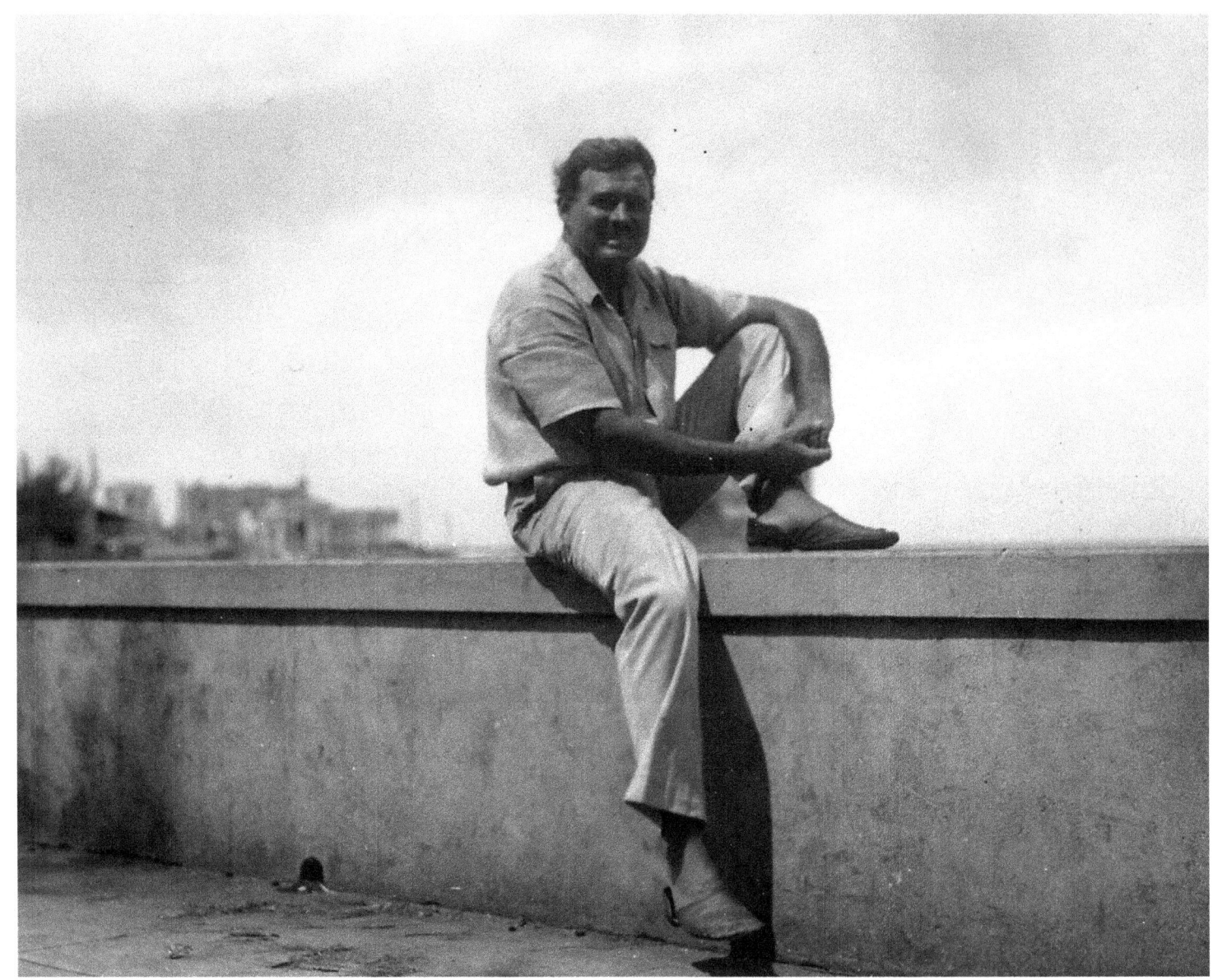

When Hemingway posed for this photo on one of his first trips to the fishing village of Cojímar, there was no way he could have known he would become a Cuban national hero—or that after his death, the fishermen of Cojímar would donate their propellers and other bronze from their boats to build a bust of Hemingway that would rest in a place of honor not far from where he sits now.

ACKNOWLEDGMENTS

This volume, *Historic Photos of Ernest Hemingway,* is the result of the cooperation and efforts of many individuals, organizations, and corporations. It is with great thanks that we acknowledge the valuable contribution of the following for their generous support:

John F. Kennedy Presidential Library and Museum
Landov Media
Oak Park and River Forest High School
Princeton University Library

The author would also like to thank Laurie Austin, Jessica Caum, Steven Cox, Valerie Hemingway, Gunnel Leavens, Forrest MacMullen, Michael McCalip, Bill Smallwood, René Villarreal, and Don Vogel of Oak Park and River Forest High School for their assistance.

to Michael Whalton and Lorian Hemingway,
for the Hemingway Days that turned into years

PREFACE

Like Mark Twain before him, Ernest Hemingway became the most celebrated writer of his time. After cameras found the nineteen-year-old in Milan, where he was lauded as the first American wounded on the Italian front during World War I, and after *The Sun Also Rises* became known as the quintessential novel of the Lost Generation, he remained in the public eye for most of his life. Everything Hemingway did was news, whether it was writing another article or book, hunting in Africa and the American West, big-game fishing in the Gulf Stream, skiing with socialites and movie stars, covering four different wars as a correspondent, following bullfighters on the summer circuit, or just traveling with one of his four wives (or rumored mistresses). He was a creative genius, certainly, but he was also a public figure and the embodiment of American robustness and vigor—a two-fisted drinker, brawler, and adventurer the world came to know as "Papa."

Hemingway, like Twain, did not shrink from publicity. He reveled in it, as attested by more than 10,000 photographs in the Ernest Hemingway archive at the John F. Kennedy Library and another 2,000 at the Museo Ernest Hemingway in Cuba that are not as yet public. Hemingway usually gave photographers what they wanted, allowing them to document his every move and every mood, and he frequently signed photos for friends and admirers, as they did for him. Often the photographers were friends and admirers. But he was so conscious of his image that he sometimes wanted to approve photos that appeared in magazines, and he was an enigma to even his closest pals: a mixture of truth and lies, of put-downs and put-ons, of understatements and exaggerations. One minute he needed people around him, and the next he required solitude. At times he could be extremely generous or tolerant, at other times he was quick-tempered and vindictive. He could be bombastic and blustery, or soft-spoken and congenial. The only constants were his desire to write "one true sentence" and a spirit of adventure that was patterned after his boyhood hero, Teddy Roosevelt, which led him to live in scenic places like Key West, Cuba, and Idaho and to test his mettle almost constantly.

Hemingway's Papa persona was a ruggedly romantic figure that dispelled the image of a mild-mannered, solitary writer whose only world was words. Though some, like writer Max Eastman, would accuse him of having "false hair" on his chest, and though a feminist backlash would later come, the public was fascinated by Hemingway's macho personality and adventurous life-style because it meshed well with the ideal man projected on the big screen by actors like John Wayne, Clark Gable, and Humphrey Bogart. But if his man's man persona was timely, his writing was way ahead of its time. Hemingway's prose style was so distinctive that *Transatlantic Review* editor Ford Madox Ford declared after reading only six of his sentences that he would publish anything the young author would ever write. Just as he was a life force, Hemingway quickly became a literary force whose stripped-down prose was imitated on college campuses and writers' garrets all across the country. He shunned adjectives and strived for objective writing that could capture the actual feel of a thing rather than simply describing it, and he created dialogue that was unmistakably stylized. Like modernist artists who railed against the notion that art must be beautiful, Hemingway frequently turned to society's down-and-outs for his characters. His themes caused critics like Philip Young to take note of a Hemingway hero who lived by a code and the young aspirant who tried to learn that code. Quickly, Hemingway's novels and such short stories as "Hills Like White Elephants" and "The Short Happy Life of Francis Macomber" became staples in high school and college classrooms.

Acclaim came early in his career, while awards came late. Critics praised *The Sun Also Rises* (1926) and *A Farewell to Arms* (1929), but *For Whom the Bell Tolls* (1940) was a blockbuster best-seller that prompted mixed reviews. Then came a literary drought that had critics claiming Hemingway the writer was down for the count. It wasn't until he bounced back with *The Old Man and the Sea* (1952) that Hemingway received his first major literary award—a Pulitzer Prize. The Nobel Prize in Literature followed, honoring him for a body of work that included seven novels published during his lifetime, six collections of short stories, and four works of nonfiction.

Since his death in 1961, Hemingway has remained a literary force. No fewer than six books of his writings have been published posthumously, and he remains as famous today as when he appeared on the covers of *Time, Look,* and *Life* magazines. There are busts and monuments to him in Italy, Spain, Idaho, Cuba, Paris, Key West, and practically every place Hemingway spent any length of time. More literary criticism devoted to Hemingway and his work is published every year than is devoted to any other American author, and festivals celebrating his life and life-style continue to thrive. His face, commemorated on United States—and Cuban, Czechoslovakian, and Central African—postage stamps, remains one of the most recognizable, and although *Time* named him one of the century's most influential people and Hemingway consciously played the role of Papa, what mattered to him most was the company of ordinary people, as many of these photos illustrate. Hemingway granted photographers far more access than reporters, whom he mistrusted and often misled. But it's hard to lie to a camera.

—*James Plath*

Ernest Miller Hemingway was named for his maternal grandfather and uncle. He weighed 9.5 pounds and measured 23 inches at birth, with blue eyes and dark hair. Of this earliest photo taken professionally when he was four weeks old, his mother said he looks "sweetly satisfied"—perhaps because her second child and first son was breast-fed on demand and, she implied, he could be quite demanding.

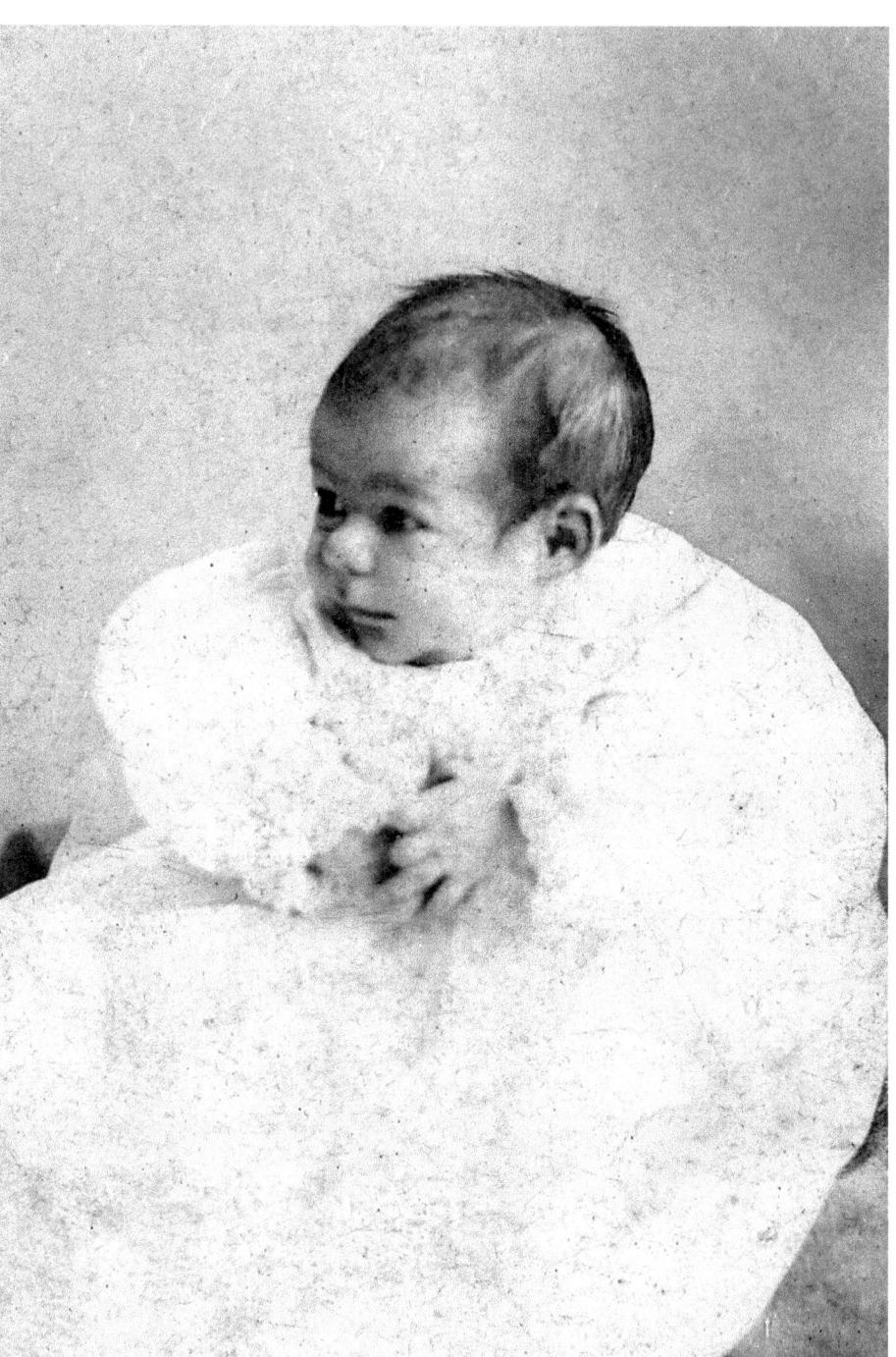

From Oak Park to Paris

(1899–1925)

Ernest Miller Hemingway came into this world on July 21, 1899, the second of six children born to a respected doctor and a society matron who had trained to become an opera singer. Both parents worked out of their home in Oak Park, Illinois, with Dr. Clarence "Ed" Hemingway practicing medicine and Grace Hall Hemingway giving music lessons. Ernest's siblings were Marcelline (1898), Ursula (1902), Madelaine or "Sunny" (1904), Carol (1911), and Leicester (1915). By all accounts, their family life was a normal one. Like others of their social standing, the Hemingways had two live-in servants, one of whom was assigned to help with the children.

Ernest attended Oak Park and River Forest High School but felt that college wasn't as useful as life experiences, especially for what he wanted to become: a writer. Partly that proved true, but Hemingway also had excellent instruction every step of the way. His father was his first great teacher. An accomplished woodsman and naturalist, Ed Hemingway taught Ernest everything he knew about the outdoors and inculcated in him a love of nature, hunting, and fishing. In high school, Ernest's talent was discovered and nurtured by two English teachers, Fannie Biggs and Margaret Dixon. And when he joined the staff of the *Kansas City Star* fresh out of high school, Ernest had the good fortune of being able to observe a legendary newsman named Lionel Moise, who was the highest paid reporter everywhere he worked, for good reason.

Later, when Ernest was trying to break into print and patterning his fiction after stories he saw in popular magazines like *Red Book, Vanity Fair,* and *Argosy,* he found another mentor in Sherwood Anderson, a writer he met in Chicago. Anderson told Ernest that slick fiction was "a perversion of life" and that modernism was the wave of the future. He helped Hemingway discover literary magazines like *The Dial, Poetry,* and *The Little Review,* and advised him to go to Paris, where Hemingway would find another mentor in Gertrude Stein. Then F. Scott Fitzgerald would lead him to Max Perkins, one of the best editors of their time. From 1899 until 1925, the year he finished writing the first draft of *The Sun Also Rises*—the novel that would launch his literary career—Hemingway learned by doing, but also by being a willing pupil.

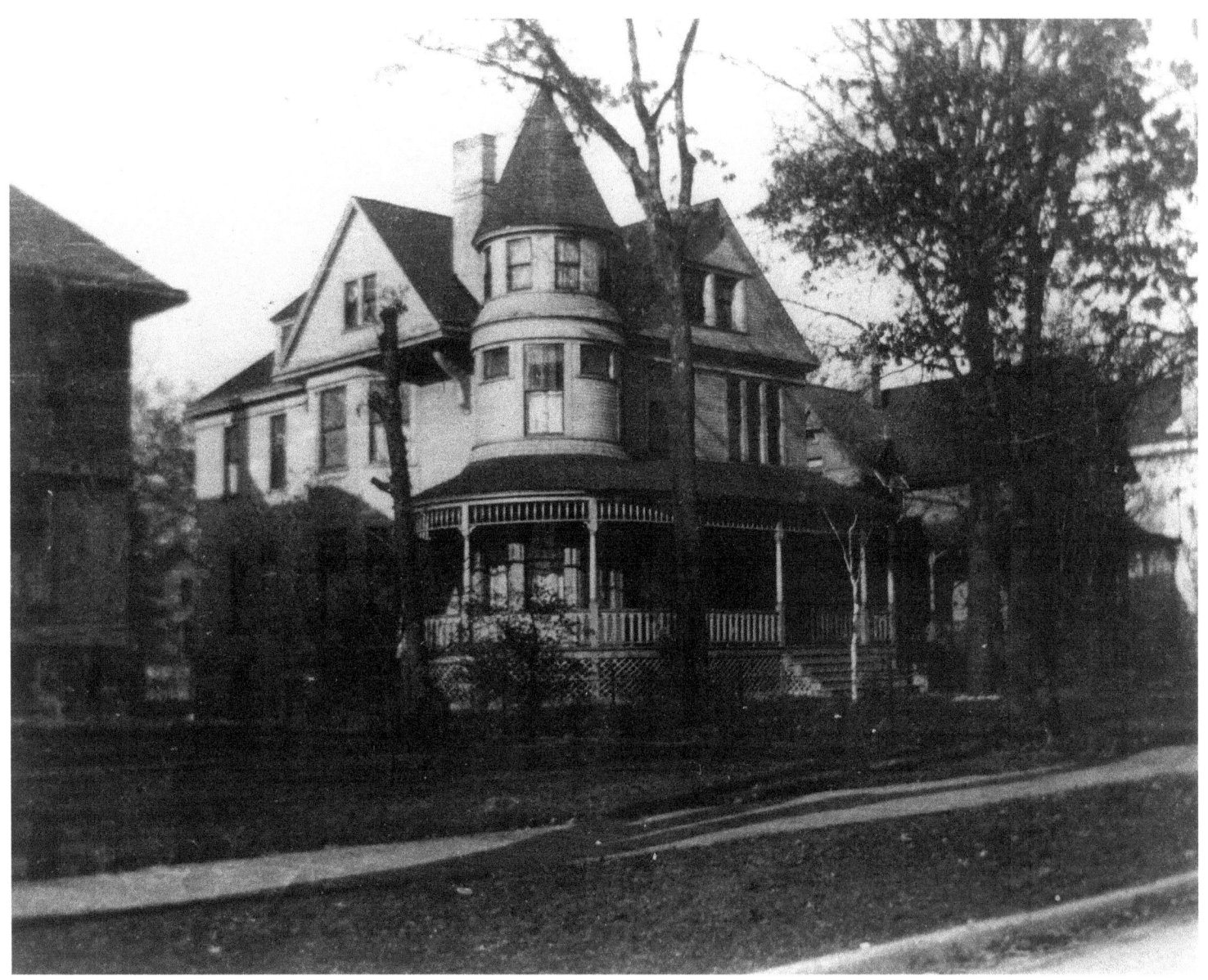

Ernest was born in the house at 439 N. Oak Park Avenue (now 339), which was owned by his maternal grandfather. His parents, Dr. Clarence and Grace Hall Hemingway, had been living with the recently widowed Ernest Hall since they married in 1896. Dr. Hemingway, who specialized in obstetrics, probably handled the delivery himself. The house is now a museum owned and run by the Ernest Hemingway Foundation of Oak Park.

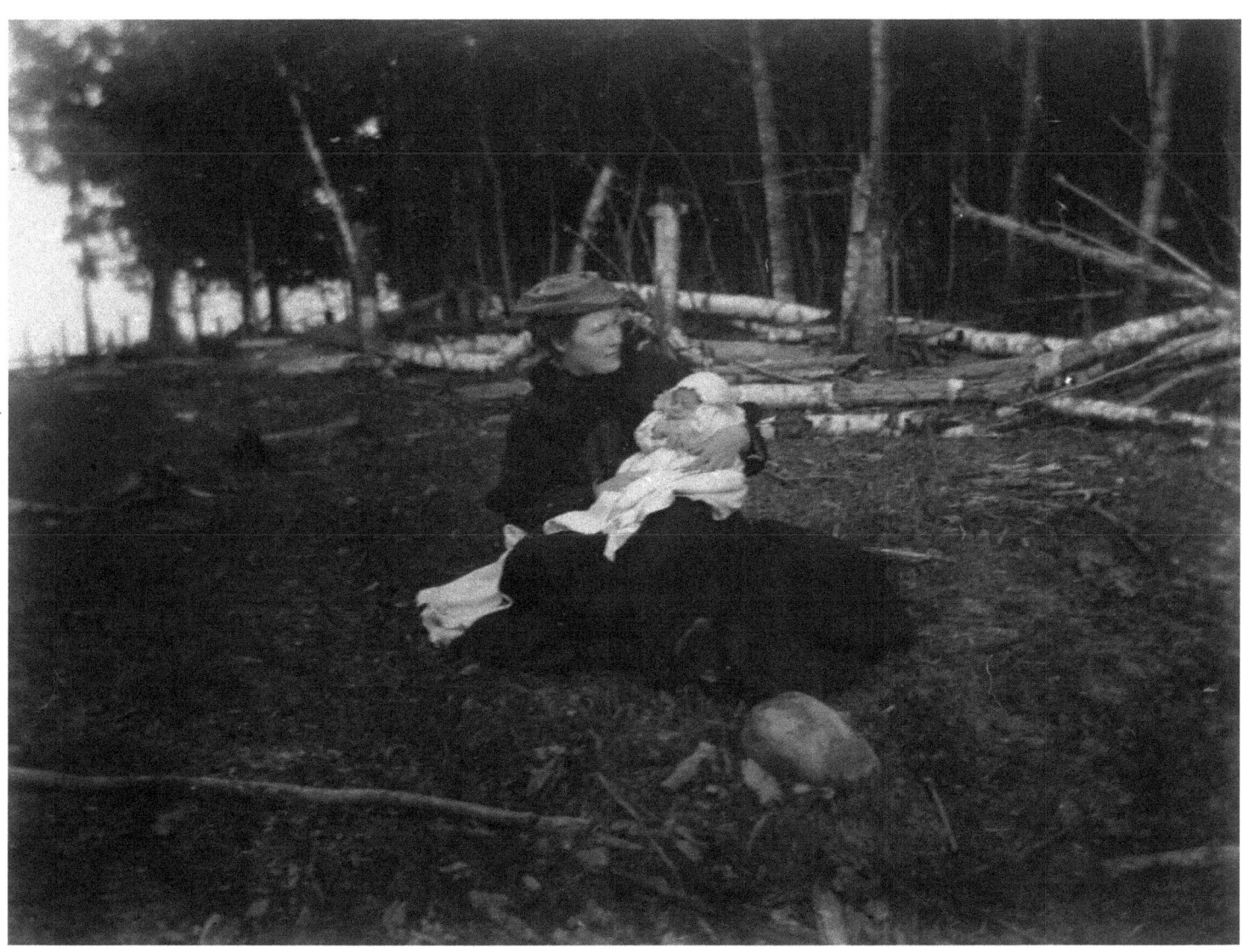

Before his birth, the family had plans to go to Bear (now Walloon) Lake in upper Michigan, where they had built a cottage the previous year. When he was old enough to travel (age seven weeks), Hemingway had his first adventure, for the trip from Oak Park to the family's favorite lake near Petoskey was a grueling one, requiring travel by horse and buggy, trains, steamship, and a rowboat. This photo was taken at Bear Lake on September 6, 1899.

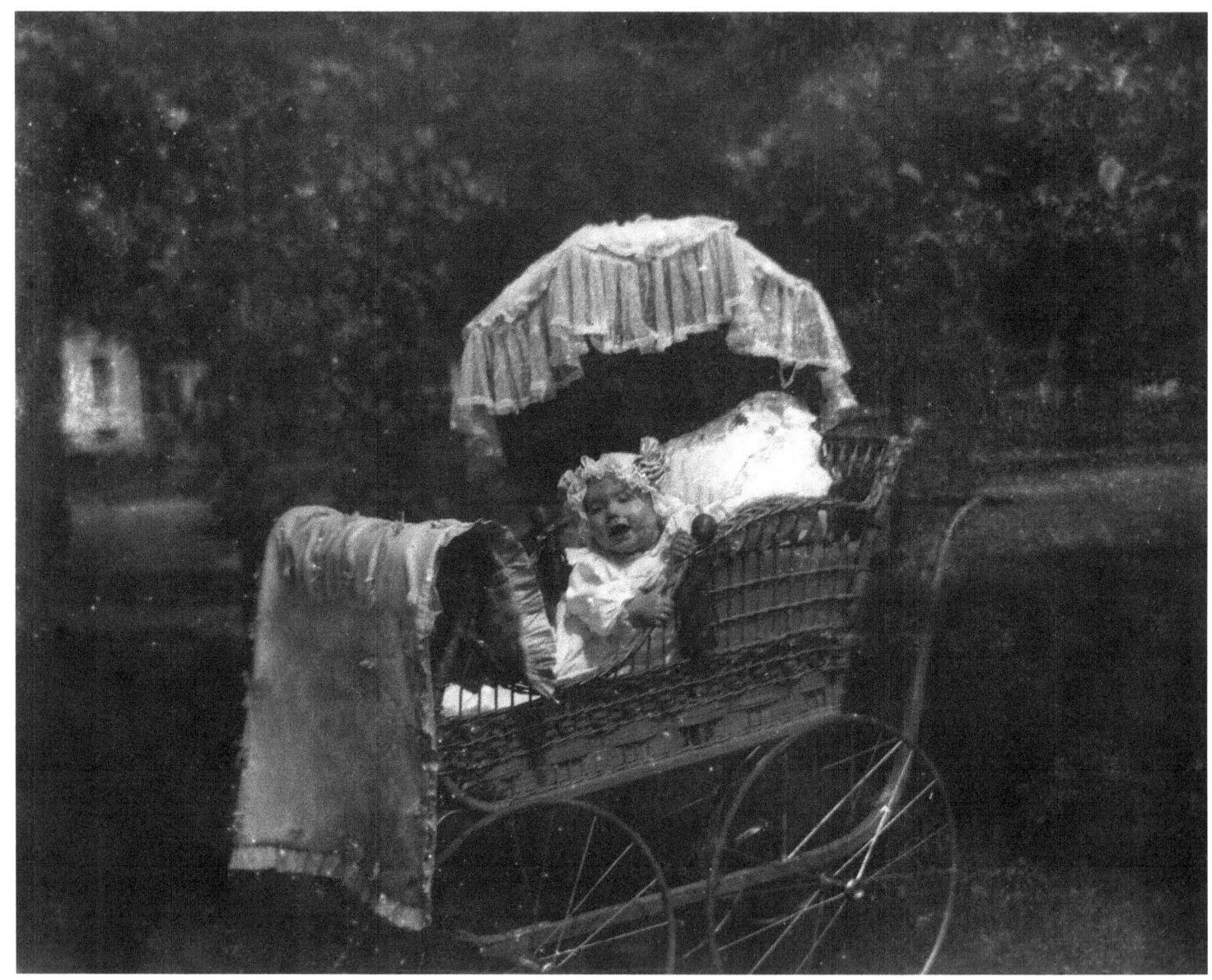

In his carriage back home in Oak Park, baby Ernest seems inclined to escape, ready for another adventure. Hemingway's first toys were exotic dolls: an American Indian papoose and an Eskimo, the latter given to him by his father. His first sentence? "I don't know Buffalo Bill."

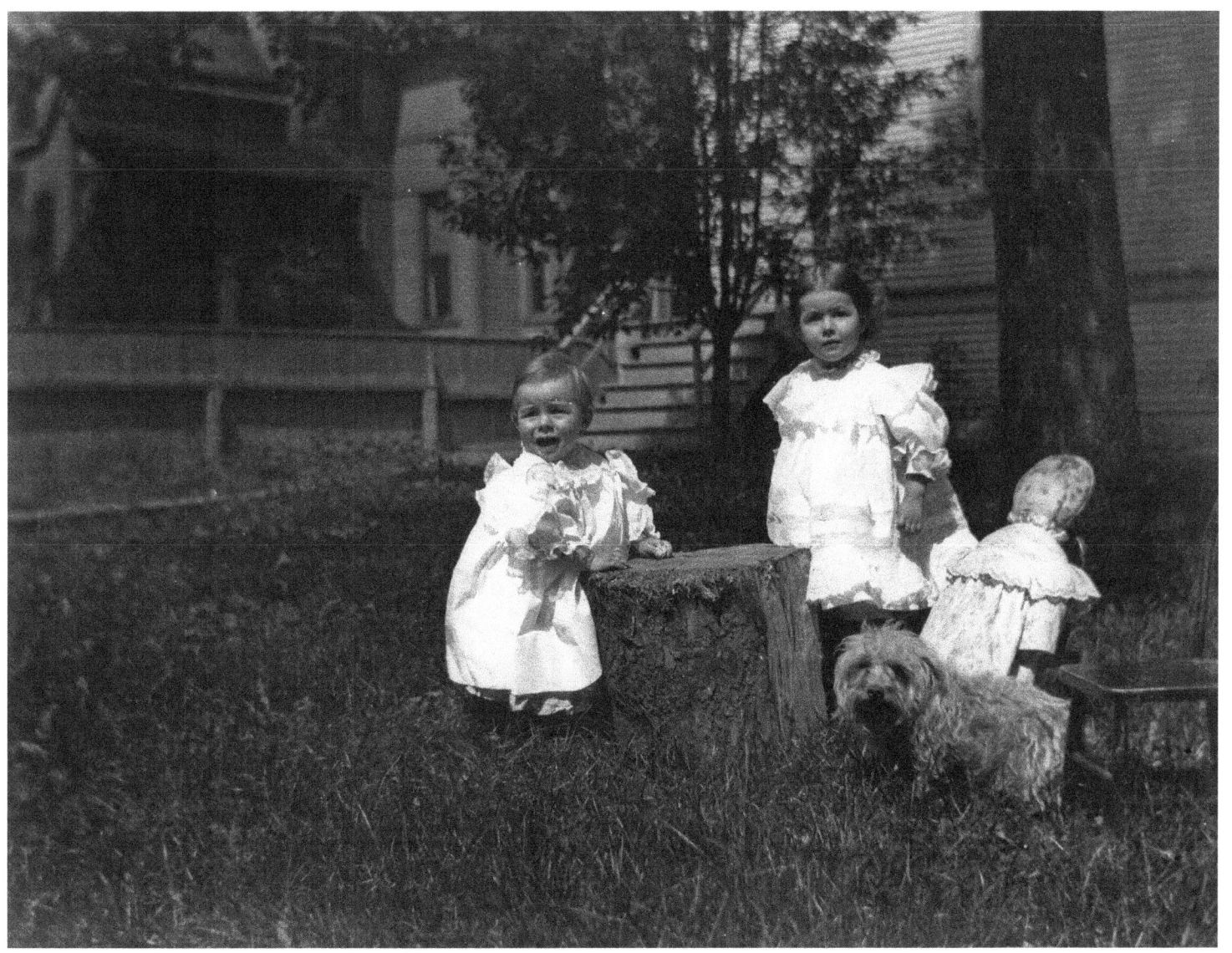

In the backyard at 439 N. Oak Park, Ernest (left) plays with big sister Marcelline, a doll, and the family dog. As an adult, Hemingway would complain about the village's broad, manicured lawns and narrow minds, which he couldn't wait to put behind him. It was a community so conservative that no alcohol could be sold within village limits from the time it was incorporated until the law was changed in 1973 to accommodate restaurants.

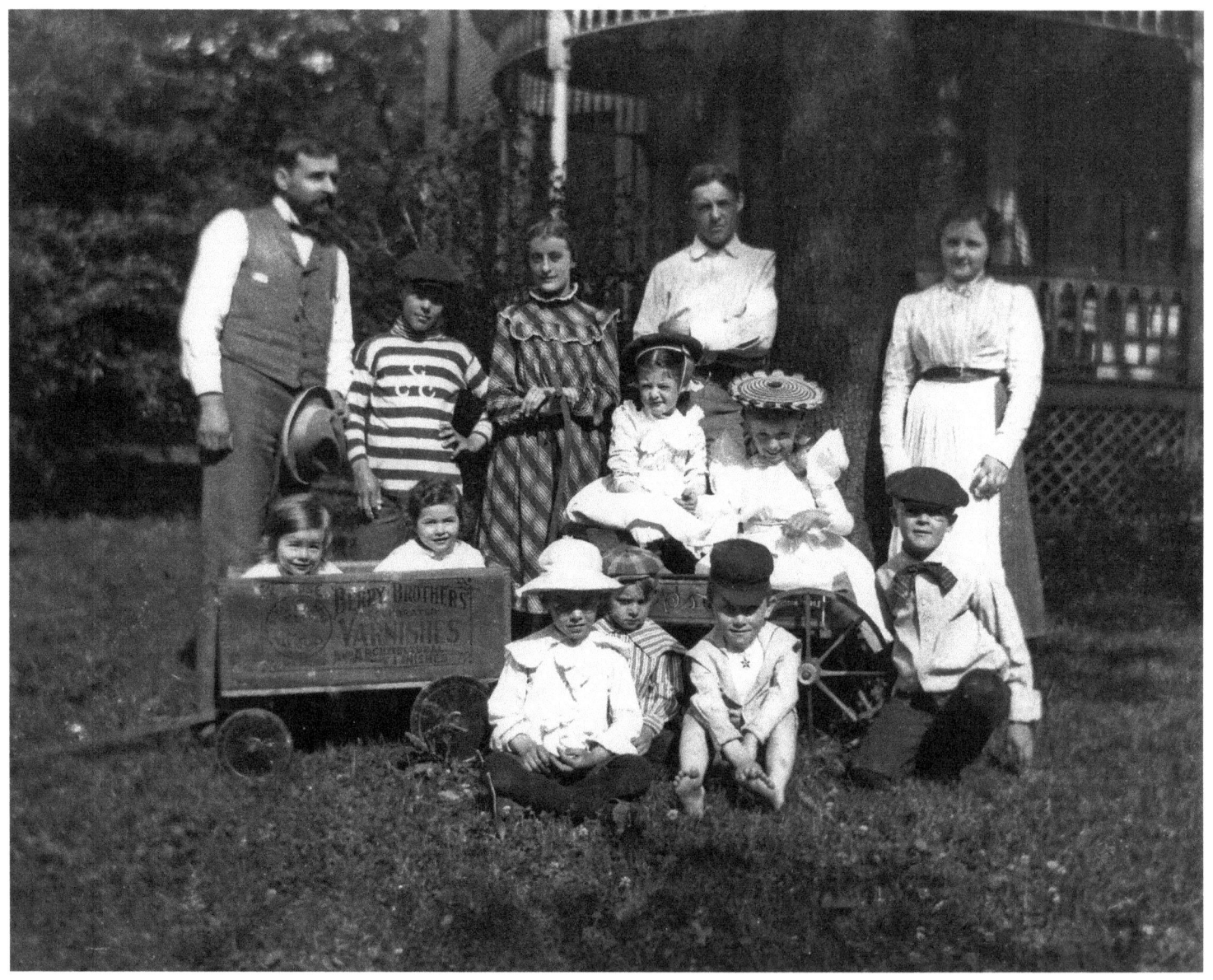

In 1901, the first nickelodeon was built in nearby Chicago, causing an uproar among parents worried about the effect that storefront amusements might have on their children. Though Oak Park was only nine miles west, it was far removed from such concerns. Here, neighbors gather for a photograph. Dr. Hemingway is on the left, while in front of him in the wagon are his two children, Ernest (left) and Marcy.

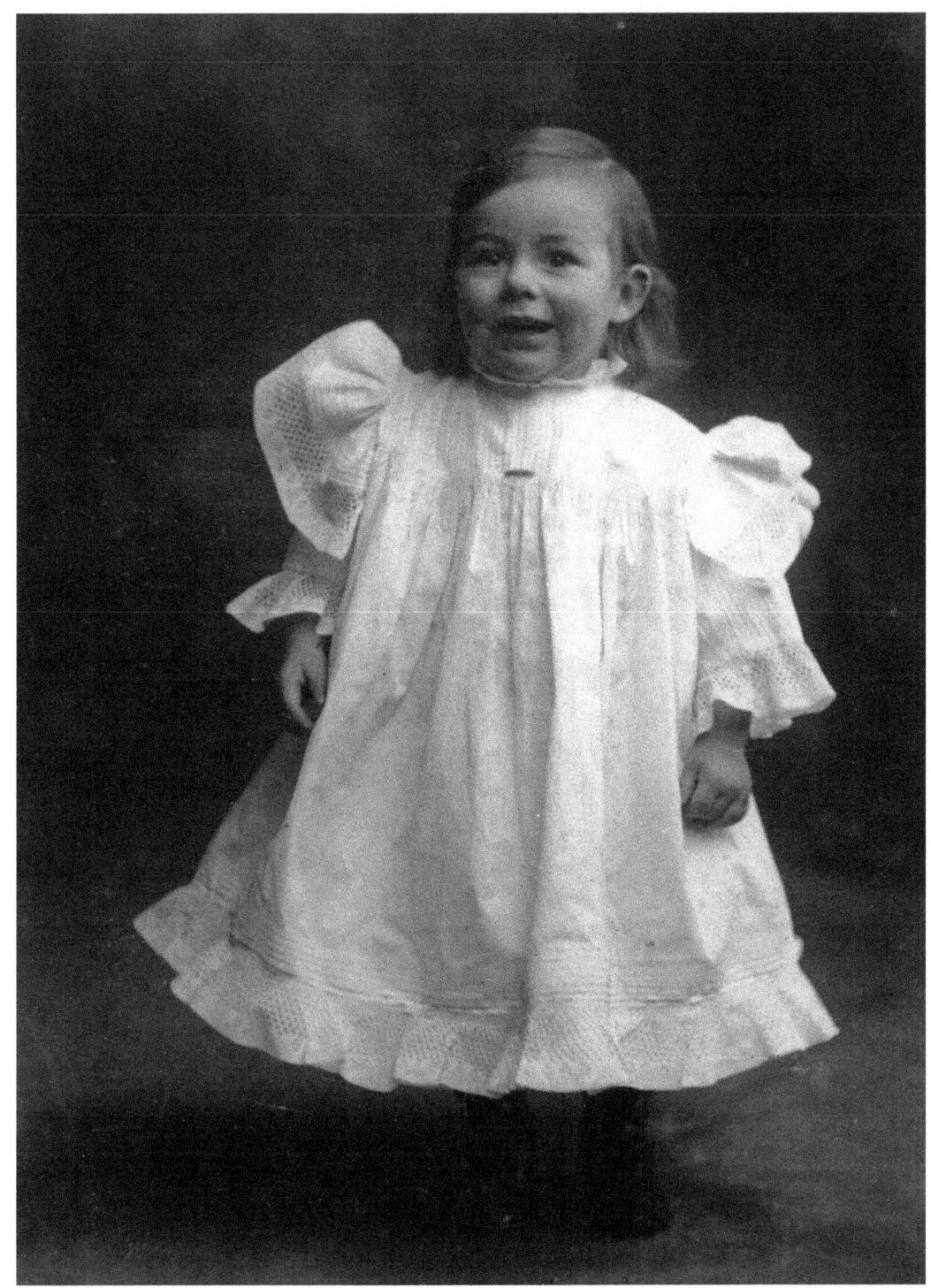

Hemingway at age two. It was customary in Victorian times to clothe and photograph baby boys in dresses until they were able to walk, but Grace Hemingway dressed Marcelline and Ernest alike until he was three, and was so fascinated by the concept of twins that she would later cut both children's hair "boy style." She would also hold Marcelline back one grade so they could enter high school together, and if Marcy wasn't asked to a dance, Ernest would have to escort her.

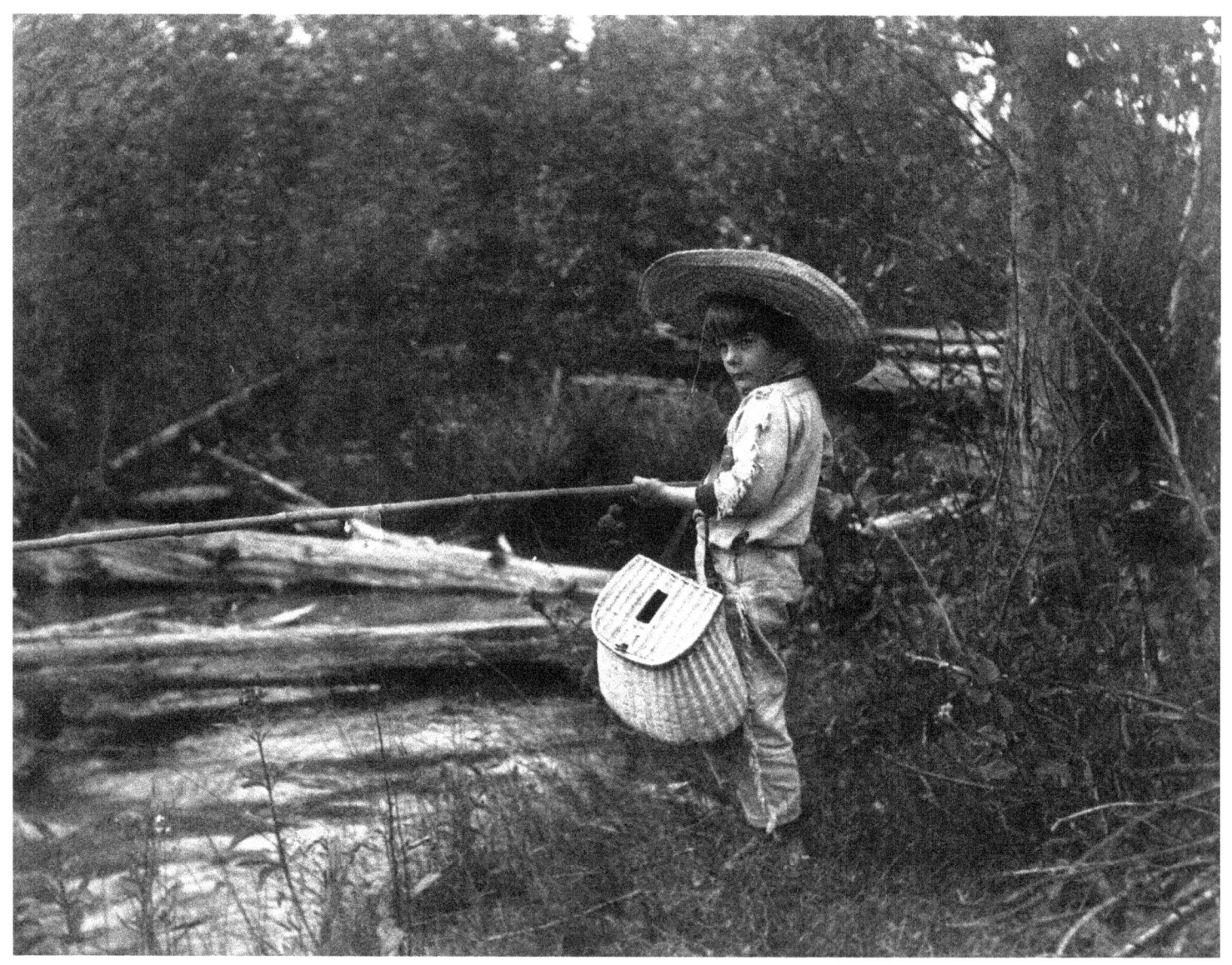

An adult Ernest Hemingway would insist that "all modern American literature" came from Mark Twain's *The Adventures of Huckleberry Finn* because of the realistic way that Twain handled character and dialogue. In 1904, fishing Horton's Creek with a cane pole, creel, and straw hat, young Hemingway looked a lot like Twain's hero. But his early reading background was almost exclusively Victorian and Romantic-period British literature—the books taught in school and stocked in the Oak Park library.

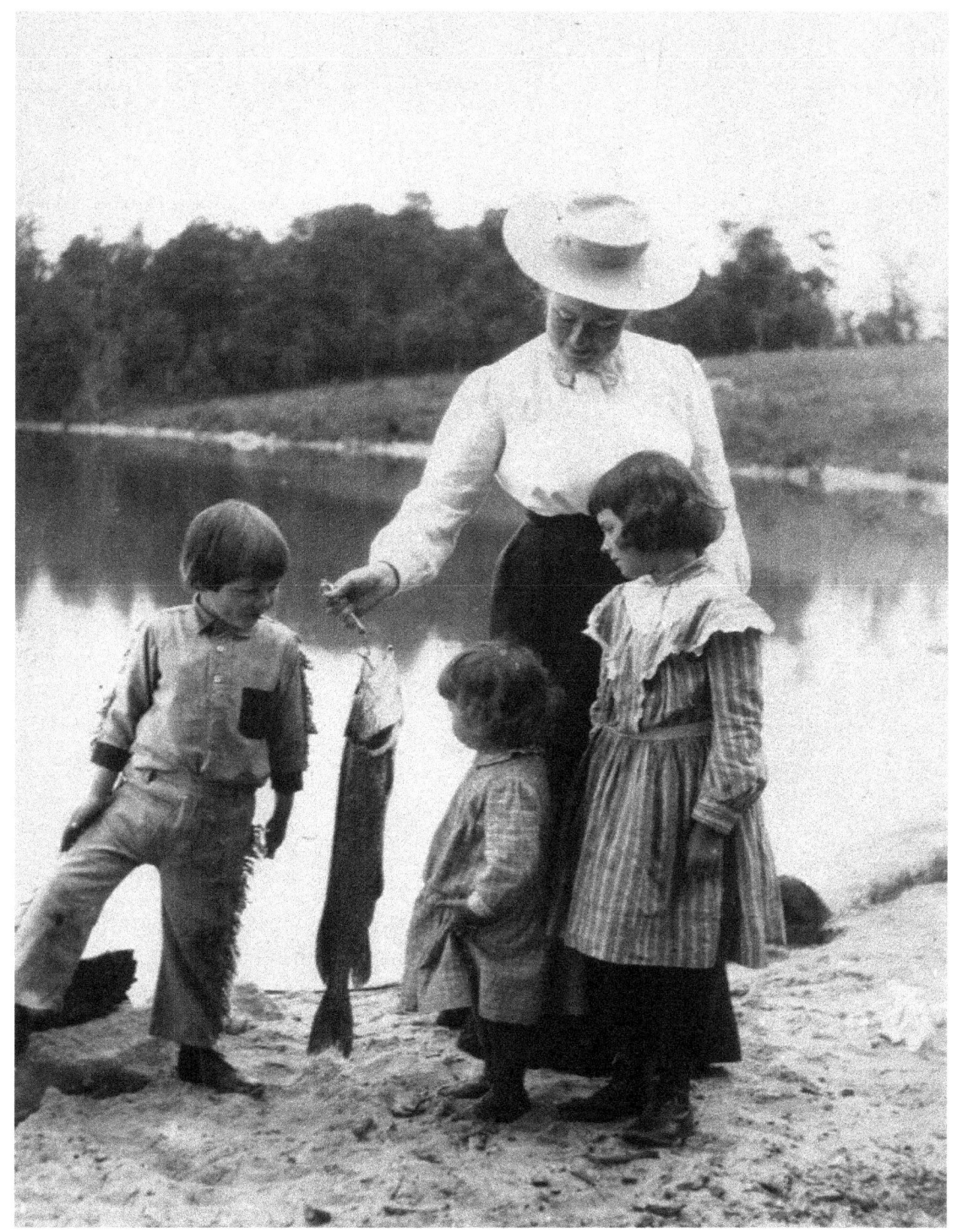

Although Grace Hemingway was the artistic one—the parent who took her children one at a time to the Art Institute of Chicago, and who insisted they each learn to play an instrument (Ernest was forced to learn cello)—she felt almost as comfortable at Walloon Lake as her husband. Here, during the summer of 1904, she holds a nice northern pike while Ernest, Ursula, and Marcelline look on.

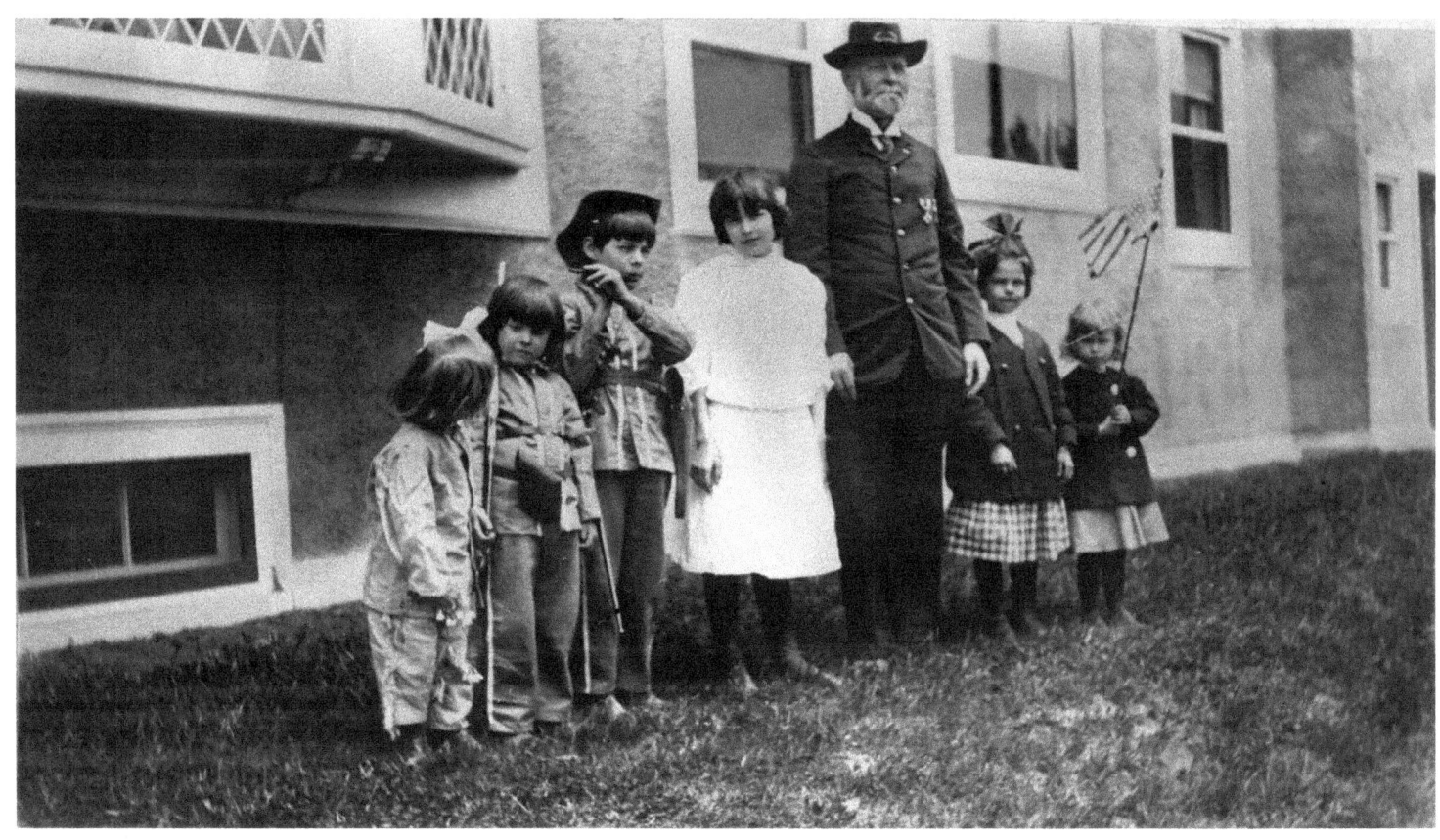

On Memorial Day 1907, a proud Anson Hemingway poses for a photograph with his grandchildren (left to right): Madelaine, Ursula, Ernest, Marcelline, and two cousins. Anson Hemingway lived just across the street from the Hall house, at 444 N. Oak Park Avenue. Like Ernest Hall, he was a Union Army veteran of the Civil War, and Hemingway grew up listening to their stories, including Anson's favorite exaggerated tale about getting hit on the noggin by a cannonball.

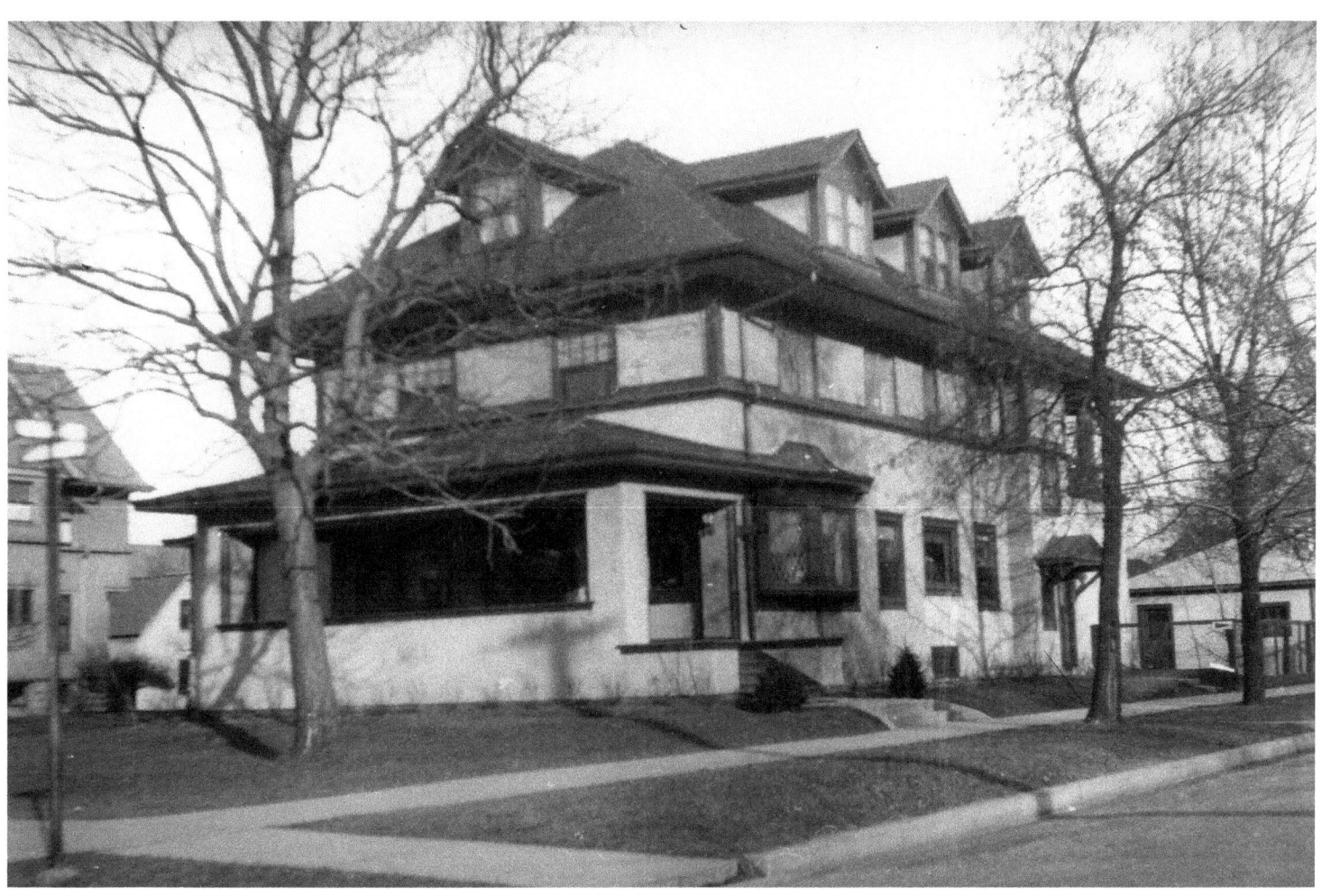

A look at 600 N. Kenilworth Avenue, 1907. After her father died, Mrs. Hemingway built a more spacious house that included a doctor's office and waiting room, along with a 30 × 30–foot music room she could use for lessons and recitals. There was also space for two live-in servants and a bedroom for Uncle Tyley Hancock—but no room for Dr. Hemingway's collection of Indian relics and specimens in jars, which Grace relegated to the basement and later burned.

On October 1, 1912, the Hemingways celebrated their 16th wedding anniversary and posed for a picture. Carol sits on Dr. Hemingway's lap, while Ernest has his hands on his hips, Marcelline towers over him, and Sunny and Ursula flank Mrs. Hemingway. Though Ernest looks uncomfortable in a white shirt and tie, seven months earlier he voluntarily wore boots and a velvet cap for a 7th grade version of Robin Hood.

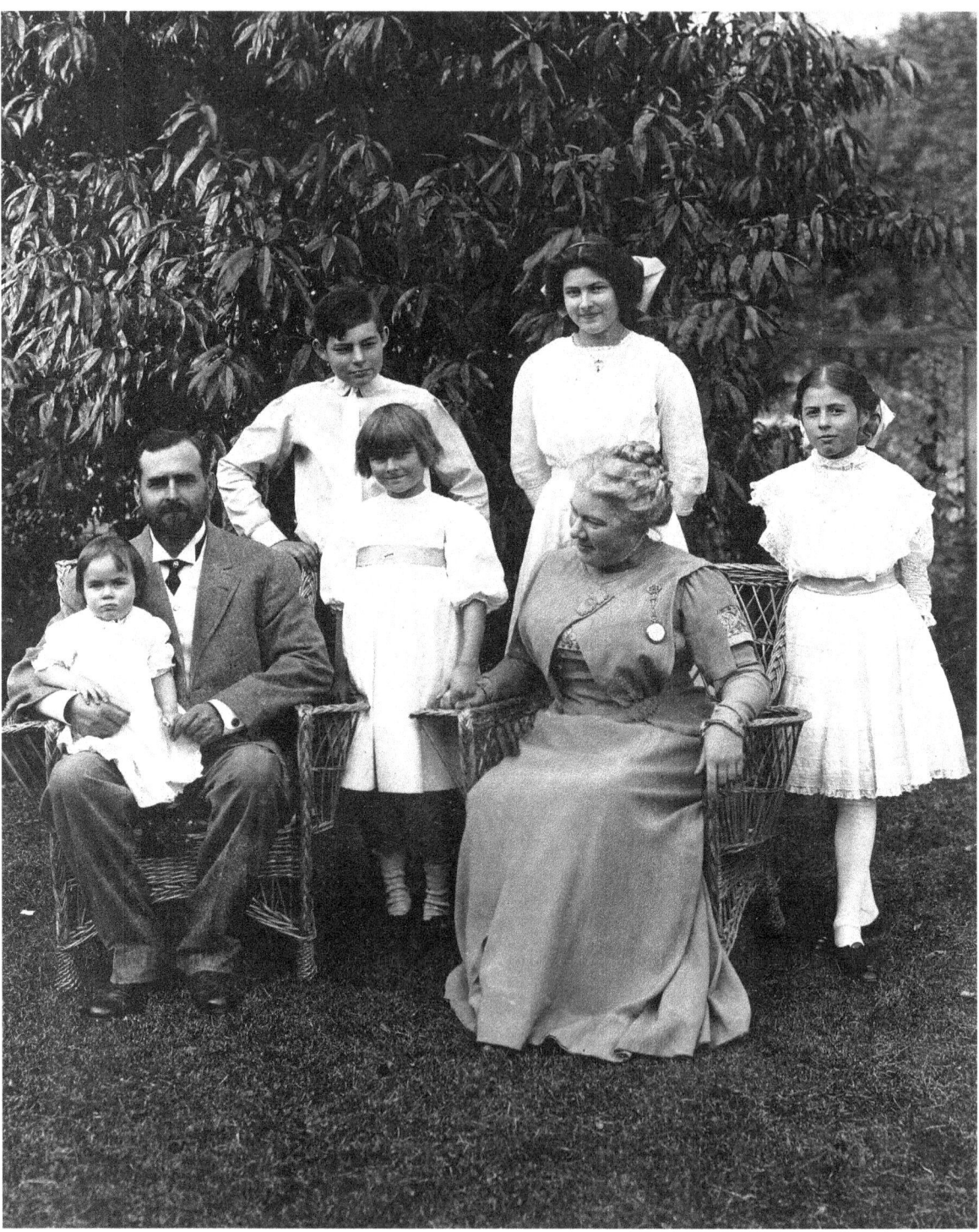

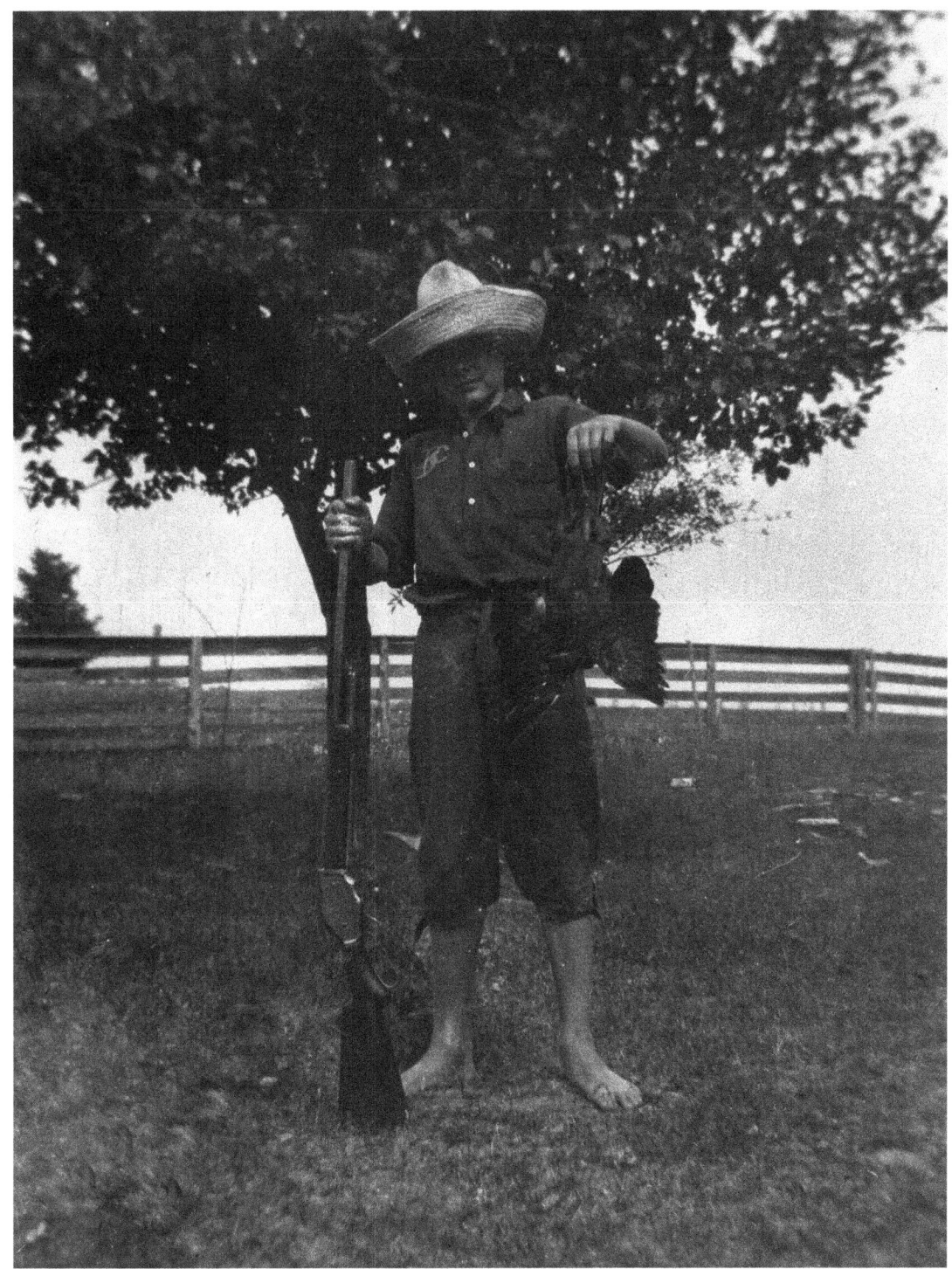

Ernest received his first gun when he was twelve, a 20-gauge single-barreled gift from Grandpa Hemingway. Dr. Hemingway gave Ernest just three shells a day to practice with to emphasize that every shot counts. Here, two years later, Ernest proudly holds a willow grouse he shot at Walloon Lake. His father was a complete woodsman who tried to instill a moral code: do everything properly, make no creature suffer, and eat what you kill.

Until his freshman year, Ernest was stuck at 5 feet 4 inches, but then he quickly grew a head taller than most of his friends. Standing at the bow of the *Missouri,* a Lake Michigan steamship bound for Petoskey in June 1915, he looks every bit the confident world traveler—though without parents this time, he and Lewis Clarahan got into plenty of mischief onboard. Hemingway would journey to Michigan every summer of his youth but one.

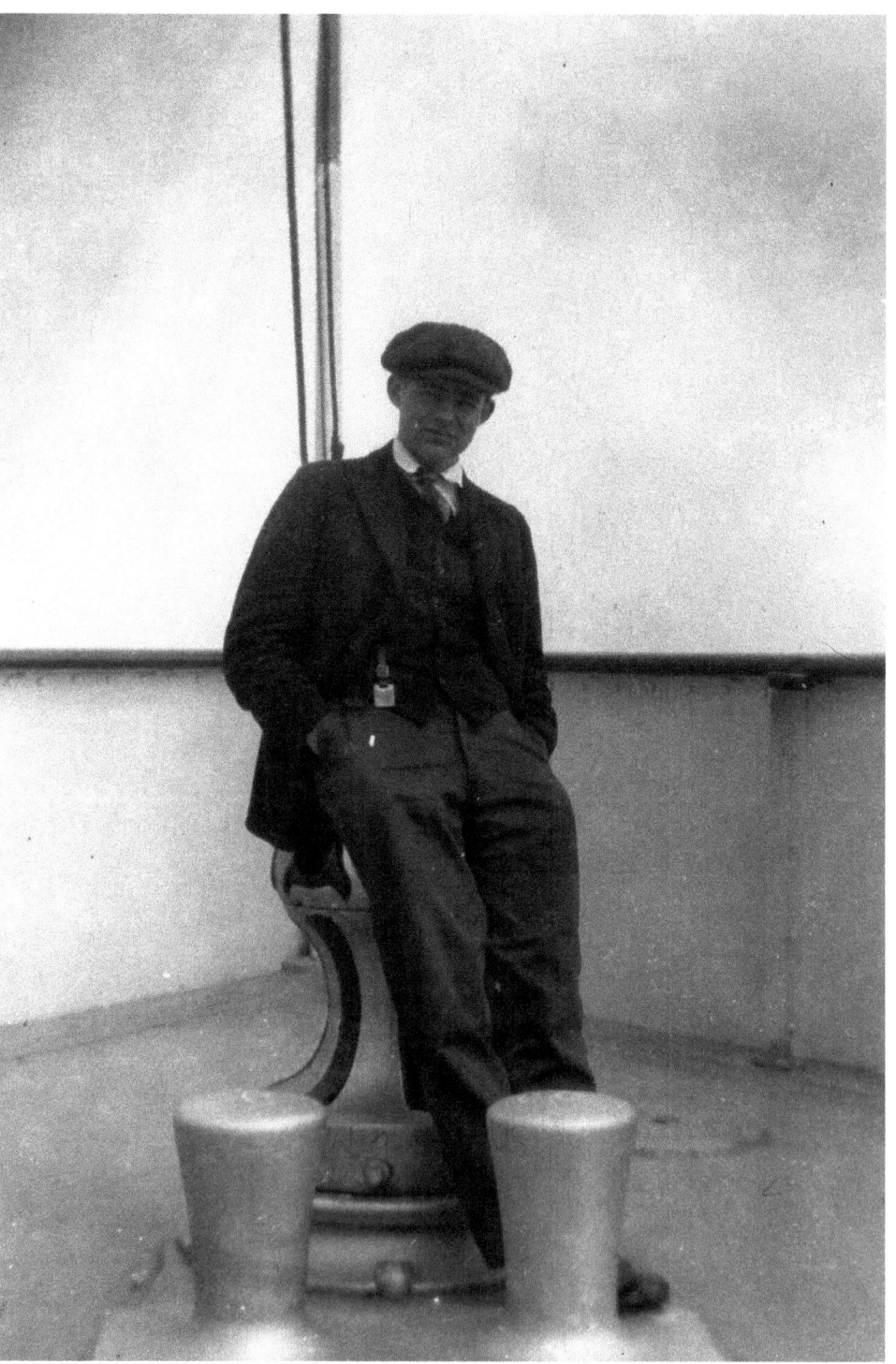

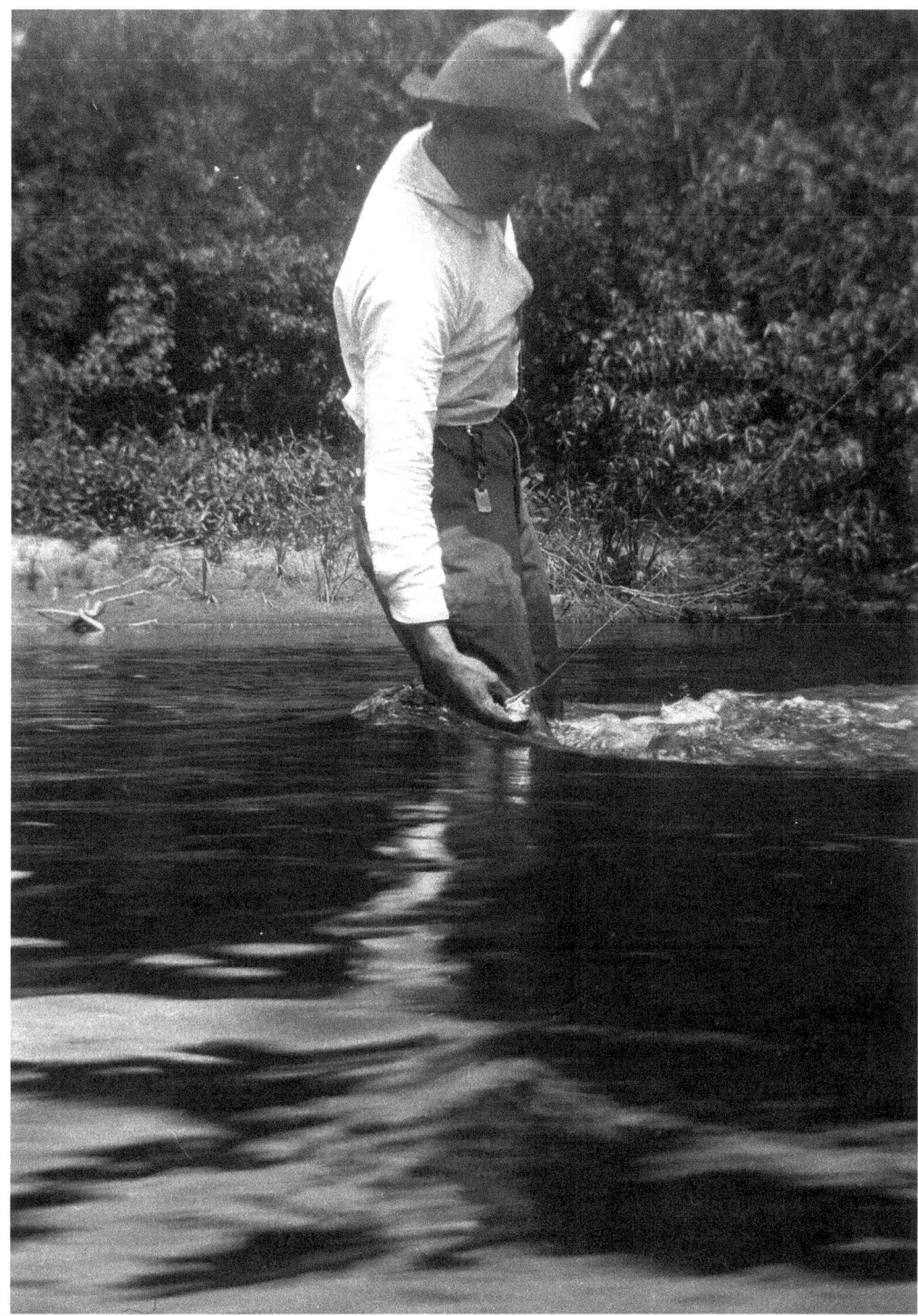

Ernest knew every stretch of Horton's Creek, which was a three-mile hike from Walloon. The creek was mentioned in Hemingway's short story "The End of Something," in which a teenage Nick Adams, Hemingway's first fictional alter ego, feels guilty at having to break up with his girlfriend—something he tells her when they take a break from fishing, and which he later discusses with his friend, Bill.

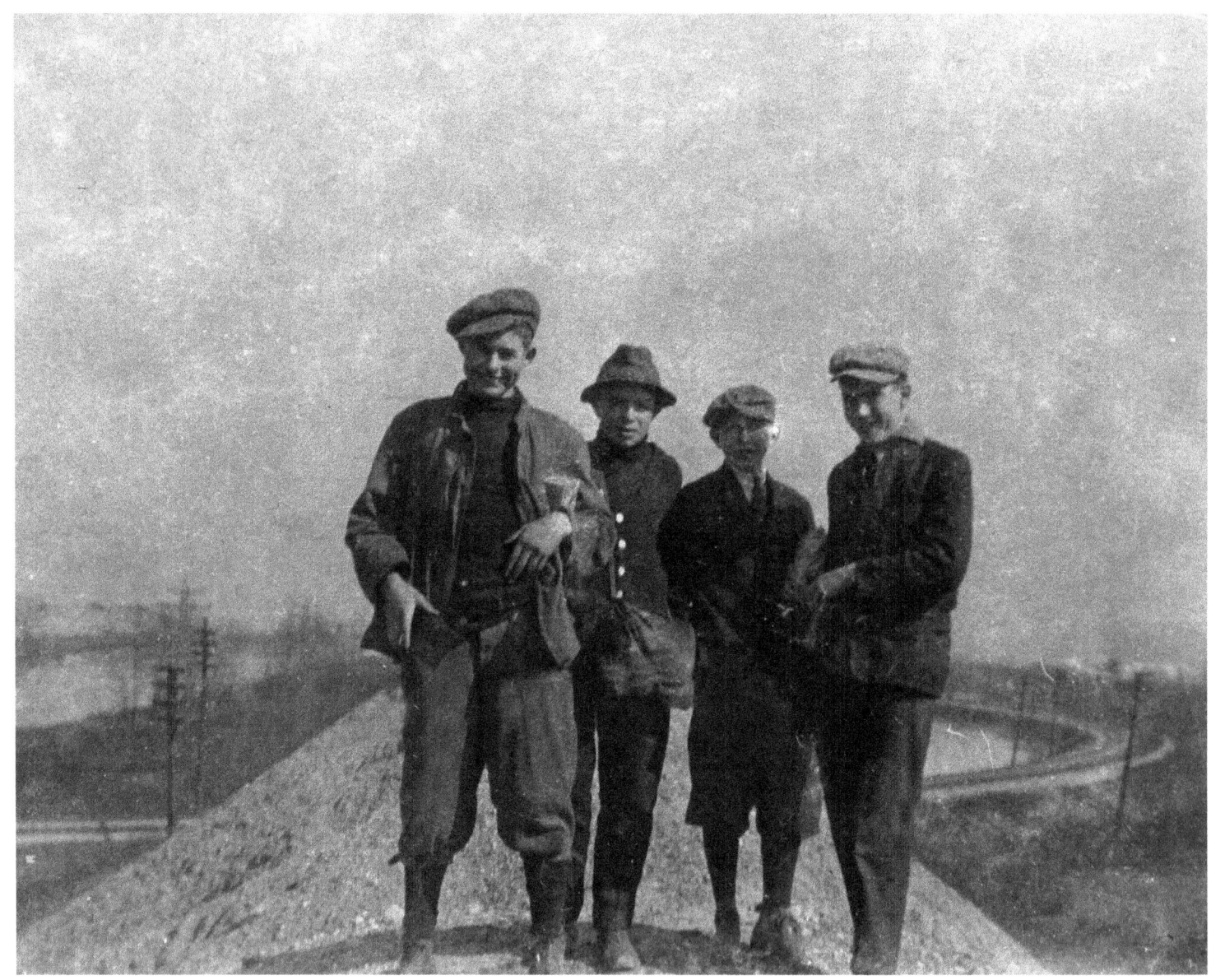

Summer 1915. Friends were important to Hemingway (left) because adventures needed to be shared, and if you experienced one alone you needed an audience. One of his best friends was Lewis Clarahan (second from left), who often fished, hiked, and "fought" with him. Others were Procter Gilbert and Morris Musselman (far right), the latter who aspired to write a play and talked Hemingway into collaborating with him briefly when he returned from the war. Apart from the trips to Michigan and his own clandestine jaunts to experience the seamier side of Chicago, such excursions with friends were the main travels Ernest managed as a youth.

In summer 1916, Hemingway poses by the shoreline near "Windemere," as the family cottage was named. That school year his first article ("Concert a Success") was published in the *Trapeze* student newspaper and his first short story ("Judgment of Manitou") appeared in the *Tabula* literary magazine. His story evoked Jack London's world and involved a Canadian trapper who causes his partner to be killed by wolves, then finds himself caught in a trap and also ironically doomed.

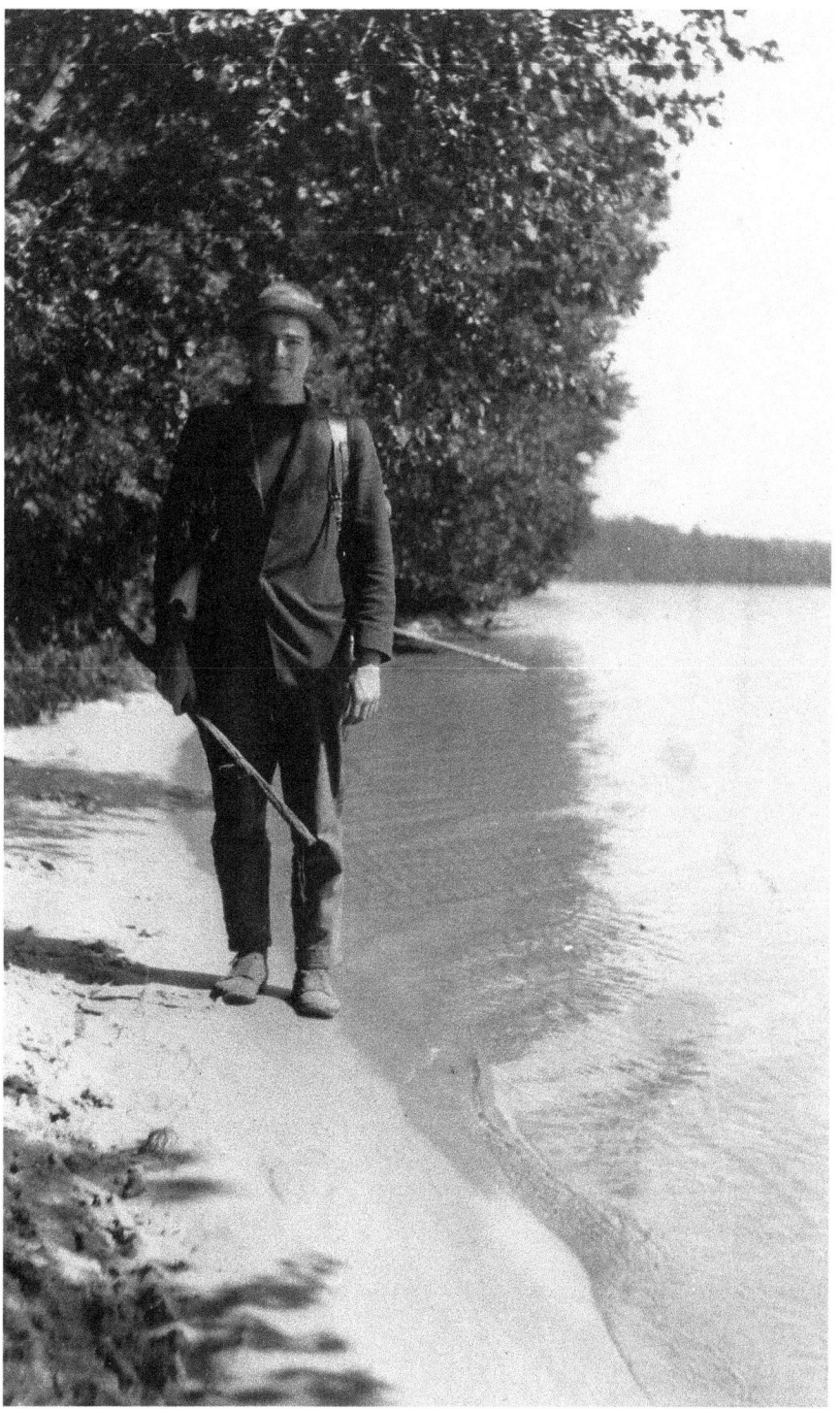

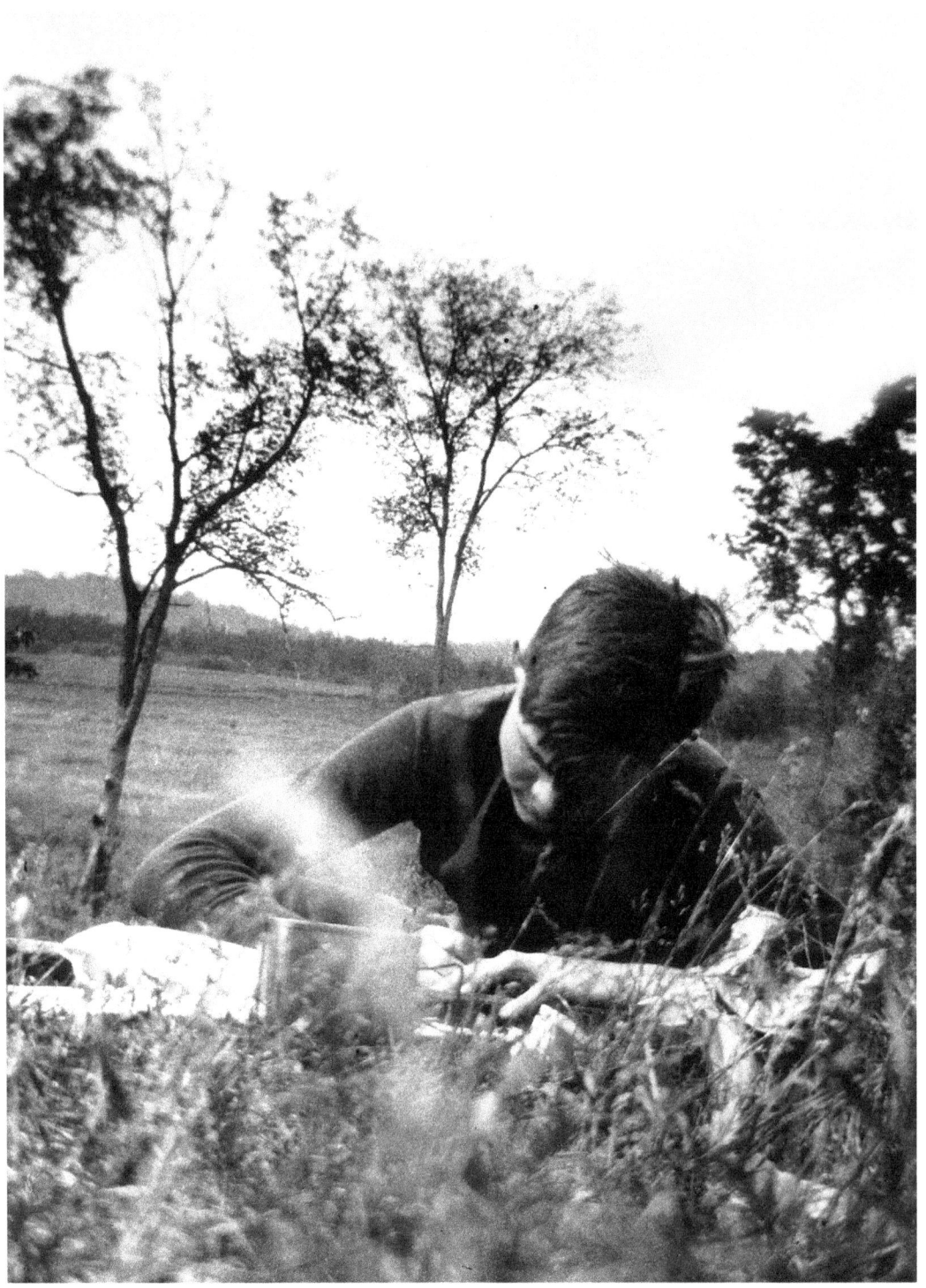

From the time he was young, Hemingway made a habit of writing while he traveled in order to get details down on paper while they were still fresh in his mind. It was a habit that would serve him well as a journalist and novelist. Here, during a fishing trip in summer 1916, he takes pen to paper in what would become one of his requirements for writing well: a different, often exotic place to inspire him.

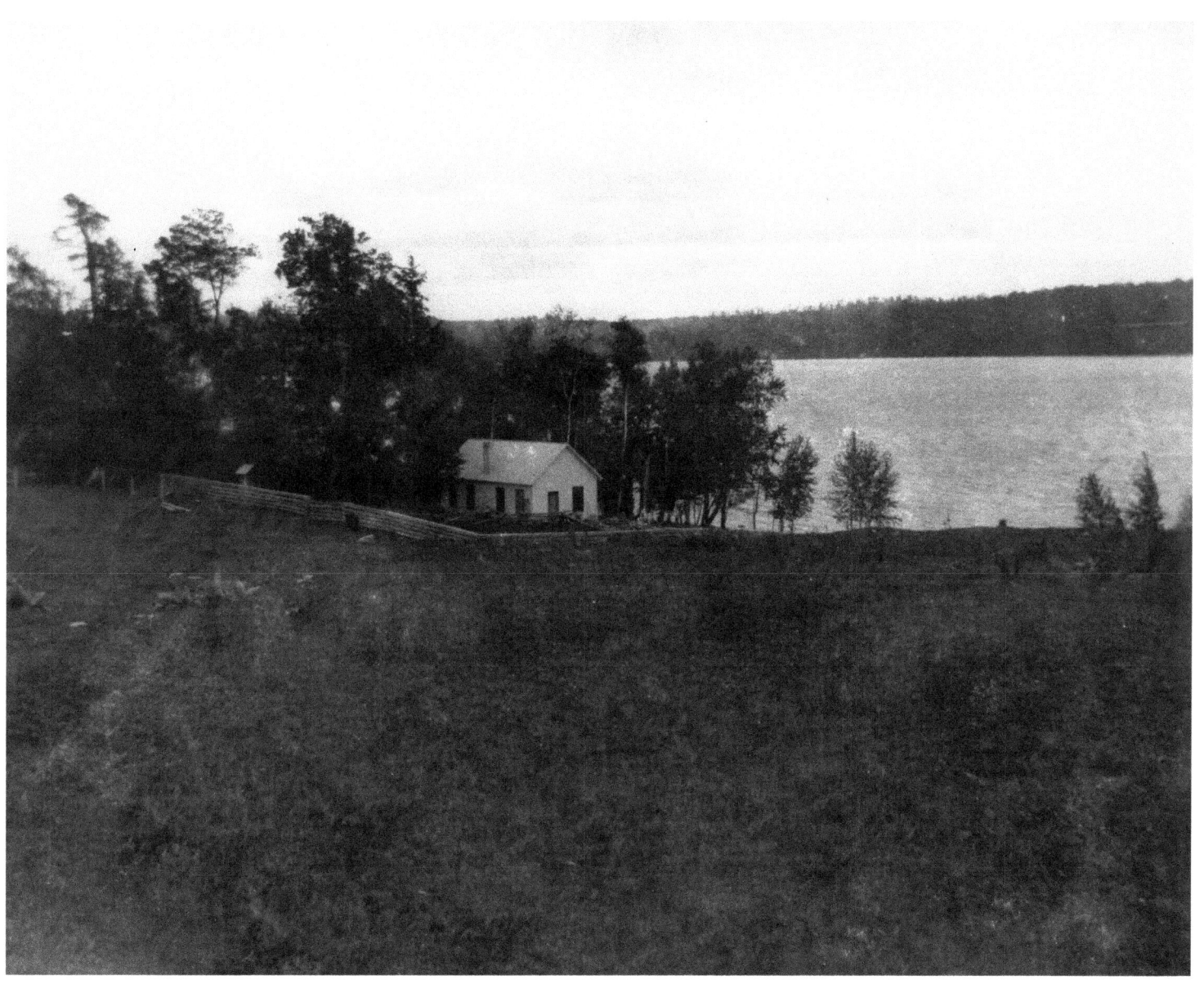

Walloon Lake when Hemingway was growing up had passed its prime as a logging area, but there was still a logging camp, sawmill, and an Indian camp nearby, and Ernest often played, hunted, and fished with Ojibway children. In November 1916, his story about an Indian and his dog, "Sepi Jingan," would be published in the *Tabula,* and later Nick Adams stories like "Indian Camp" and "Ten Indians" would reveal the profound impression such experiences had on him.

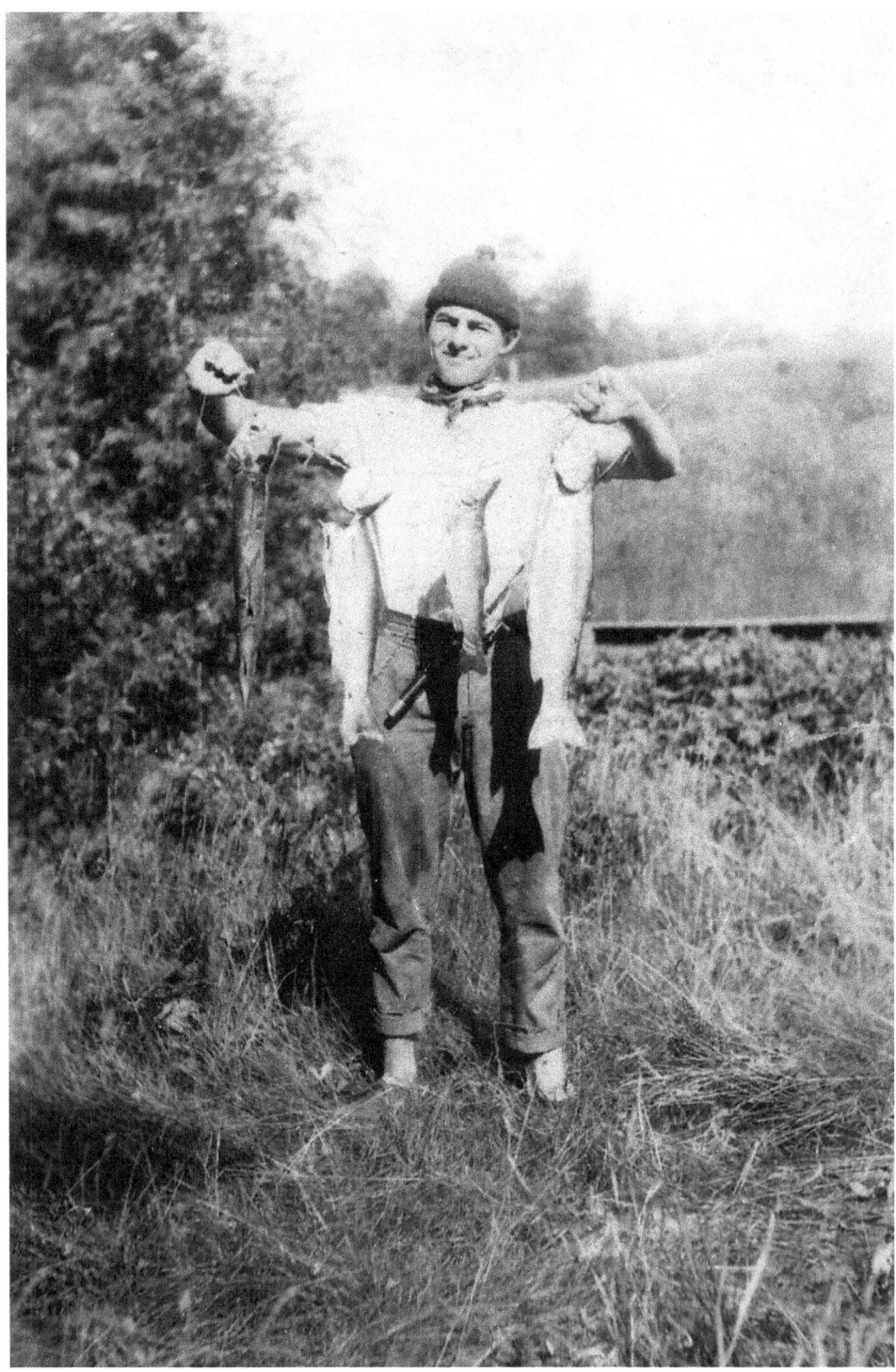

Ernest with a fine stringer of rainbow trout. Like his father, who showed him how to fly cast and tie his own flies, Ernest was part naturalist and part fisherman. He learned as much about habits and habitats as he could, and usually it paid dividends. For the remainder of his life he would gravitate toward people who had knowledge of pursuits that interested him, learn all he could, then pass on that knowledge to others.

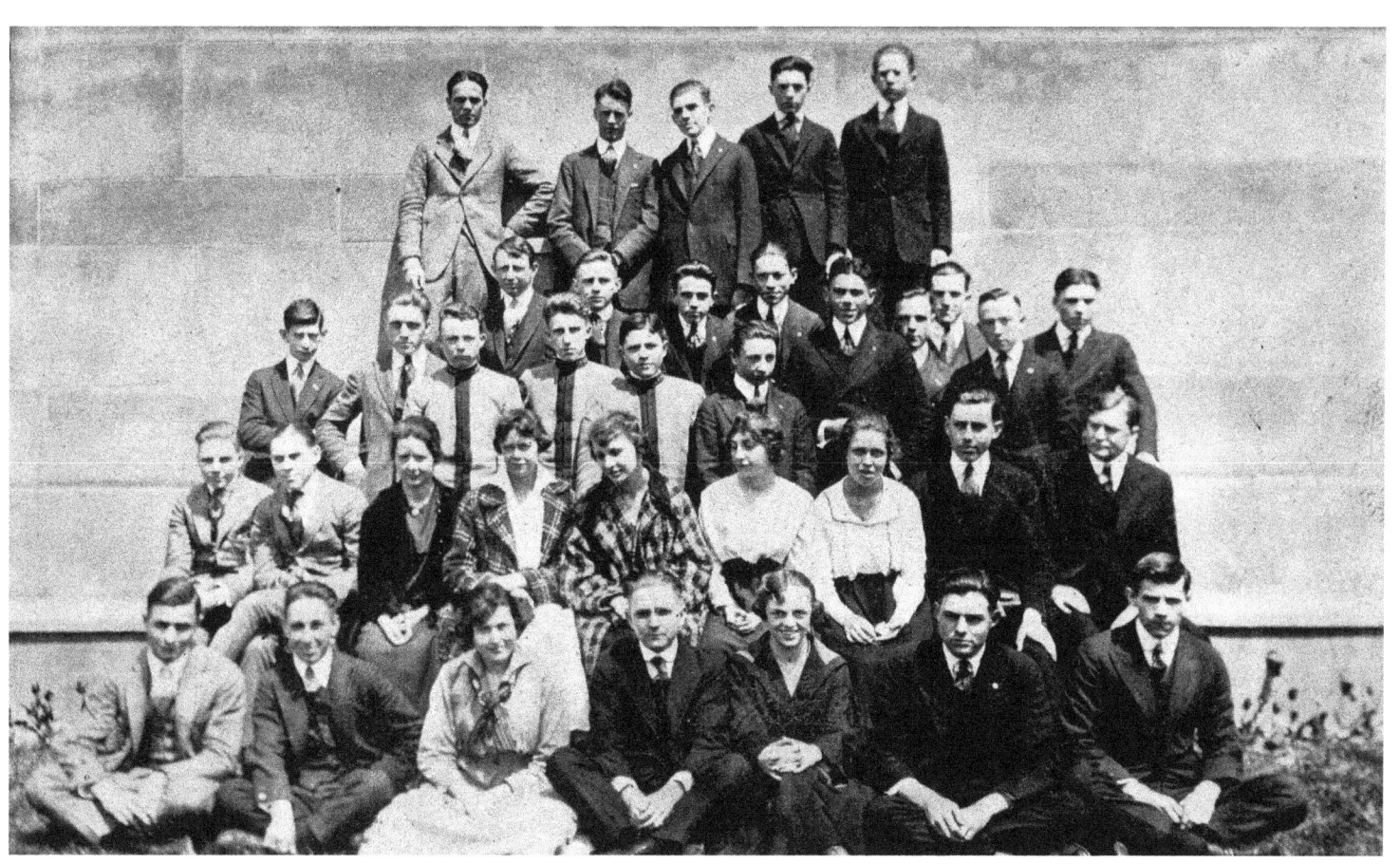

Marcelline (front row, third from left) and Ernest (second from right) were co-editors of the *Trapeze* their senior year, and Hemingway was elected to deliver the Class Prophecy at graduation. While his friends were all going off to college, Ernest knew he wanted to be a writer and chose to work as a cub reporter for the *Kansas City Star*—a job his Uncle Tyler arranged with his connections at the newspaper.

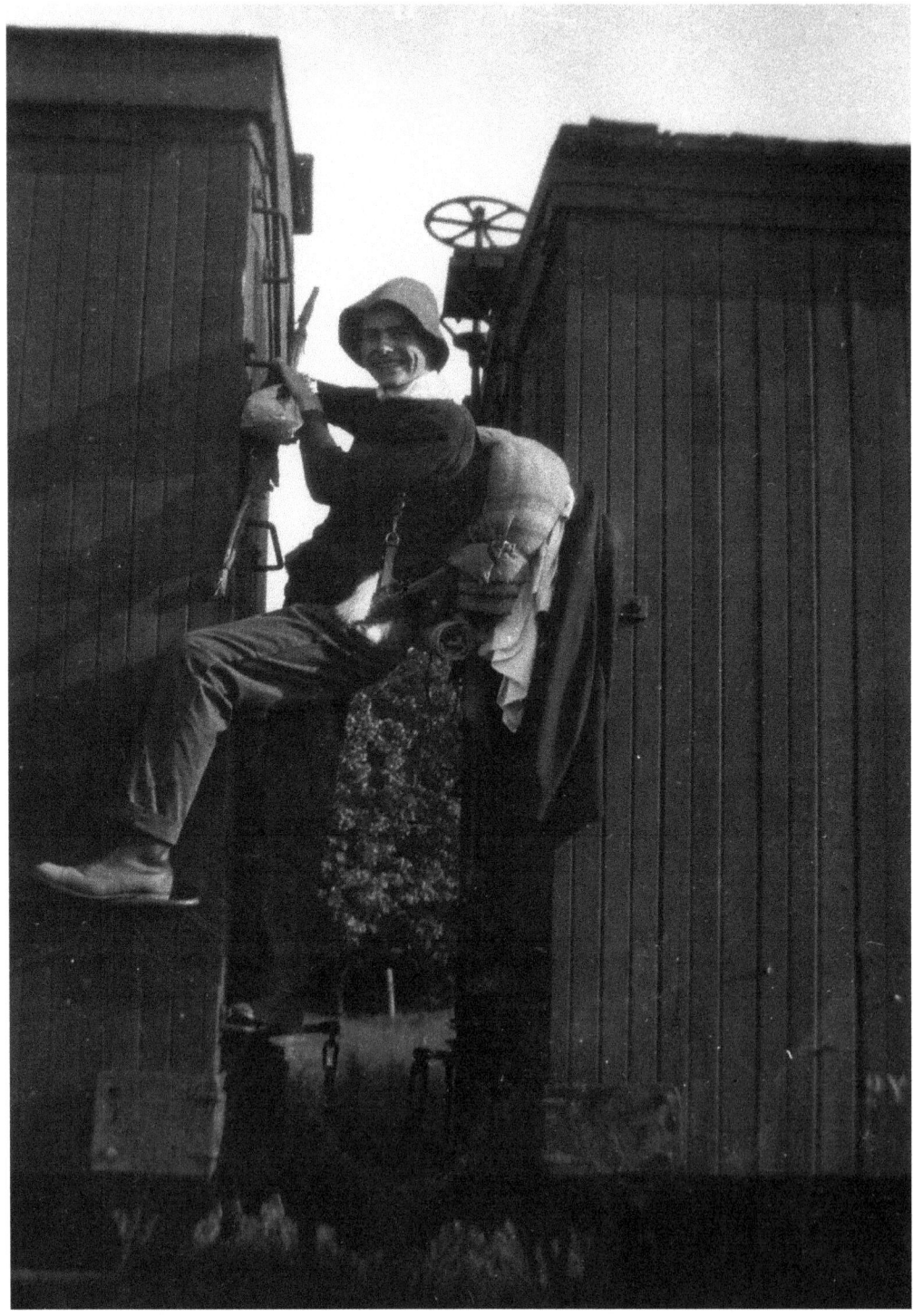

In "The Battler," Hemingway writes about how Nick Adams, heading for northern Michigan, is thrown off a freight train by a sucker-punching brakeman. It's not clear if Hemingway ever hopped freight trains himself or if it was just part of his active imagination and exaggerated storytelling. Often, though, there are pictures like this one to "prove" it.

Hemingway's career at the *Star* spanned less than seven months and he produced only a dozen stories, most of them police beat. But the experience was crucial on two counts. The *Star* stylebook taught him the importance of short sentences and "grabber" leads. Also, it was Ted Brumback at the *Star* who told Hemingway even guys like him with eye trouble (inherited from Grace) could drive ambulances for the Red Cross. Both enlisted. Here Hemingway sits in his Section 4 ambulance in Italy, 1918.

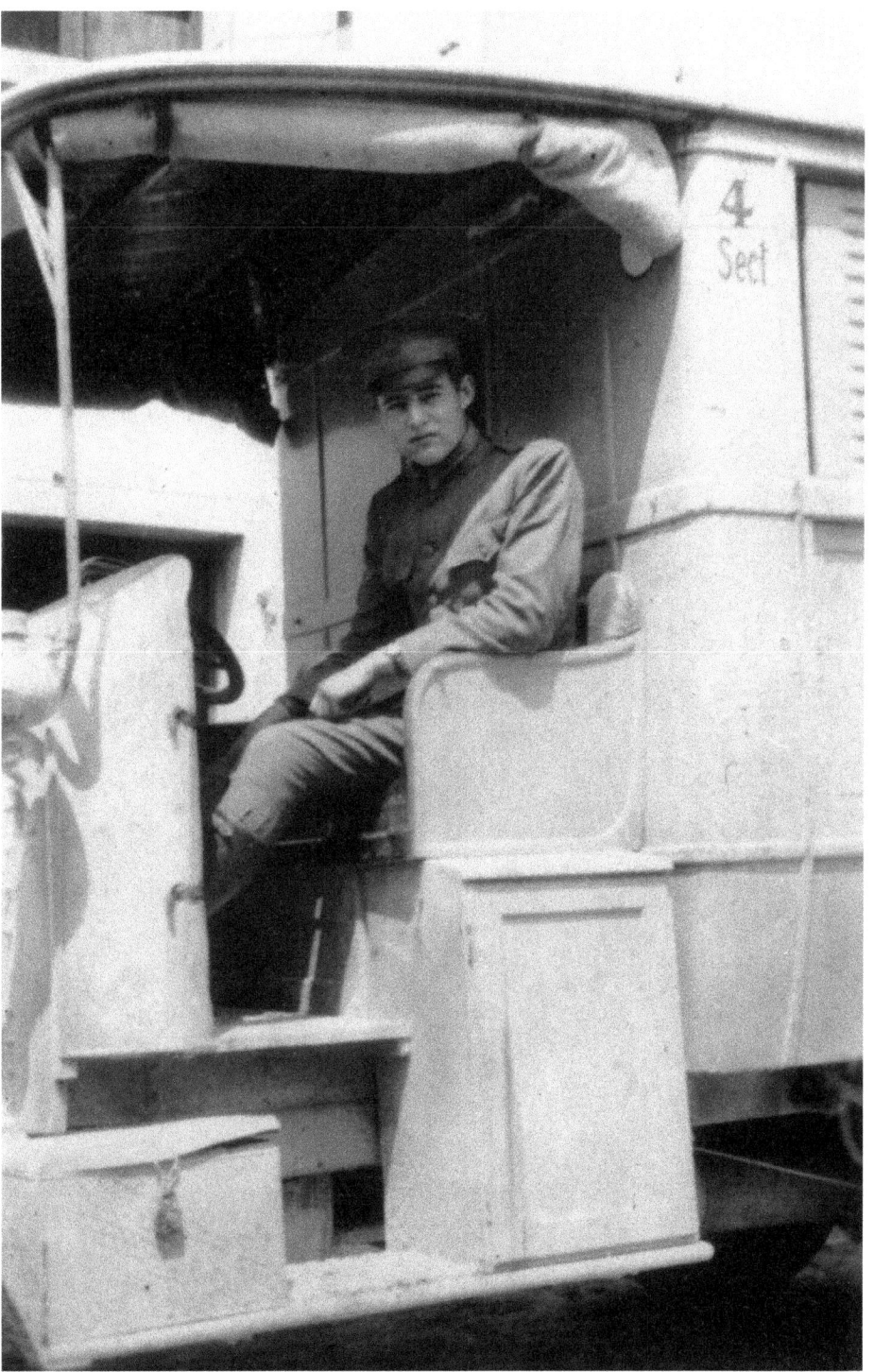

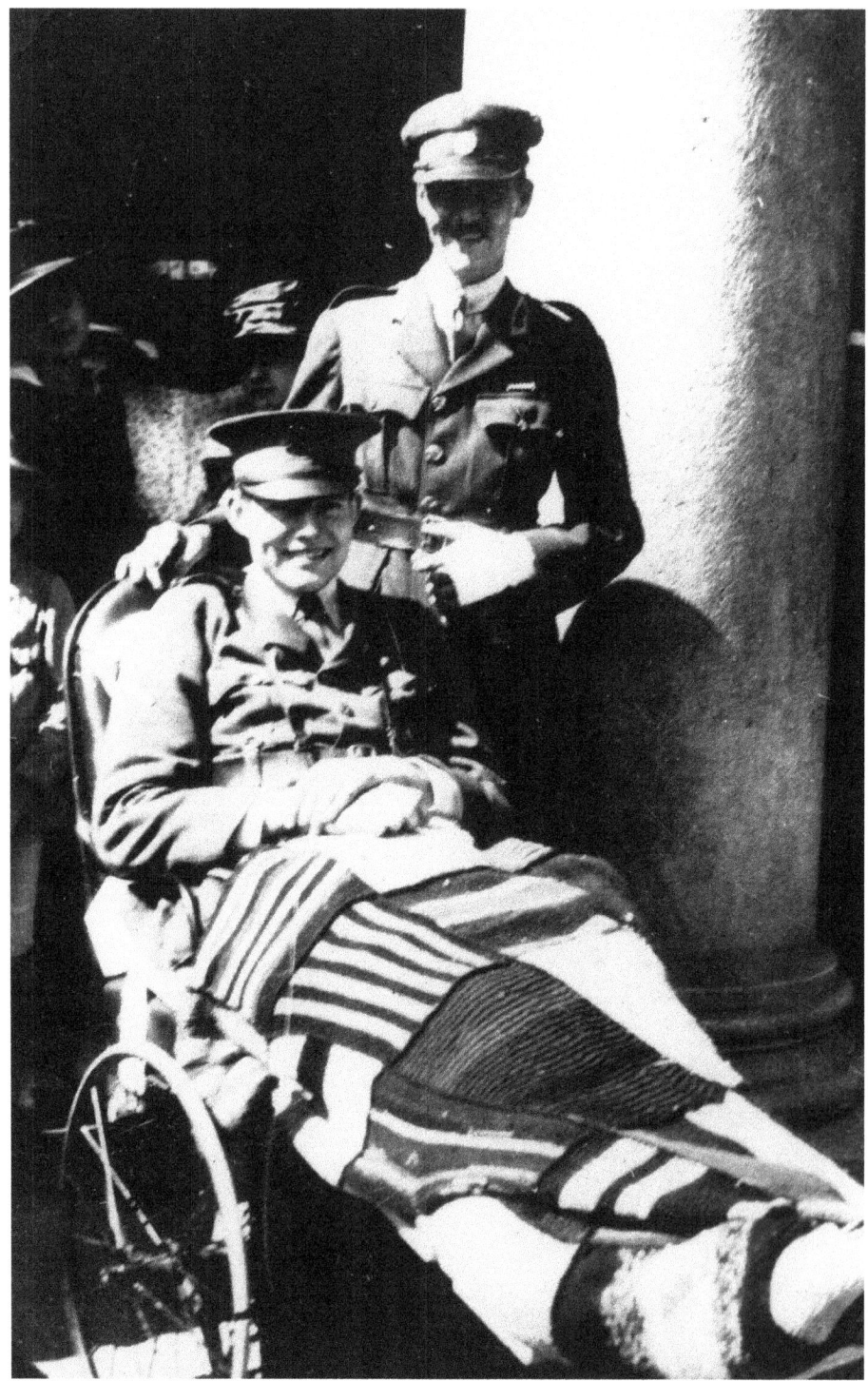

On July 8, 1918, a little more than two weeks after he had volunteered for frontline duty, Ernest had ridden a bicycle to distribute chocolate and cigarettes near Fossalta when a trench mortar shell exploded nearby, killing one man and badly injuring the rest. Ernest stumbled to an aid station while carrying an injured soldier on his back—this, despite receiving more than 227 shrapnel wounds to both legs and the bottoms of his feet.

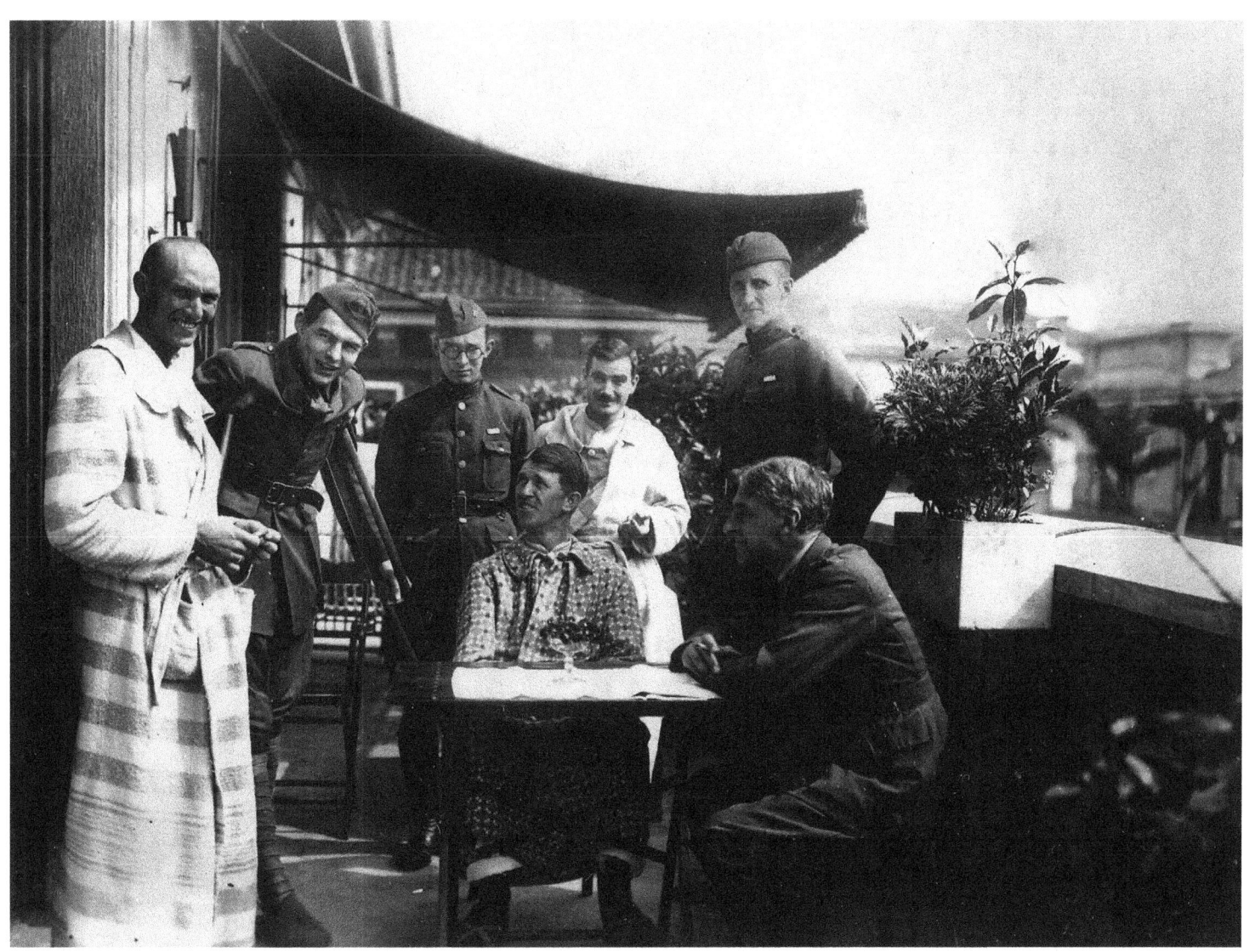

Hemingway (on crutches) spent three months at the Red Cross Hospital, during which time he underwent numerous surgeries. In the summer of 1918 he gets some sunshine on the balcony of the hospital, which was a converted villa in a fashionable part of Milan. By Hemingway's side in uniform is Bill Horne, a fellow driver who would become Ernest's roommate in Chicago after the war.

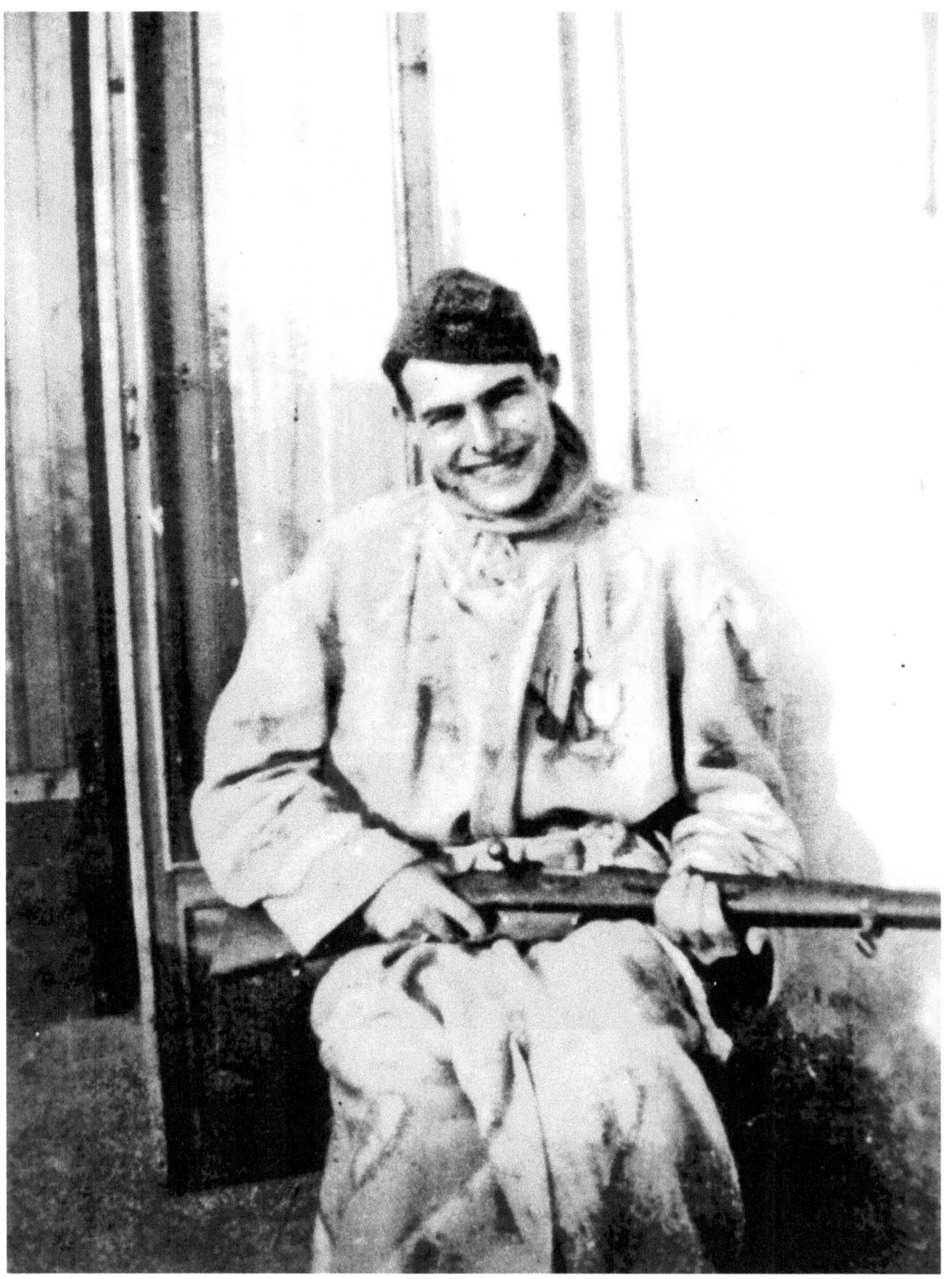

Hemingway enjoyed the notoriety that his wounding brought. He was never content to be on the sidelines. He always wanted to be in the thick of things. Here, even though Red Cross volunteers were not issued or authorized to carry weapons, Ernest poses with a rifle—a clear case of wishful thinking, since he had been rejected for military service because of his eyesight.

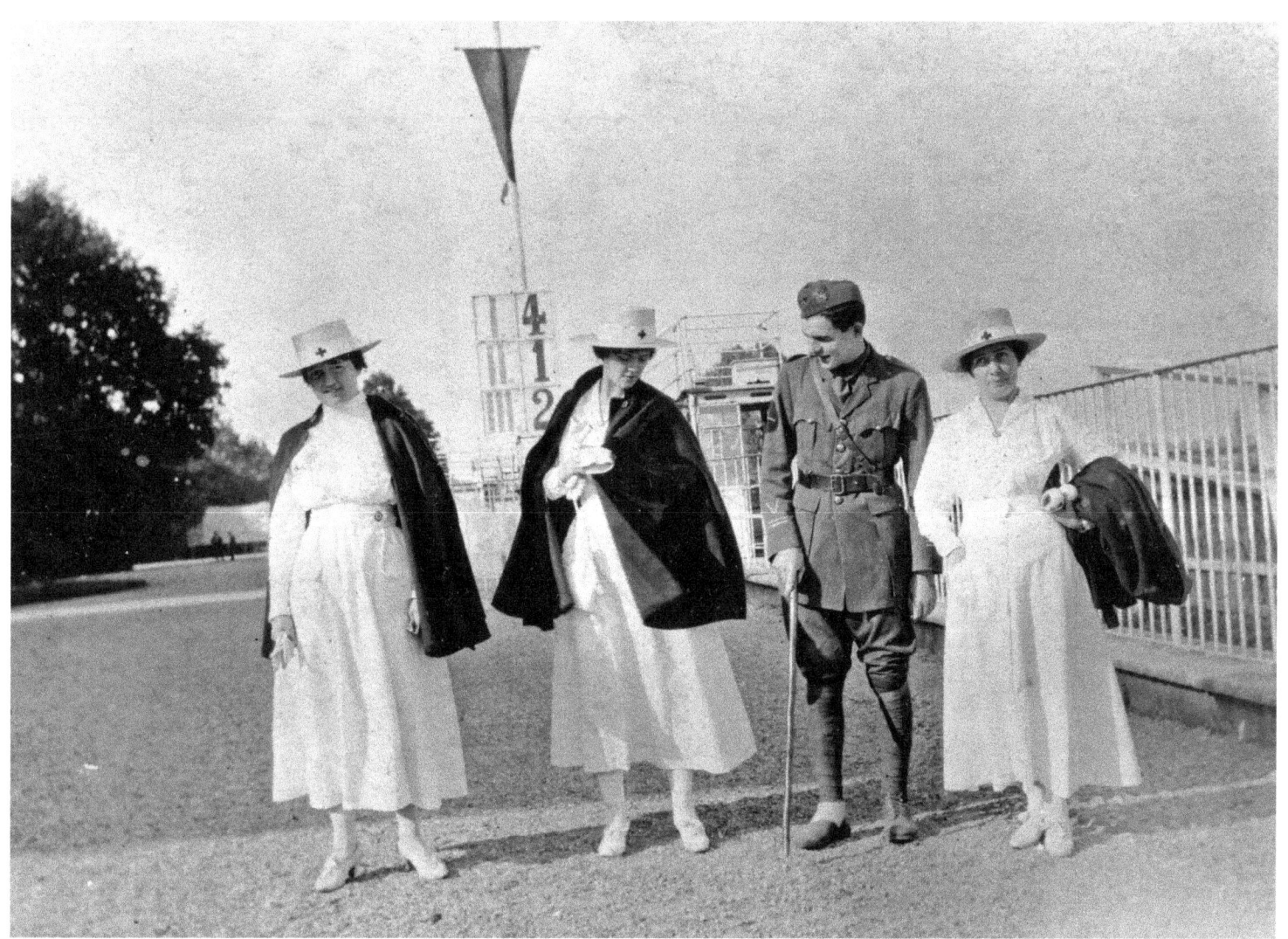

By far the wounded soldiers' favorite excursions were the outings to the San Siro racetrack, which admitted Red Cross volunteers free. The ratio of nurses to patients was indeed roughly three-to-one, and one nurse in particular, Agnes von Kurowsky, caught Ernest's eye. Here the coy game seems to have begun, he looking at her and she glancing downward.

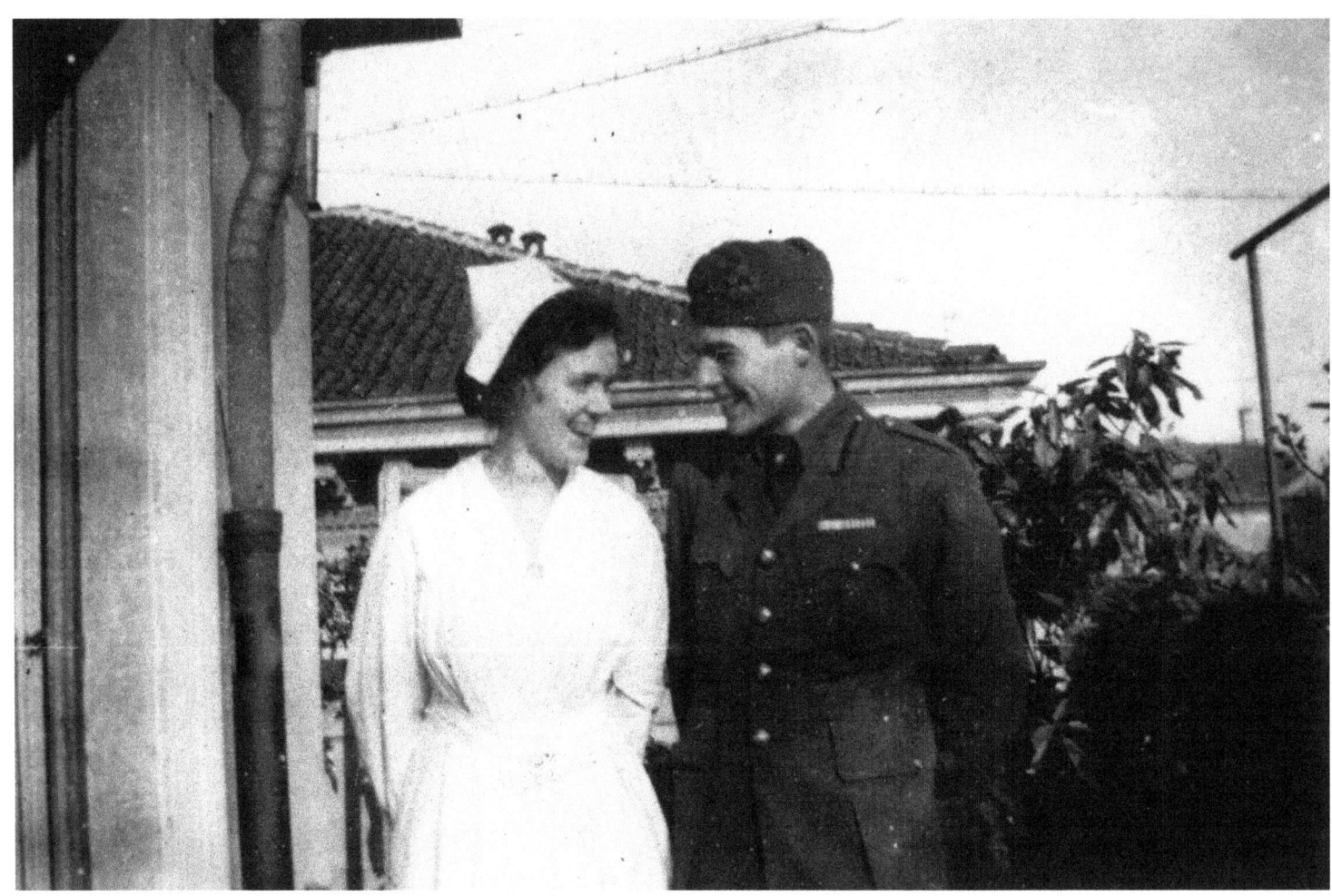

Agnes von Kurowsky, an American-born nurse nearly eight years Ernest's senior, flirted with all of her patients to make them feel better and dated several. Most biographers agree that while Ernest may have had his first sexual encounter in Michigan, his first real love was Agnes, though the relationship was never consummated. Agnes would become the model for Catherine Barkley in *A Farewell to Arms*, but years would pass before Ernest could write about her objectively.

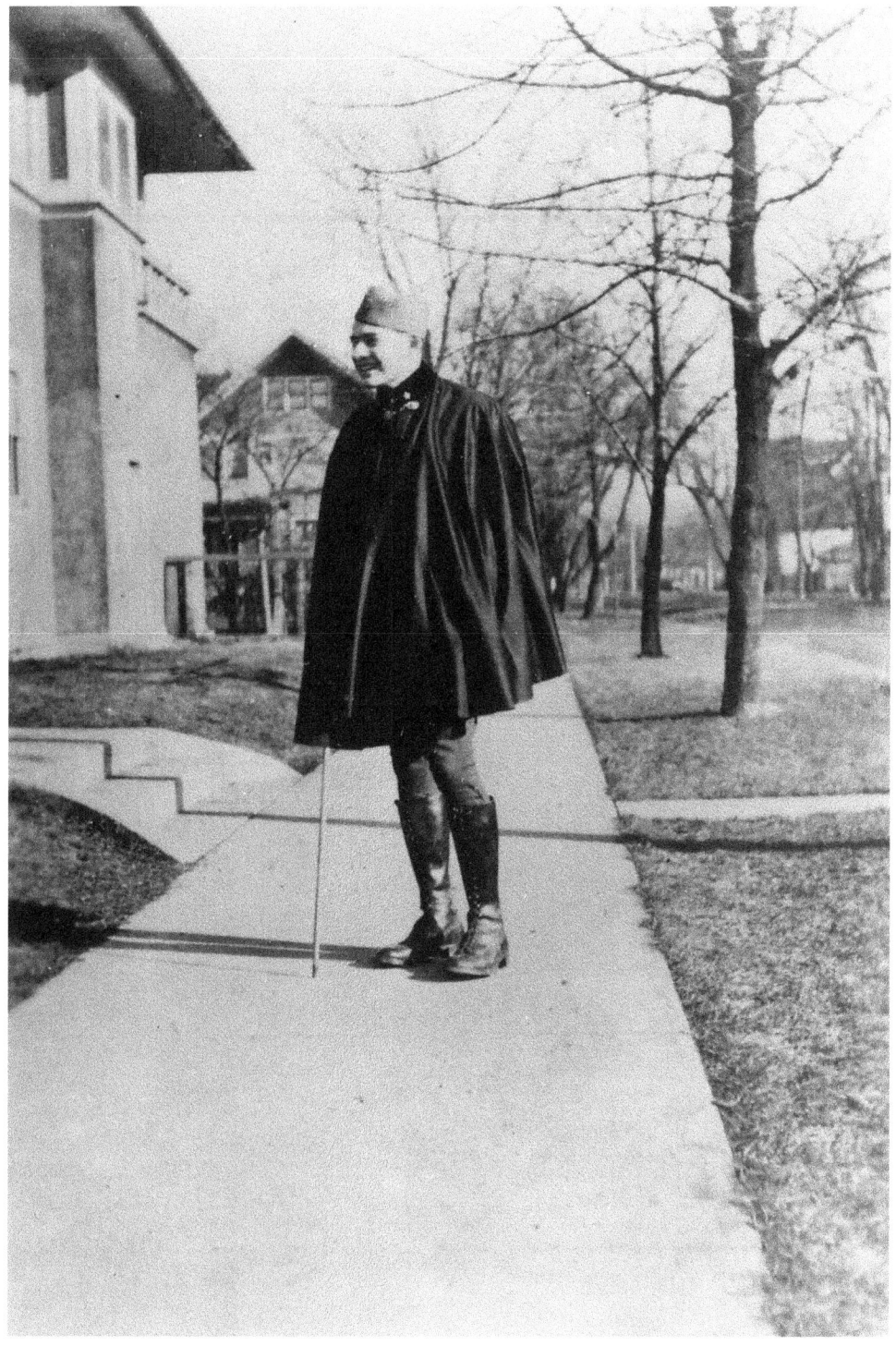

When Hemingway returned to Oak Park in January 1919, he had already been interviewed for a big *New York Sun* story and he was treated to the same sort of homecoming as Sergeant York. He paraded around town in an Italian officer's cape and boots, shot off a star shell for the neighborhood girls, gave more interviews, and spoke at a school assembly at his old high school, clearly relishing playing the part of the war hero.

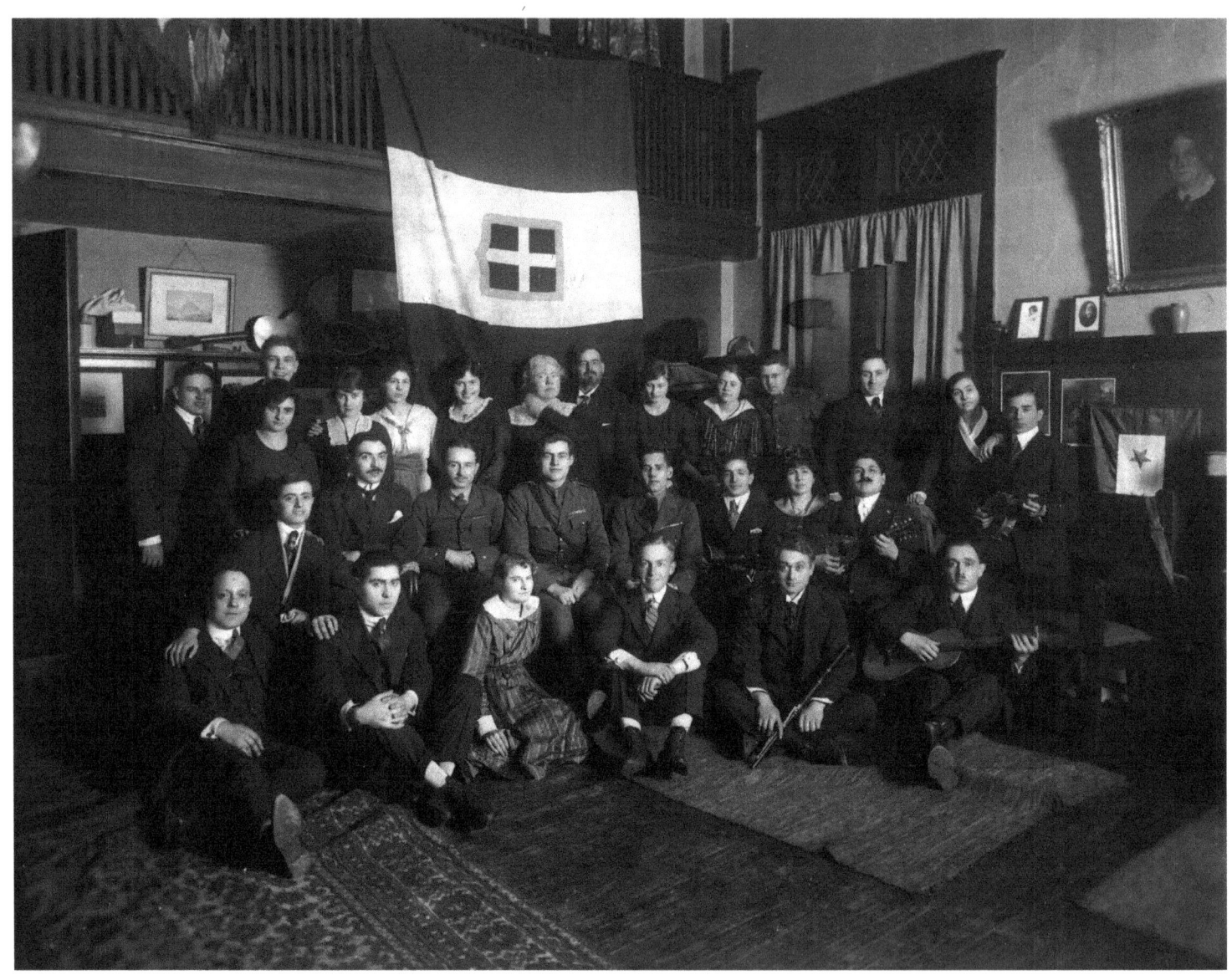

The Italian-American community from Chicago and Oak Park came to the Hemingway house on two occasions, bringing food and wine and toasting Ernesto with wine and song . . . all of which made him homesick for Italy and drove the quiet, non-drinking Dr. Hemingway half mad.

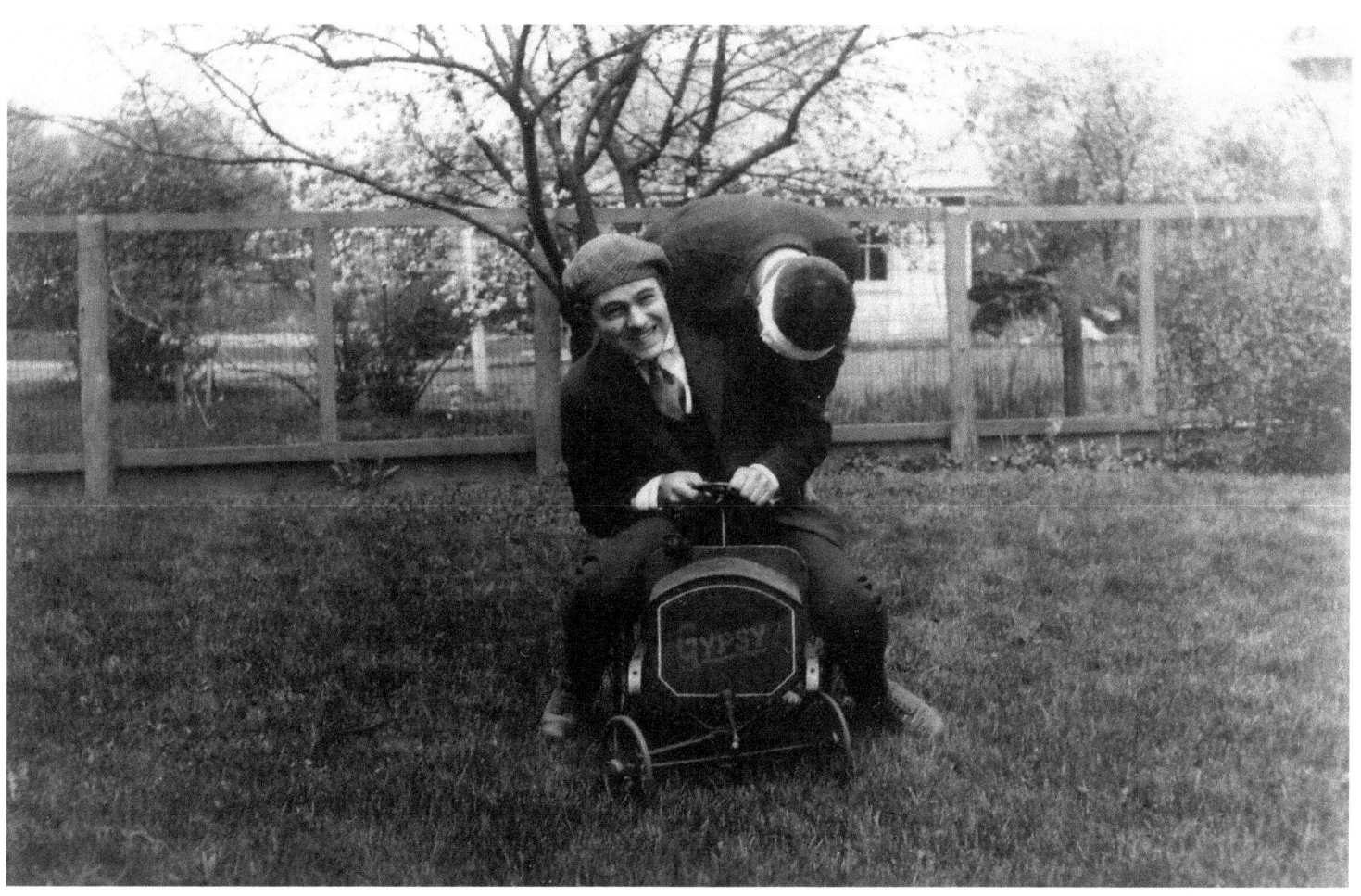

Ernest and one of his friends playing "ambulance driver" on brother Leicester's toy car. In Schiao, Italy, drivers called their headquarters the Schiao Country Club and published a newsletter to which Ernest contributed breezy, clipped-style "Dear Al" letters that imitated sports columnist Ring Lardner—the same kind Ernest wrote in high school. Modified to suit his personality, it would become his way of speaking and letter-writing, this mixture of cleverness, silliness, shorthand, and understatement.

While in Italy, Ernest had written his father that what bothered him most wasn't the war or his wounds, but that he was missing out on the fishing up in Michigan. Once home, he missed Agnes. But in March she wrote him a "Dear John" letter, and Ernest was devastated. He went alone to Horton Bay, where he stayed with friends, fished, and lived an experience that would later be described in "Big Two-Hearted River."

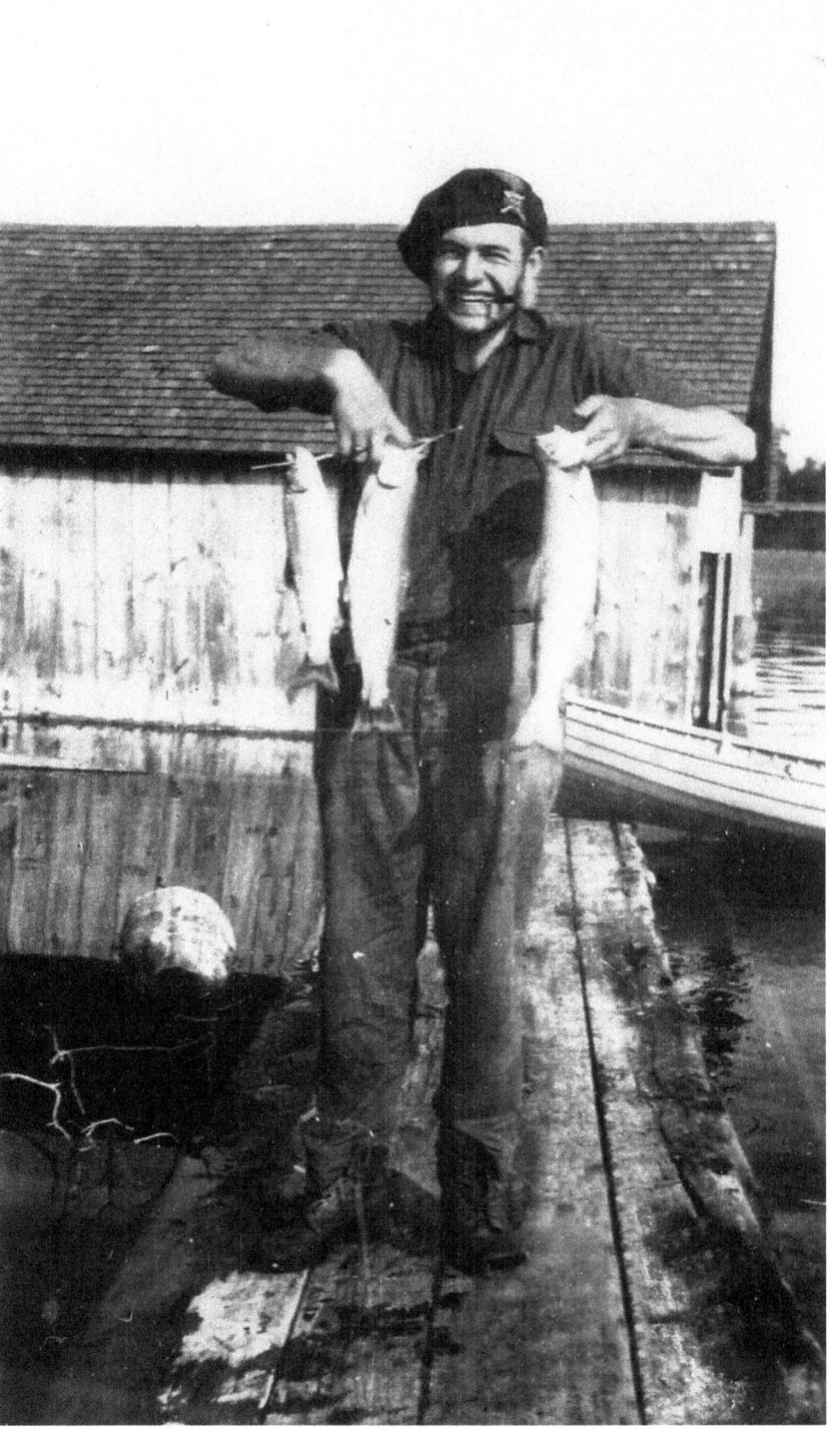

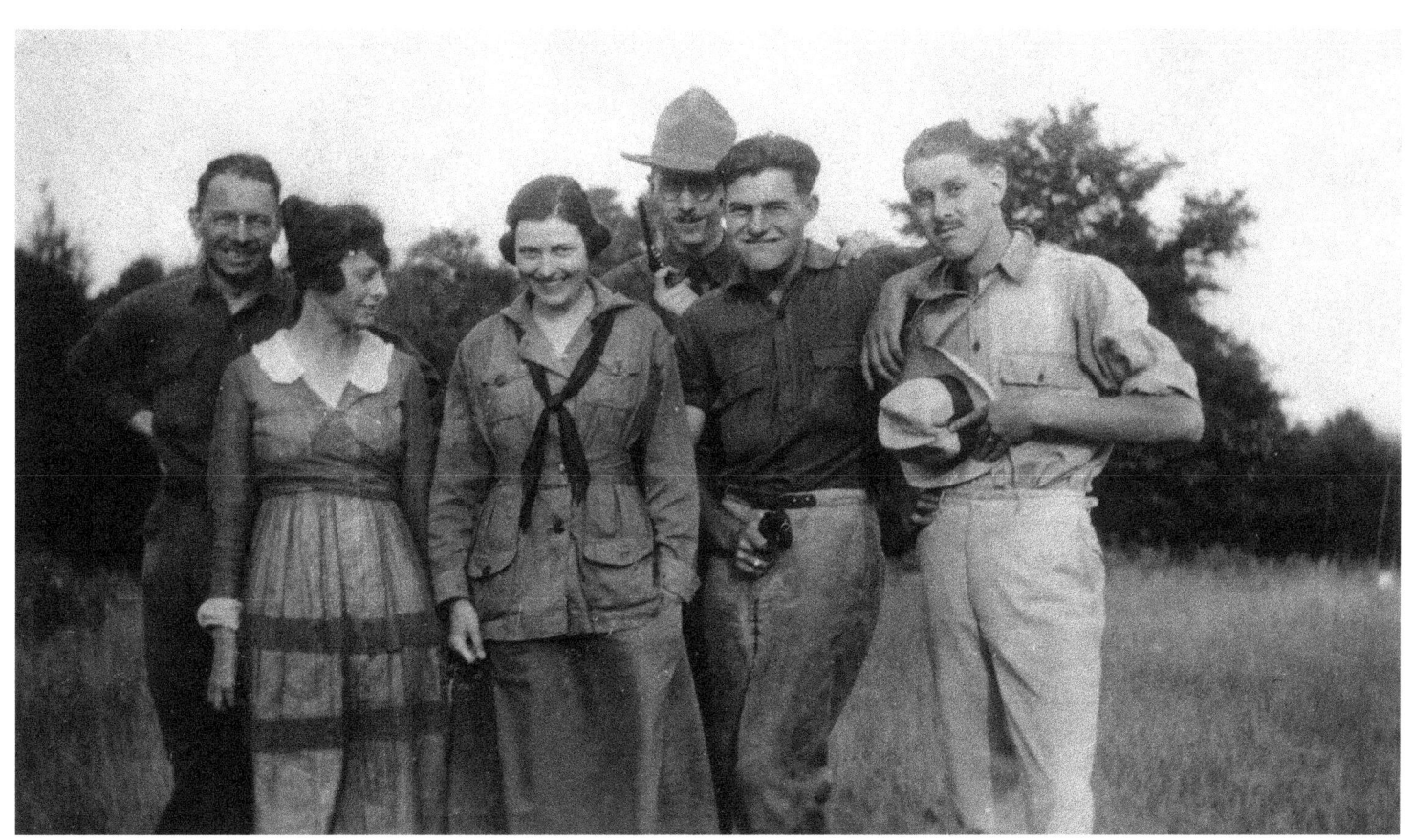

Ernest's mother became fed up with his postwar attitude and, blaming him for an incident involving the Hemingway sisters and neighbor girls, banished him and his ambulance driver friend from Windemere. In 1920, the "summer people" regulars who vacationed with the Hemingways since childhood were more important to him than ever. From left: Carl Edgar, Katy Smith, Marcelline, fellow driver Bill Horne, Ernest, and Charles Hopkins.

In this photo, from around January 1921, Ernest dons a fake mustache and strikes a John L. Sullivan pose in Y. K. Smith's apartment, where he and Bill Horne landed after the summer fireworks up in Michigan. Smith was the older brother of Hemingway's friends Katy and Bill, and in his apartment Hemingway met Sherwood Anderson, who encouraged him to go to Paris and provided him with a letter of introduction to Gertrude Stein.

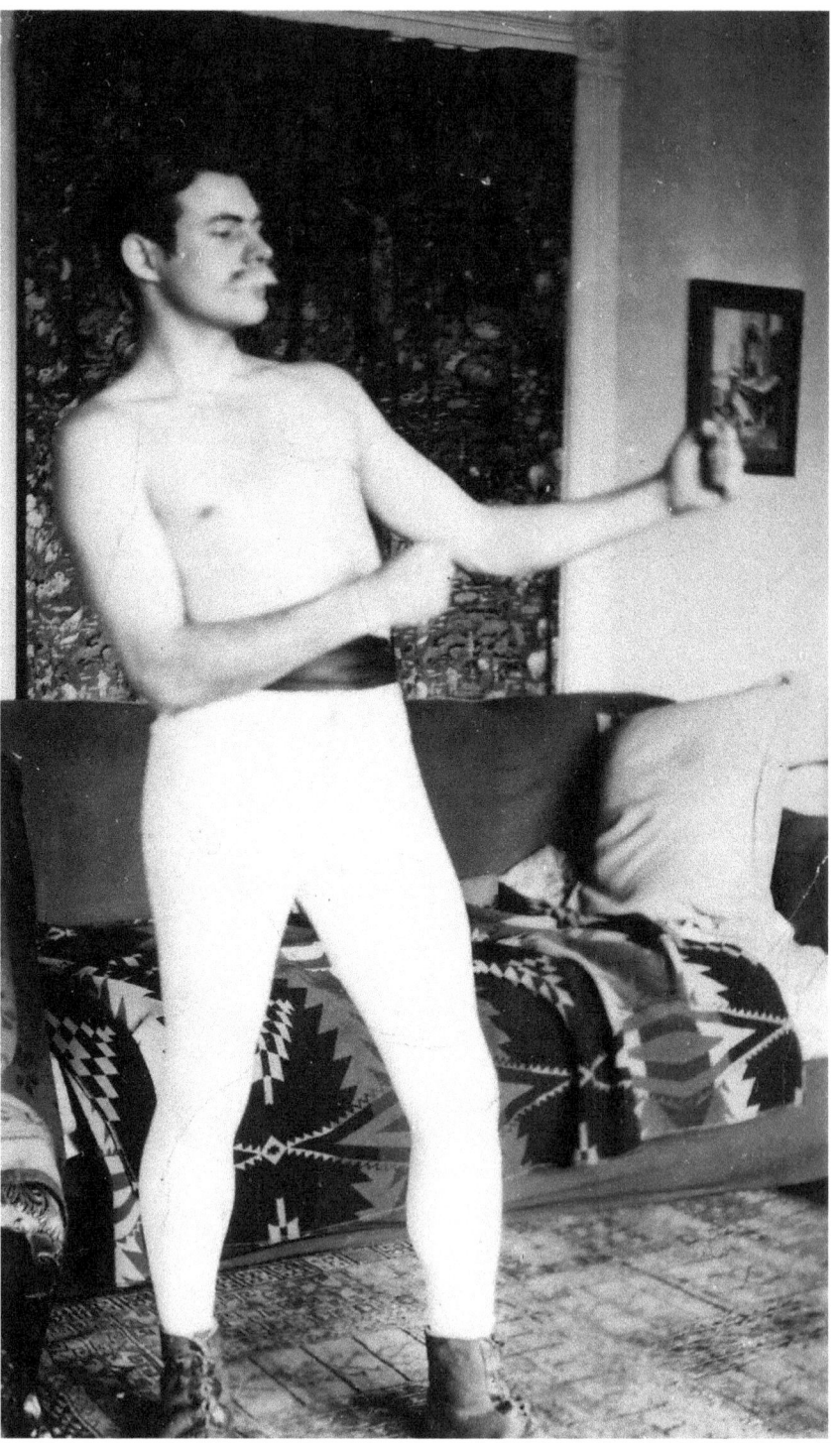

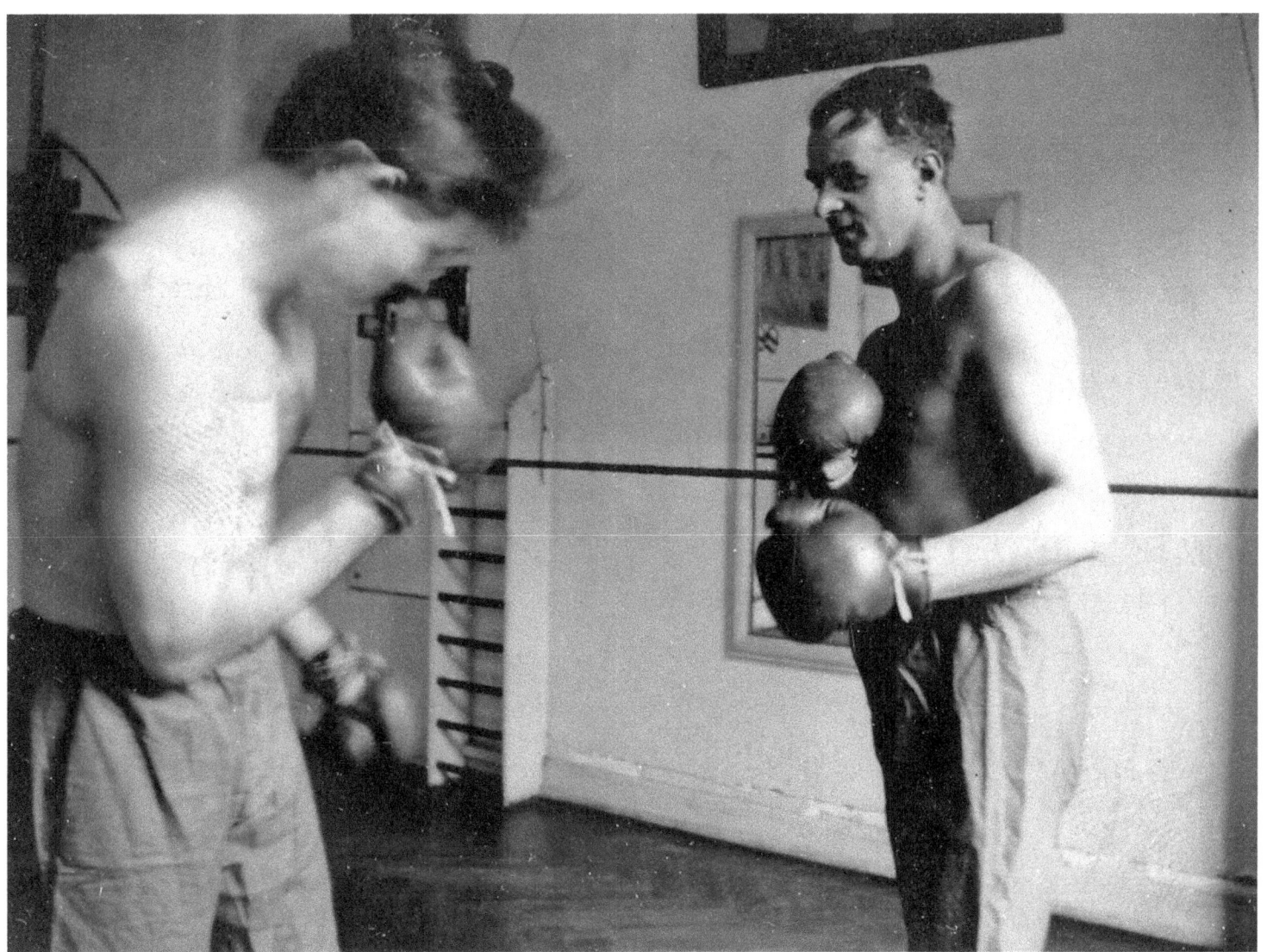

Since the age of 16, Hemingway (left) had taken a keen interest in boxing, and one of three stories he published in the *Tabula* concerned a boxing manager. Hemingway claimed to have learned how to box at Kid Howard's and other Chicago gyms, and he used the music room at the Hemingway house to challenge his friends to friendly bouts—until Grace kicked them out. Odds are, there was real boxing at Y. K. Smith's apartment, too.

At another Y. K. Smith party on Chicago's north side, Ernest met Hadley Richardson, who, like Agnes, was eight years his senior. Hadley was visiting from St. Louis and the two hit it off so spectacularly that she stayed three weeks in a spare bedroom so they could spend more time together. Then Ernest visited her in St. Louis to continue their courtship. This photo was taken March 1921 in the backyard of Hadley's home on Cates Avenue.

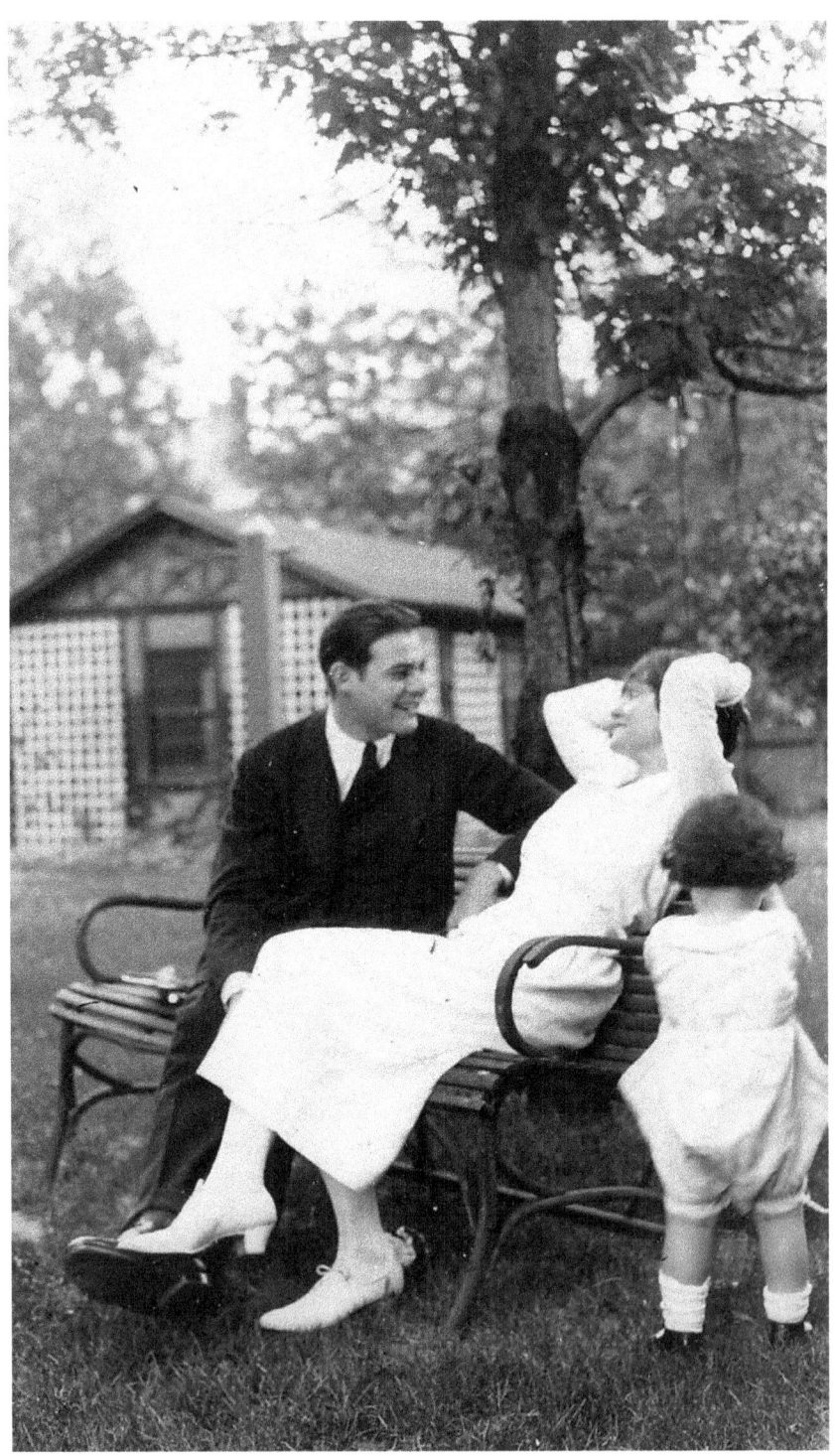

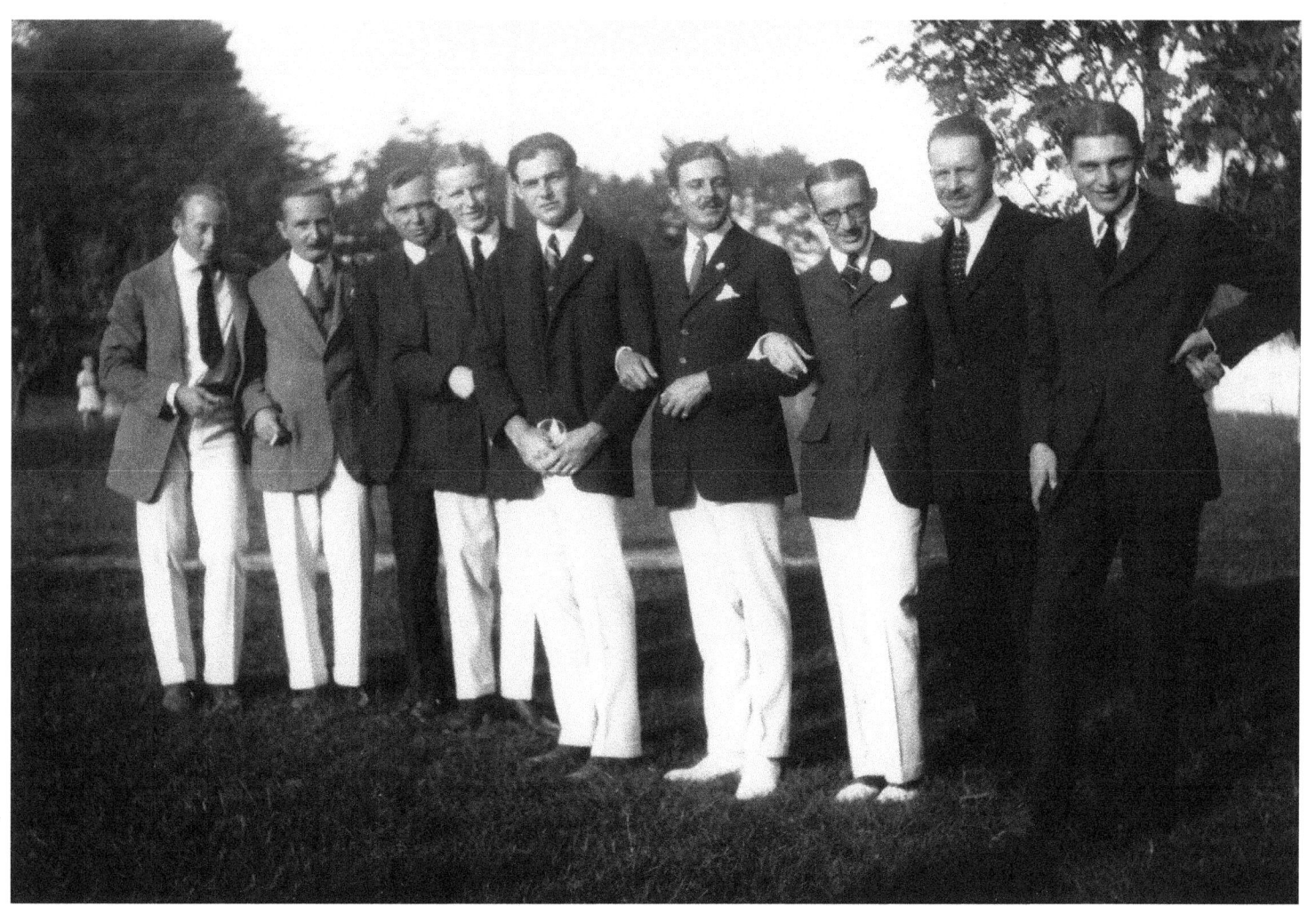

Ernest Hemingway married Hadley Richardson on September 3, 1921, in Horton Bay. Attending the groom (fifth from left) were a few familiar faces, like Bill Smith and Bill Horne, on his left. Over the summer, buoyed by romance, Ernest was inspired to write "Up in Michigan," a story Gertrude Stein would later say was not publishable because it dealt with what's now considered date-rape.

No doubt they loved each other, but each was ripe for romance. Hadley's mother had just passed away, and her father had committed suicide when she was 14. Ernest, meanwhile, was still on the rebound from the Agnes affair, and getting thrown out of the family cottage didn't help. His friends were opposed to the marriage, but his mother took it as a sign of his maturing, so the whole Hemingway clan happily attended.

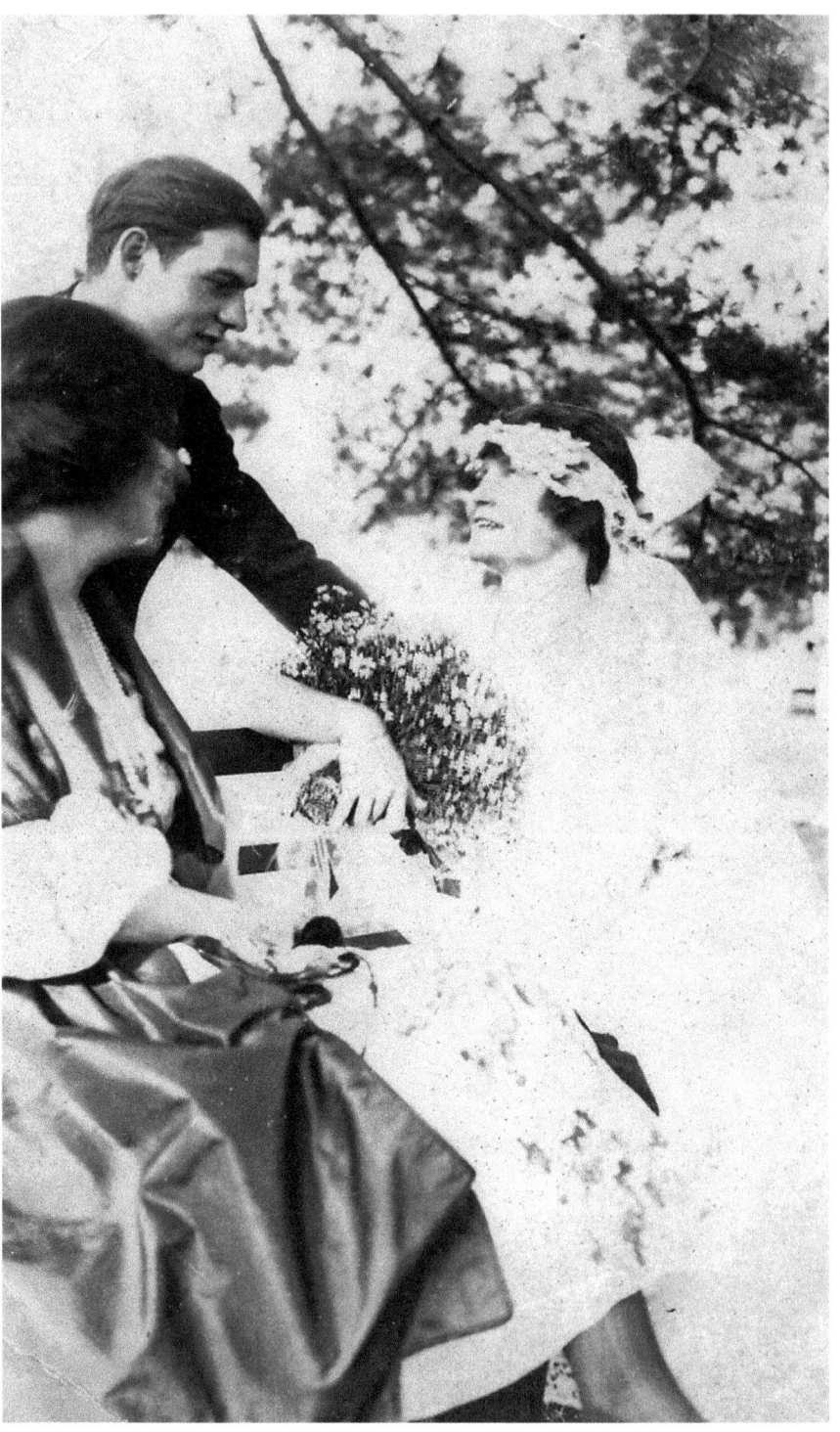

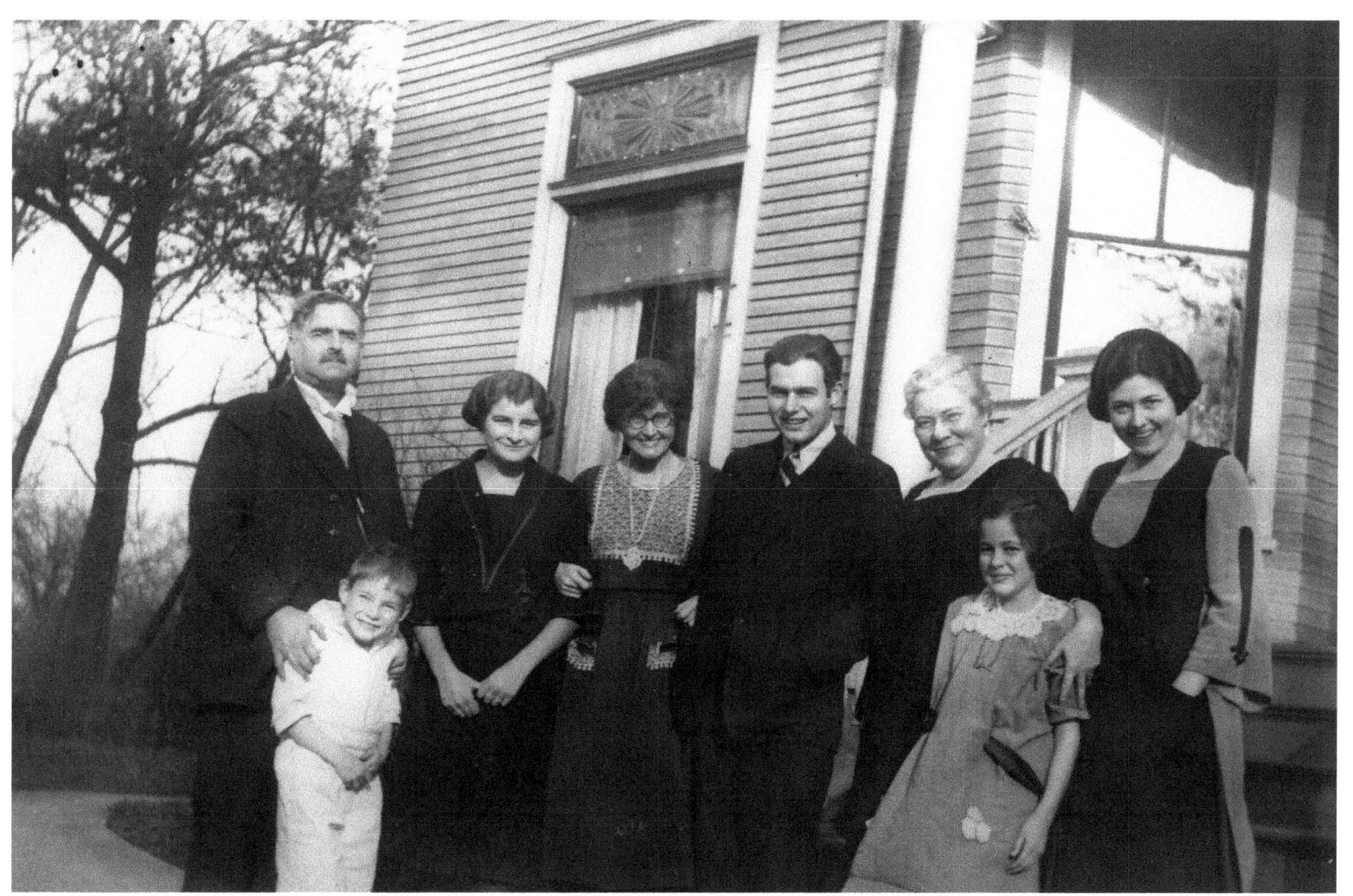

The Hemingways pose for a picture with the newlyweds in fall 1921 (left to right): Clarence, Leicester, Sunny, Hadley, Ernest, Grace, Carol, and Marcelline. Hadley admired Ernest's boxing and fishing skills and was supportive of his writing, willing to use her trust fund to give Ernest the chance to follow Sherwood Anderson's advice. The couple would set sail for France in December.

After landing in Paris, the newlyweds left for Chamby sur Montreux for a belated honeymoon in January 1922. In Paris, Hemingway said his goal was to write "one true sentence." During the year he'd finish "My Old Man" but find their marriage tested in December after Hadley, en route to join him in Switzerland again, lost a suitcase containing all but two of the short stories he had written, representing two years of work.

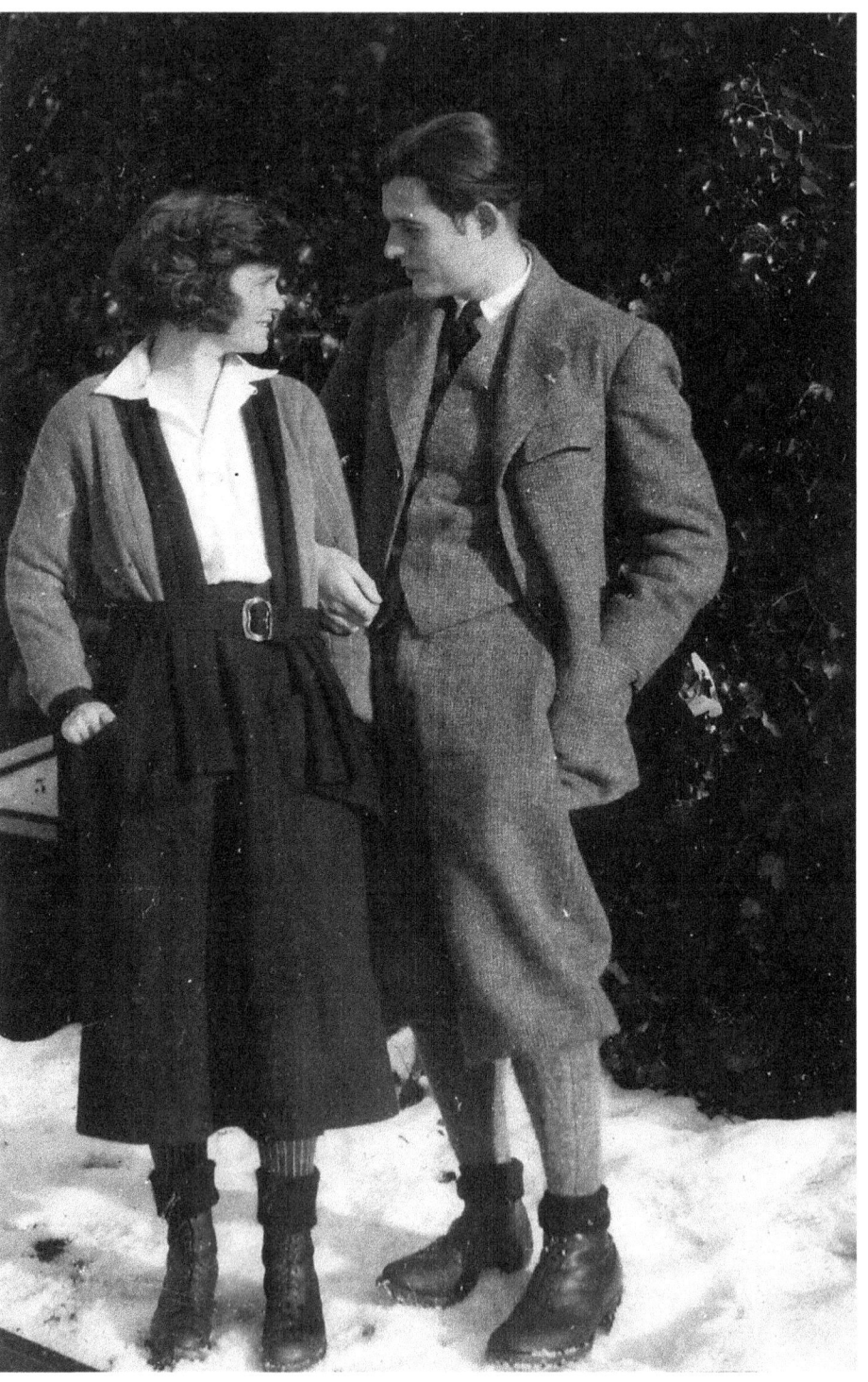

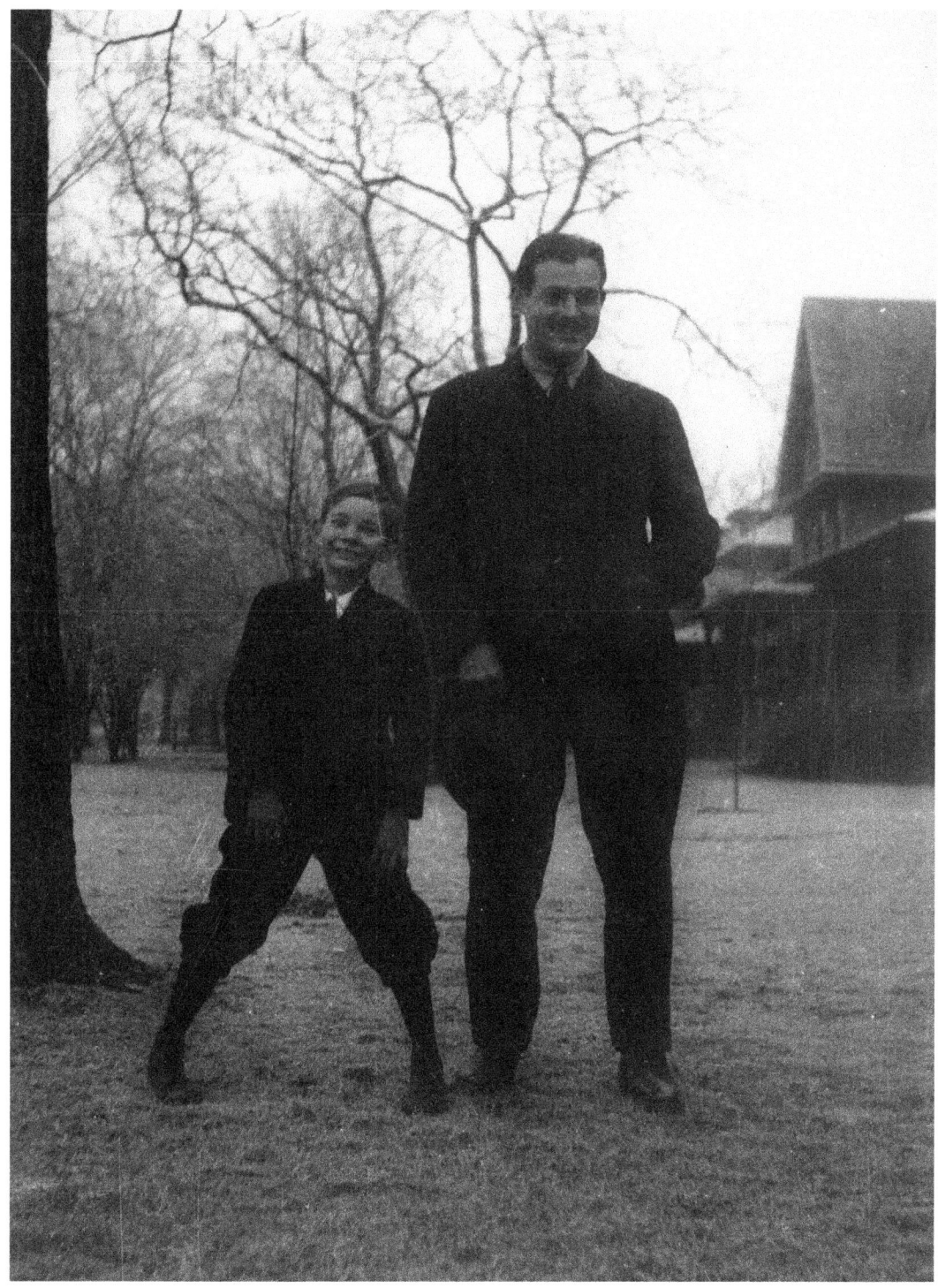

By the time the Hemingways returned to Oak Park in 1923 for a Christmas visit, Ernest had published his first poems in *Poetry* magazine, as well as a first book *(Three Stories & Ten Poems)*. He also covered two world conferences and the Greco-Turkish war for the *Toronto Star* and became a father for the first time. John Hadley Nicanor Hemingway was born on October 10, so little brother and new uncle Les had plenty to admire.

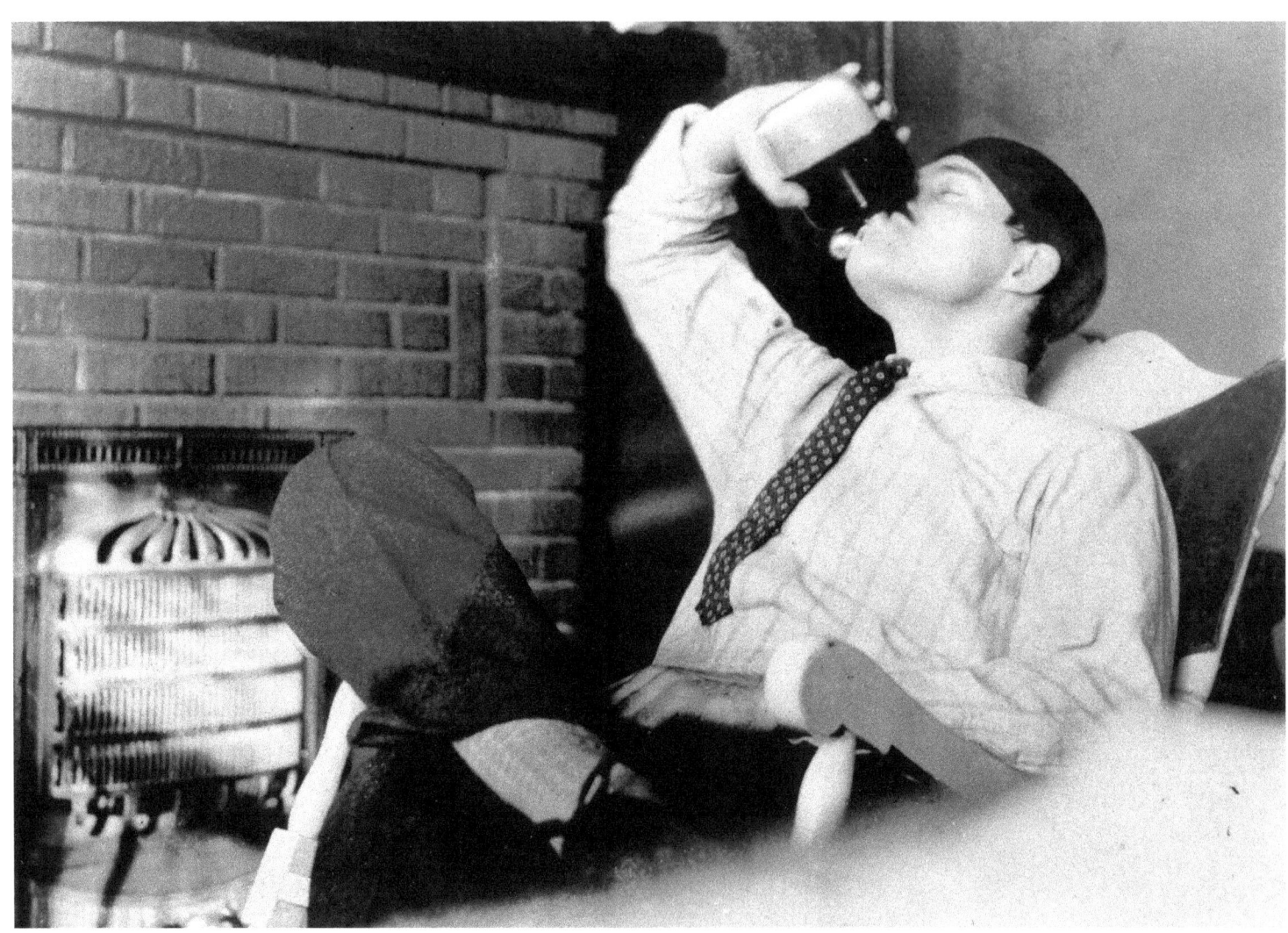

February 1924. Hemingway took to Paris, and vice versa. His writing was going well, *In Our Time* was being published and hailed a masterwork by all who read it, and he was part of a vibrant expatriate scene that included Stein, Alice B. Toklas, Ezra Pound, F. Scott Fitzgerald, Sylvia Beach, and James Joyce. This photo was taken not long after he and Hadley moved into their new apartment—a carpenter's loft above a commercial sawmill at 113 rue Notre-Dáme-des-Champs.

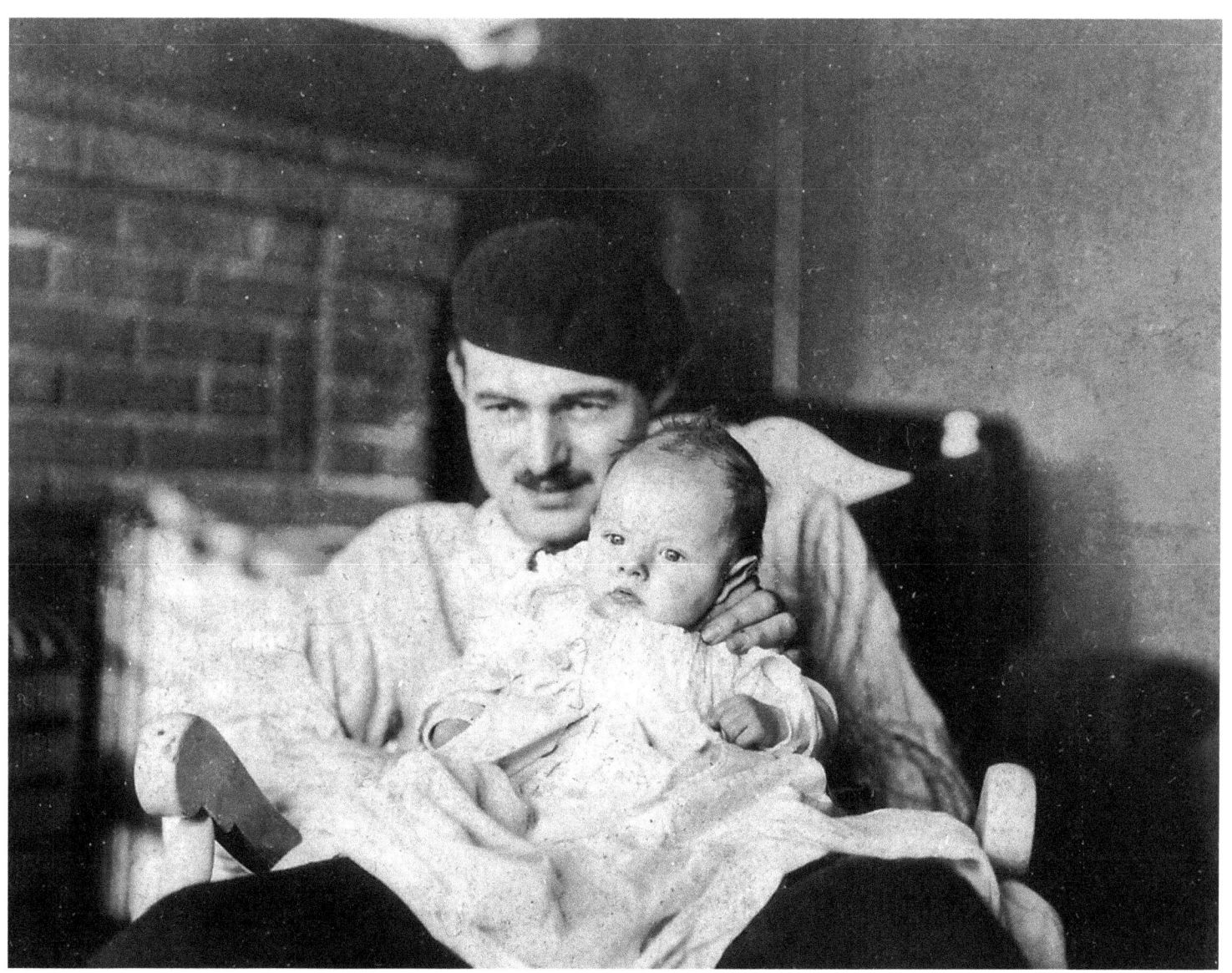

Ernest with baby John, whom he nicknamed "Bumby." The writing continued to go well, with Hemingway just finishing "Cat in the Rain" and "The End of Something." When the saws grew too loud, he would walk to the nearby Closerie des Lilas to work on his writing in that clean, well-lighted café, while Hadley enjoyed taking Bumby on walks to the nearby Luxembourg Gardens. Ernest's favorite sections of Paris were Montparnasse and the 5th and 6th arrondissements.

Gertrude Stein and Alice B. Toklas were named godparents when Bumby was baptized in spring 1924, and Stein attends to him here—an unexpected image, considering that this imposing woman hosted some of the biggest painters and writers of the century in her salon and is credited with coining the term "Lost Generation" to describe all of the jaded postwar writers.

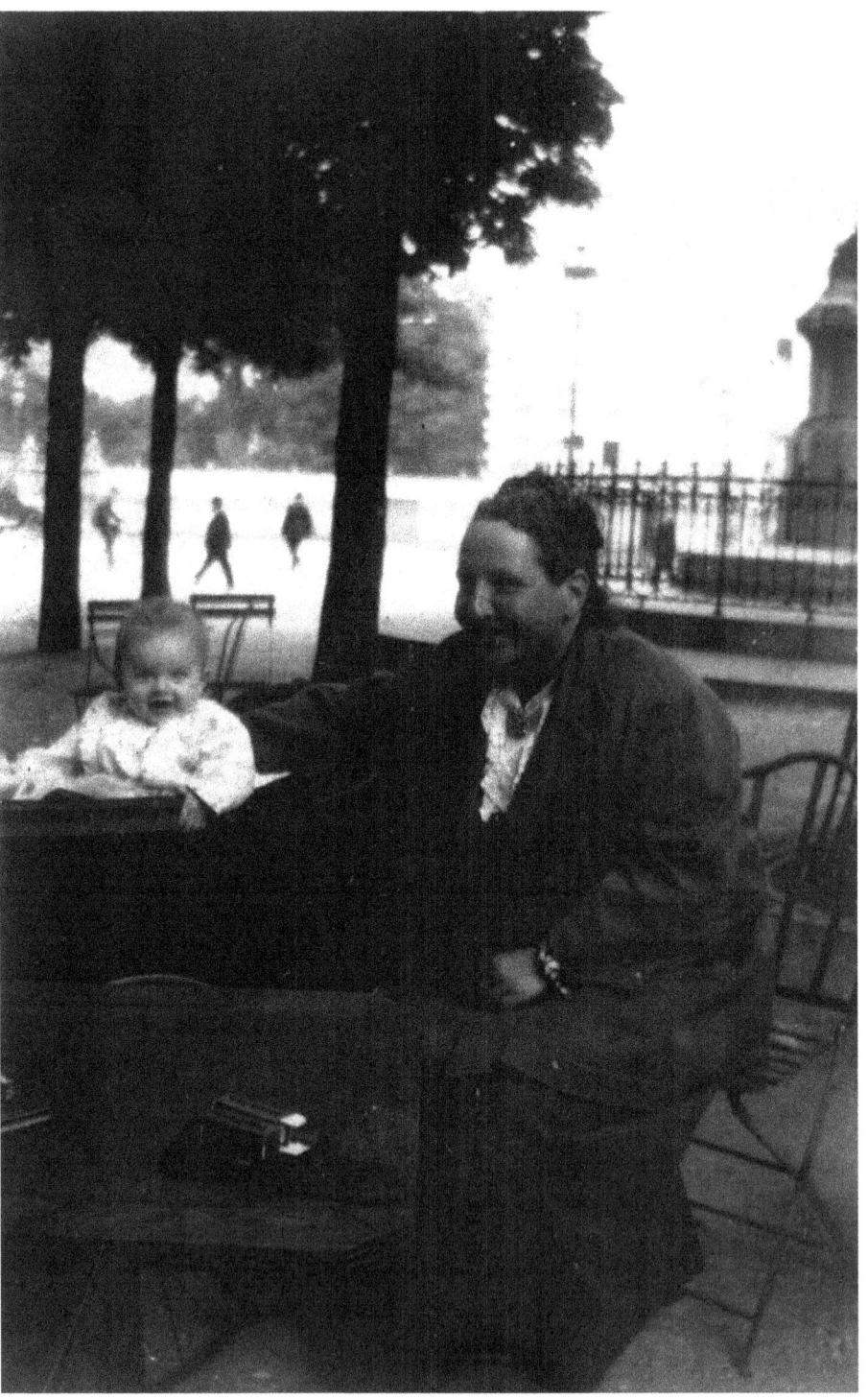

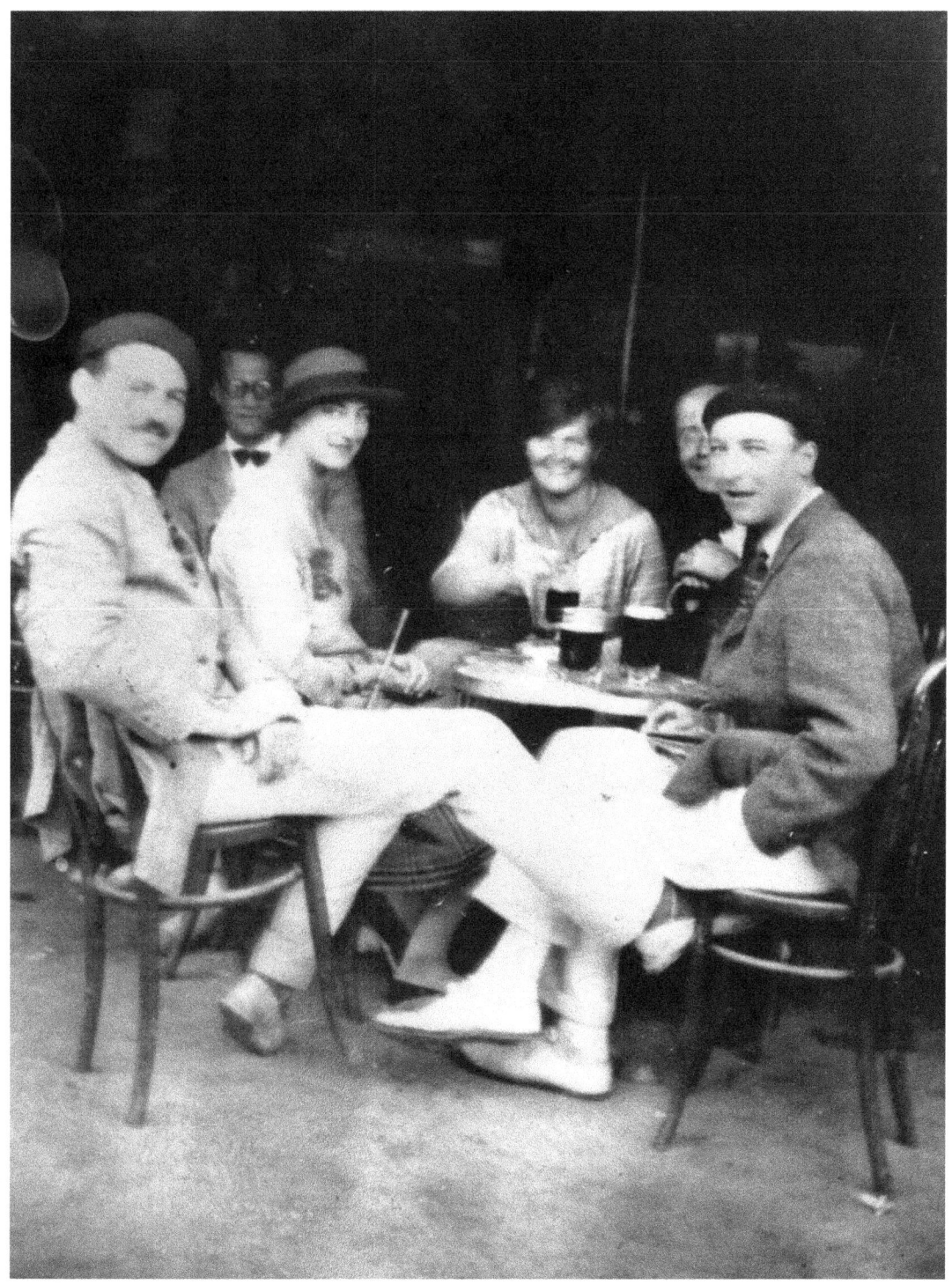

It was Stein who suggested Pamplona, and Ernest was immediately hooked. July 1925, when this photo was taken, marked his third San Fermin fiesta, the one to become immortalized in *The Sun Also Rises*. Here at an outdoor café sits Hemingway (left) with Lady Duff Twysden (model for Brett Ashley), Hadley, and Pat Guthrie (model for Mike Campbell). Driving the novel was Hemingway's disappointment that 1925 never measured up to the magic of their first San Fermin.

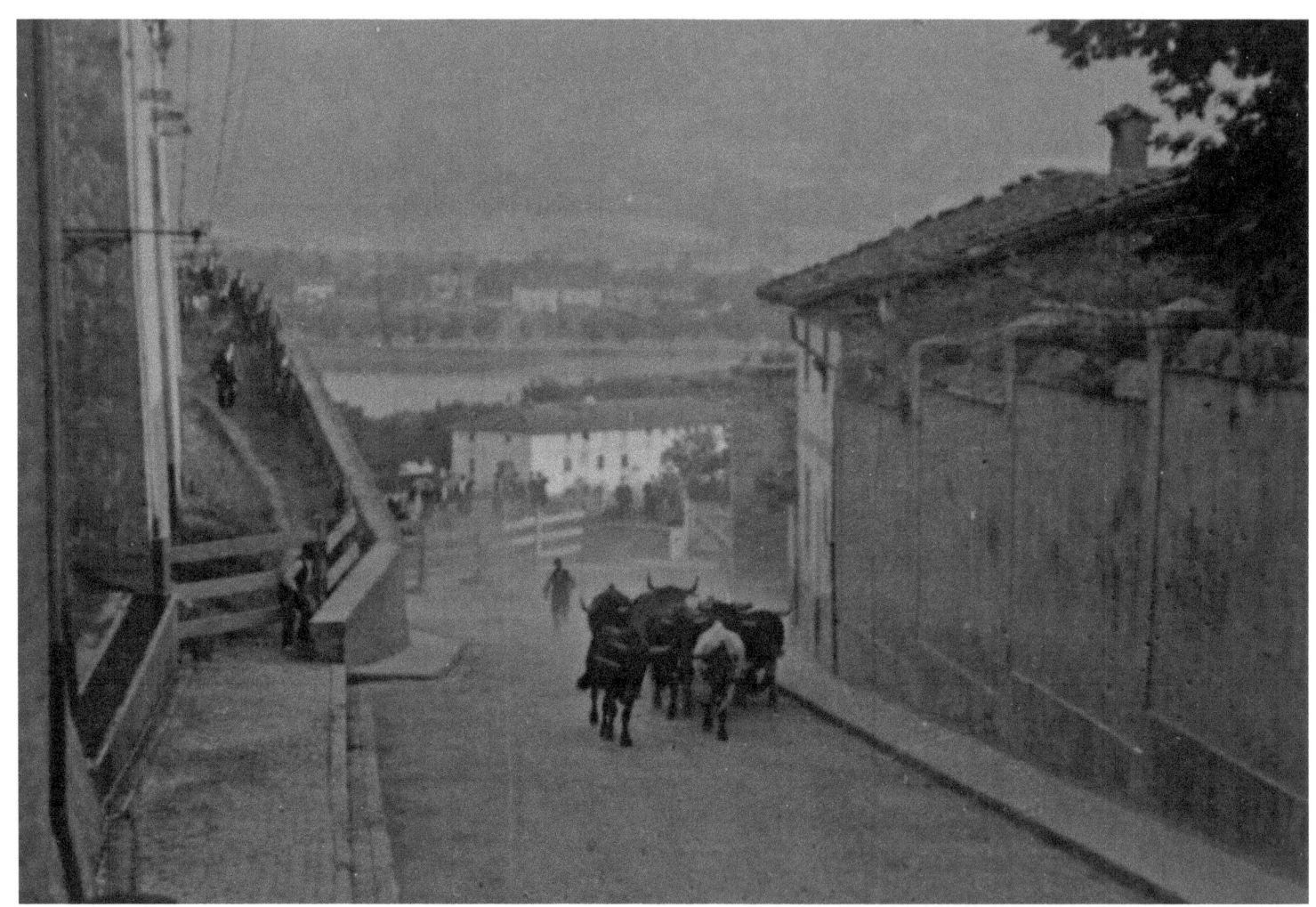

For eight of the nine days of the Pamplona festival, bulls corralled near the top of the old city are released at 8:00 A.M. and participants run with them until they're all funneled into the Plaza de Toros a little over a mile away. Barricades keep the bulls on-course and give crowds a relatively safe place from which they can watch the spectacle. Because of his war injuries, it's almost certain that Hemingway did not run.

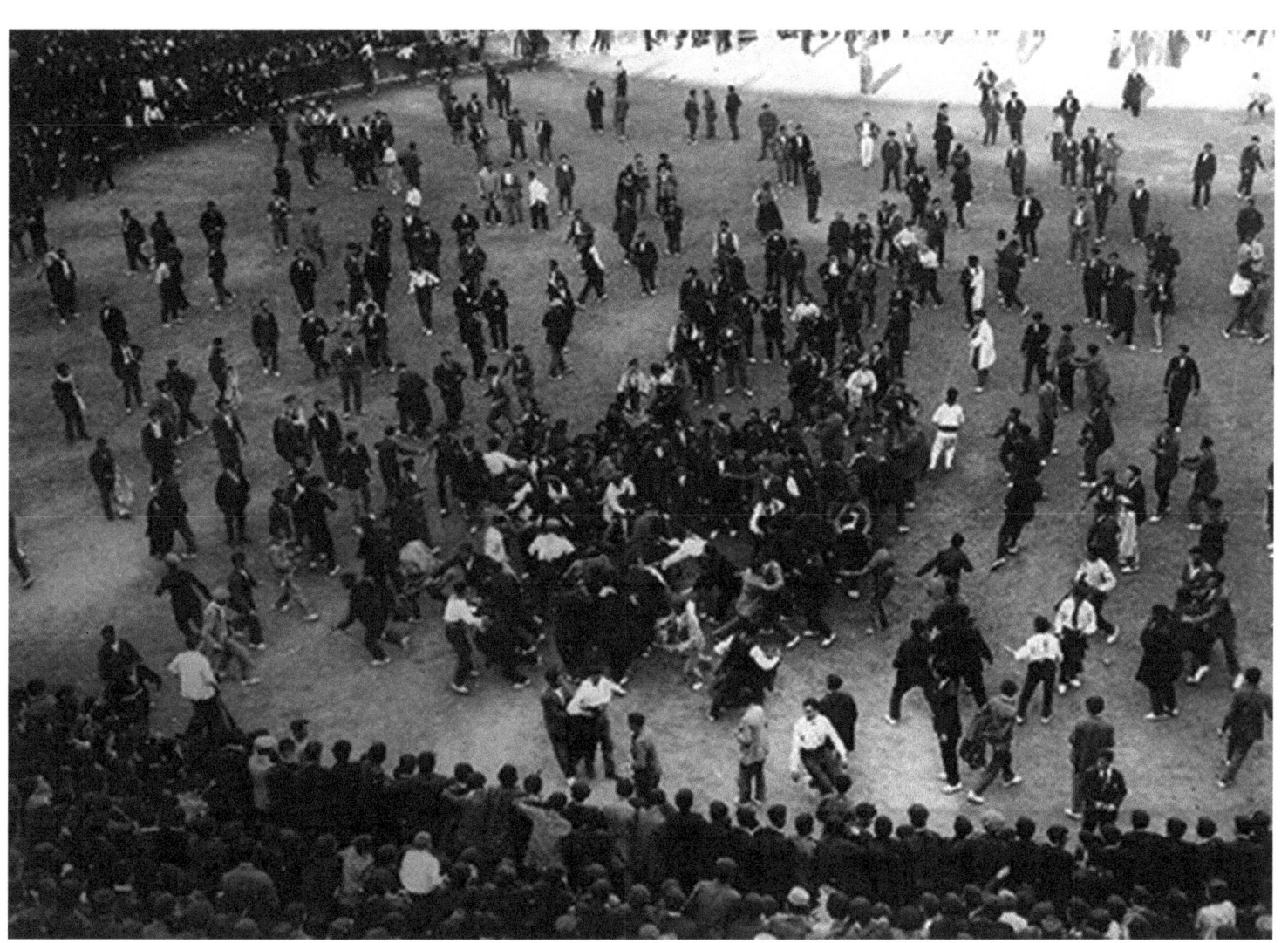

Hemingway relished participating in the encierro, or amateur bullfights, which he described as "unorganized as a riot." To do so he had to position himself near the end of the run and climb through the barricade to follow the bulls and runners into the ring. But everything about San Fermín was exciting to him, from the all-day, all-night drinking to the colorful riau-riau bands that led impromptu parades of revelers down the narrow cobblestone streets of Old Pamplona.

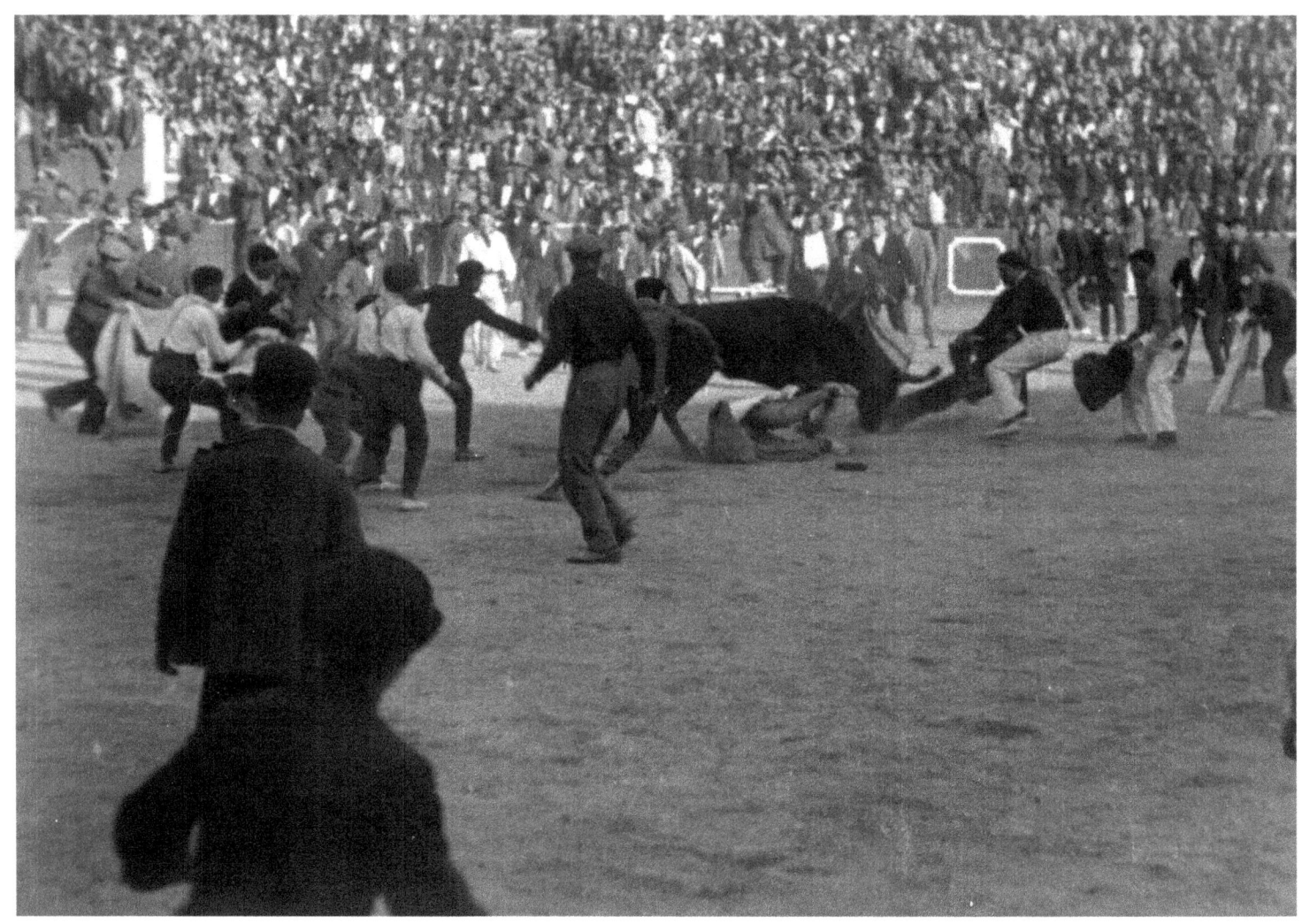

In the amateur bullfight, Hemingway, wearing white pants and a dark top, confronts the bull and goads him
to charge. This San Fermin was considerably less eventful than his first, when Ernest and his friends made the
newspapers—including the *Chicago Tribune*—because Donald Ogden Stewart was thrown into the air and Ernest
was gored when he tried to help his friend.

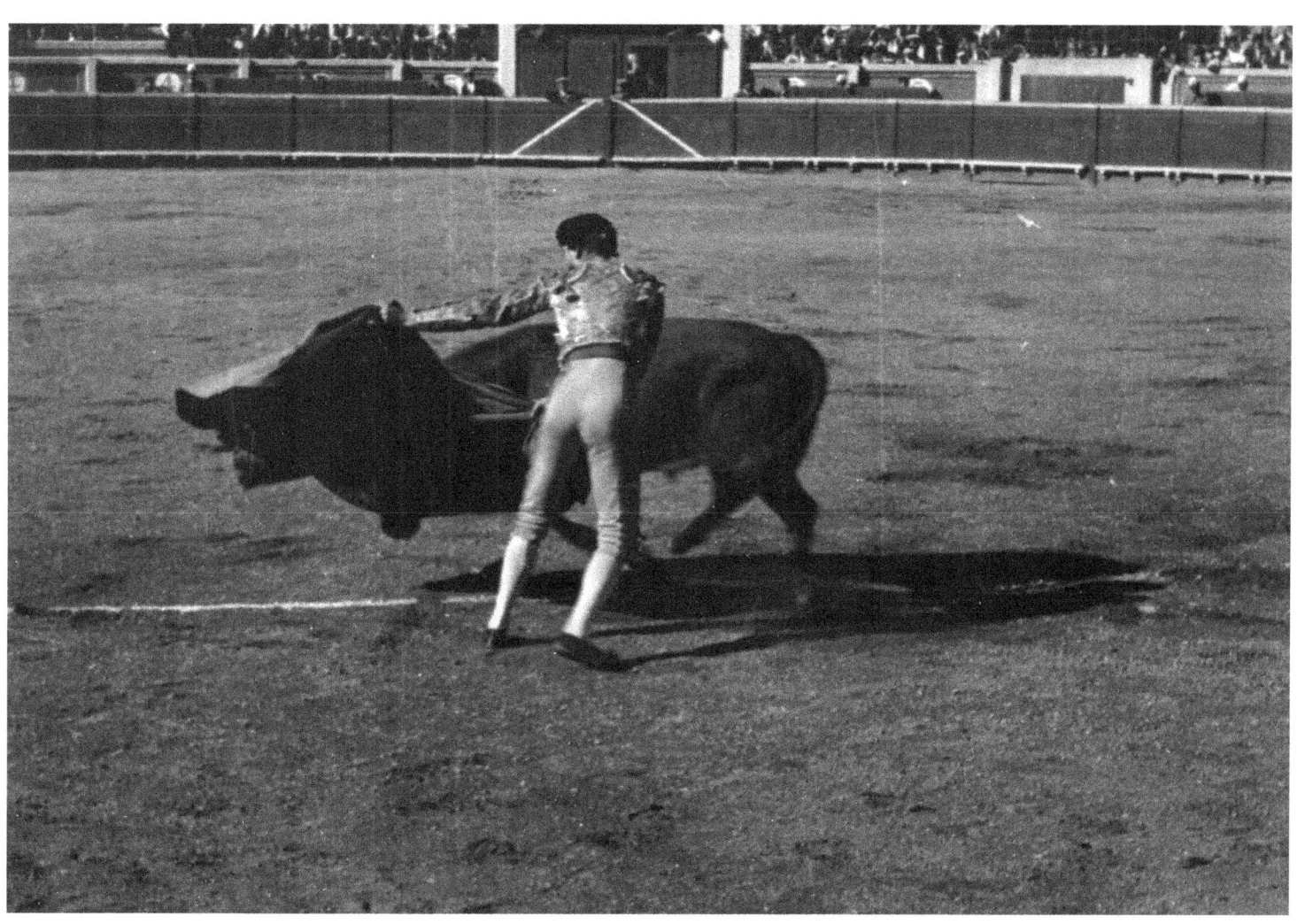

Hemingway finished the first draft of *Fiesta* (as it was titled in England) in September 1925. Though *The Sun Also Rises* would become a best-seller and enjoy critical success on two continents, it clashed with Midwestern values. The *Chicago Tribune* called it "exactly what you would expect a mediocre young man from Oak Park, Ill., and not one with real talent, to write about," and Grace wrote her son that every page filled her with "a sick loathing." Afterward, she referred to it only as "that book."

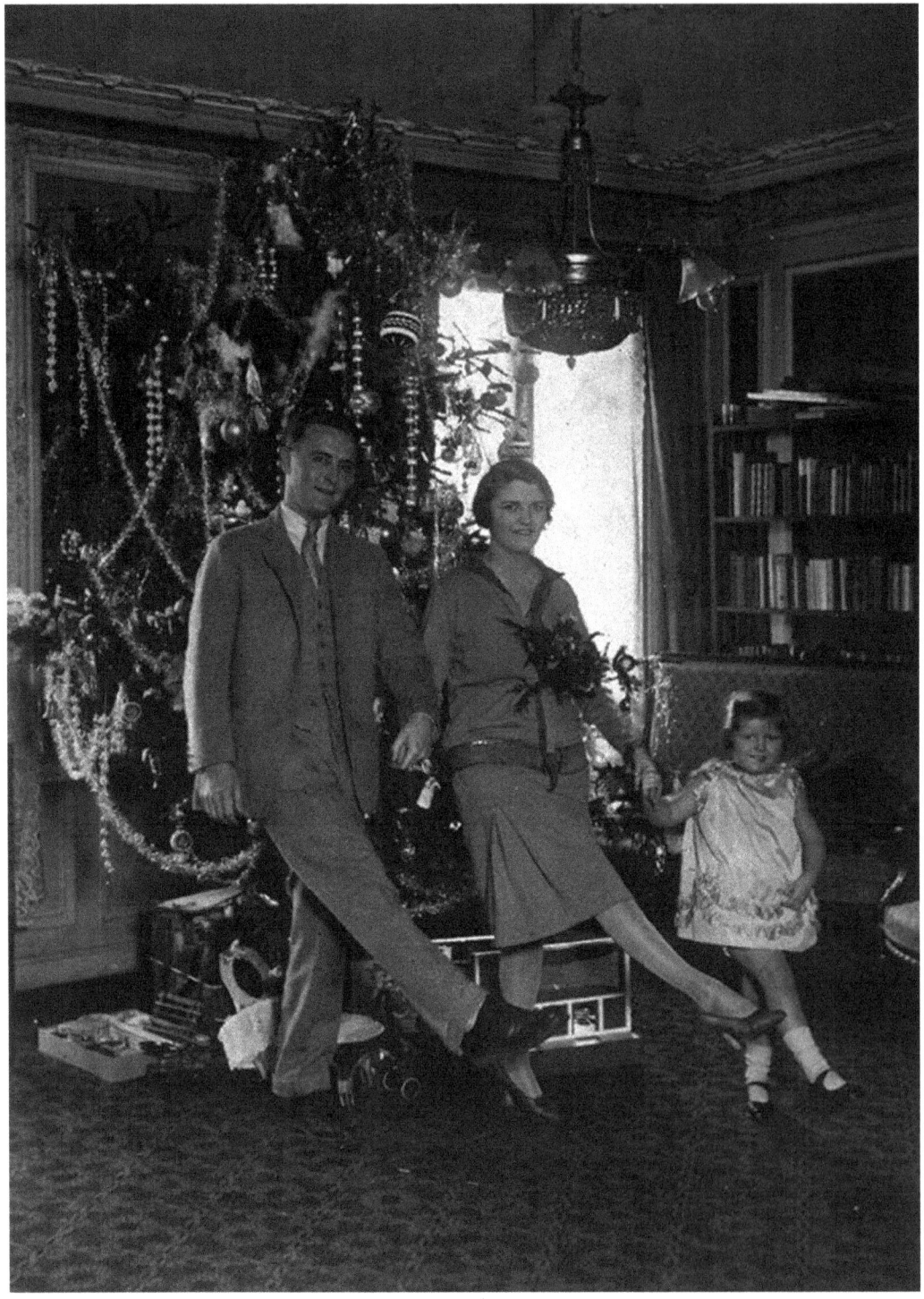

Scott, Zelda, and Scottie Fitzgerald celebrate Christmas 1925 in their posh Paris apartment. Having met in Paris earlier that year, Hemingway and Fitzgerald had a long, complicated relationship. Fitzgerald recommended him to his editor at Scribner's, and would also suggest cuts to *The Sun Also Rises,* which Hemingway would grudgingly make. But Hemingway's penchant for seeing everything as a competition often got in the way of friendships, as it would with Scott.

The Hemingways spent Christmas 1925 and part of the new year in Schruns, Austria, where they skied with friends. Here at the hotel, Hemingway poses with socialite Gerald Murphy and former ambulance driver and fellow writer John Dos Passos, who seems uncomfortable enough with the linked-arms pose that he's thrust his hands into his pockets.

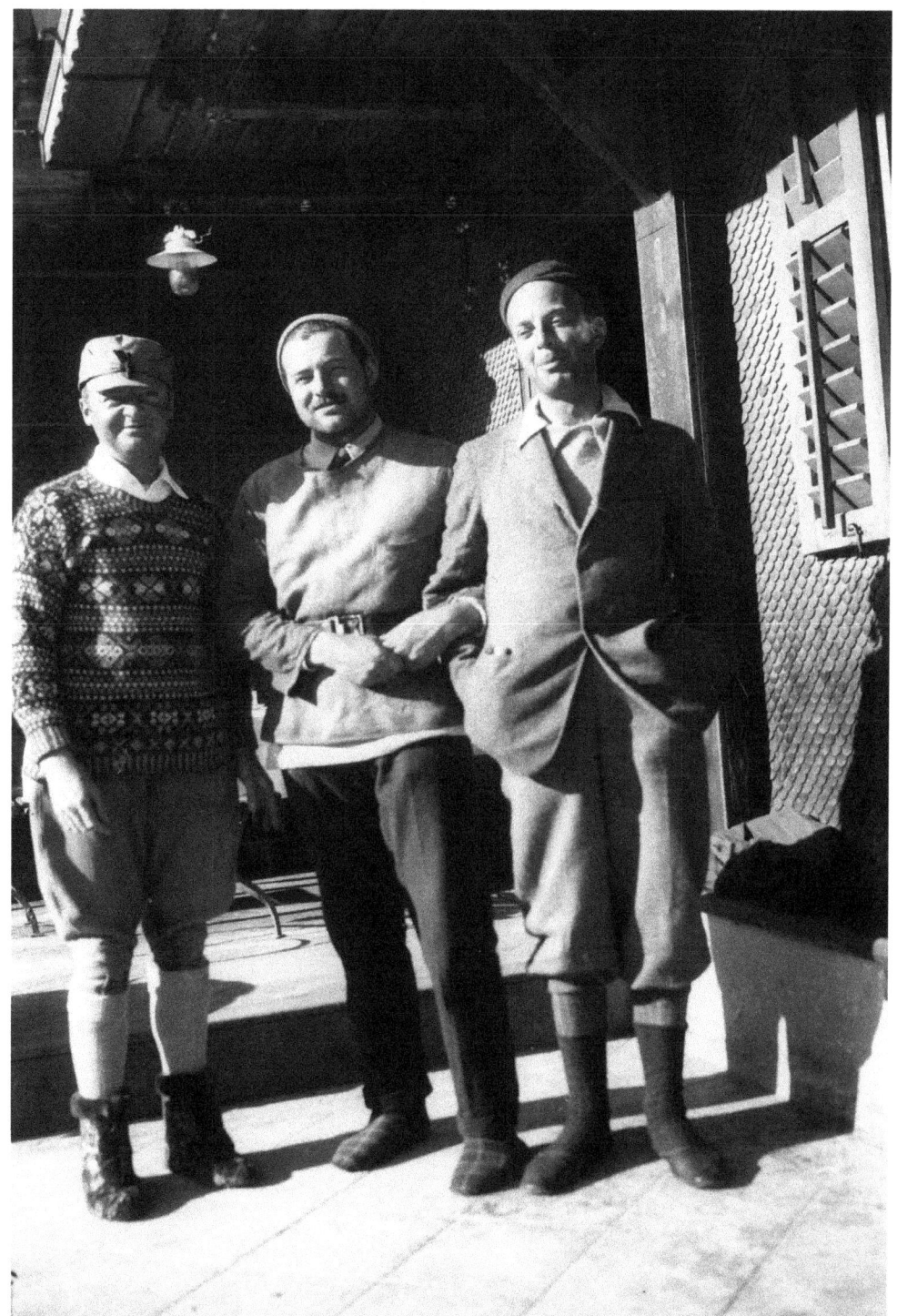

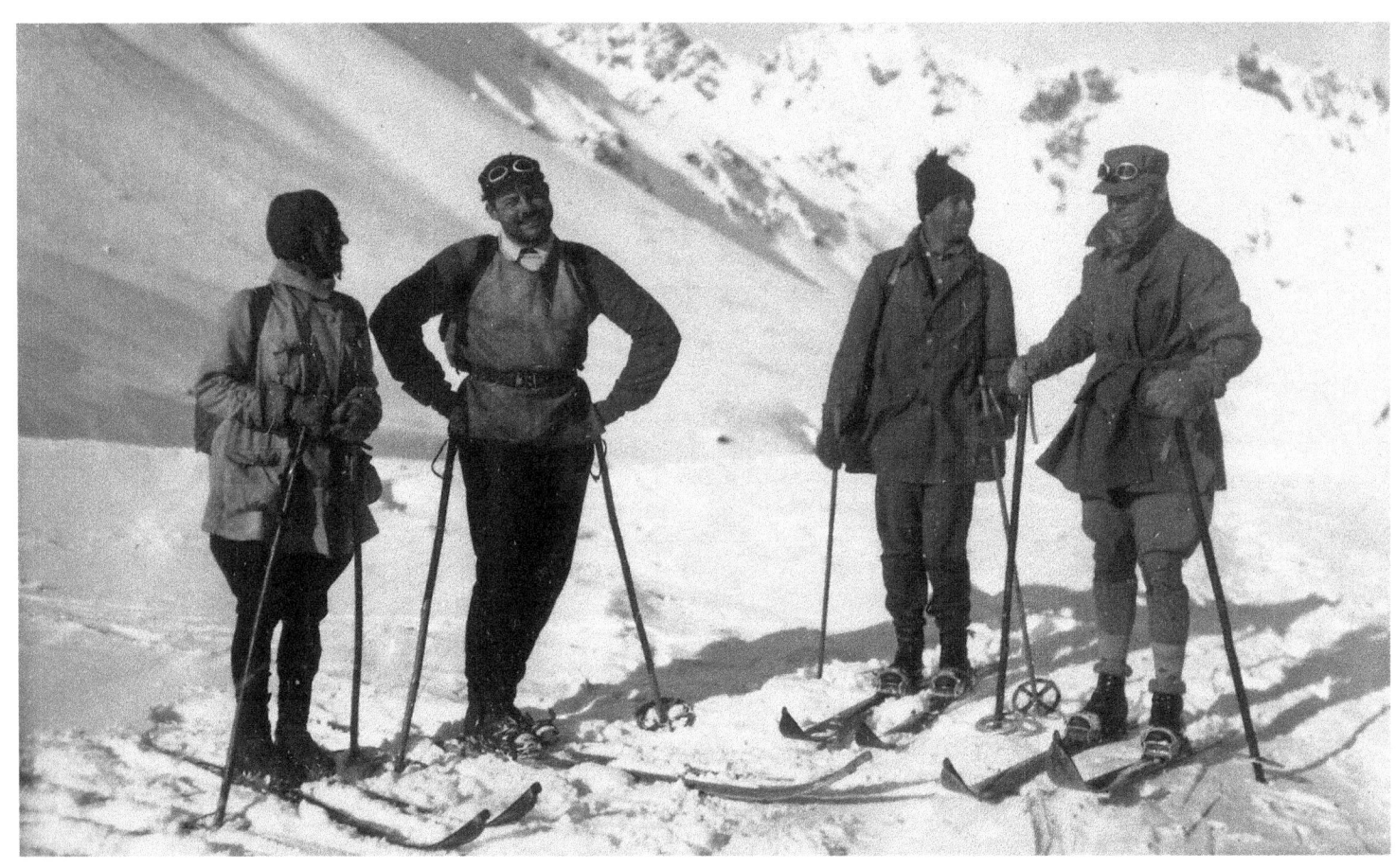

On the slopes near Schruns (left to right): a ski instructor, Hemingway, John Dos Passos, and Gerald Murphy. When Hemingway liked a place, he wanted to share it with friends and often returned again and again.

Ernest with Bumby. Hemingway would later admit that he wasn't comfortable around children, something perhaps inherited from his mother, who had her own cabin built across the lake from Windemere as a private sanctuary. Though Hemingway's father handled most of the housekeeping and child-raising chores, Hemingway, often as not, left the children in the care of others when he went on his adventures—at least until they were old enough to shoulder a gun.

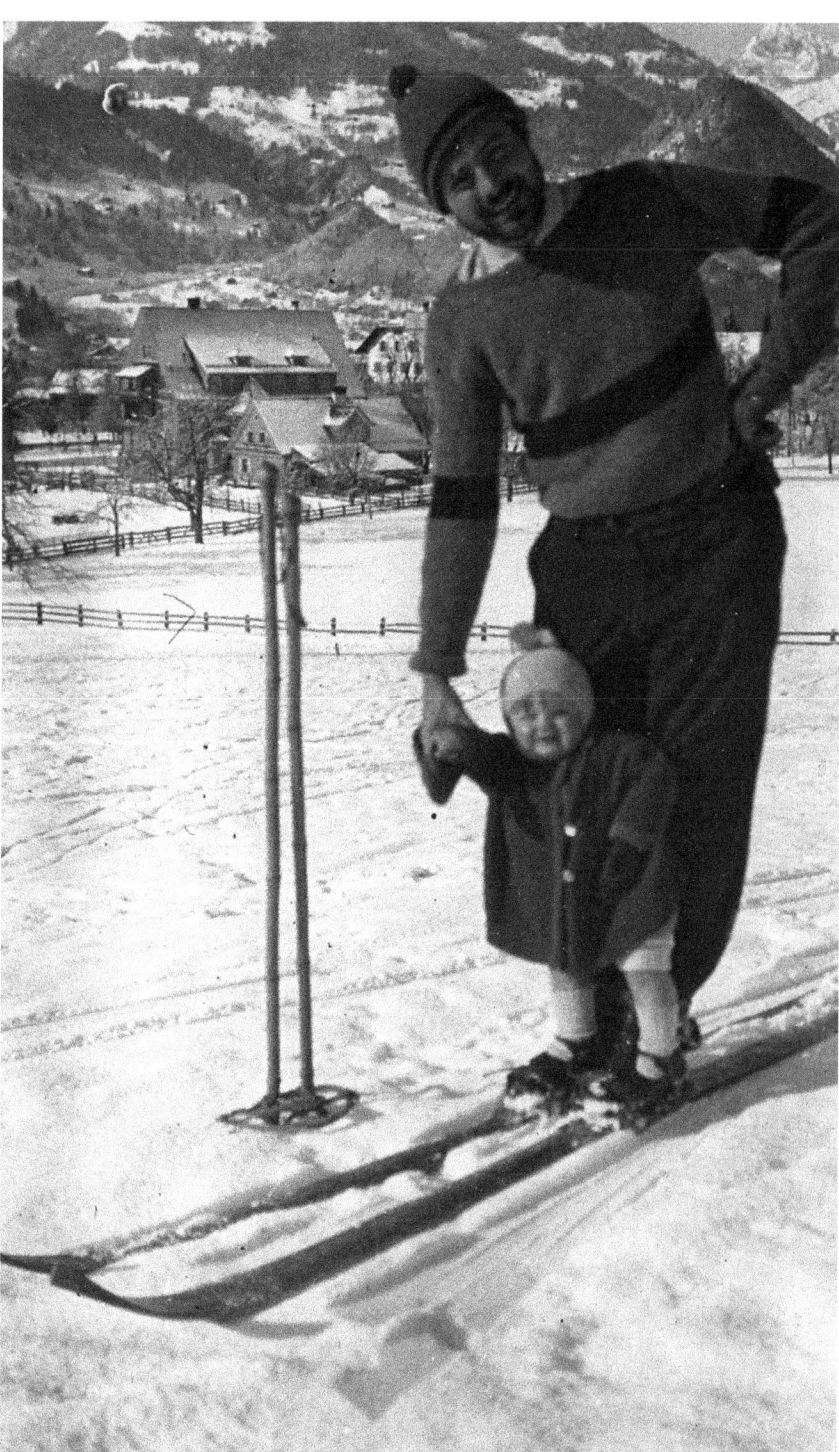

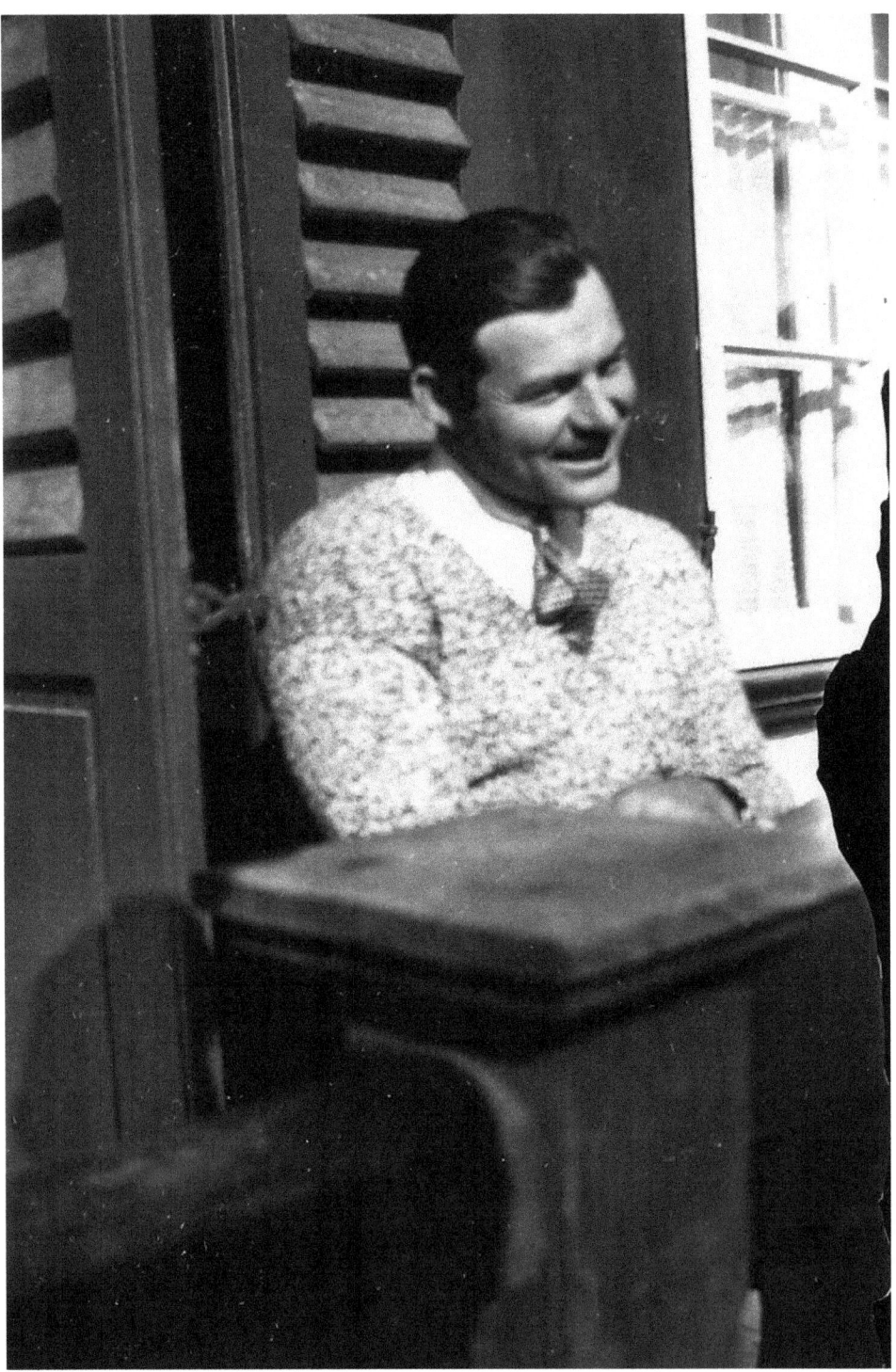

Hemingway on the balcony of their hotel, December 1925. By this time he had thrown together a novel that parodied Sherwood Anderson, all but forcing their mutual publisher, Boni & Liveright, to reject it or risk insulting Anderson, their biggest author. The break allowed him to switch to Scribner's at Scott's urging, but there was another break coming.

The Hemingways in Schruns, Austria, winter 1925-26. Though they look happy enough, the Hemingways' marriage was in trouble. Ernest had invited Pauline Pfeiffer, the Paris *Vogue* editor whom he had met at the home of a mutual friend, to join them so he could teach her how to ski. Pauline arrived on Christmas Day, but for Hadley, who may not have sensed it yet, her visit wasn't much of a present. Ernest and Pauline were immediately attracted to each other.

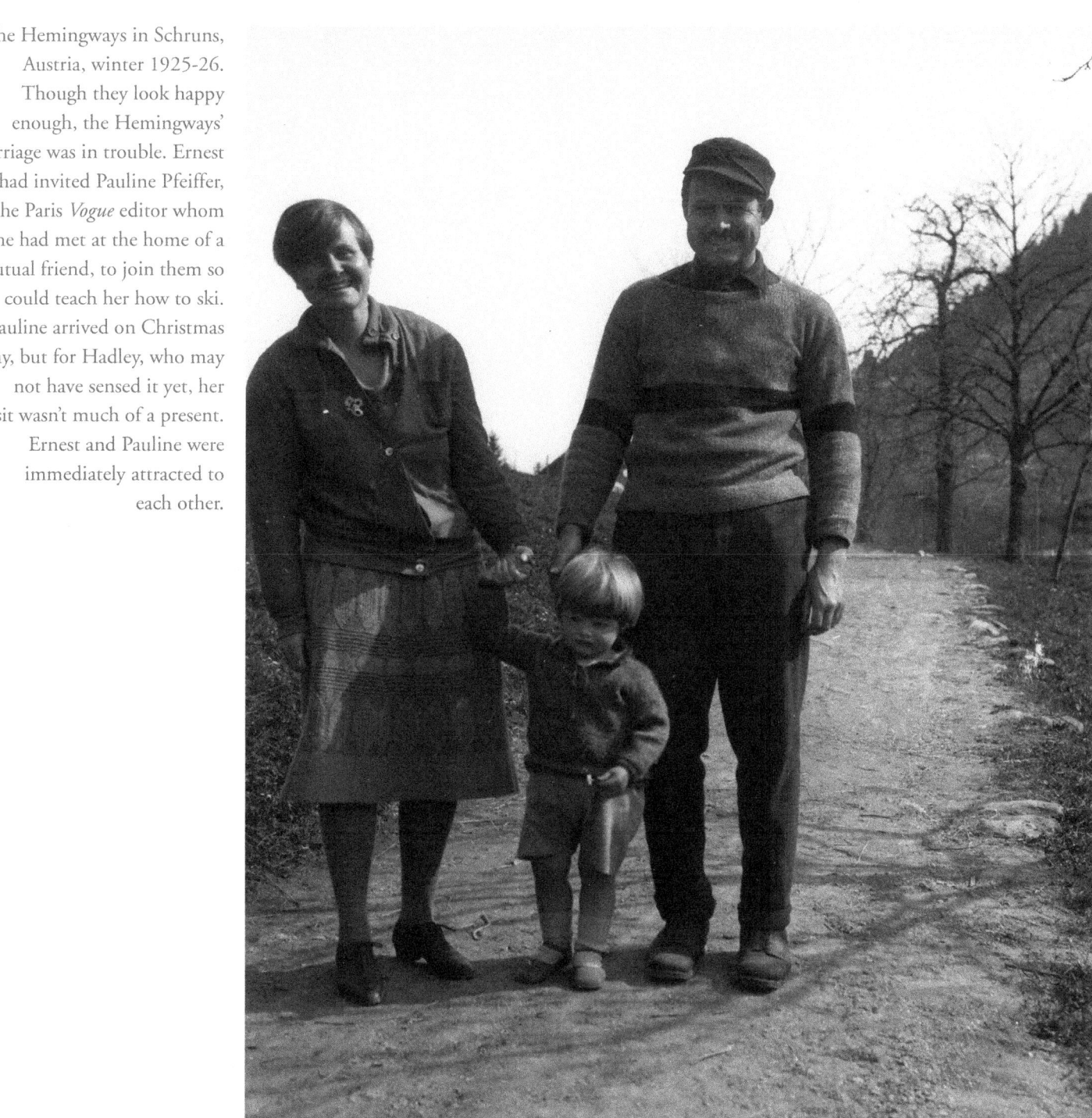

March 1926. Though still married to Hadley, Hemingway spent time in Paris with his new lover, Pauline. Fitzgerald was convinced his friend needed "a new woman for each big book," which certainly seems true. Ernest was in love with Hadley when he began *The Sun Also Rises,* and in love with Pauline when he began work on *A Farewell to Arms.* In 1926, Scribner's published his contract-breaker *Torrents of Spring* and *The Sun Also Rises,* and Ernest wrote "The Killers," one of his best stories.

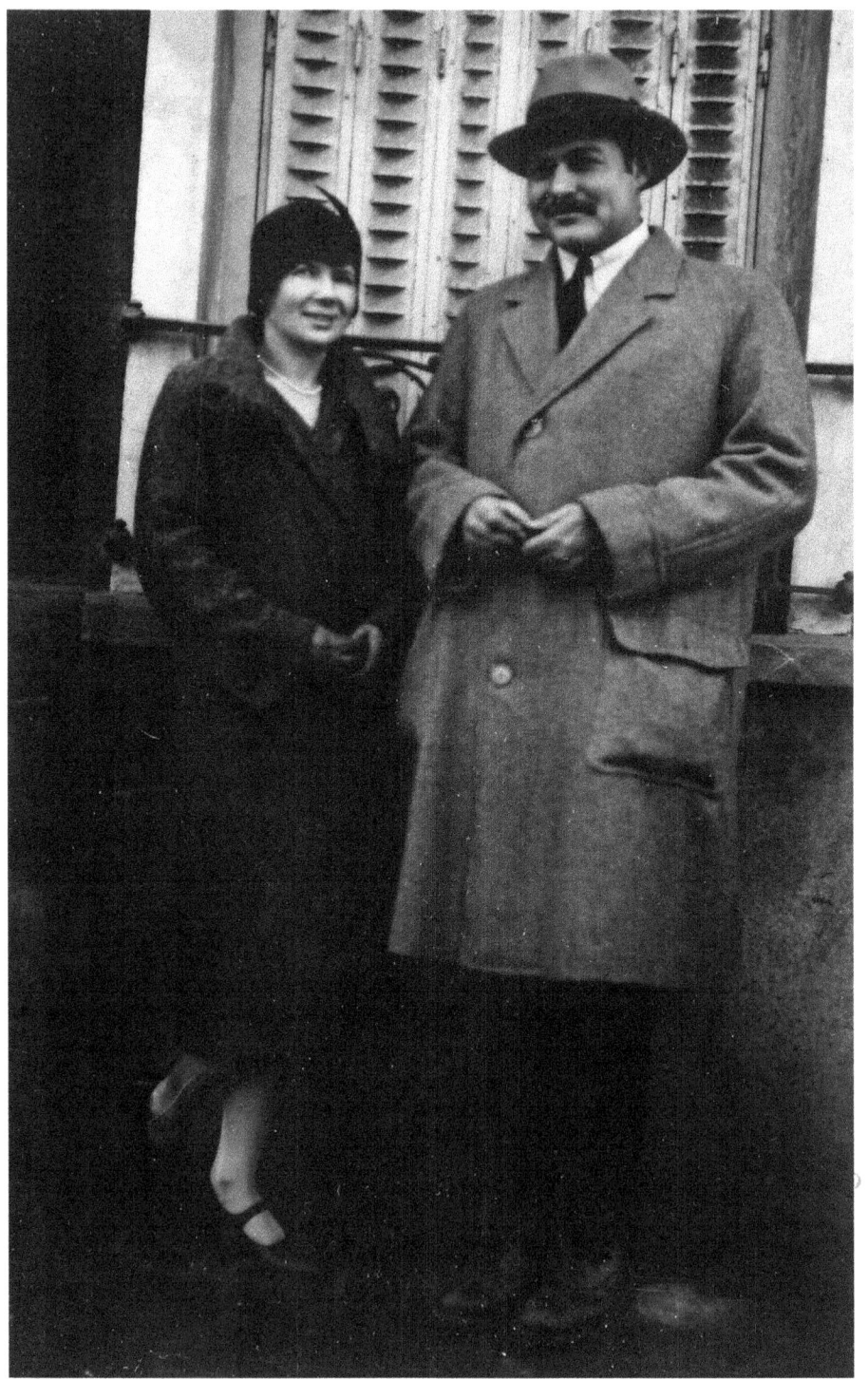

WRITING AND OTHER ADVENTURES

(1926–1938)

Late in life, Hemingway told *Paris Review* editor George Plimpton that the best training for an aspiring writer was to hang himself, because writing is "impossibly difficult." After that he should force himself to write, because "at least he will have the story of the hanging to commence with." Though it sounded flippant, Hemingway was revealing one of his core philosophies: writers should experience life. As Ernest told his sister Sunny, he traveled, hunted, and fished as much as he did because otherwise he'd have nothing to write about. That may be oversimplified, but with Hemingway the line between autobiography and fiction was always blurred.

Ernest was wounded and fell in love with his nurse in Milan, and not coincidentally the same things happen to Frederic Henry in *A Farewell to Arms* (1929). Hemingway went on safari with his wife and best friend from Key West, and soon afterward the "nonfiction" *Green Hills of Africa* (1935) features a character named Karl who sounds an awful lot like Charles Thompson, while P.O.M. ("Poor Old Mama") is unmistakably wife Pauline. Harry Morgan, the hero of *To Have and Have Not* (1937), has exploits and traits that evoke Hemingway's rumrunner friend Josie Russell, while the knowledge Hemingway gained from three trips covering the Spanish civil war would become important resources later when he would begin work on *For Whom the Bell Tolls* (1940). All writers incorporate their own experiences, but it was somehow different with Hemingway. Every blurring of his life and fiction added to the mystique of his emerging public image as writer-adventurer—a larger-than-life character, which was reinforced by his first *Time* magazine cover in October 1937. It depicted a painting of Hemingway trophy fishing, rather than sitting at his typewriter.

Between 1926 and 1938, Hemingway flourished. The author had adventures in Austria, France, Spain, Cuba, the Bahamas, and the American West, while generating two of his acknowledged "big books" and a good many of the short stories that are now regarded as classics—stories like "A Clean, Well-Lighted Place." Hemingway also wrote what many consider to be the most knowledgeable book about bullfighting written by a non-Spaniard, and he became world-renowned as a legitimate sportsman, with a lasting impact on international trophy fishing.

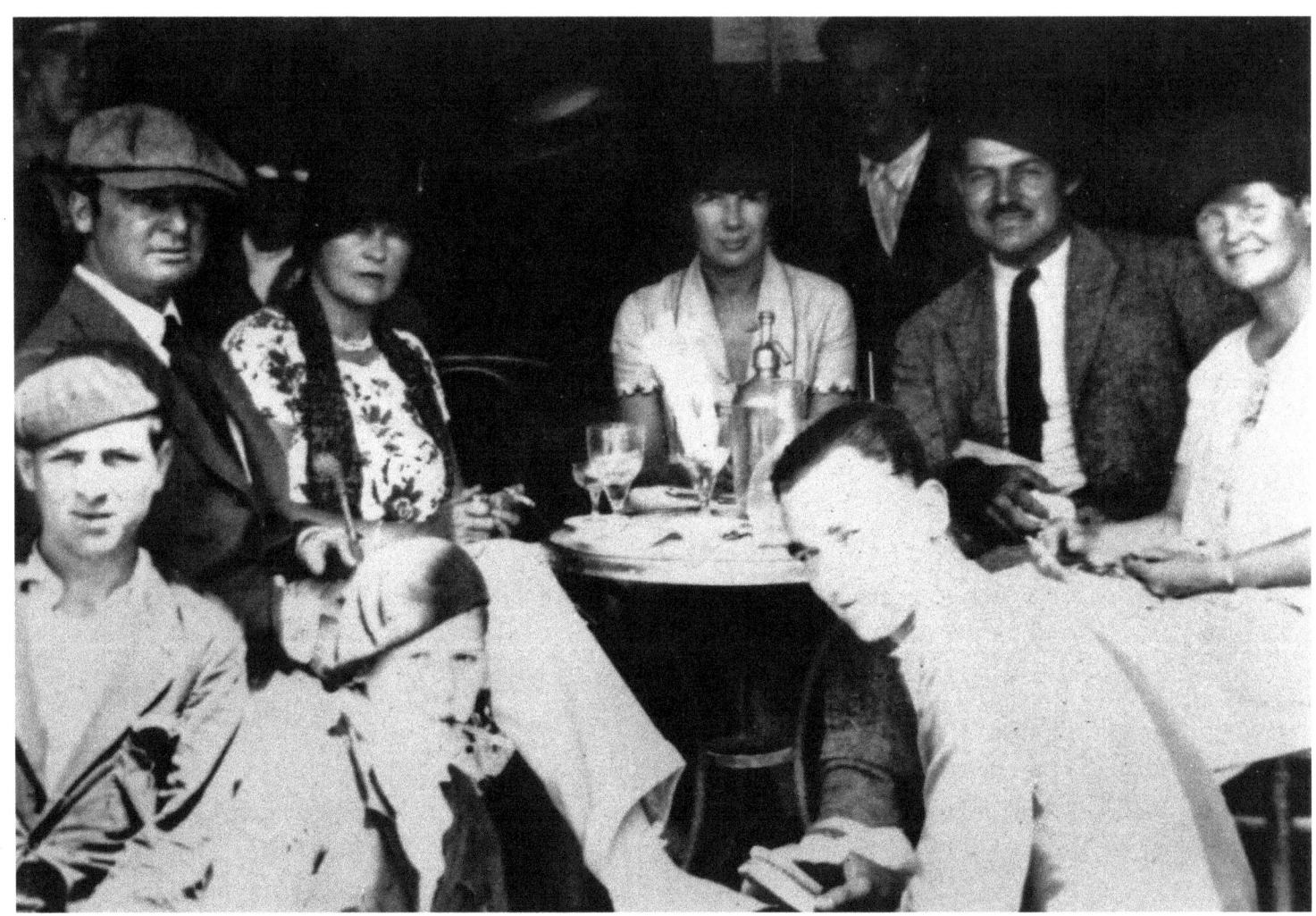

Summer wasn't summer without Pamplona, and the Hemingways were joined for the 1926 San Fermin festival by then-ubiquitous Pauline and the couple's friends, Gerald and Sara Murphy, who approved of the new woman in Hemingway's life and even encouraged her. Like a referee, Ernest sits between Pauline and Hadley, who almost presciently is cropped partially out of the picture.

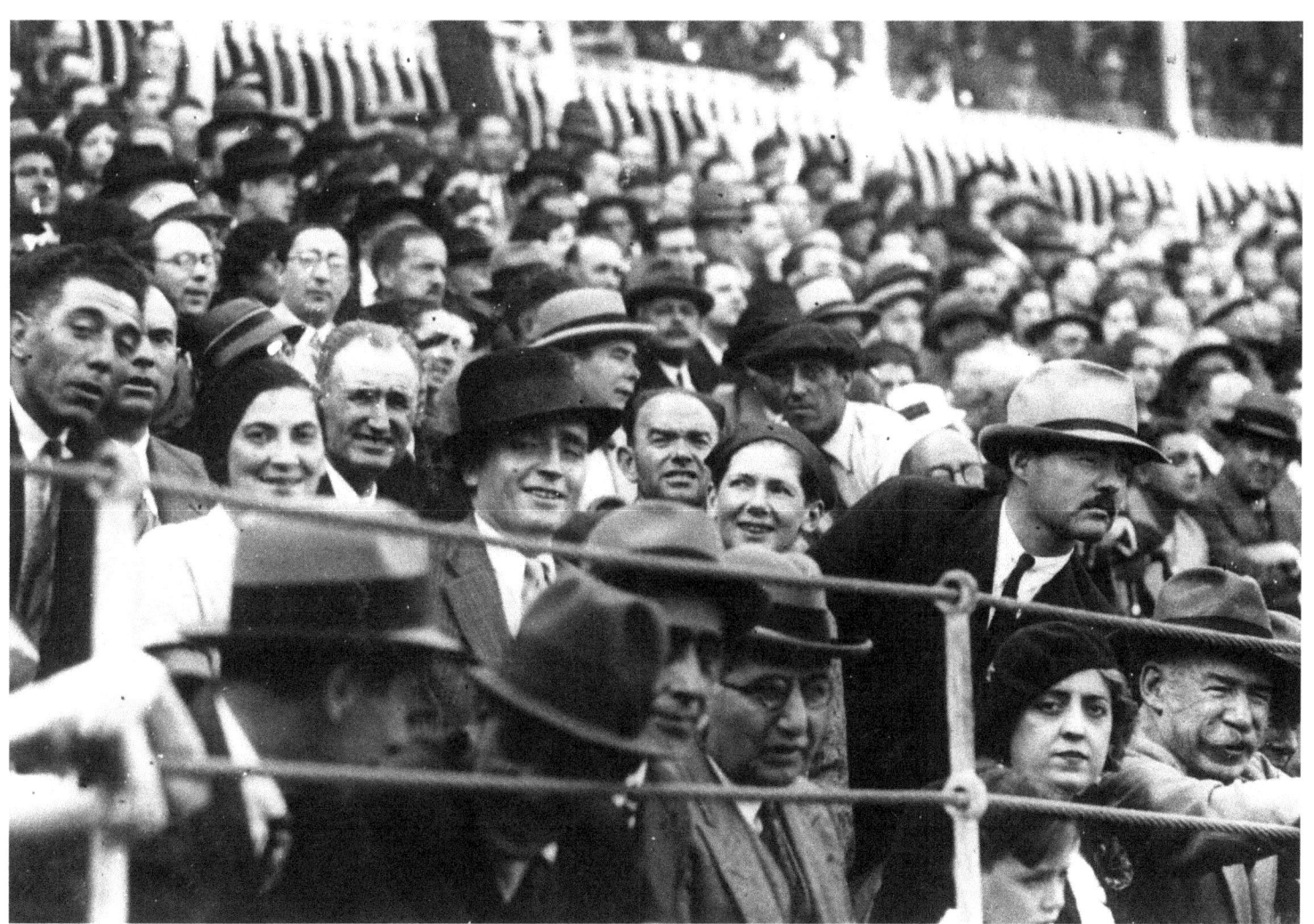

At the corrida, Ernest (foreground, right) leans forward while Pauline sits to his right. Hemingway preferred the sombre or shade seats to the cheaper sol seats. In the sombre section, aficionados wore their best clothes. The men often smoked cigars and brought bota bags of wine, while the women sometimes packed picnics and cooled themselves with decorative fans.

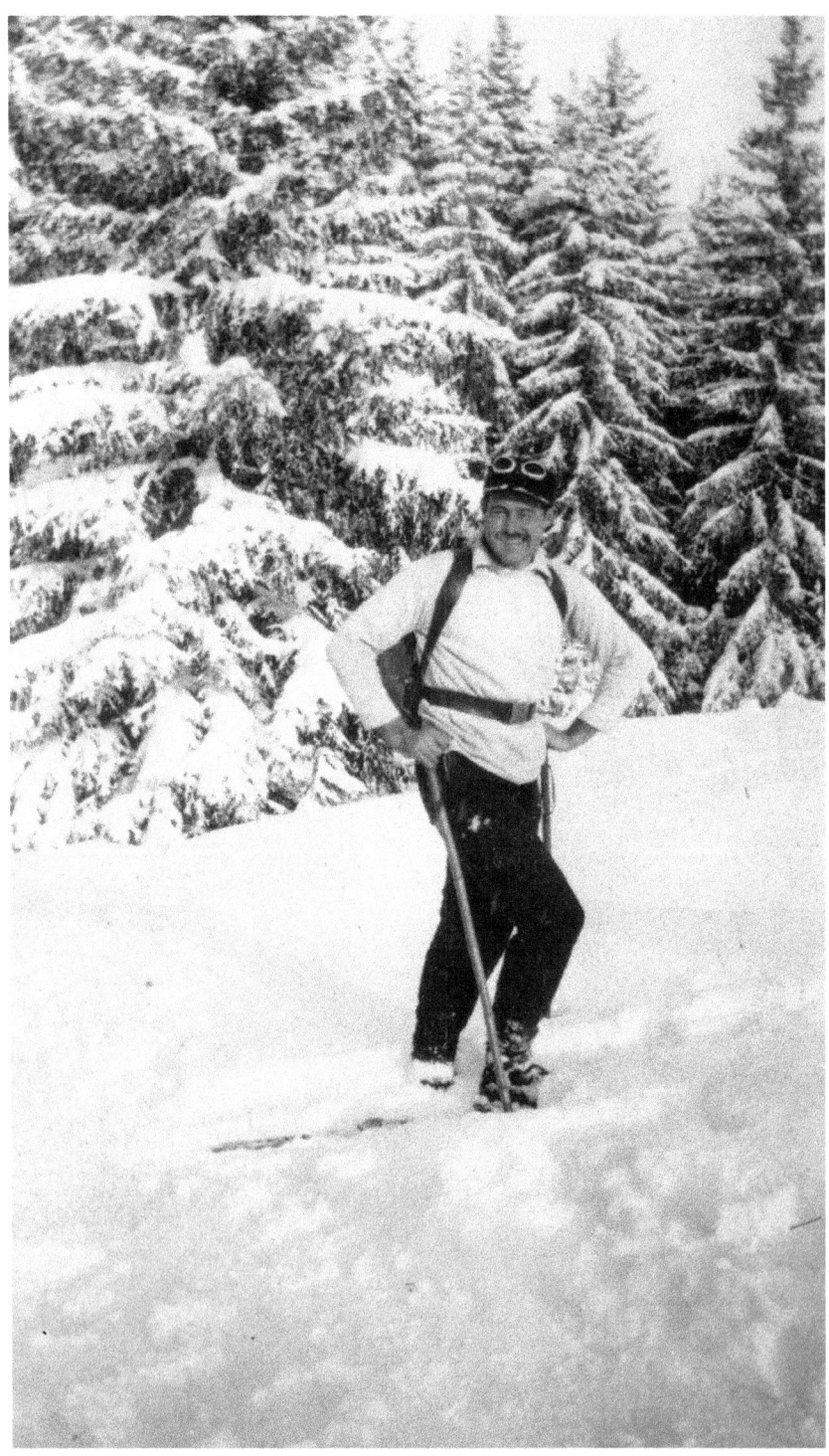

For someone with an adventurous spirit, Hemingway was also a creature of habit. Winter skiing trips quickly became one of his traditions. In February 1927, a smiling and rejuvenated Ernest strikes a pose on the slopes at Gstaad, Switzerland. By this point he was already engaged to Pauline; Hadley, who had insisted that he and Pauline spend 100 days apart before she would grant a divorce, had finally capitulated.

In July 1927, Ernest and Pauline relax on the beach at San Sebastian, Spain, which is mentioned in *The Sun Also Rises*. Ernest and Pauline had married in Paris on May 10, 1927, and here the newlyweds enjoy their holiday away from Paris . . . and, one suspects, Hadley.

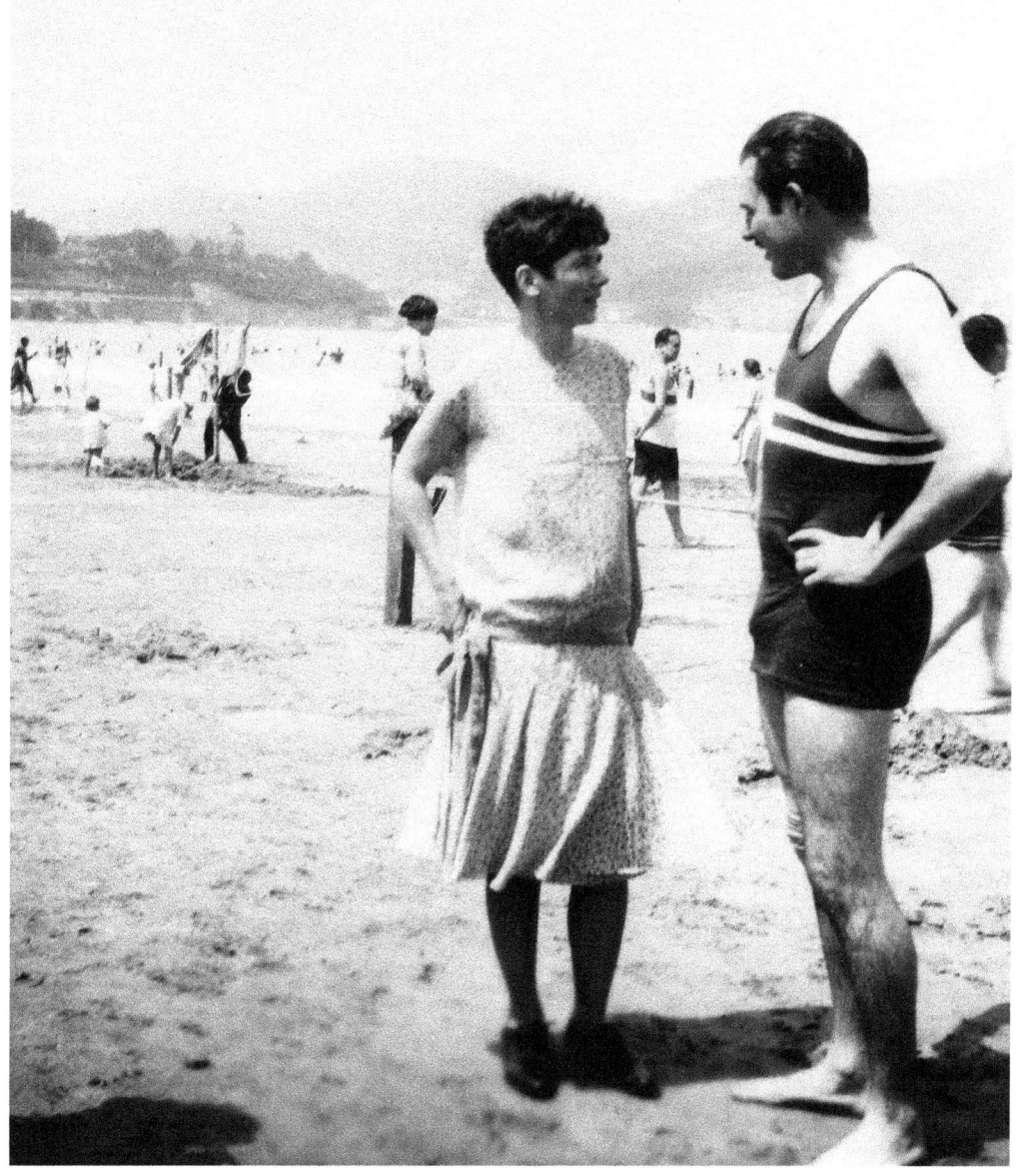

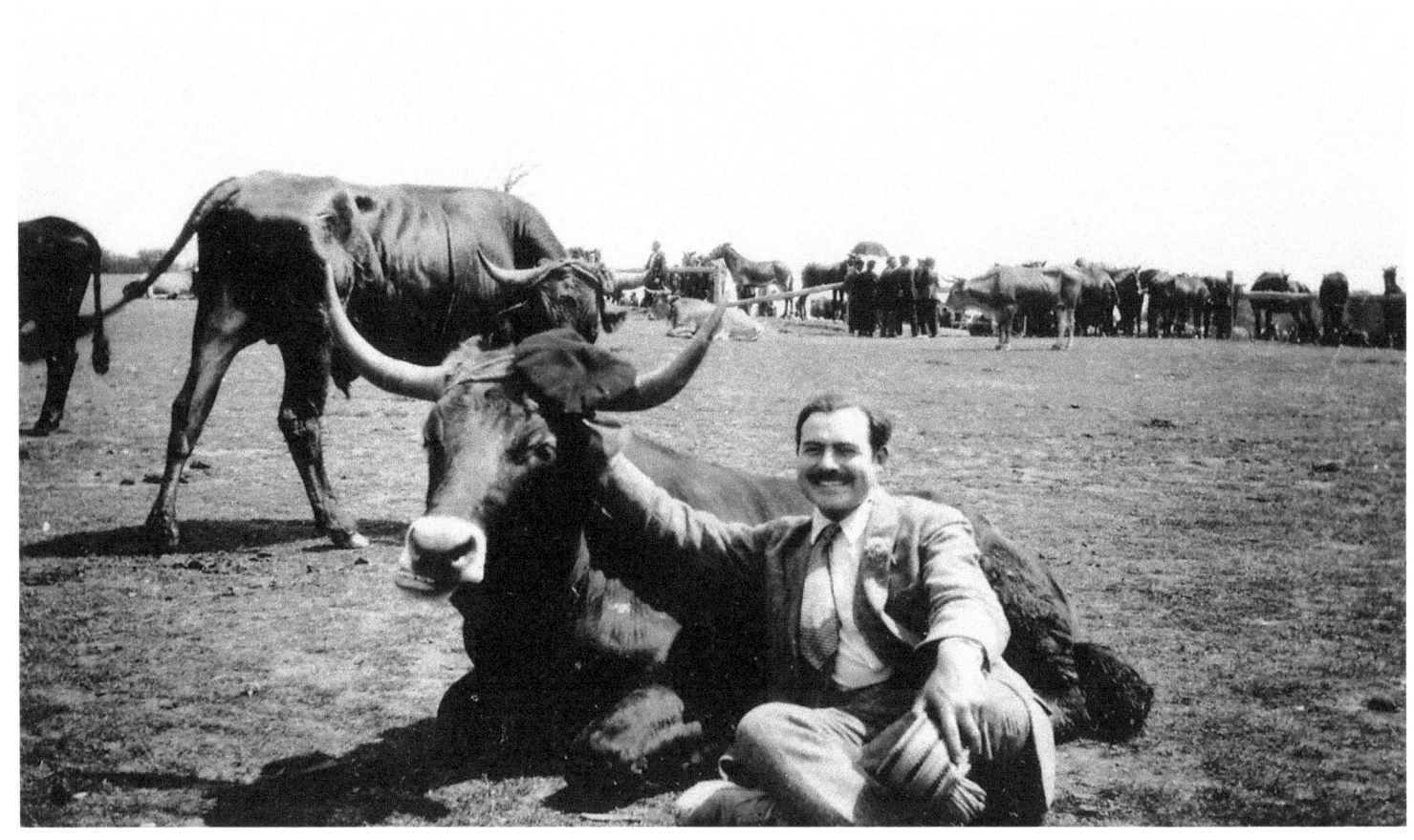

Ernest with oxen, summer 1927. Along with the bulls that were run each day from the corrals to the bullring, oxen were released to keep the bulls from goring one another, which Hemingway used as a metaphor in *The Sun Also Rises.* His first several San Fermins sparked a lifelong interest in bullfighting that would inspire Hemingway to write *Death in the Afternoon,* a nonfiction treatise and meditation on bullfighting—which he called a "tragedy" acted out, rather than a sport.

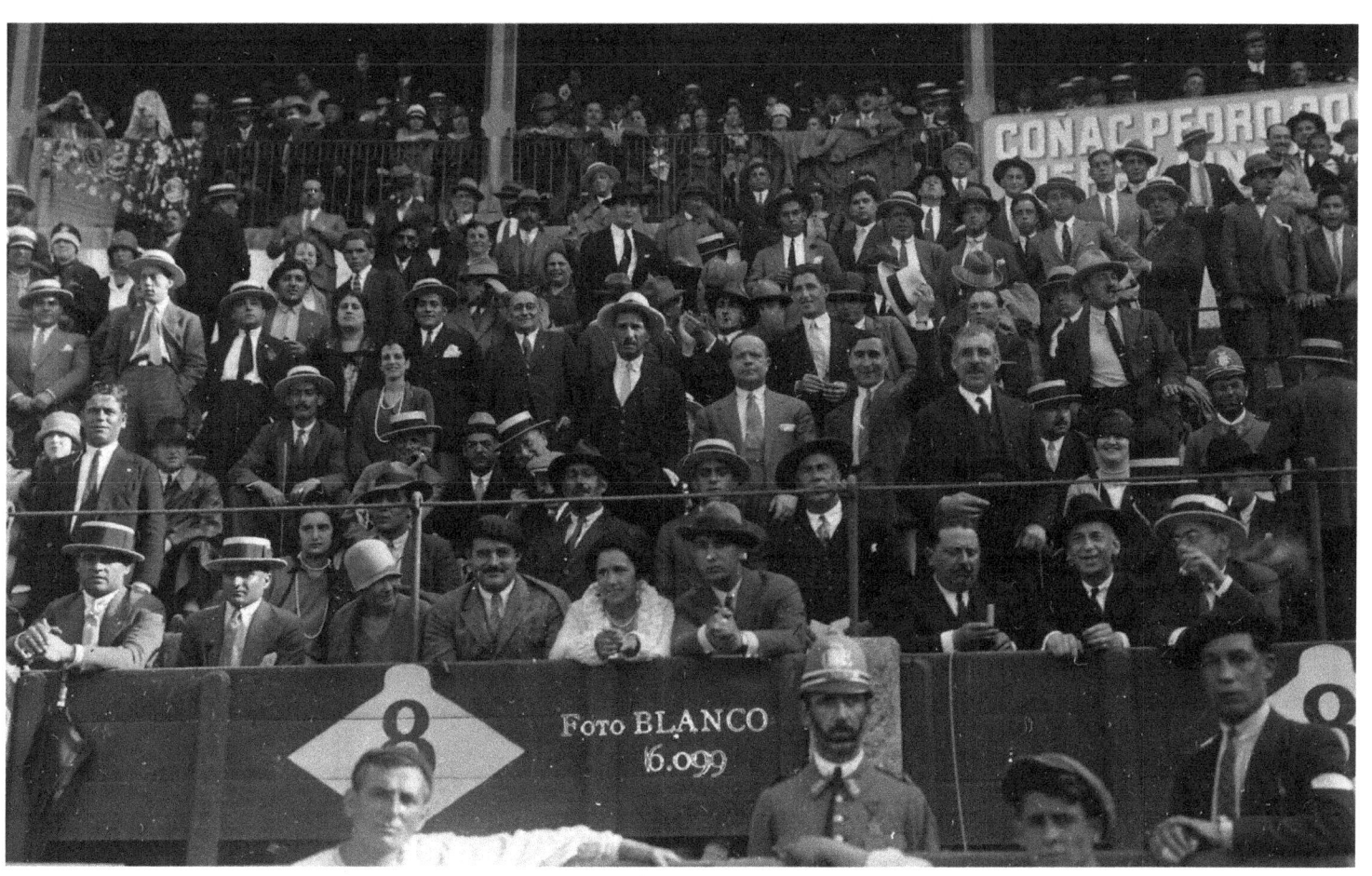

After San Fermin, Ernest and Pauline visited Valencia, Madrid, La Coruna, and Santiago de Compostela. Hemingway was drawn to the bullring because he felt it was the "only remaining place where valor and art can combine." In a letter to Scott Fitzgerald he remarked that his idea of heaven would be a pair of front-row barrera seats (which he has here) and two houses—one for his wife and children, and another for his mistresses.

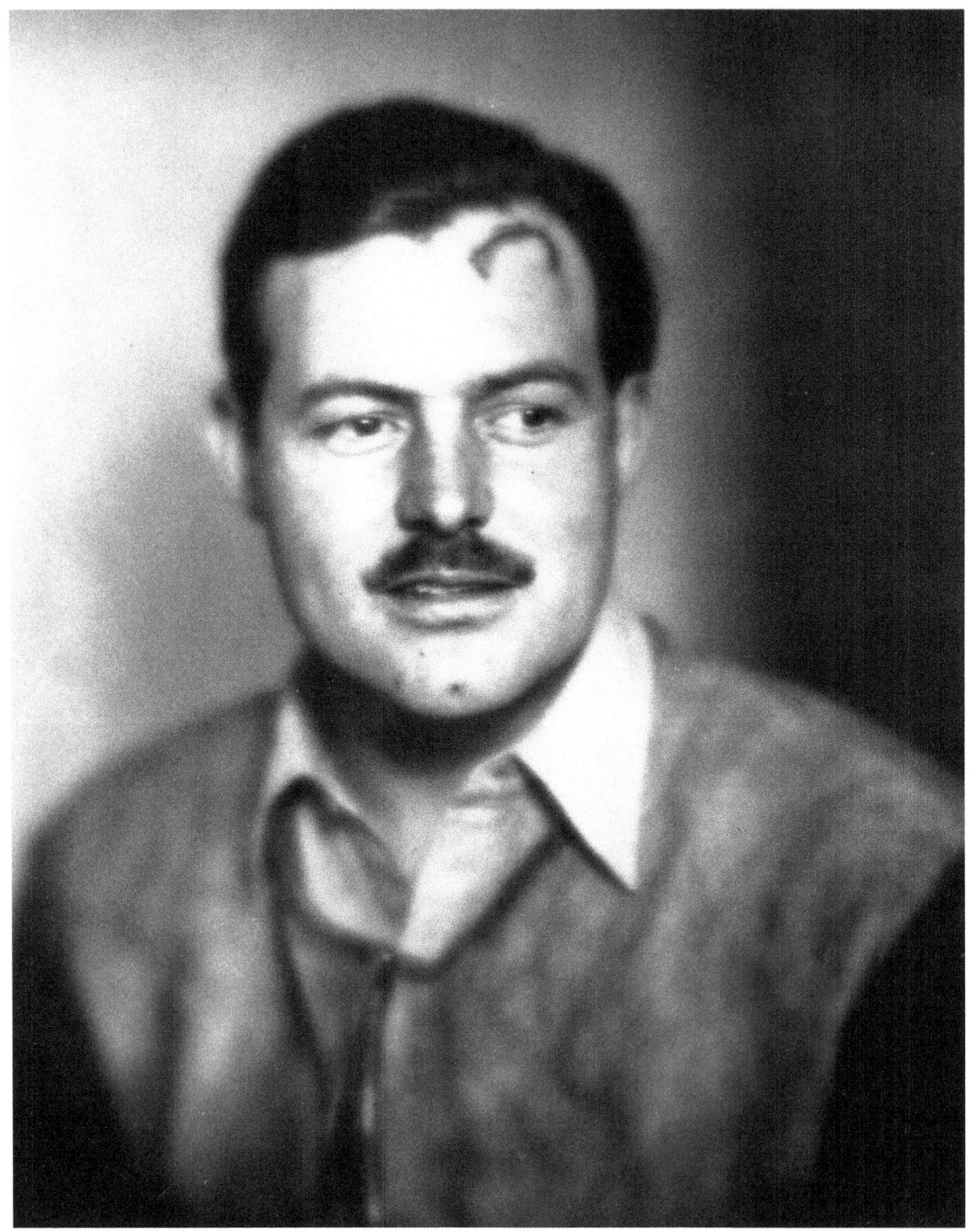

Rugged as Hemingway looked, he was accident-prone throughout his life. In March 1928, he was trying to repair a skylight in their Paris apartment when the entire thing fell on his head. It took nine stitches to close the wound. Already scheduled for a portrait by Helen Pierce Breaker, one of first-wife Hadley's bridesmaids, Hemingway chose to sit for it without a bandage.

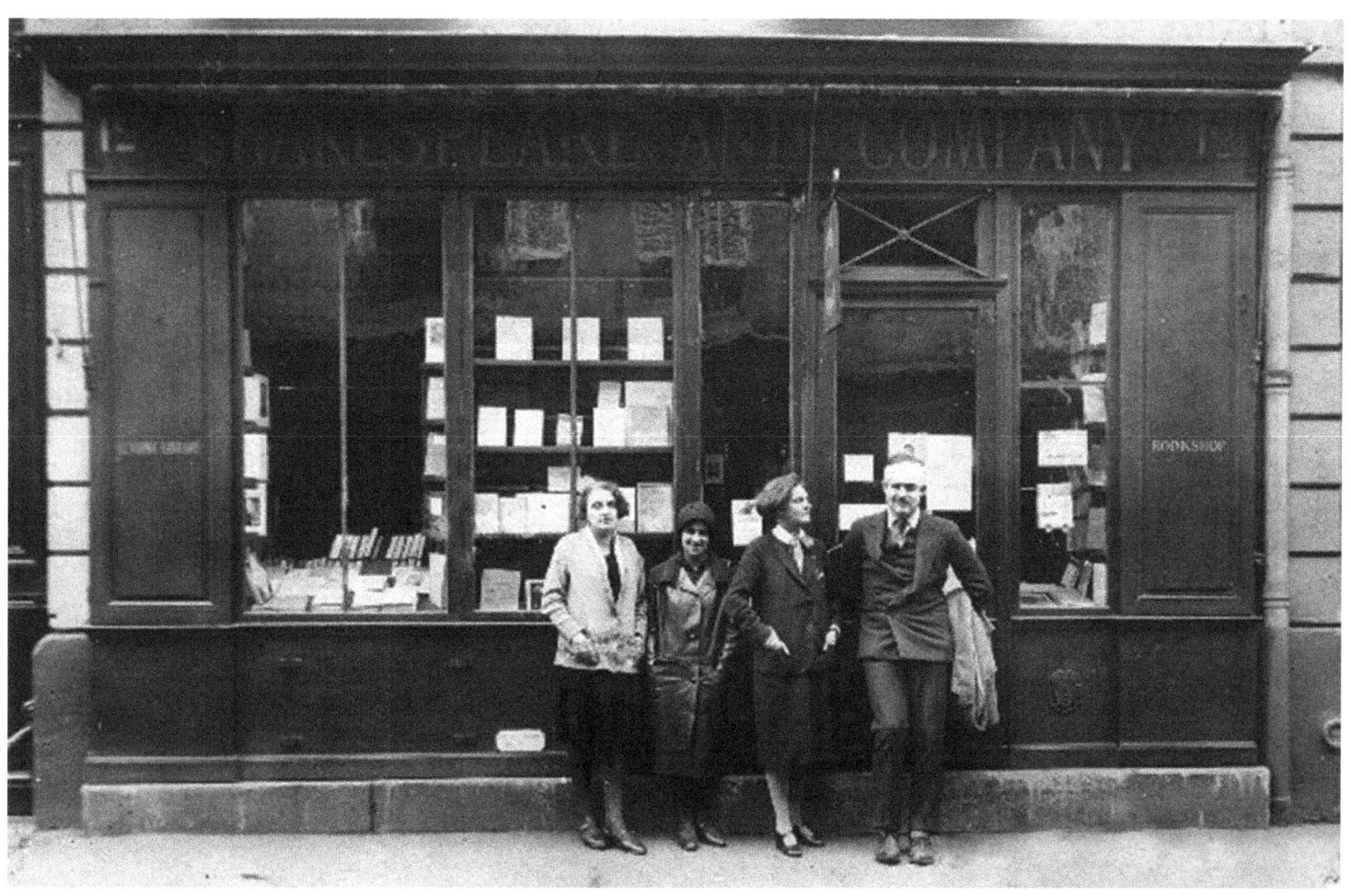

In March 1928, Hemingway poses with Sylvia Beach and friends in front of her bookstore, Shakespeare and Company, at 12 rue de l'Odéon. From the time it opened in 1919 until its doors closed in 1941 because of the war, the shop was a popular gathering place for writers and artists on the Left Bank. Books were for sale, but Beach also had a lending library, and Hemingway frequently borrowed books. He was a voracious reader.

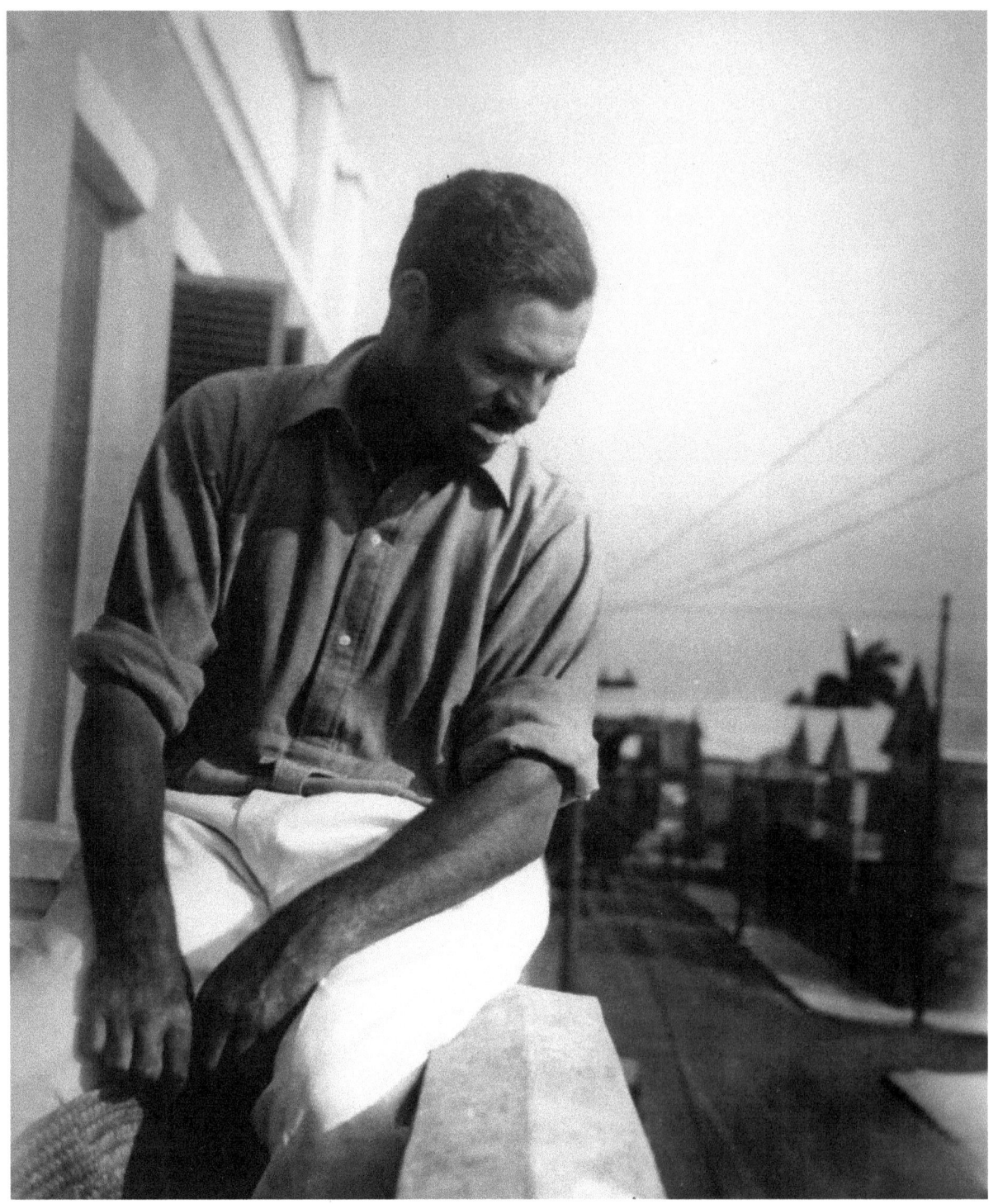

Ernest (with zinc oxide on his lips) on the third-floor balcony of the Trevor and Morris building on Simonton Street in Key West. The Hemingways were ready to come back to the U.S., but not the Midwest. John Dos Passos suggested Key West, and they arrived by way of Havana on a Peninsular & Occidental steamship the first week of April 1928. The Model A Ford that Pauline's Uncle Gus had ordered for them hadn't come in yet, so the Ford people insisted they stay in an apartment above the dealership.

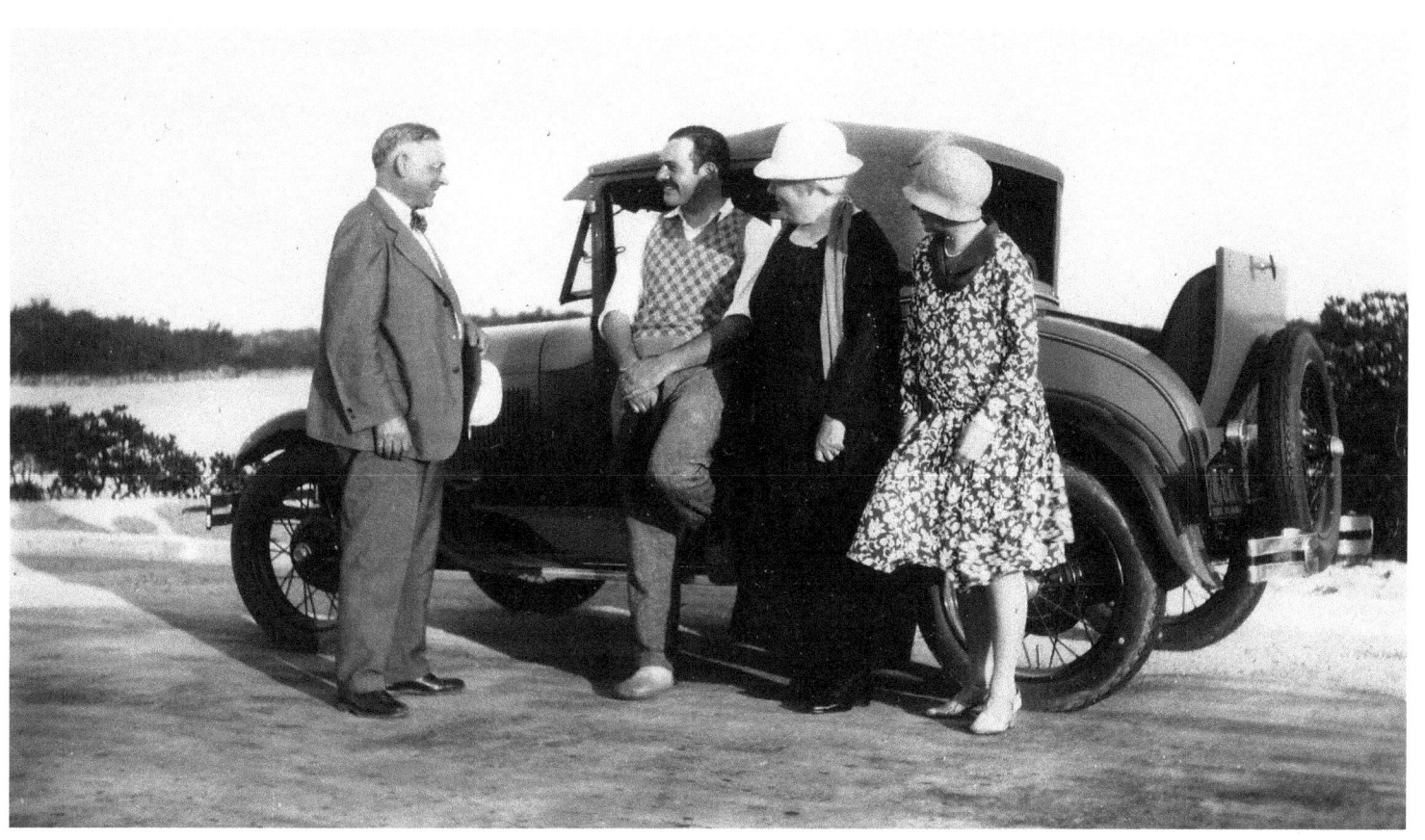

Returning from their own vacation, Clarence and Grace Hemingway leaned over the railing of their steamship, which had stopped in Key West, and were startled to see Ernest fishing from a pier. Neither had any idea the other would be there, and for the first time they met their new daughter-in-law, who was seven months pregnant. The caesarean birth in *A Farewell to Arms* would be inspired by Pauline's emergency C-section on June 28, 1928, when Patrick was born. Ernest and Pauline's Model A had finally come in, and the following month they would take the train to Piggott, Arkansas, to visit her family.

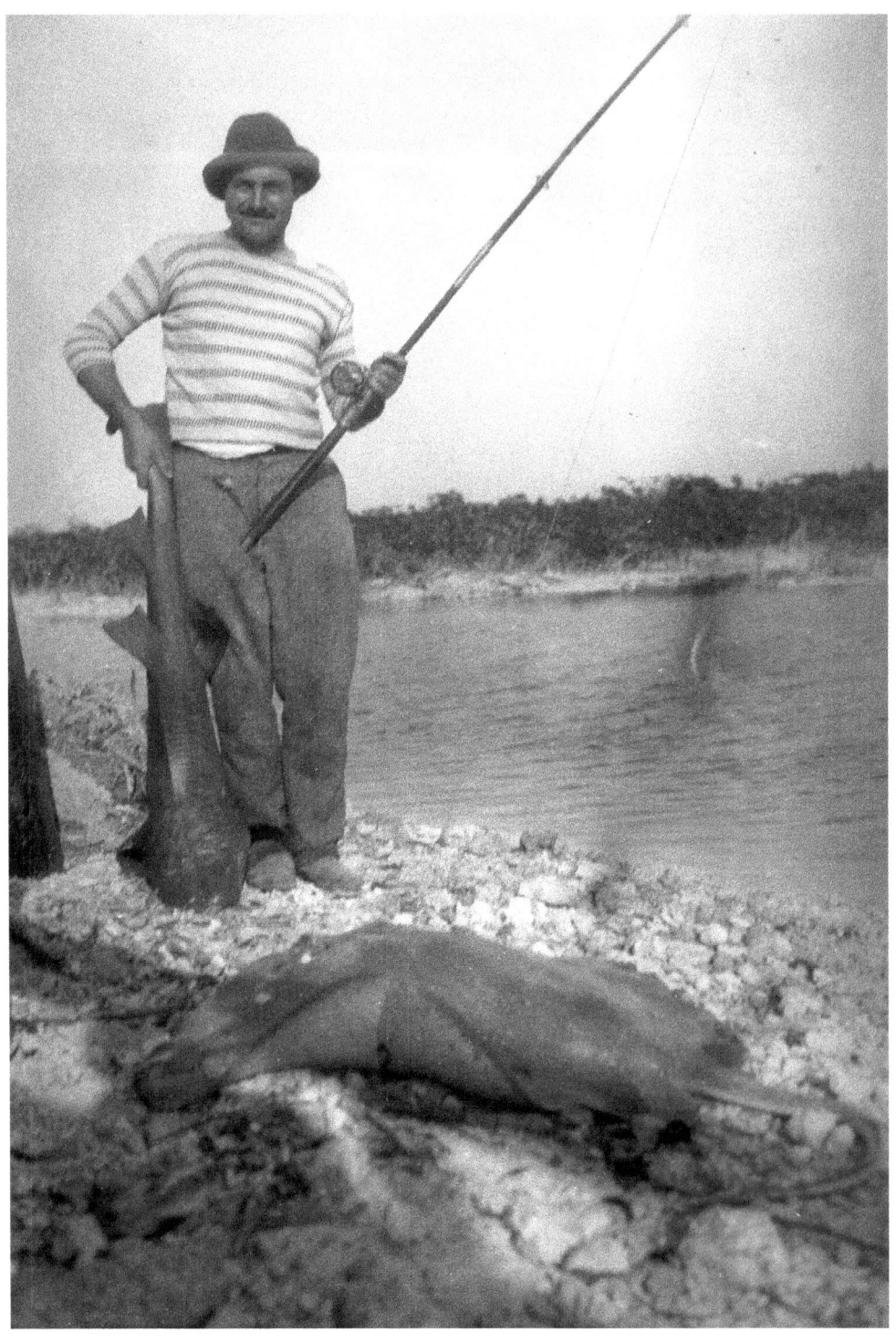

Until he met someone with a boat, Hemingway fished from piers and shore, posing here with a shark and ray. Key West was a double paradise for him. It was a tropical island with Caribbean-style architecture, exotic flora, and bountiful fauna. But in 1928 it was also a rough little town full of fishermen, boxers, rumrunners, shrimpers, spongers, and cigar makers—his kind of people. While the country was under Prohibition, local "conchs," as Key West citizens called themselves, happily ignored the law, which was just Hemingway's style.

Before the highway connected Key West to the rest of the U.S., the only way to get to another key or the mainland was by boat. A car ferry ran between No Name Key and Lower Matecumbe. Here, on an unidentified vessel heading for one of the other keys, Ernest takes a break from fishing. He had to be feeling good—work on *A Farewell to Arms* was going well about the time this photo appears to have been taken.

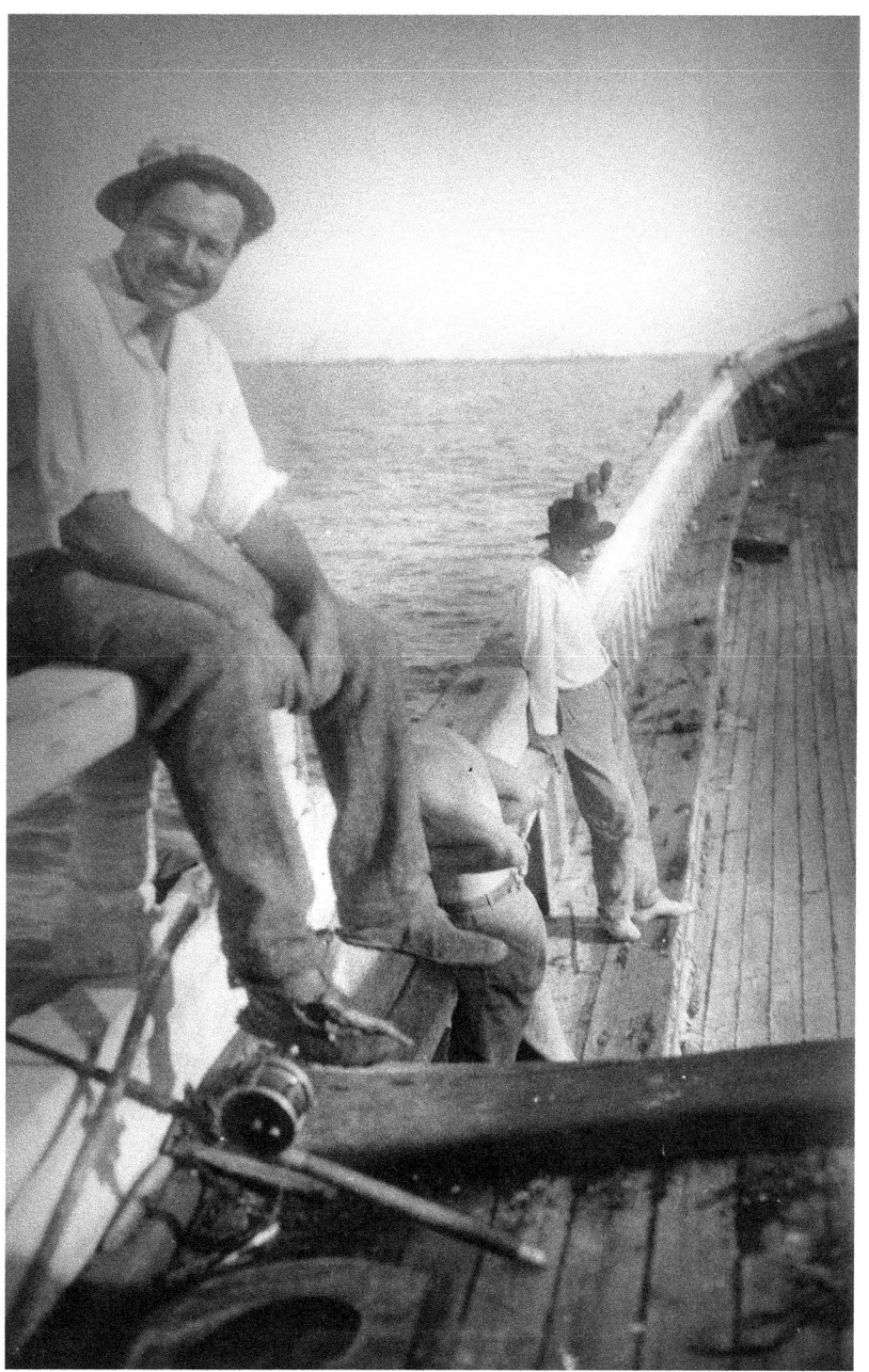

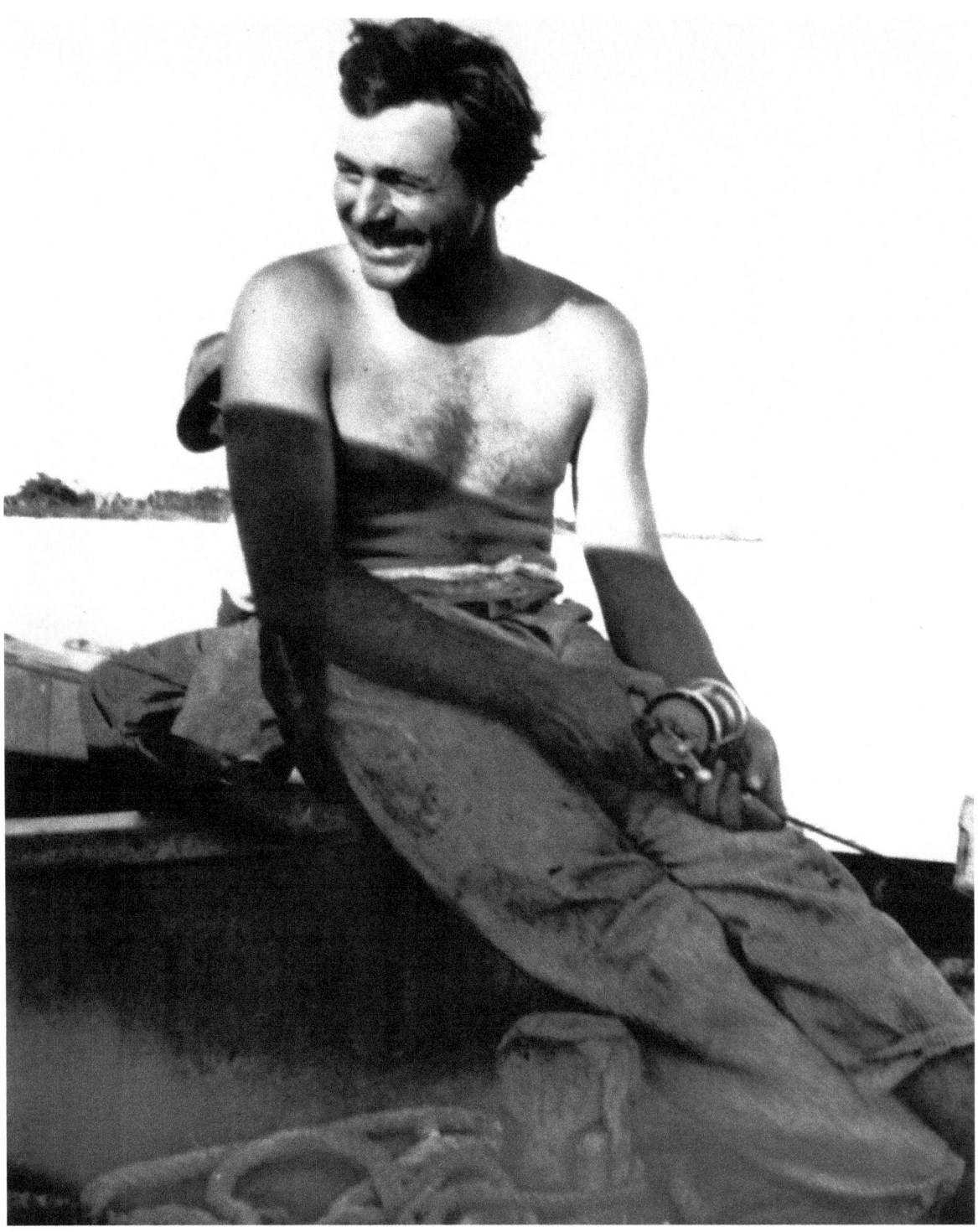

Hanging out on the docks, Ernest met Bra Saunders, a guide who had his own little boat and became one of Ernest's saltwater fishing mentors. The others were Charles Thompson, a local businessman who owned the ice house, fish market, and hardware store, and Josie Russell, who ran rum illegally from Cuba to Florida and operated a speakeasy and later a bar on Greene Street (now Captain Tony's), then Duval.

In December 1928, Hemingway left for New York to pick up his son for a non-custodial visit to Key West, but learning his father had committed suicide, he paid a porter $100 to make sure his five-year-old got to Key West while he attended to matters in Oak Park. Ernest asked his mother to get Grandpa Hemingway's impounded Civil War revolver—used by his father to kill himself—and ship it to him. Here, Pauline poses with her new son and Bumby, after his arrival.

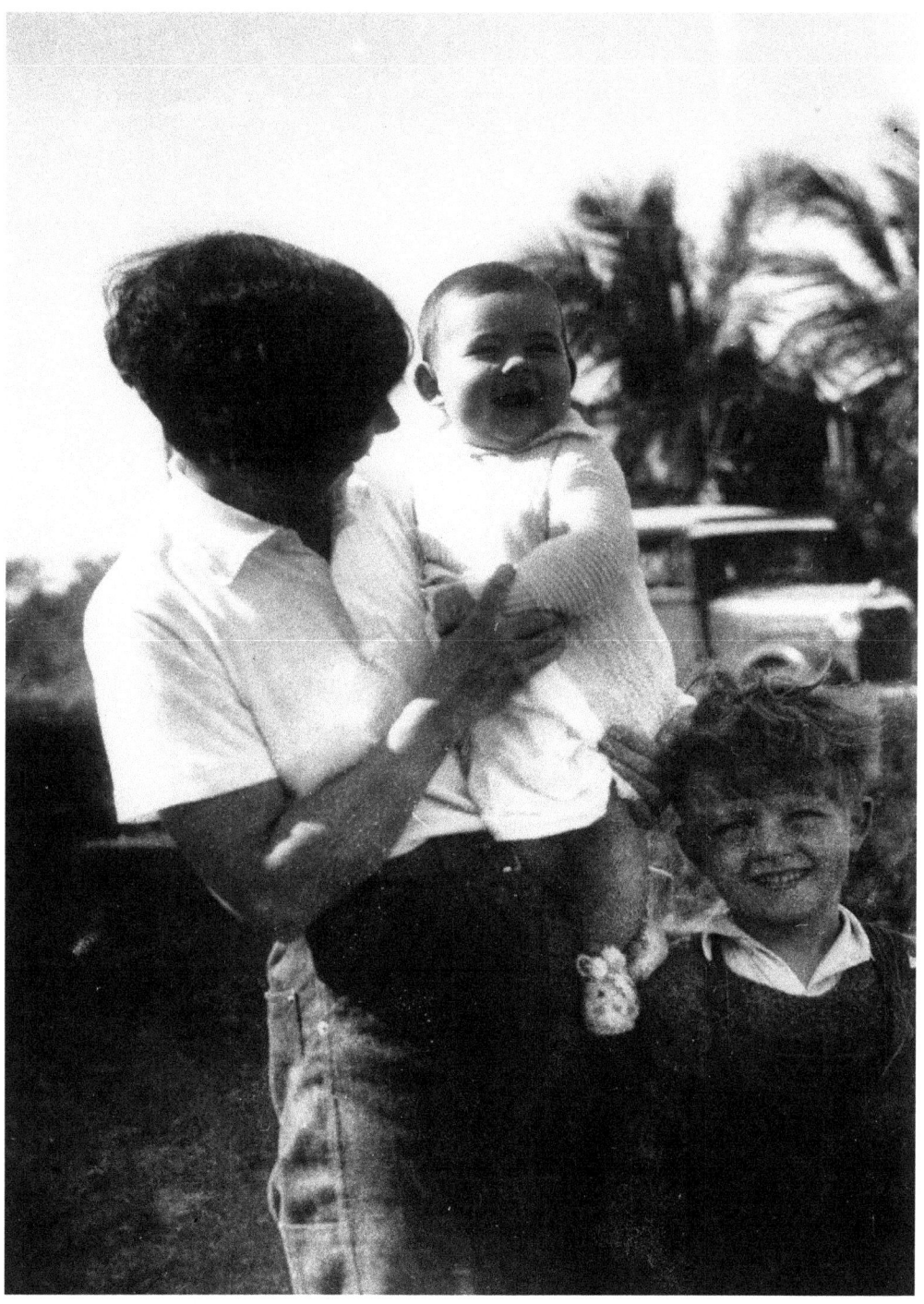

The fishing was so good that Hemingway invited all his friends to join him, as he usually did when he found paradise. In March 1929, John Dos Passos was one of those who responded to the call. Here Hemingway and "Dos" stand beside a pair of tarpon caught near Key West harbor. Hemingway landed five tarpon that season, the largest 71 pounds, and more friends came. Around town they were known as "Hemingway's Mob," because they fished, swam, drank, and raised hell together.

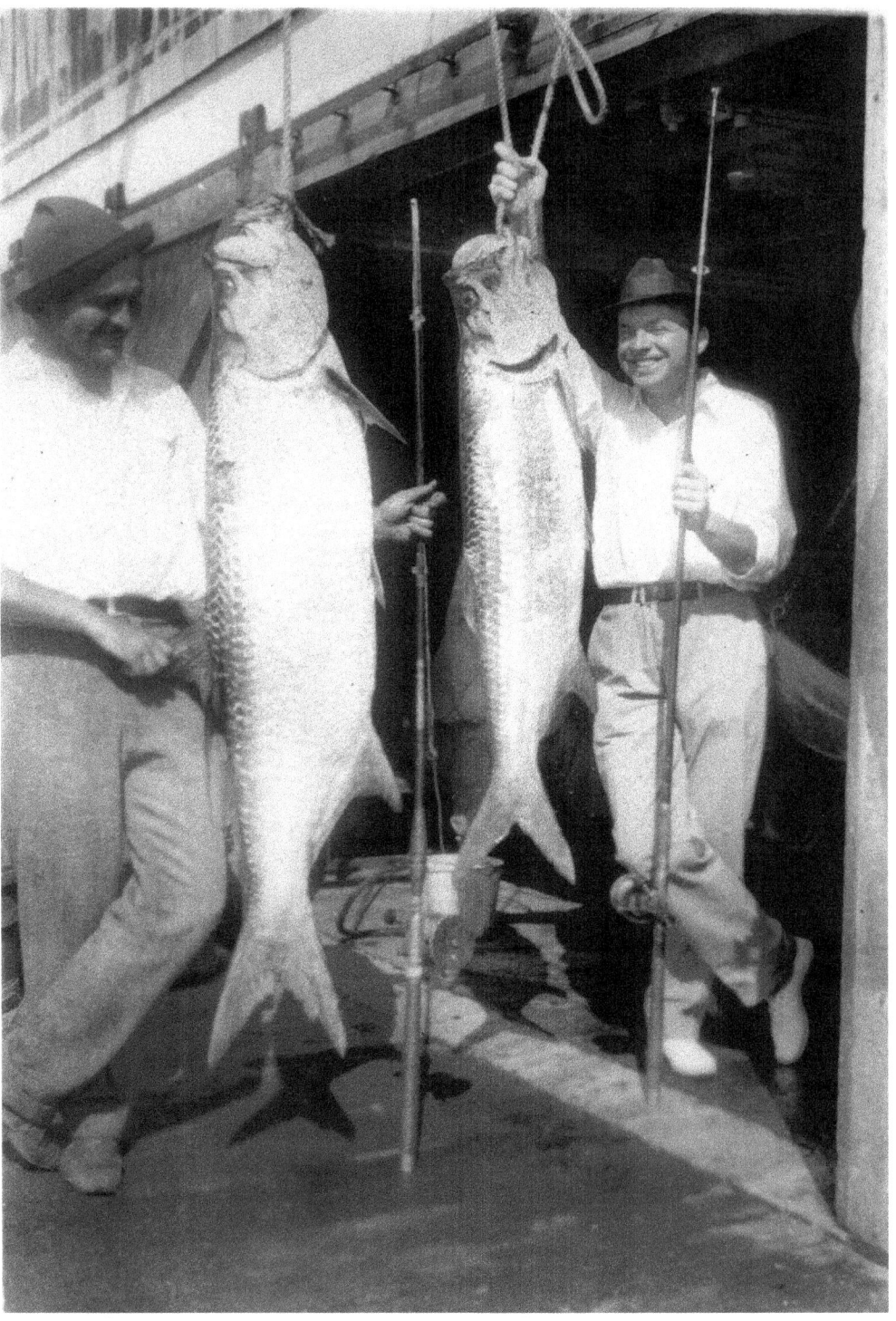

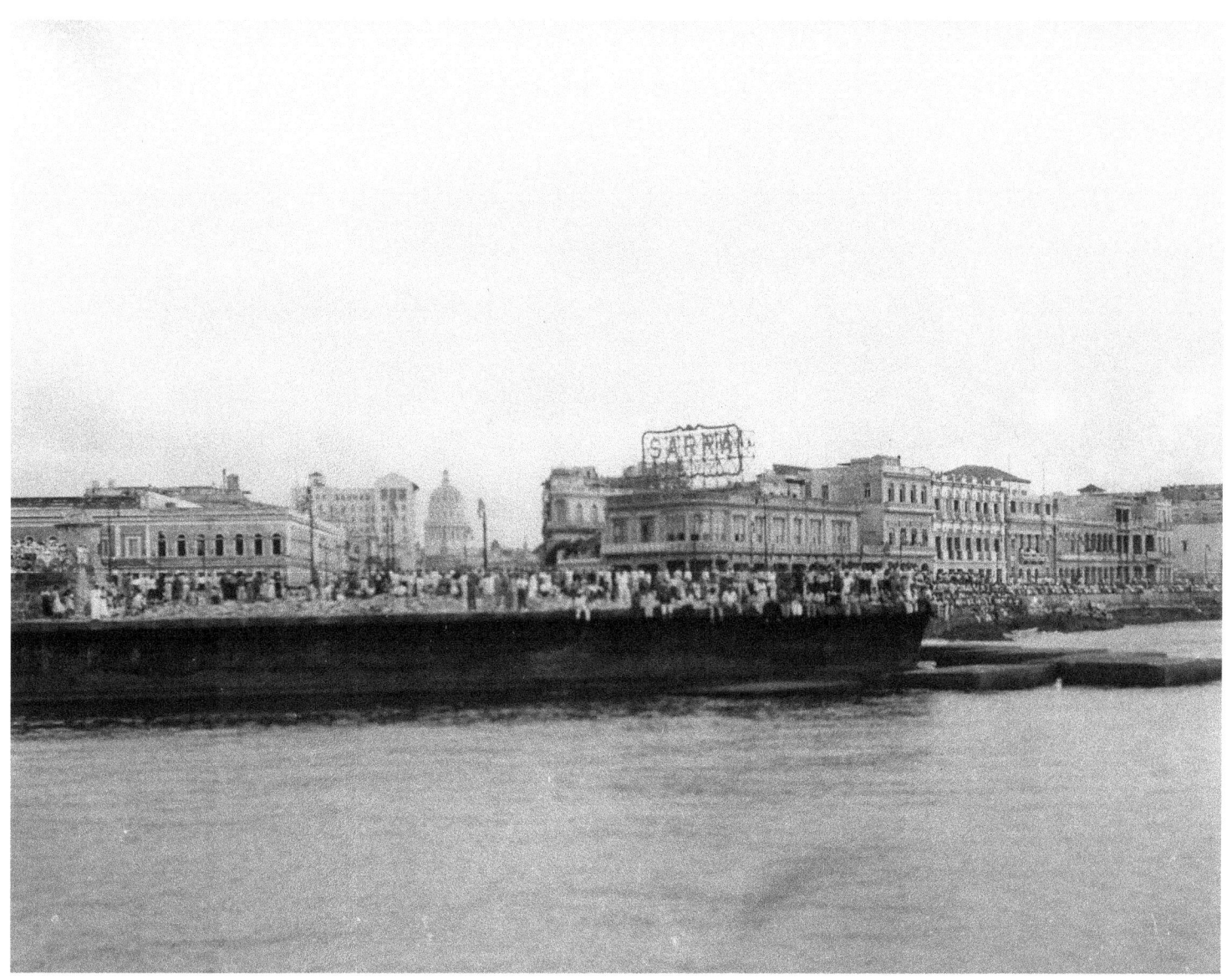

Havana, in Hemingway's time. In summer 1929 Hemingway hired Josie Russell, owner and skipper of the *Anita,* a 34-foot yacht, to take him on the first of many fishing trips to Havana and the eastern coast of Cuba. It wasn't just recreation for Hemingway. He had written his editor about this time that fishing "keeps my head from worrying" after the writing was done for the day. Thought-cleansing physical adventures like fishing were a necessary part of Hemingway's writing process.

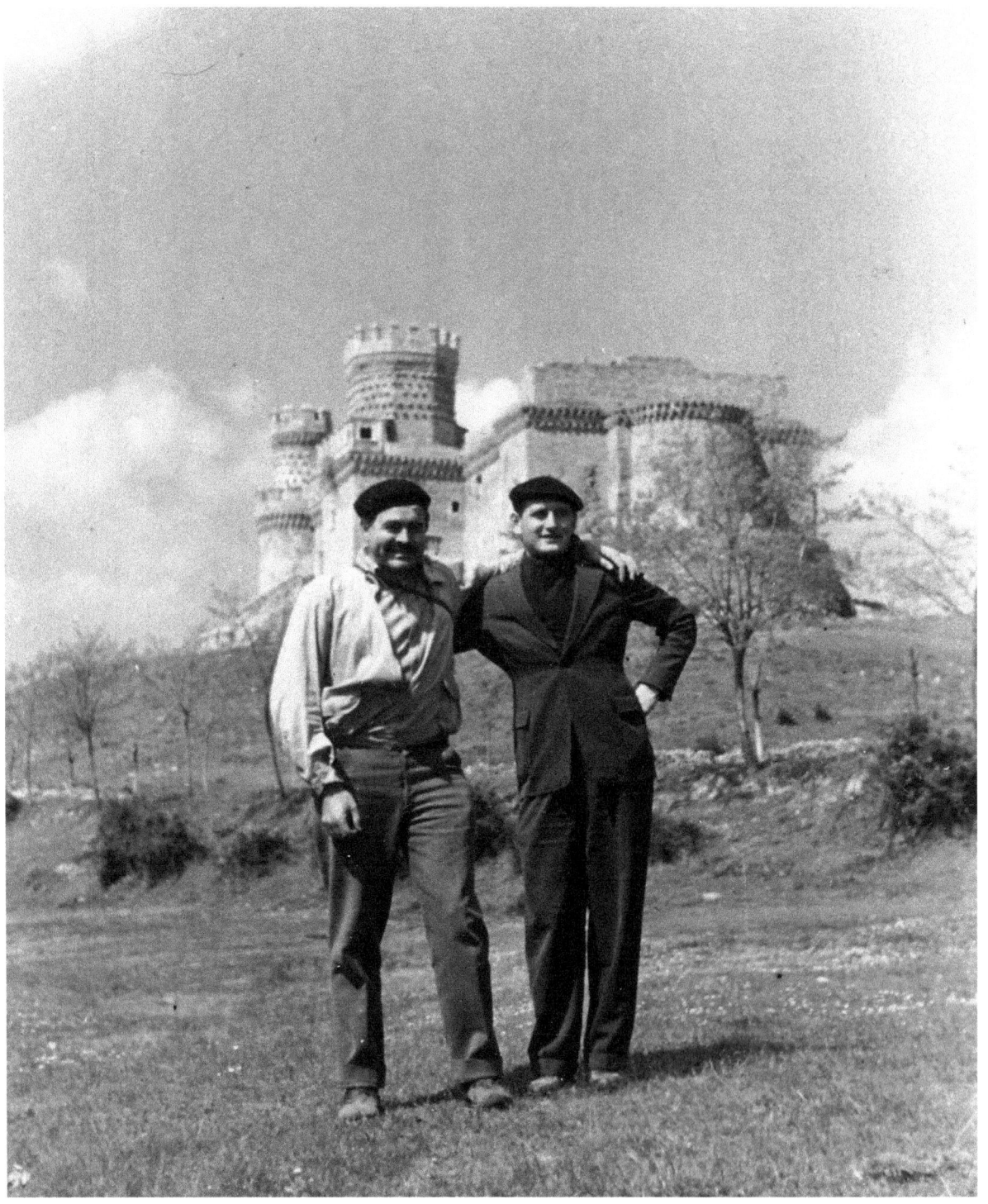

In September 1929, Hemingway was in Spain again, posing with Brooklyn-born bullfighter Sidney Franklin at the Castle of Manzanares el Real, which was built in 1475. Hemingway had been doing research for his bullfighting book and wrangled an invitation to join Franklin's entourage for three weeks. The following March Hemingway would finally begin the actual writing for *Death in the Afternoon*.

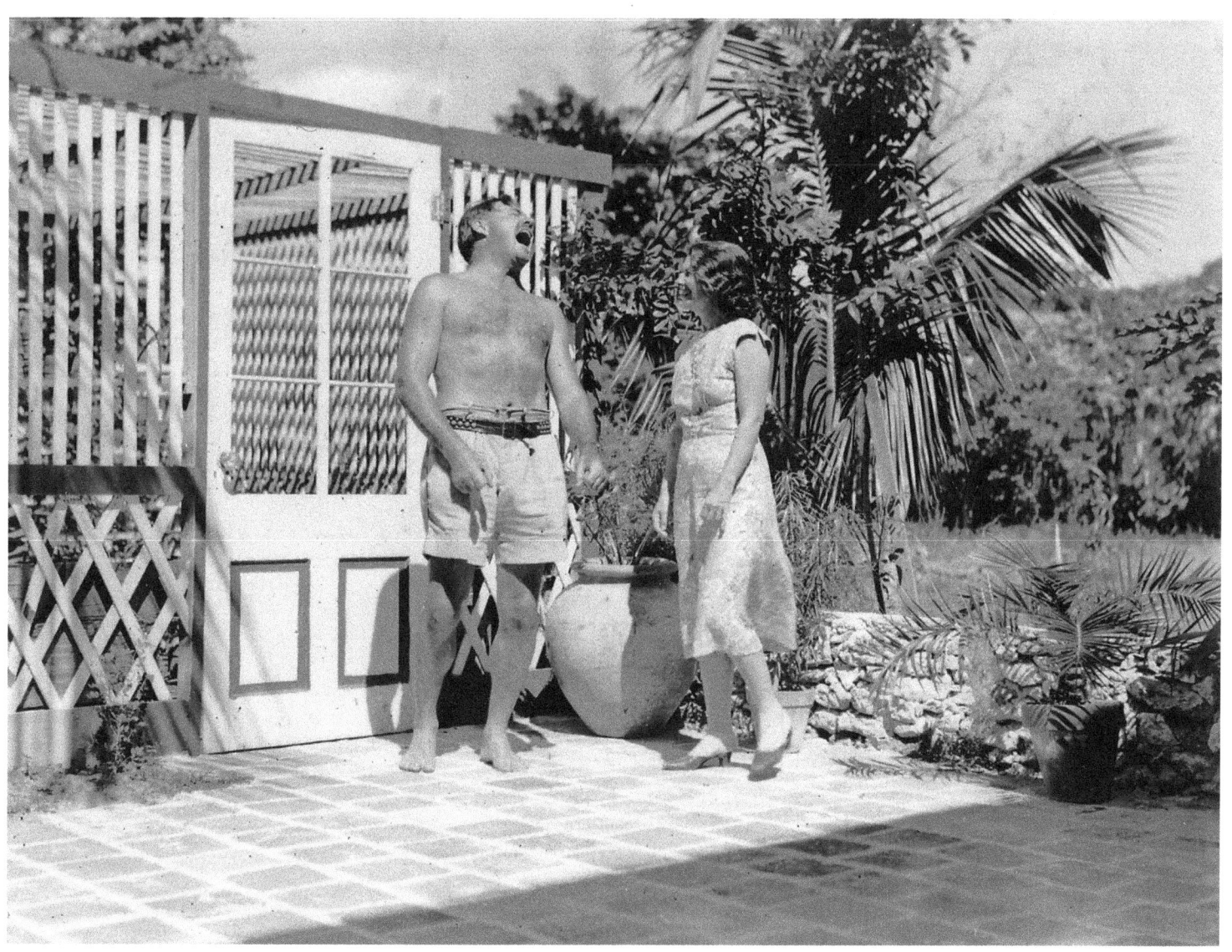

The Depression hit Key West hard, but Pauline's Uncle Gus helped the Hemingways buy an old Spanish Colonial–style mansion in need of repair. Here, the couple shares a laugh at the house on 907 Whitehead, now a privately run museum. Son Gregory was born in Kansas City on November 12, 1931, and they took up residence at the mansion a month later. Key West would become Hemingway's home base for the next eight years—until a highway connecting it to the mainland was completed and tourists started pouring in.

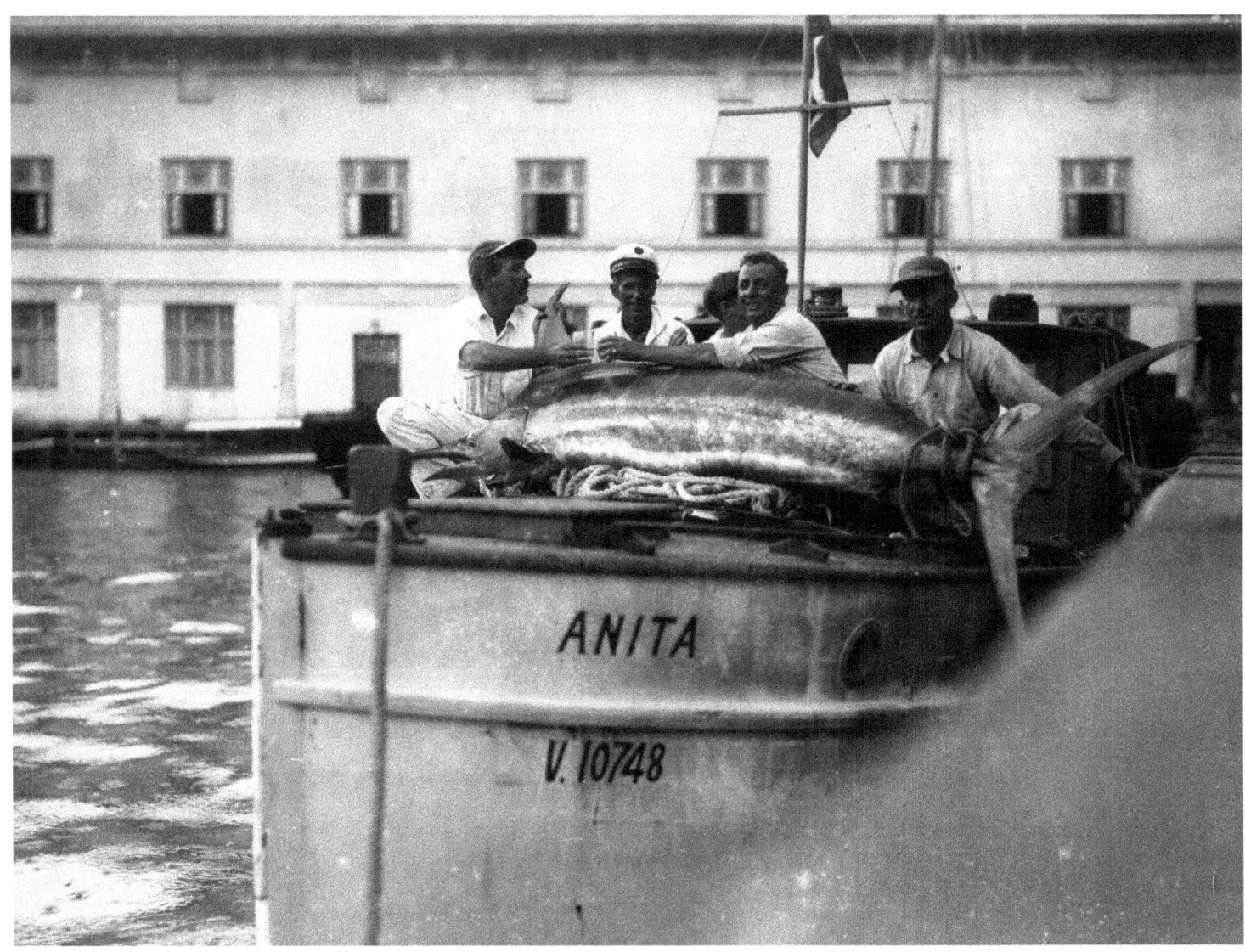

On the *Anita* with a marlin at San Francisco docks in Havana, probably May 1932. That year, Josie Russell had suggested they hire veteran Cuban fisherman Carlos Gutiérrez to act as a fishing guide, because he knew the waters of the Romano Archipelago and the eastern shores of Cuba better than anyone, and he was an expert on the habits of billfish. From left: Hemingway, Gutiérrez, Russell, and mate Joe Lowe. Hemingway was working on the story "After the Storm," inspired by a tale he heard from fishing guide and friend Bra Saunders.

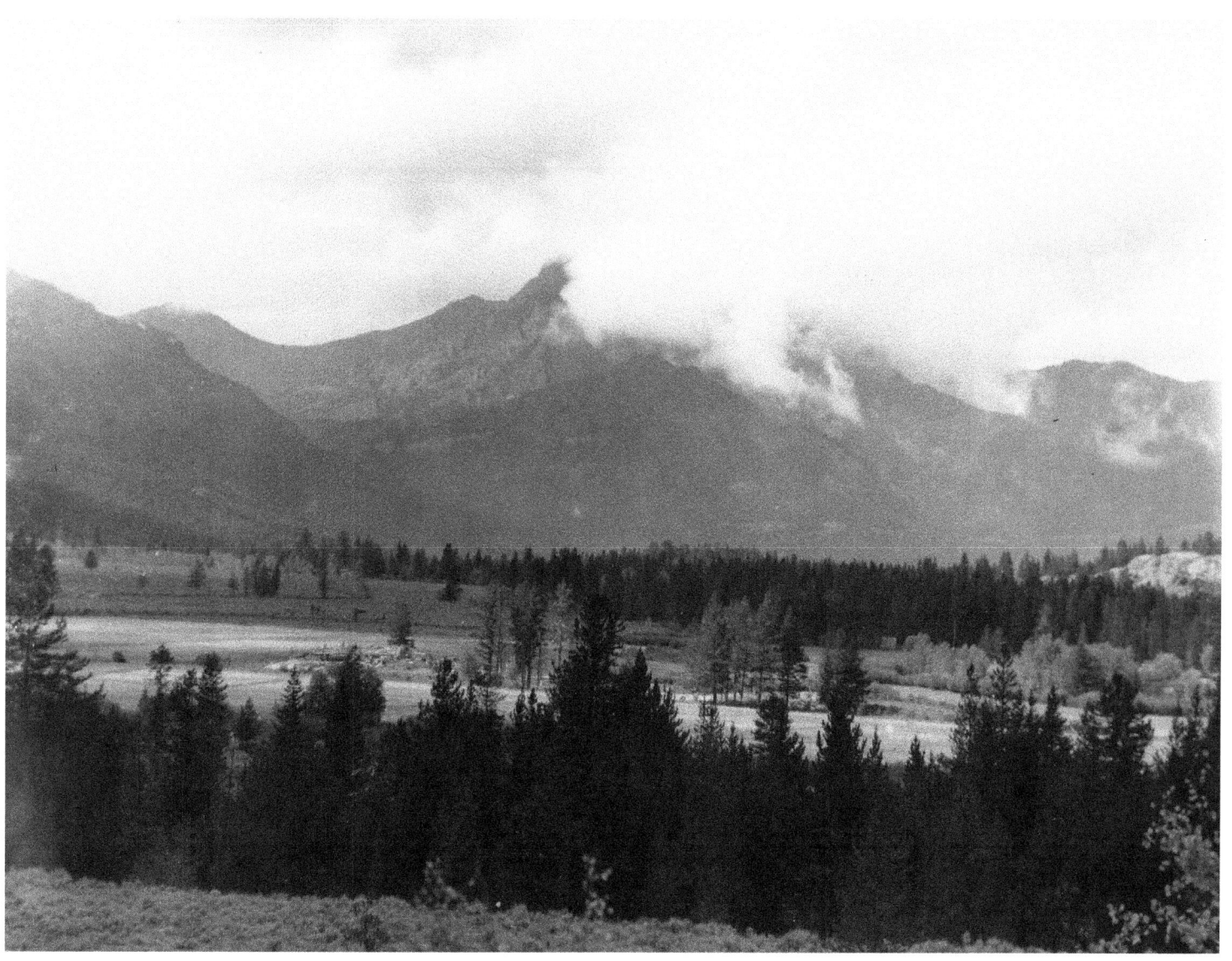

After two months of fishing, Ernest took Pauline to the Nordquist L-Bar-T ranch, where they had hunted in 1930. Nordquist's was a dude ranch on the Clark Fork Branch of the Yellowstone River, but as always it was not just a vacation. Wherever Hemingway traveled, he worked. Max Perkins, his editor at Scribner's, had sent him final proofs for *Death in the Afternoon* to correct, and Hemingway also answered correspondence his publisher forwarded.

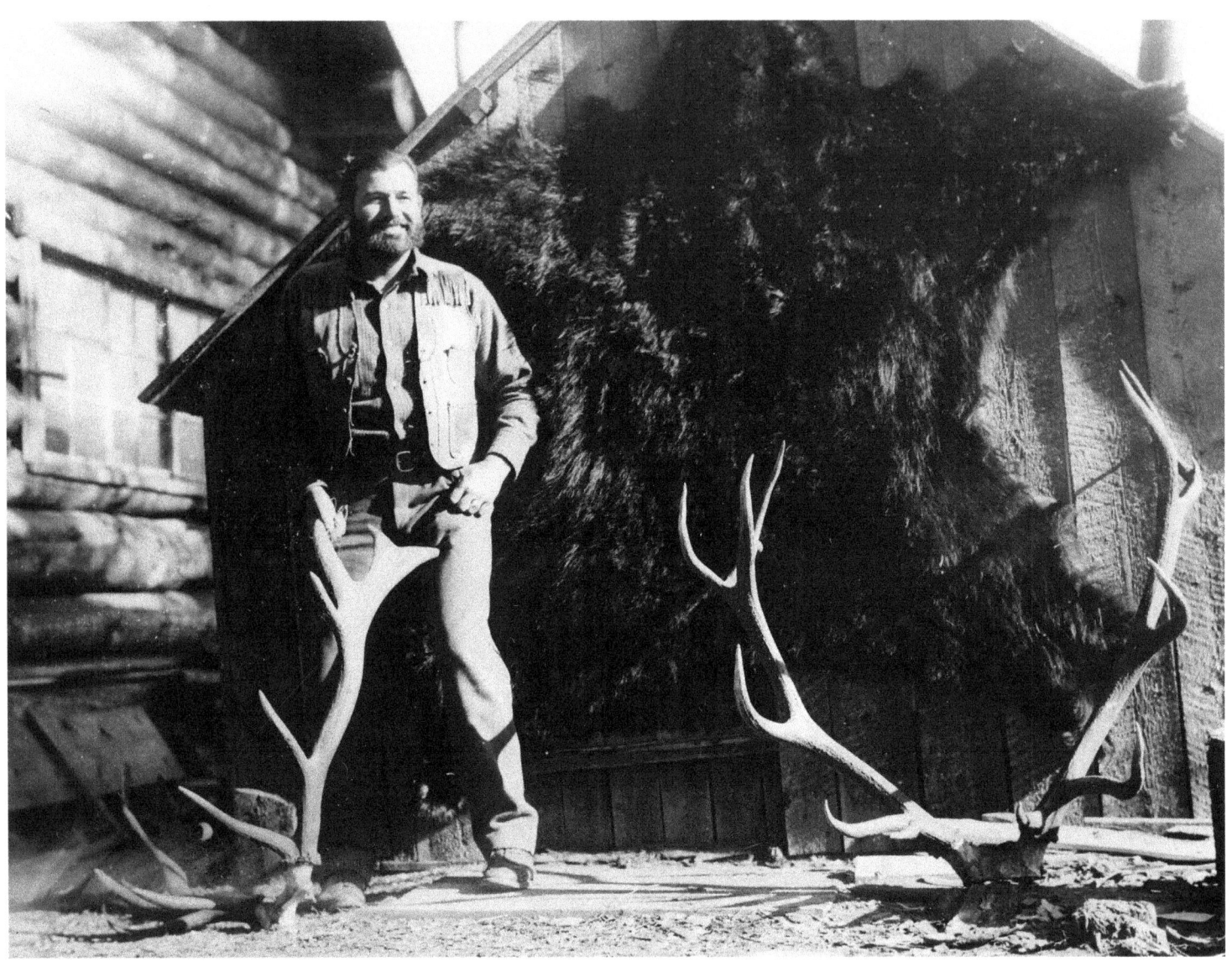

Charles Thompson, Hemingway's Key West friend, met them in Wyoming and hunted elk with Ernest at an altitude of 11,000 feet. Each got a nice bull, but Hemingway also worked on two short stories, one of them "Light of the World." Here, sometime during late summer or early fall 1932, Hemingway poses with his rack in front of the main lodge. Behind him is the hide of a grizzly bear, which were still plentiful.

Hemingway always seemed most comfortable with a drink or fishing rod in hand. After spending more time in Key West, he was off for Havana again in spring 1933. This time, aboard the *Anita,* he was gathering information for a detailed account of marlin fishing that was solicited for the first issue of *Esquire* magazine: "Marlin Off the Morro: A Cuban Letter," which he would write in his old correspondent's style.

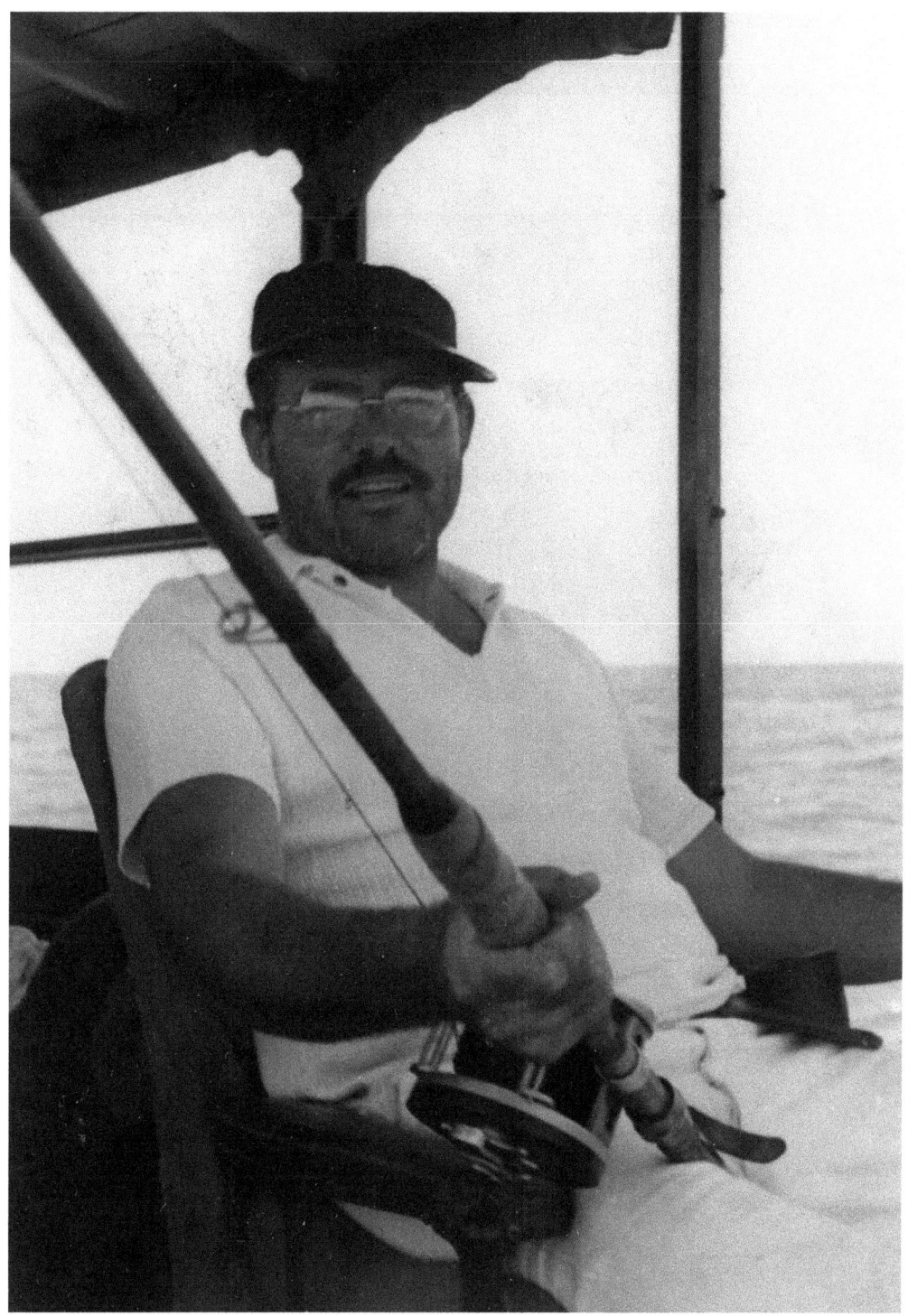

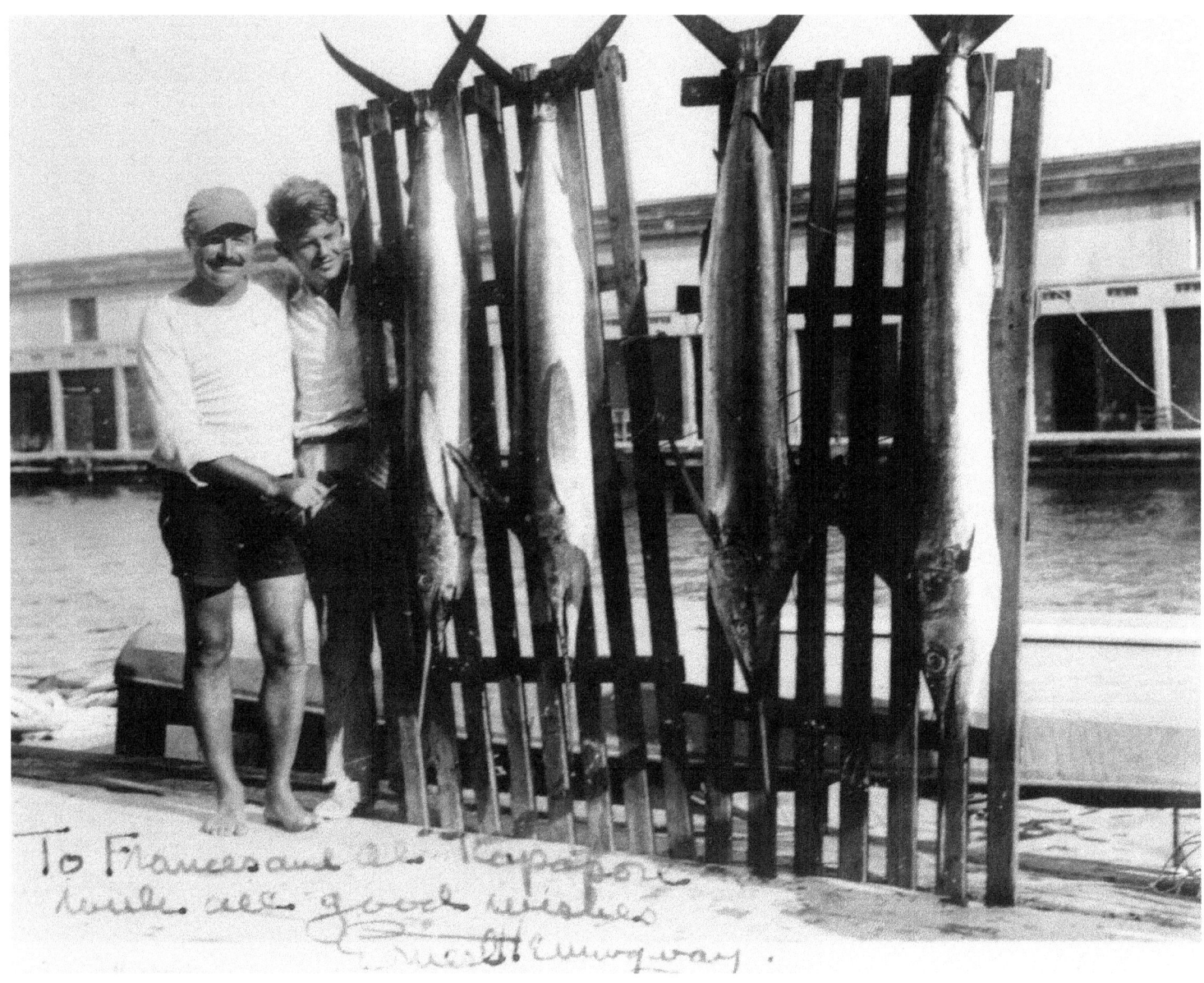

To Frances and Al Rapporte
with all good wishes
Ernest Hemingway.

Ernest and Charles Thompson with a rack of white marlin in Havana 1933. Hemingway hated to fish alone, and Thompson was easygoing and quite willing to let Ernest be alpha male. While in Cuban waters they saw 100 marlin a day and docked at San Francisco because it was close to the Ambos Mundos Hotel and two of Hemingway's favorite bars, the Floridita and the Bodeguita del Medio.

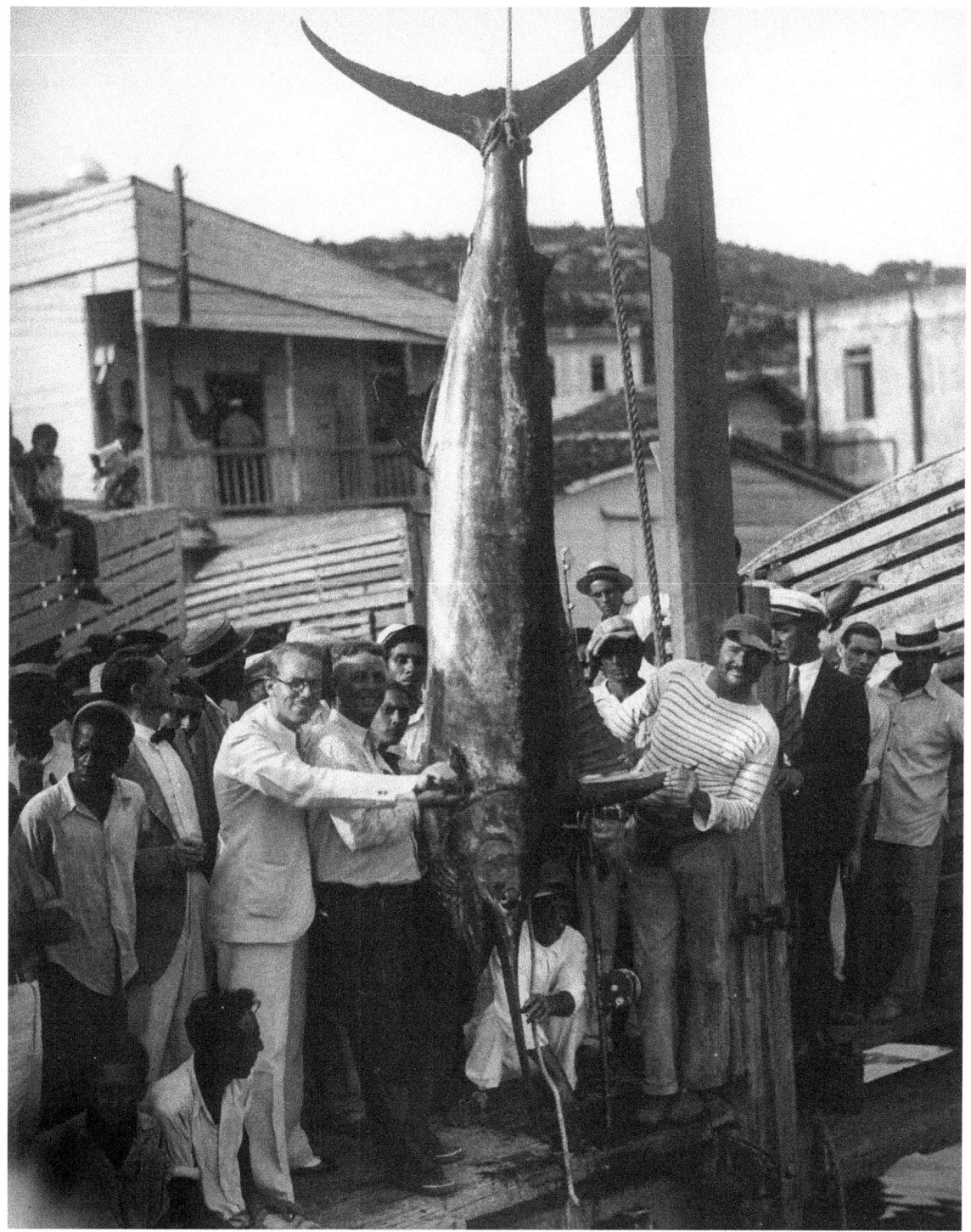

Casablanca docks, Havana. In Cuba, marlin were taken regularly by commercial fishermen, but Ernest was a rod-and-reel pioneer, first fishing there in 1929. In 1933 he boated a 468-pound blue marlin (shown) near Havana Harbor—then a record for the largest marlin taken off the coast of Cuba.

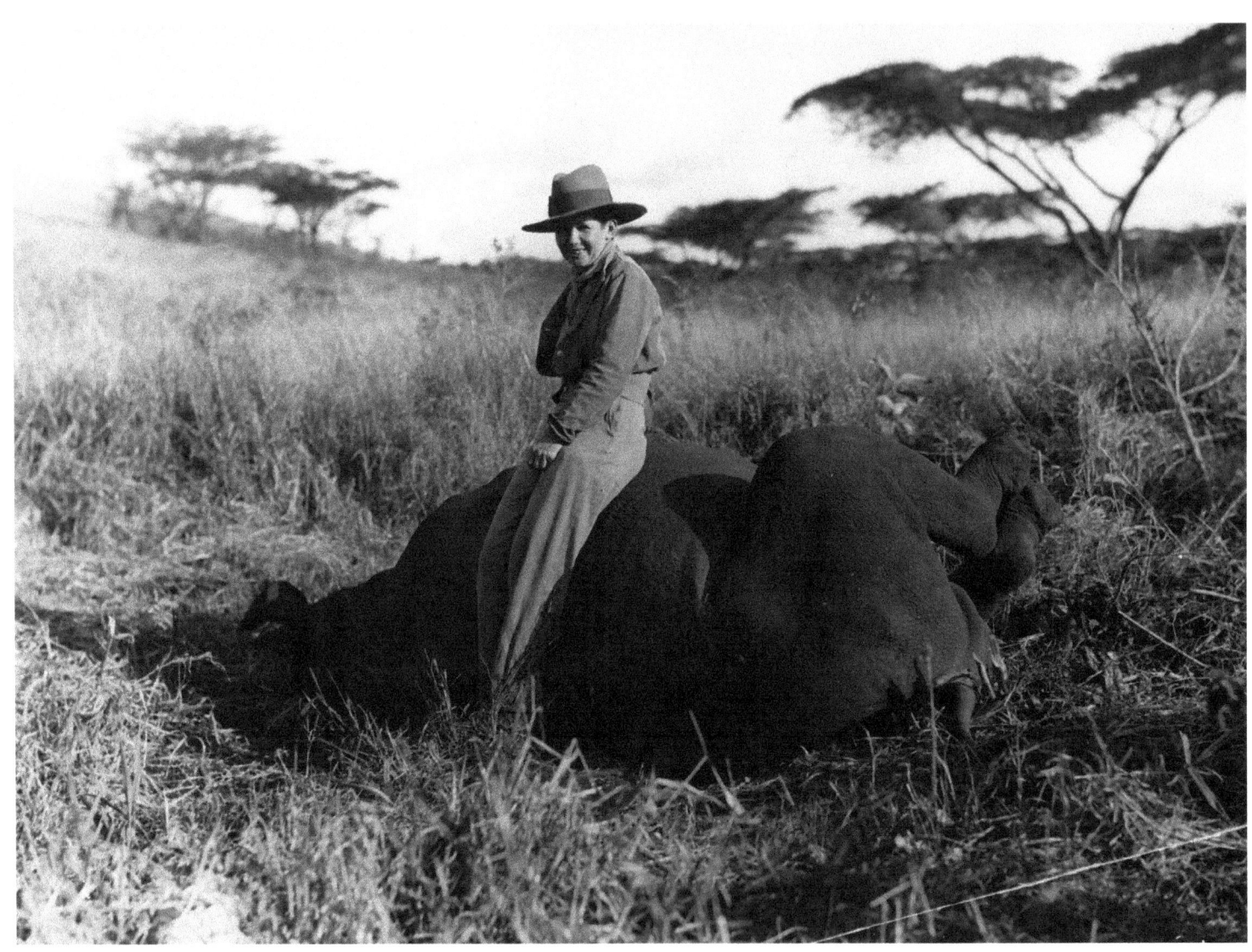

Since childhood, Ernest longed to go on safari. His father had taken him to Chicago's Field Museum, where he admired taxidermy mounts of African elephants, and his hero Teddy Roosevelt had gone on safari the year Hemingway turned ten. He planned a trip to Africa with his Key West best friend, Charles Thompson, but Pauline, whose uncle was footing the bill, insisted on going along. She turned out to be a pretty good shot, posing here with her rhino, around January-February 1934.

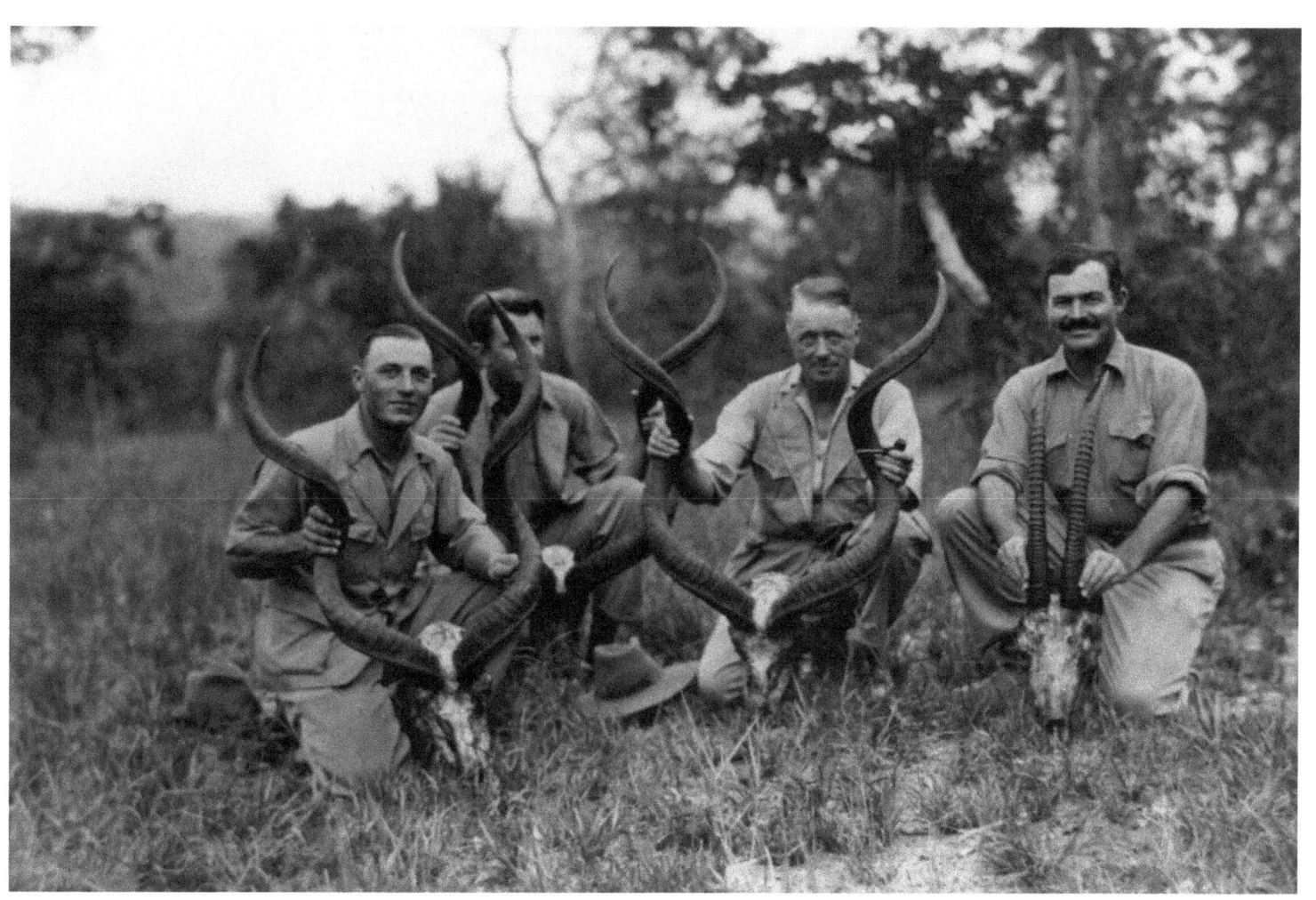

With kudu and oryx trophies, February 1934 (left to right): assistant hunter Ben Fourie, Charles Thompson, hunting guide Philip Percival, and Hemingway, who was annoyed that others kept bagging bigger trophies. He also missed part of the two-month safari when he was airlifted to a hospital because of severe dysentery. Hemingway would later write about the safari and people in it in *Green Hills of Africa* and two acclaimed short stories: "The Short Happy Life of Francis Macomber" and "The Snows of Kilimanjaro."

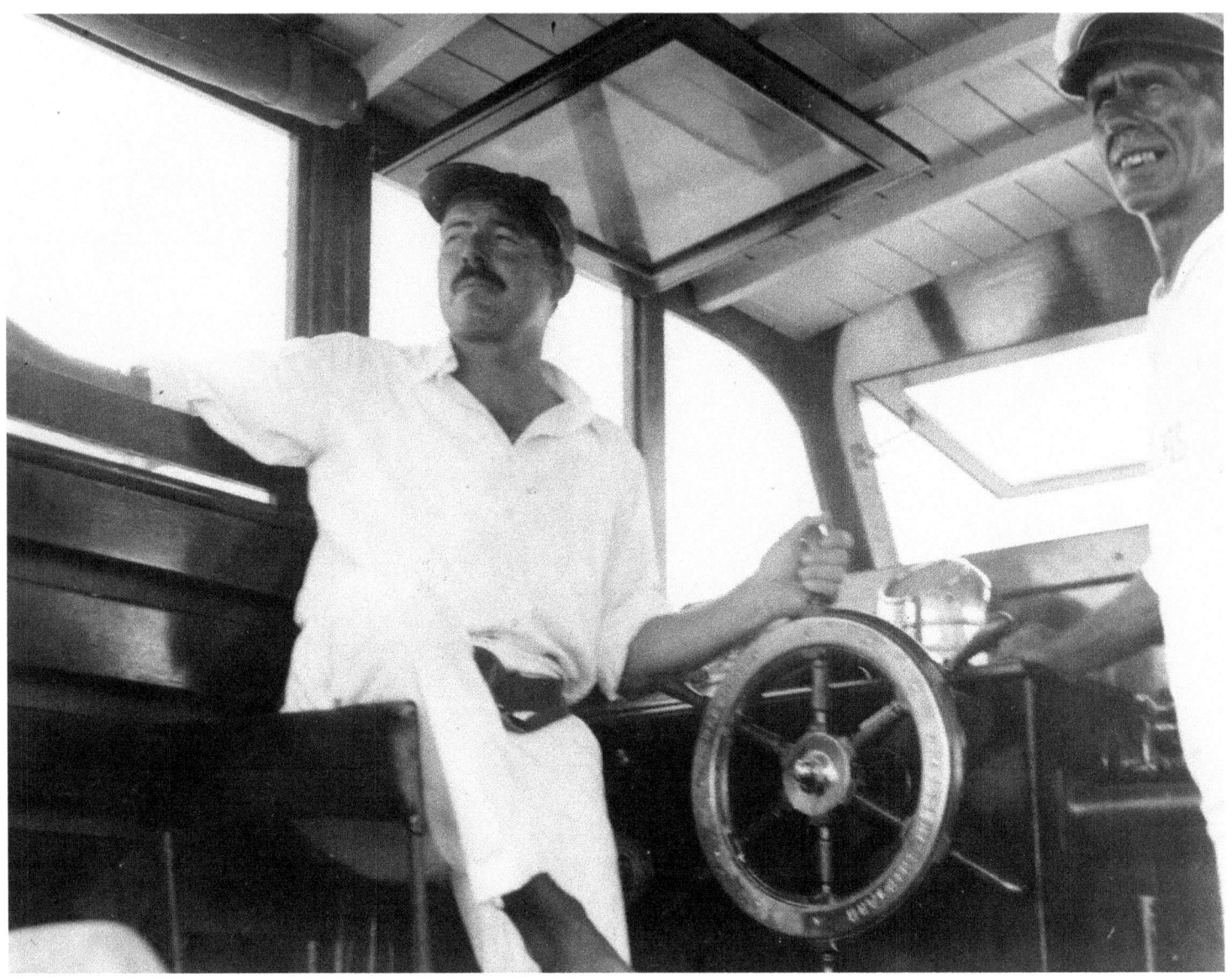

In May 1934, Hemingway received delivery of a specially designed 38-foot sport fishing boat which he named the *Pilar*, after Our Lady of the Pilar, a shrine in Zaragoza, Spain. The boat, which had a 75 hp Chrysler engine and the most expensive fighting chair available, was paid for in part with an advance check from *Esquire* for ten more articles. It slept six persons and carried 400 gallons of fuel for long trips.

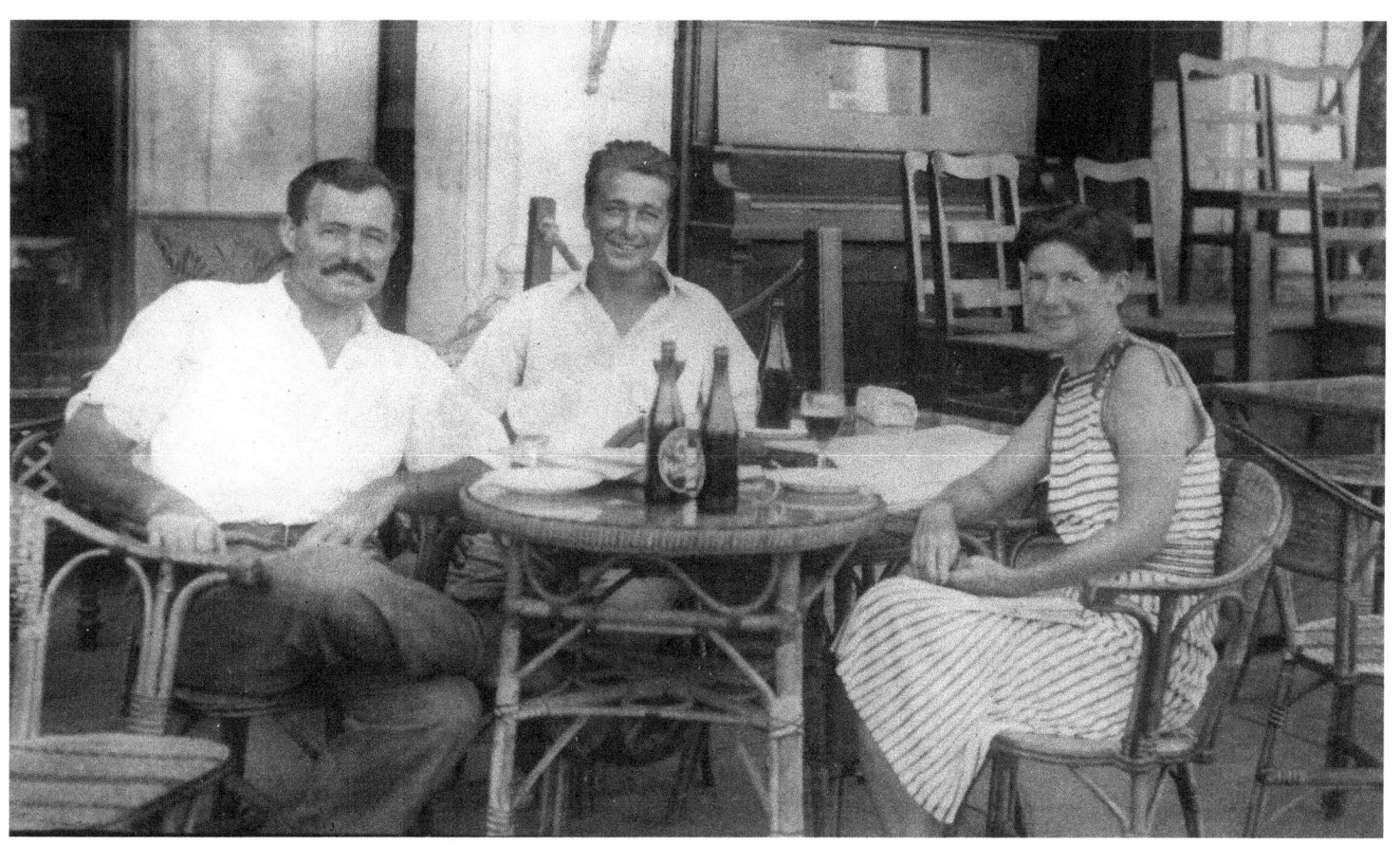

Hemingway regarded visitors and the telephone as "destroyers of work." One exception was Arnold Samuelson, an aspiring writer who had corresponded with Hemingway and hopped freight trains to get to Key West. He wanted lessons on writing from the master. Ernest admired his audacity, but it was also good timing. With an upcoming Cuba trip, the *Pilar* needed a night watchman. Here Samuelson enjoys a Havana lunch with Ernest and Pauline in summer 1934.

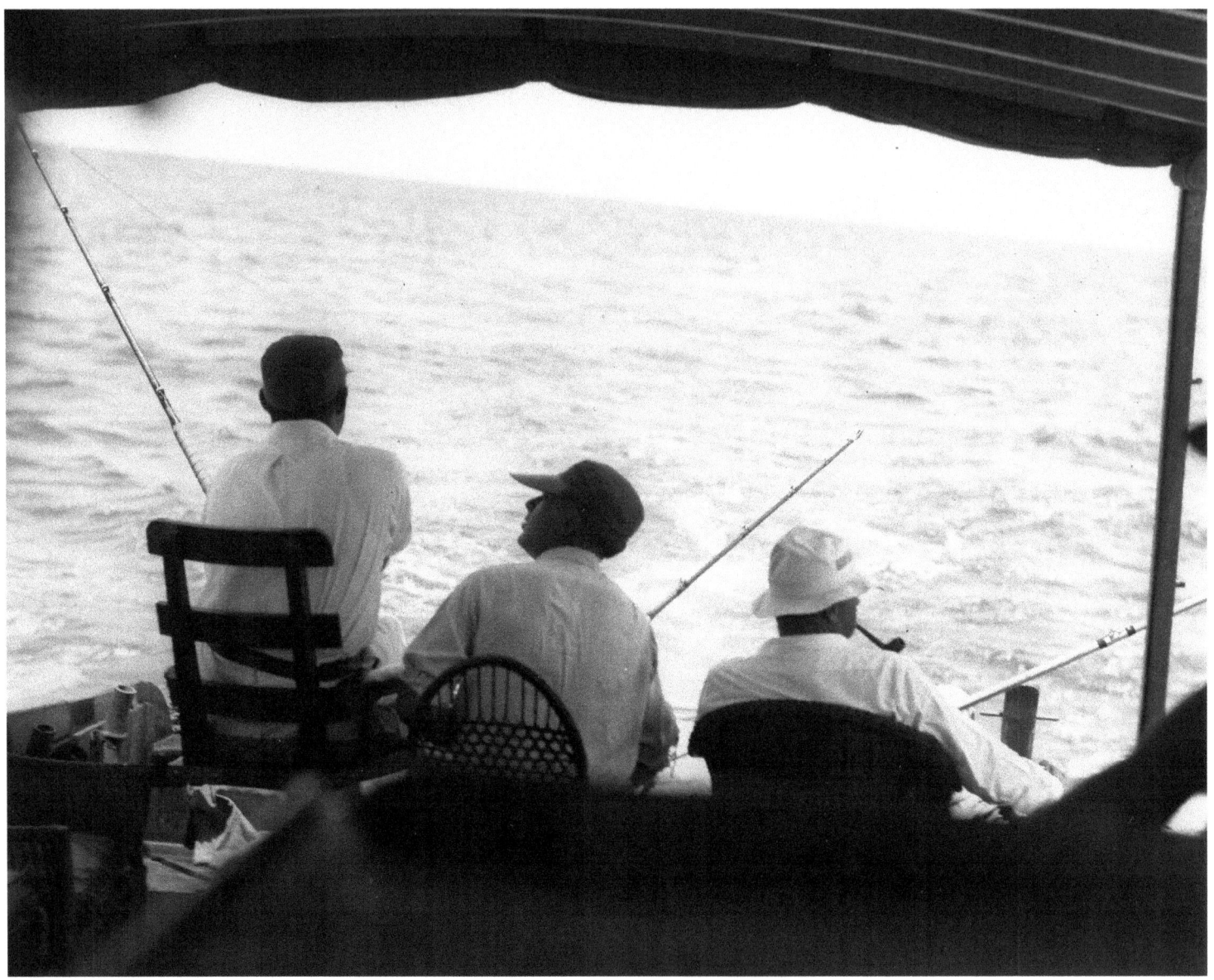

By 1934 Hemingway's fame as a sportsman was almost equal to his fame as a novelist. Writer and trophy fisherman Zane Grey even proposed a joint "world tour" that never materialized. Instead, a succession of friends joined Hemingway on the *Pilar* that first season, and at one point his expanding knowledge of marlin led to a visit from the director of the Museum of the Natural Sciences Academy of Philadelphia and his chief ichthyologist. With Hemingway's help, they reclassified marlin species.

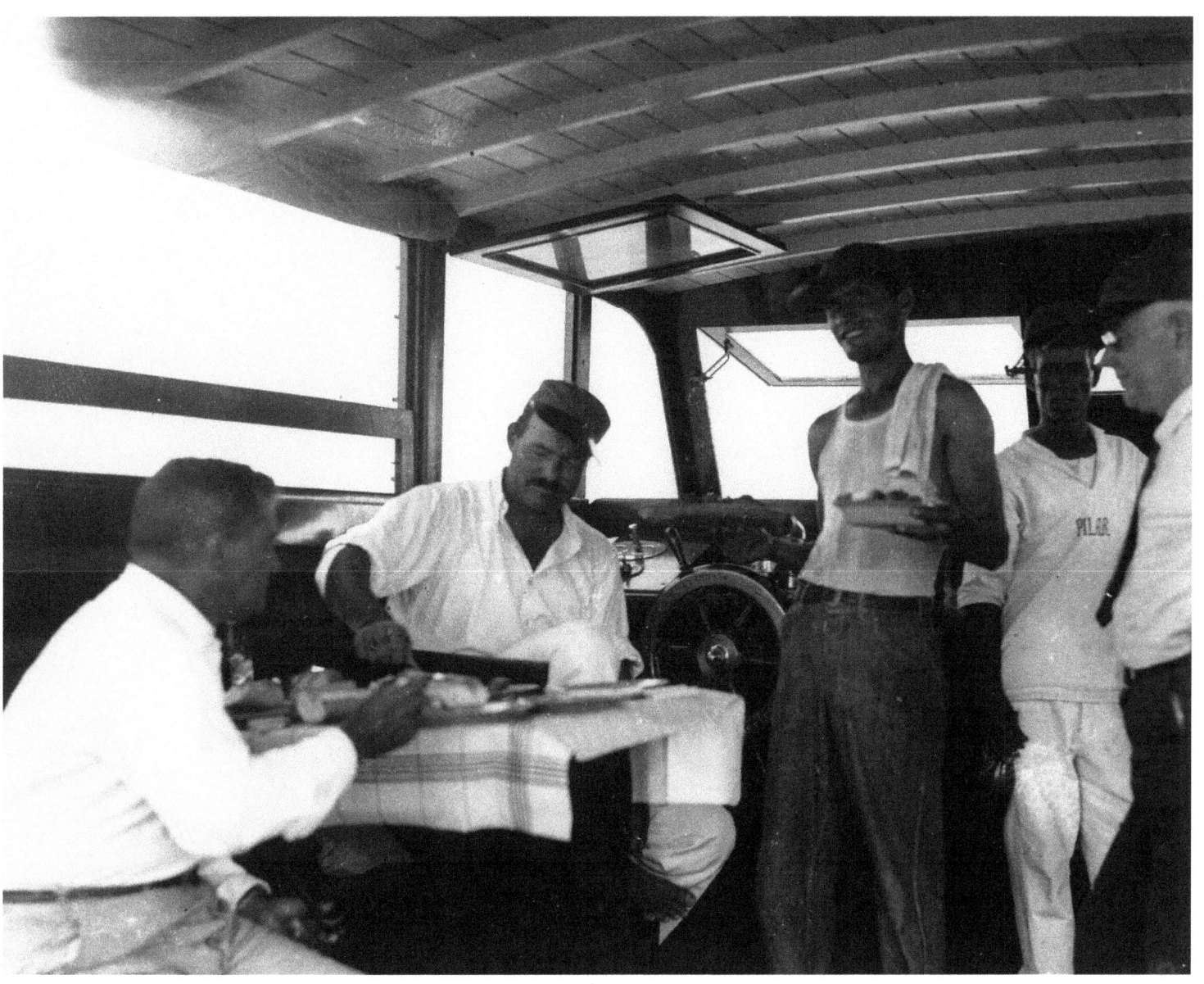

The *Pilar* was a beautiful boat with a streamlined black hull, polished mahogany woodwork, and chrome fittings. Lunch onboard was a civilized affair, with a cook named Juan preparing the food and serving it. Next to him, in a uniform that told the world he worked on Hemingway's boat, is Carlos Gutiérrez, whom Ernest had hired to be his mate.

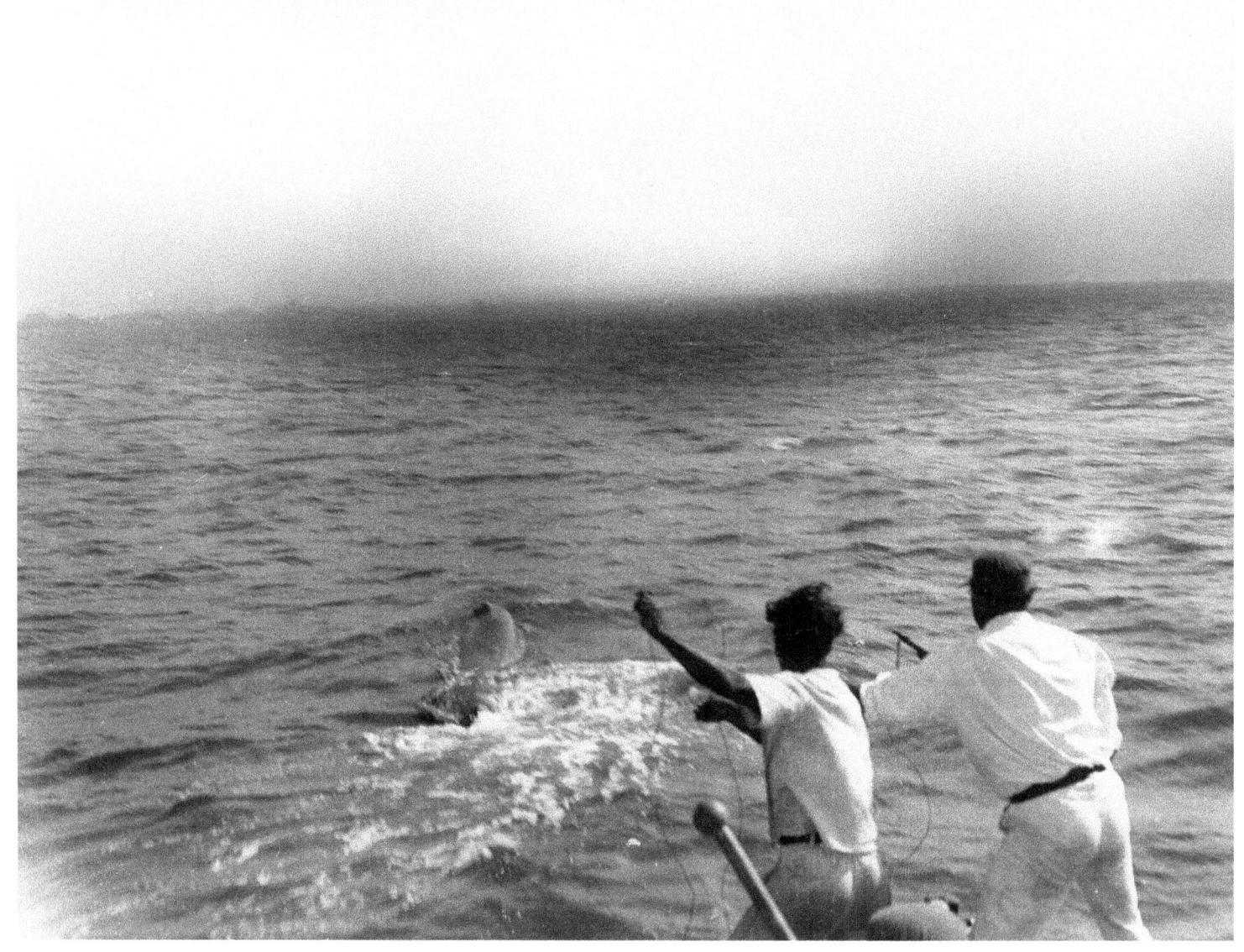

In the Gulf Stream, summer 1934, Hemingway (right, with harpoon gun) takes a shot at a whale which he later wrote was 60 feet long. When it came to hunting and fishing, Hemingway was an anarchist, despite his father's teachings. At 16 he shot a heron to mount, prompting the local game warden to come knocking. And in 1932, in Wyoming, he drew the ire of hunting companion Charles Thompson when he shot an eagle on the fly.

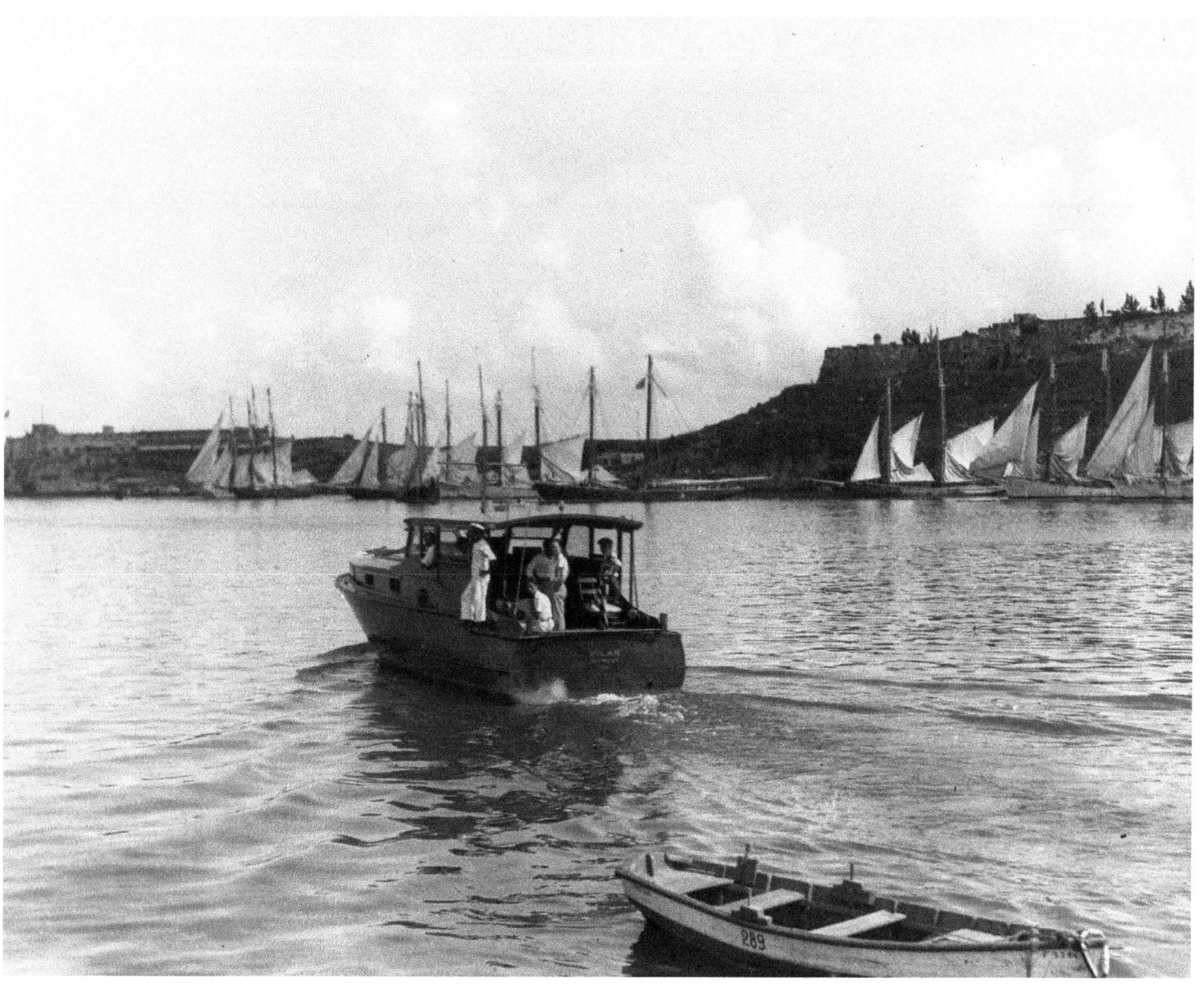

Heading out again. In summer 1934 Hemingway landed a 243-pound marlin in under half an hour and a 130-pound striped marlin in a scant three minutes. He was perfecting his technique of using brute strength to reel fish in fast and still full of fight, because when the fish were fought the traditional way and tired before being brought alongside the boat, sharks could easily attack the hooked fish. Not so when the fish were still strong and fast.

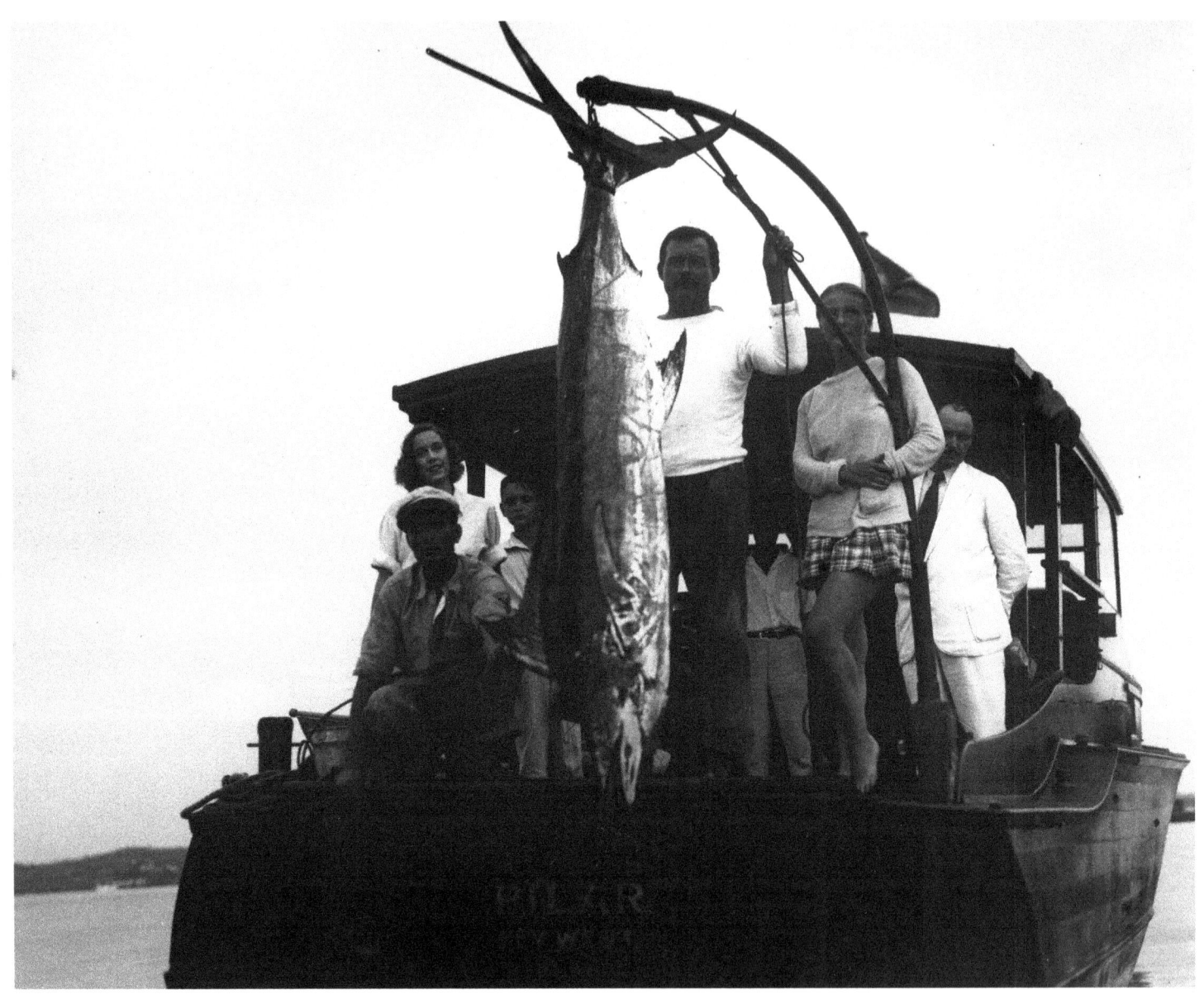

Hemingway often became friendly with other men's wives. Usually it was a harmless flirtation, but that wasn't the case with Jane Mason (in plaid). The young wife of the head of Pan American Airways in Cuba was as attracted to Hemingway as he was to her. She and her husband, Grant, lived on an estate west of Havana, and in 1934 while Pauline was in Key West and Grant out of town, she went with Hemingway on his new boat for a trip that stretched into four months.

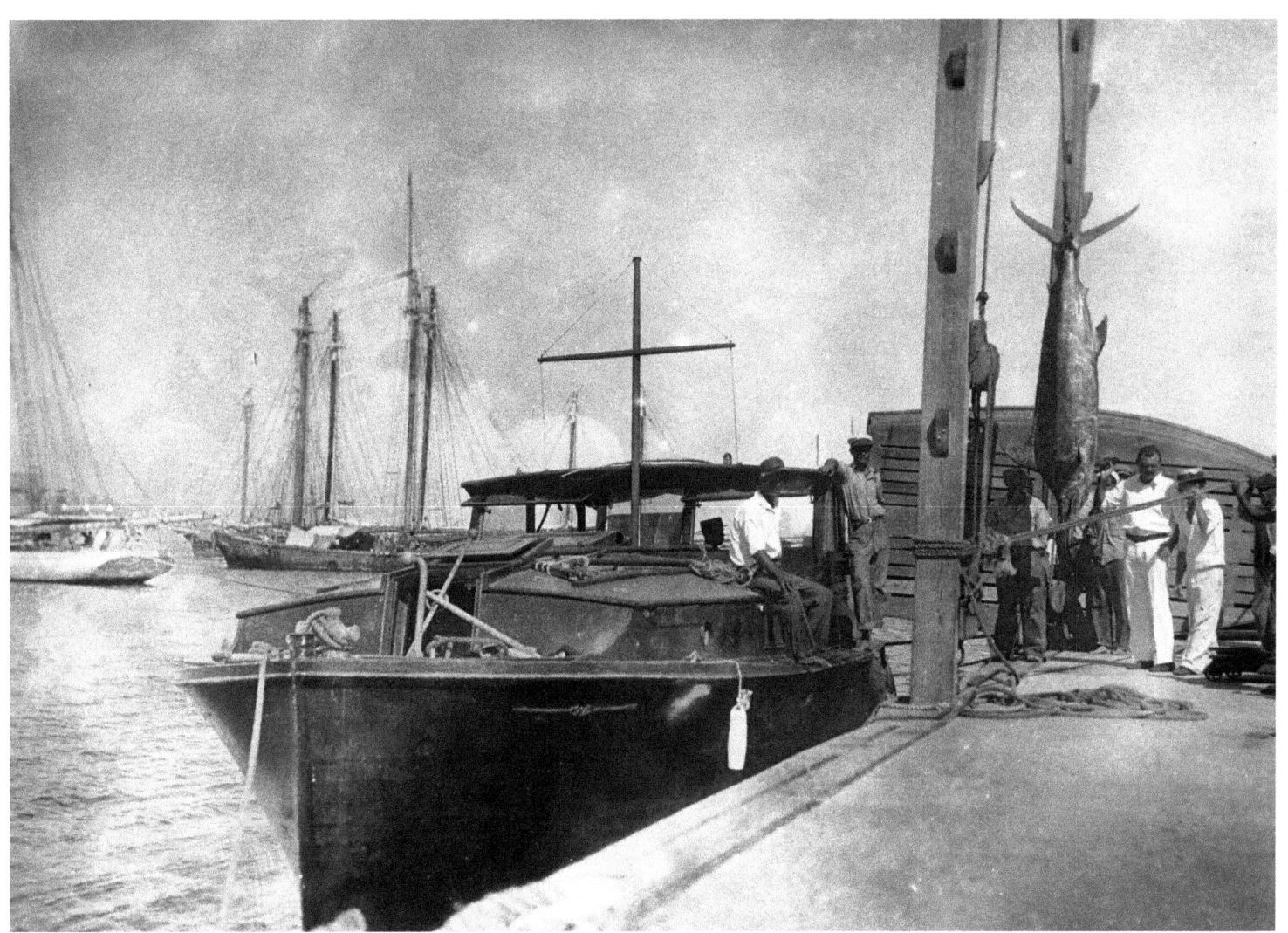

As often as it docked here in Havana in the thirties, Ernest's boat anchored off Jaimanitas, the Masons' estate. People began to talk, especially after incidents the foregoing year. In May 1933, a depressed Jane either fell or threw herself off a balcony just days after a car accident while driving the children. She broke her back, but their on-again-off-again affair was on again the summer of 1934, fueled, no doubt, by the excitement of the new boat.

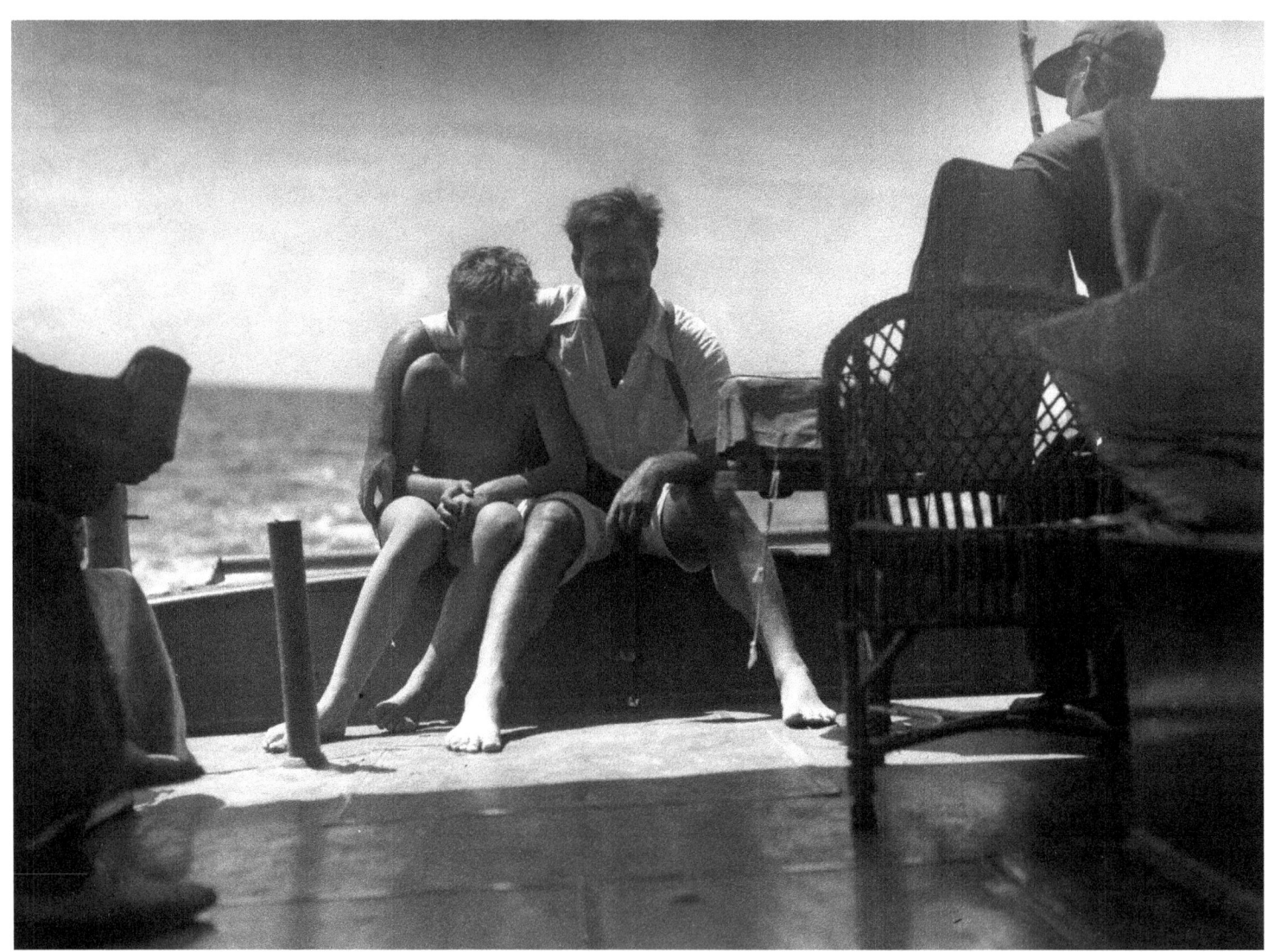

A father-son moment on the stern of the *Pilar*. Bumby, or "Jack" as he would prefer to be called as an adult, was 11 this summer. Many years later he would quip that he spent the first half of his life in the shadow of a famous father, and the last half as father to three famous daughters: writer Joan, model Margaux, and actress Mariel. Hemingway never wanted to go straight home after a day on the water. Son Patrick recalled that in Key West there were a number of times when their father would stop at Sloppy Joe's bar for drinks while the sons waited. In Havana it was the Floridita, the Bodegita del Medio, or one of the smaller bodegas.

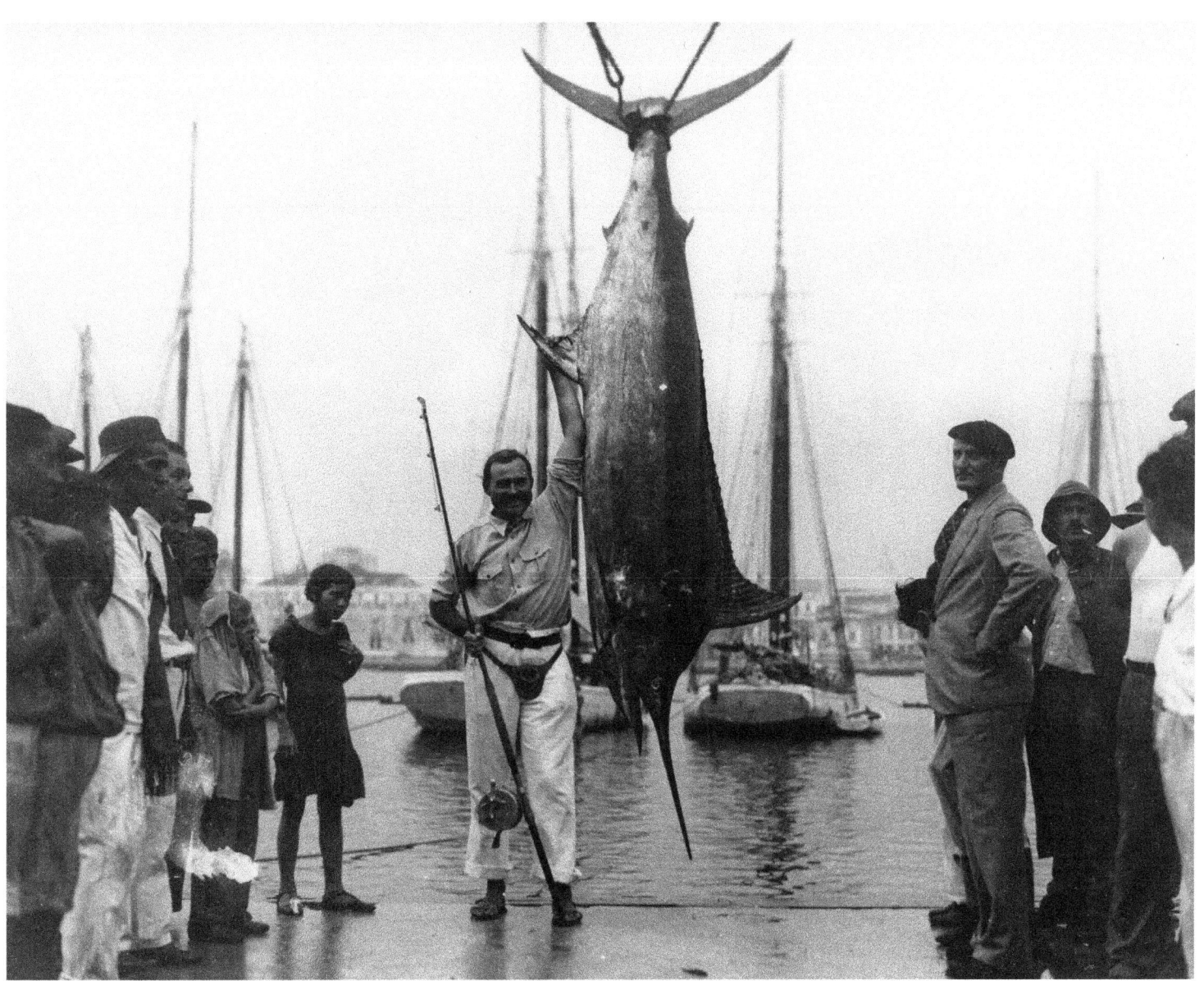

When matador Sidney Franklin was in Havana to inspect the bulls, he met up with Hemingway, who stands beside a 420-pound, 12-foot-long blue marlin while still wearing his fighting belt. Franklin is the man in the beret with his hands on his hips. It's likely that Hemingway and his politically minded friend discussed the foregoing year's collapse of the Machado regime and the new U.S.-backed government.

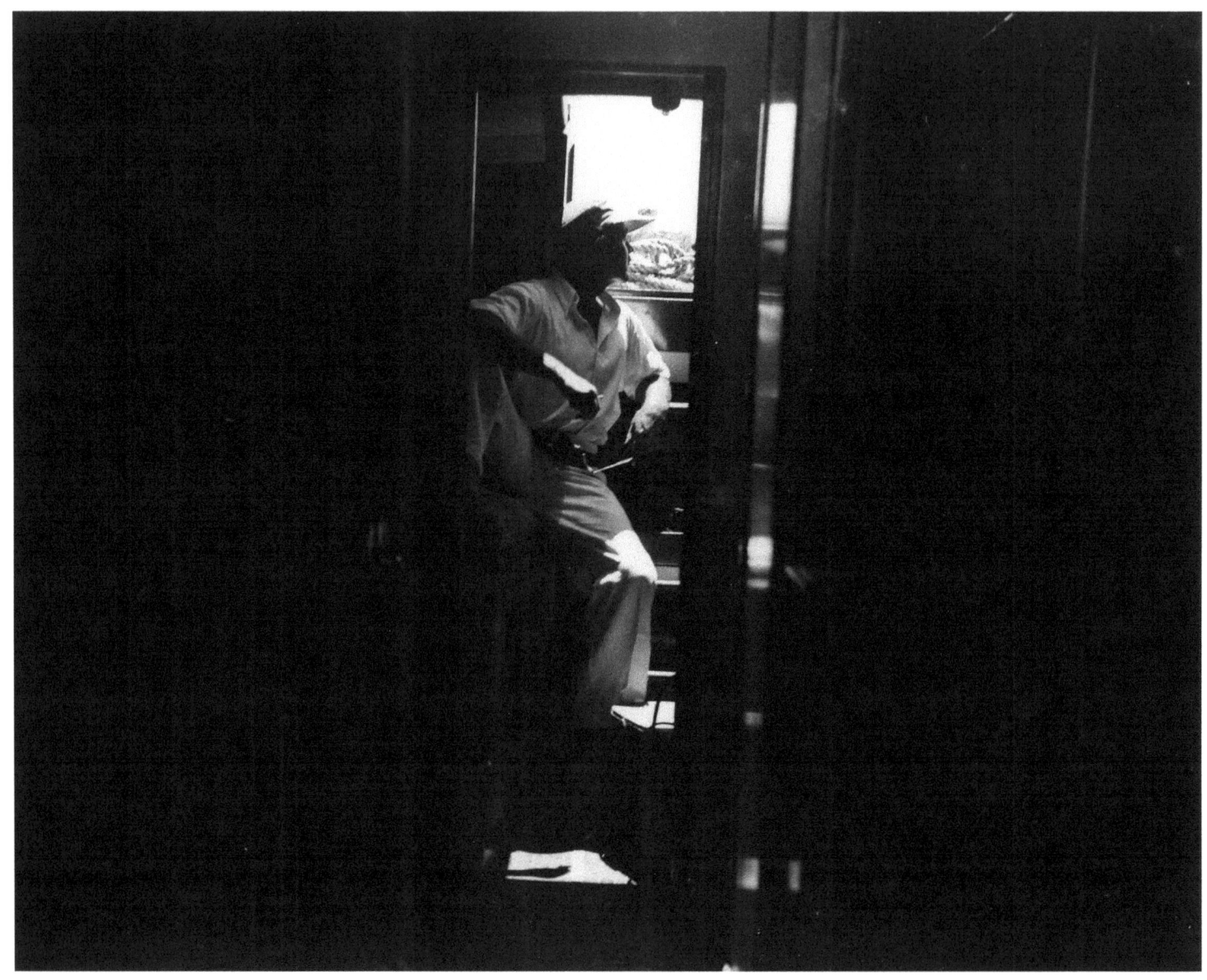

By mid-season, Hemingway had boated close to 30 marlin from his fighting chair, and he wasn't strapped in, the way fishermen are today. Seven of those fish were monsters that took a lot out of him and took off some of the weight that he put on with his daily drinking. Here, the camera captures a slender and thoughtful man aboard the *Pilar* in Havana Harbor.

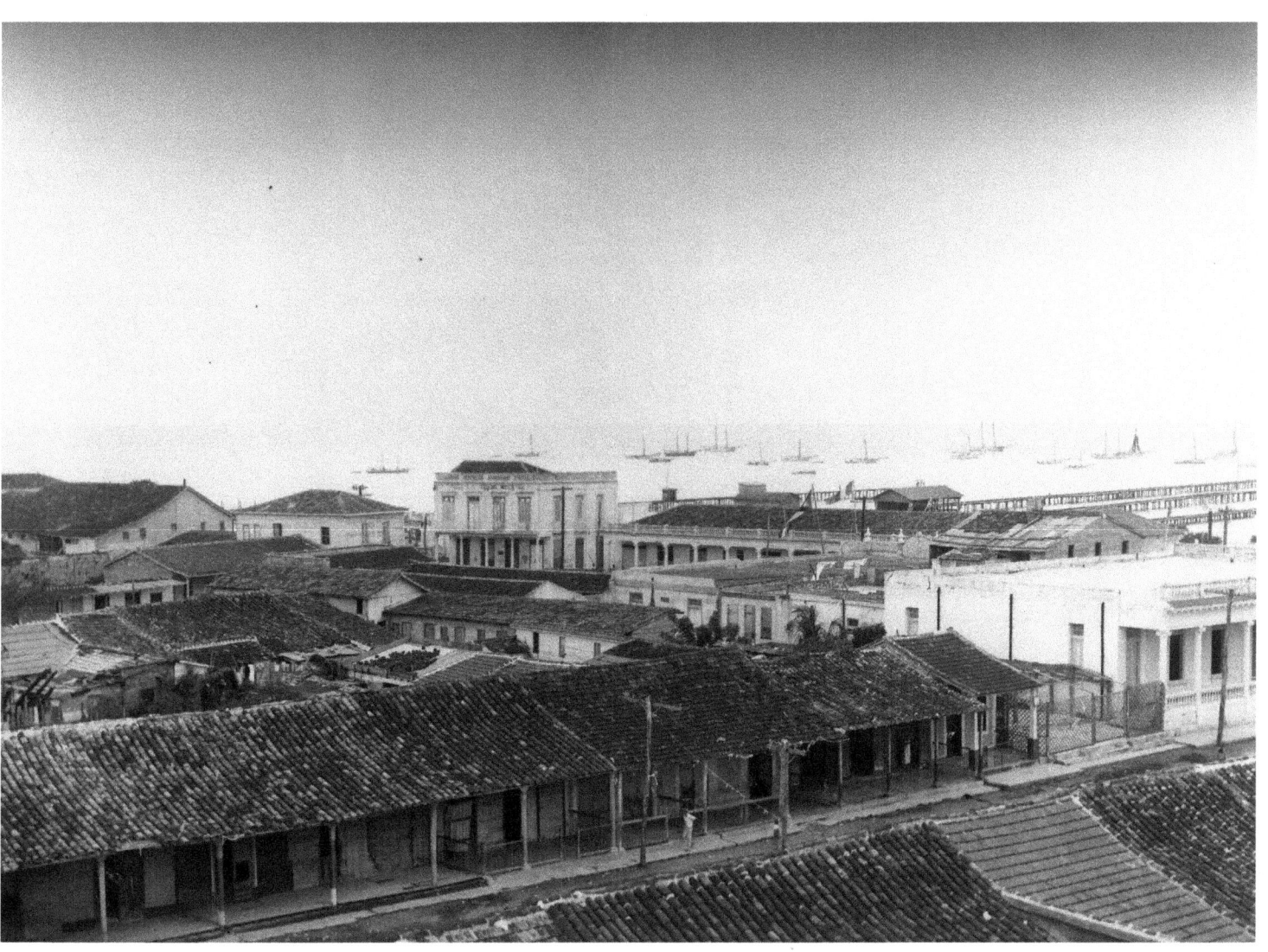

Hemingway's Cuba. He told *Esquire* editor Arnold Gingrich he had "no romantic feeling" about the "scene" in the U.S., and that he planned to live his life in places that interested him. In the thirties, it was Key West and Havana, two exotic settings where Hemingway was able to establish a routine of writing 300-500 words in the mornings (he kept count), fishing in the afternoons, and celebrating with drink afterward.

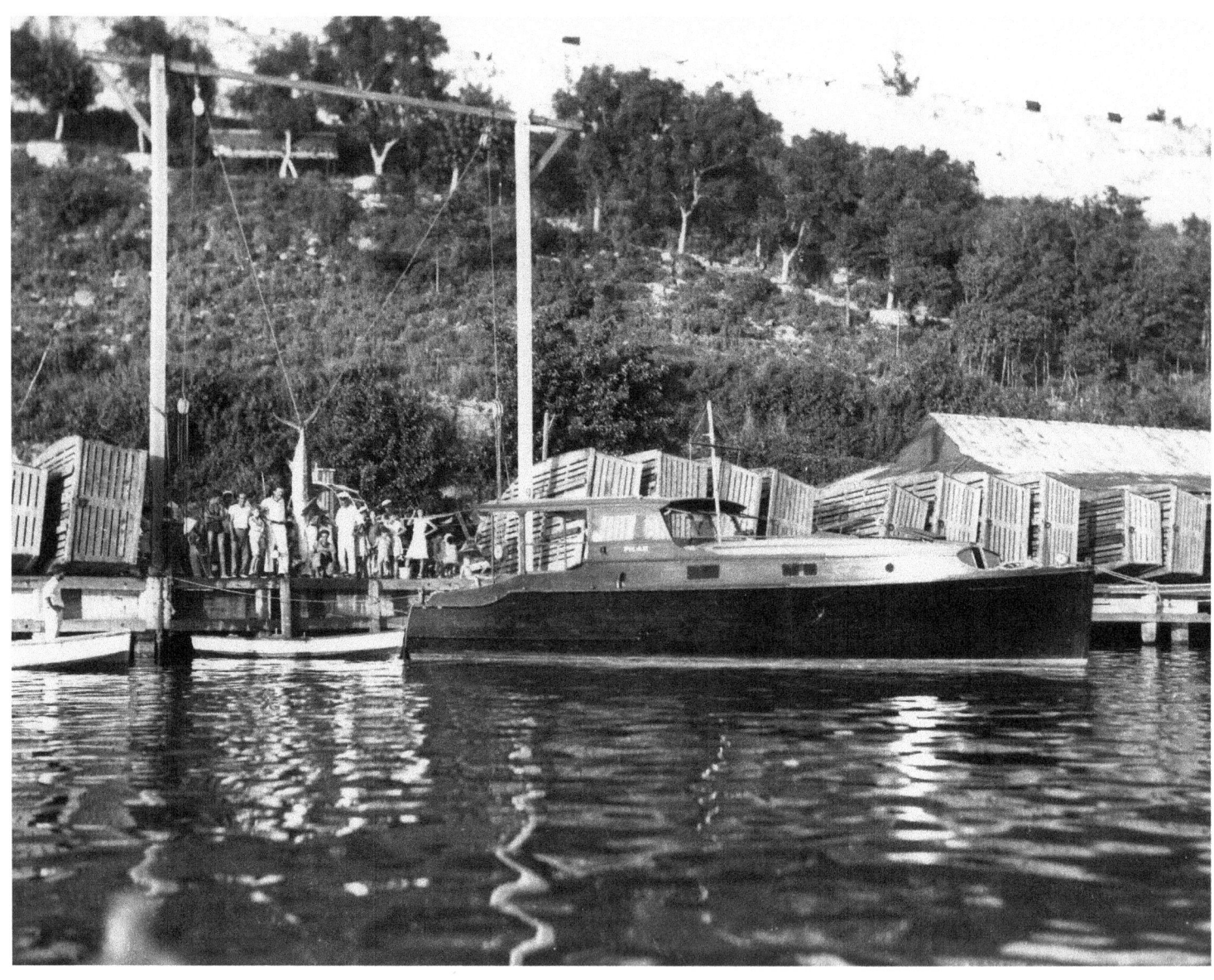

Crowds always gathered when the *Pilar* pulled in at Casablanca docks. None of the locals had read any of his novels. They only knew him as a "millionaire" who had one of the best boats in the Gulf Stream and the time to spend on it while never apparently having to work. But Hemingway became a minor folk hero because he gave away thousands of pounds of marlin meat to the locals . . . and, no fool, to the harbor guards as well.

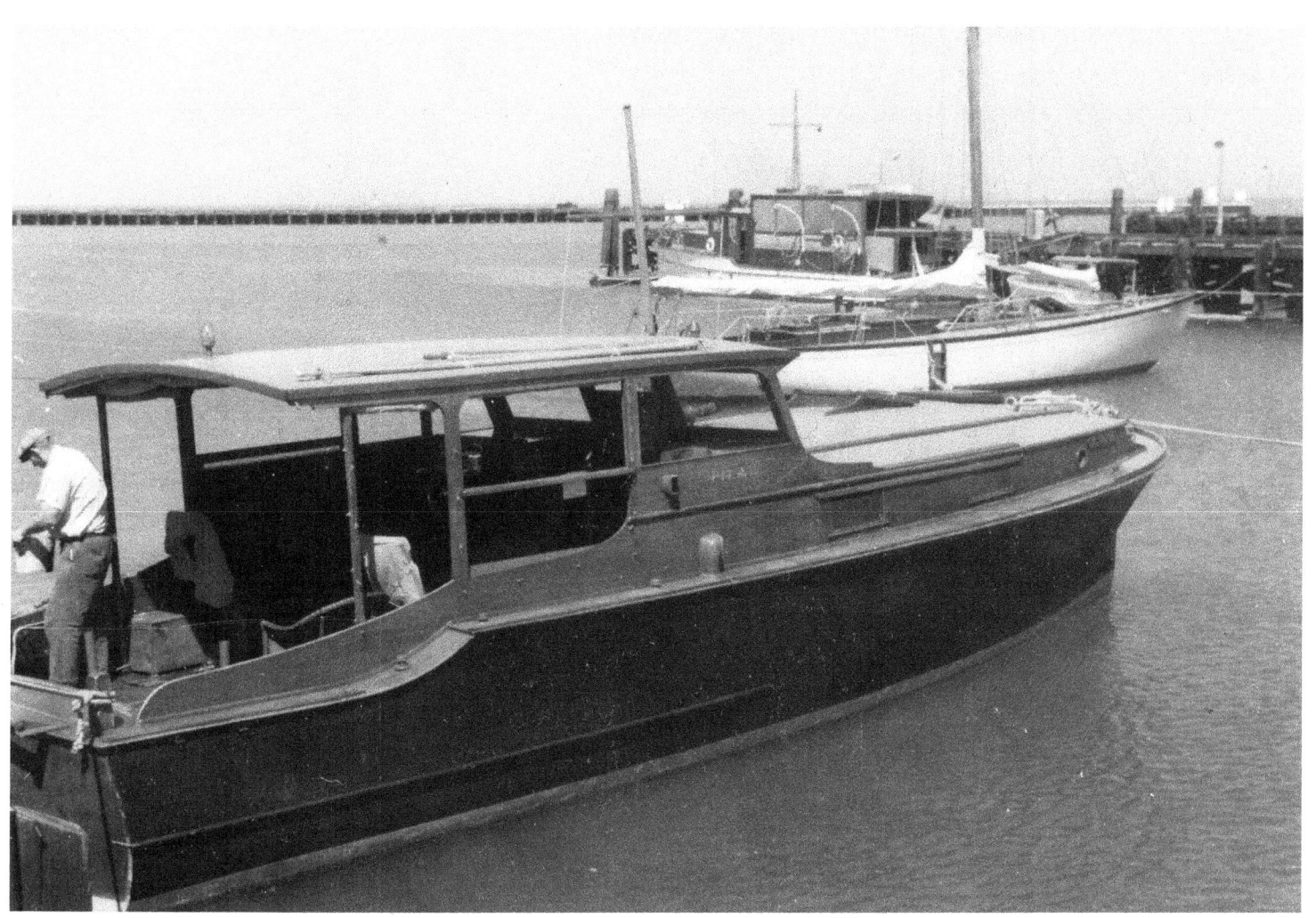

In April 1935, Hemingway planned a fishing trip to Bimini with friends, but fishing en route they caught a shark. Hemingway pulled out his Colt .22 to put a bullet in the creature's brain to keep it from thrashing on deck, but it moved as the accident-prone Hemingway fired. The bullet splintered and ricocheted, hitting both of his legs and forcing the group to return to Key West. A week later, the *Pilar* finally anchored in Bimini.

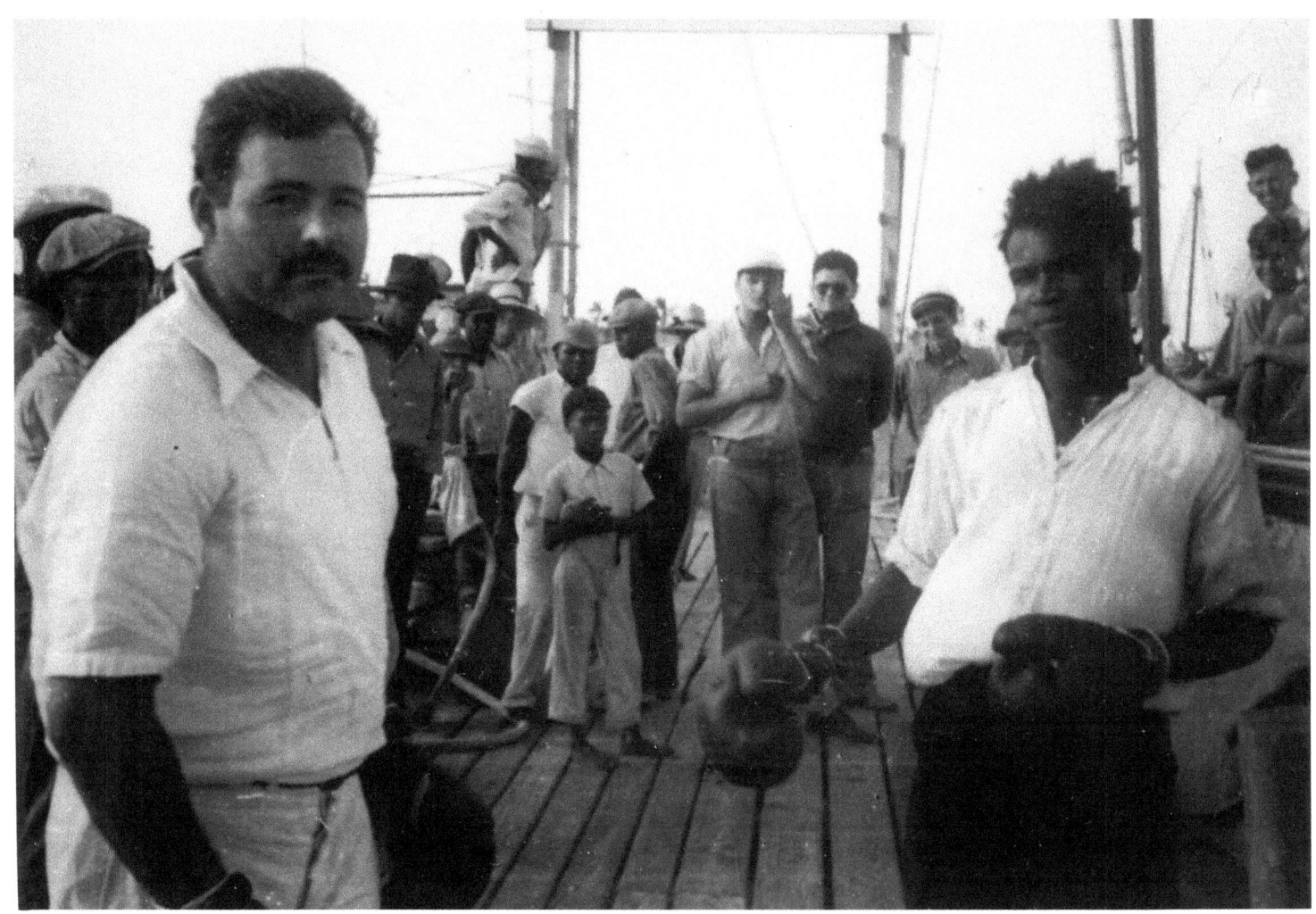

Hemingway's reputation as a brawler prompted numerous challenges, and he participated in as many fights as he avoided, besting the biggest boxer on the Bimini docks. But what impressed Bahamians so much that they made up a song was a bare-knuckle fight in which he decked a drunken challenger with just three punches. The man turned out to be publisher Joe Knapp. After Hemingway knocked him cold he joked it probably wasn't the best thing for a writer to do.

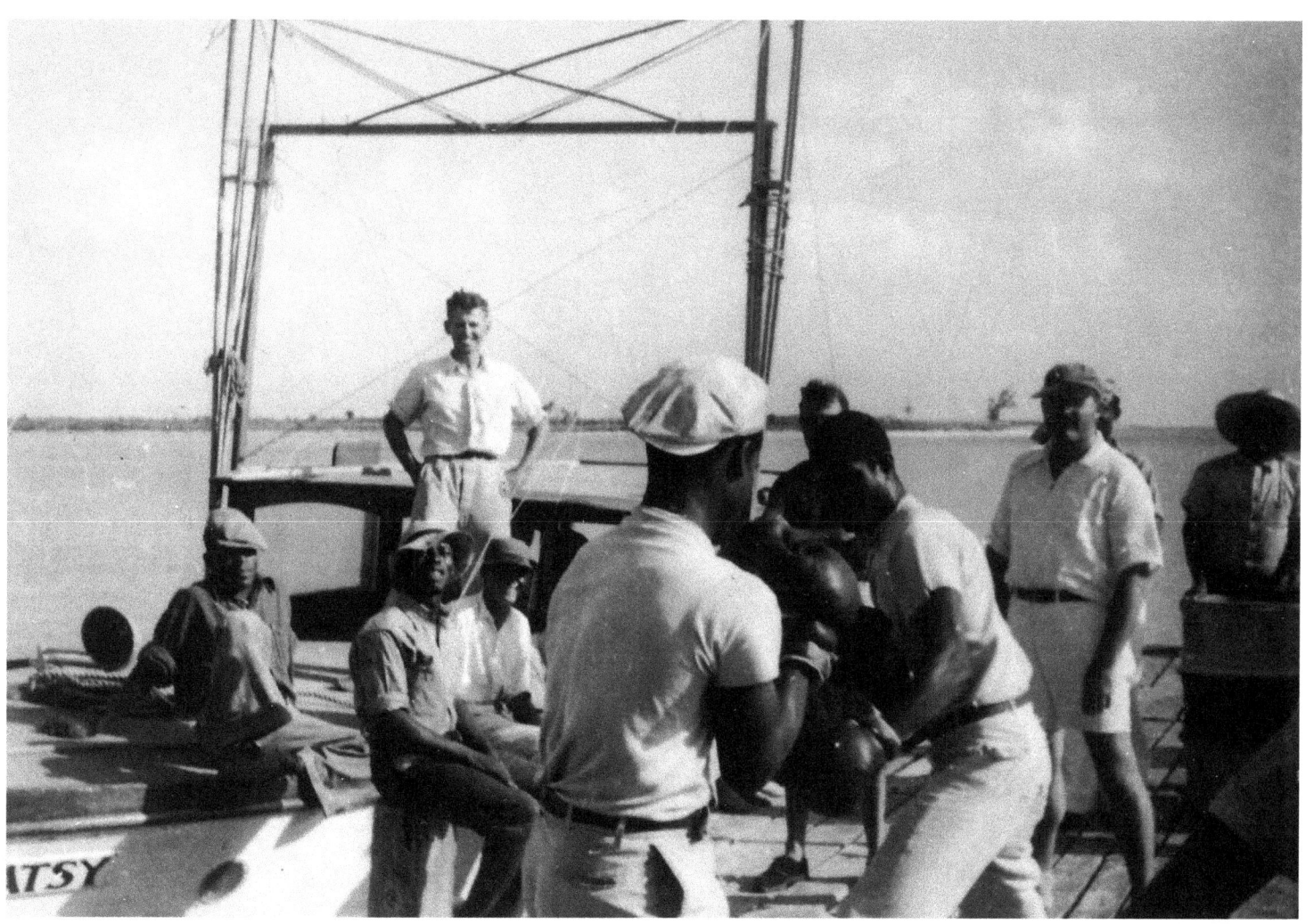

Hemingway (watching on the right) was a boxing aficionado who was a regular at the Friday night fights in Key West that were held outdoors at the Blue Goose (now Blue Heaven), serving as both referee and fighter's second. In Bimini he started the tradition of Saturday night fights and boxed for exercise on the beach with former British heavyweight champ Tom Heeney.

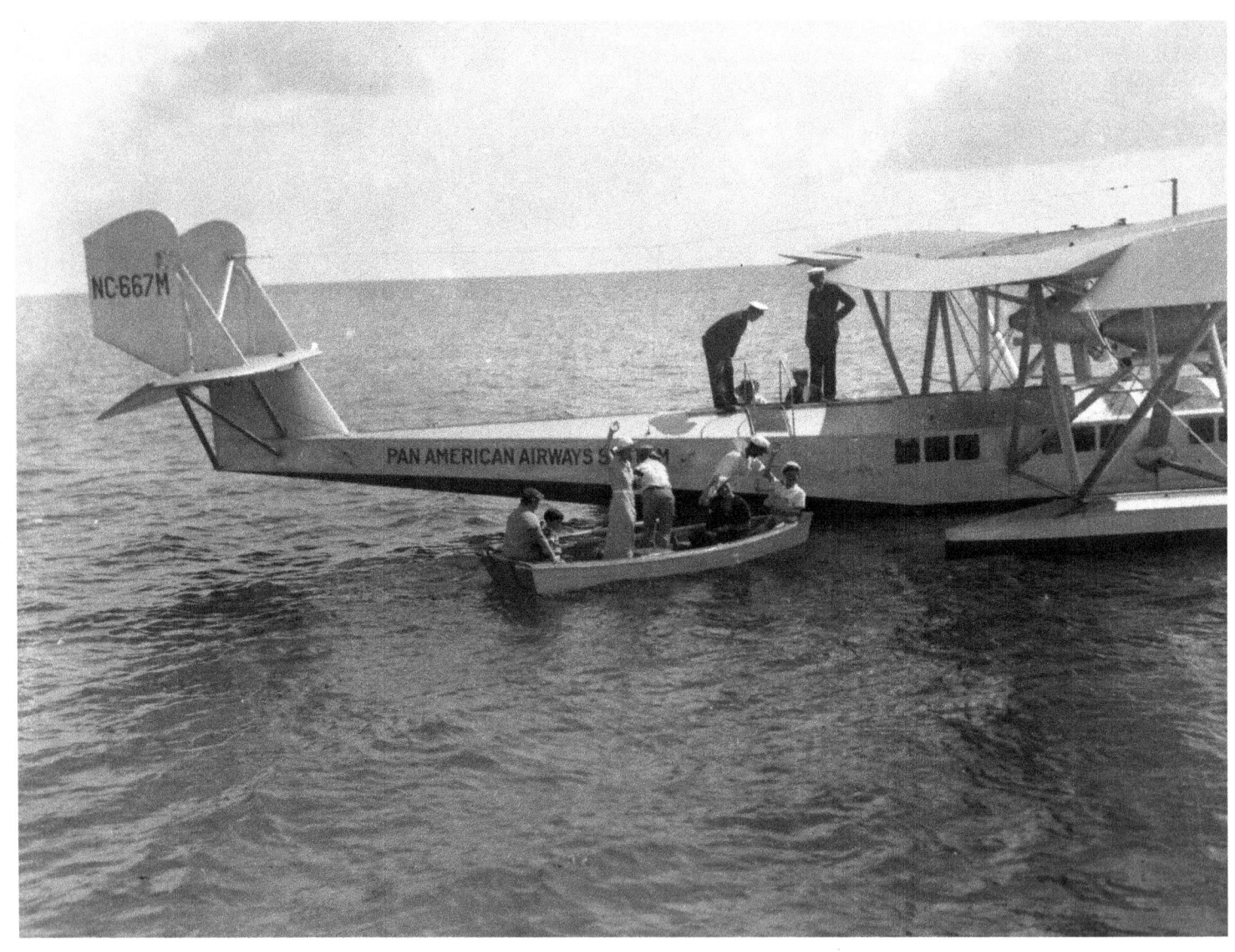

Pauline arrives by seaplane at Cat Cay with the boys to join Ernest in Bimini in late April 1935. The headquarters for Pan American in Key West was just a few blocks away from the Hemingway house on Whitehead Street.

After settling in, Pauline cuts Ernest's hair at the Compleat Angler Hotel in Bimini. By this time, Pauline knew that her husband was seeing Jane Mason, because she had cracked wise that maybe she should have her nose fixed and warts removed, since she couldn't compete with the young Cuban girls or the lovely Mrs. Mason.

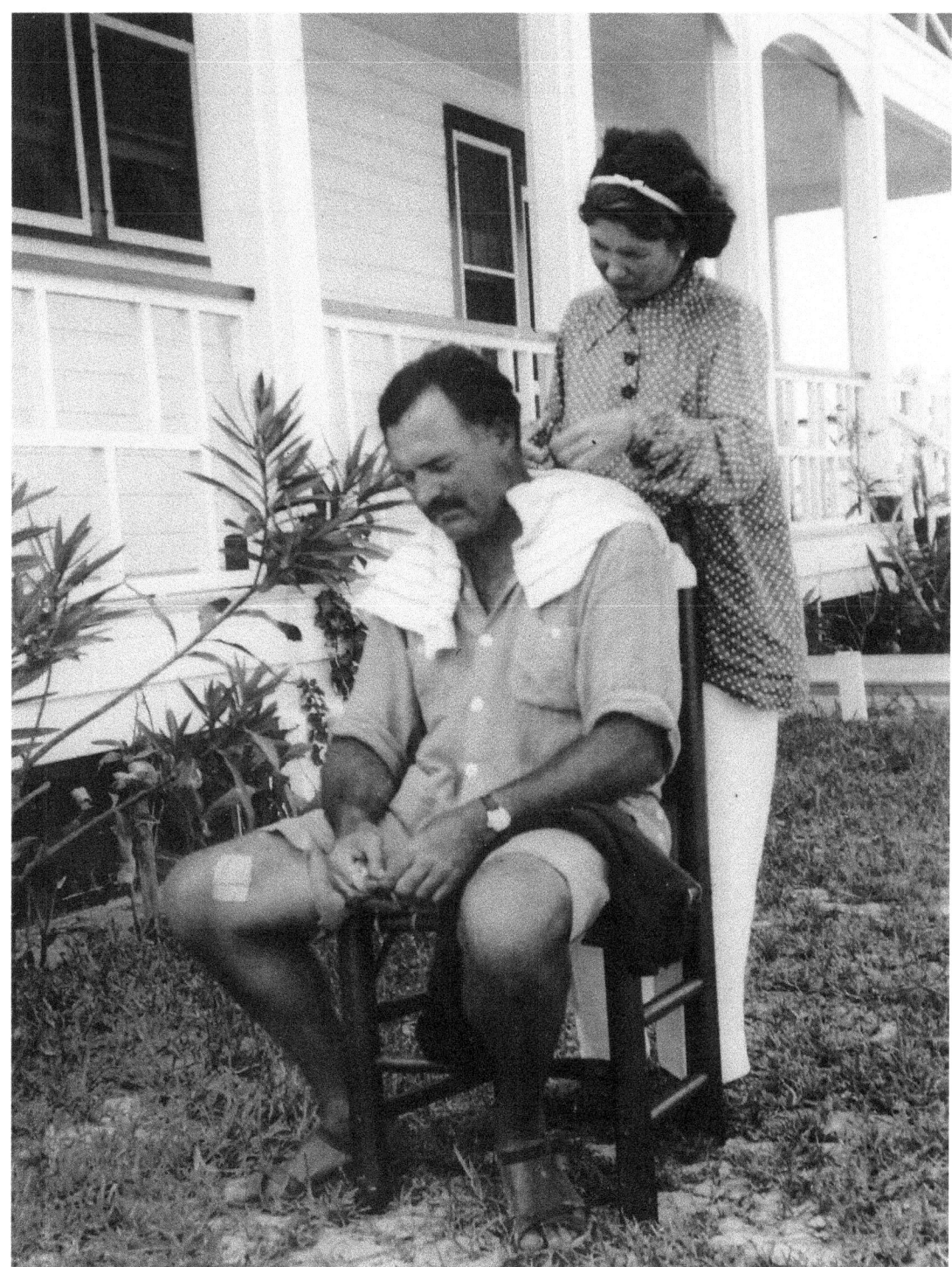

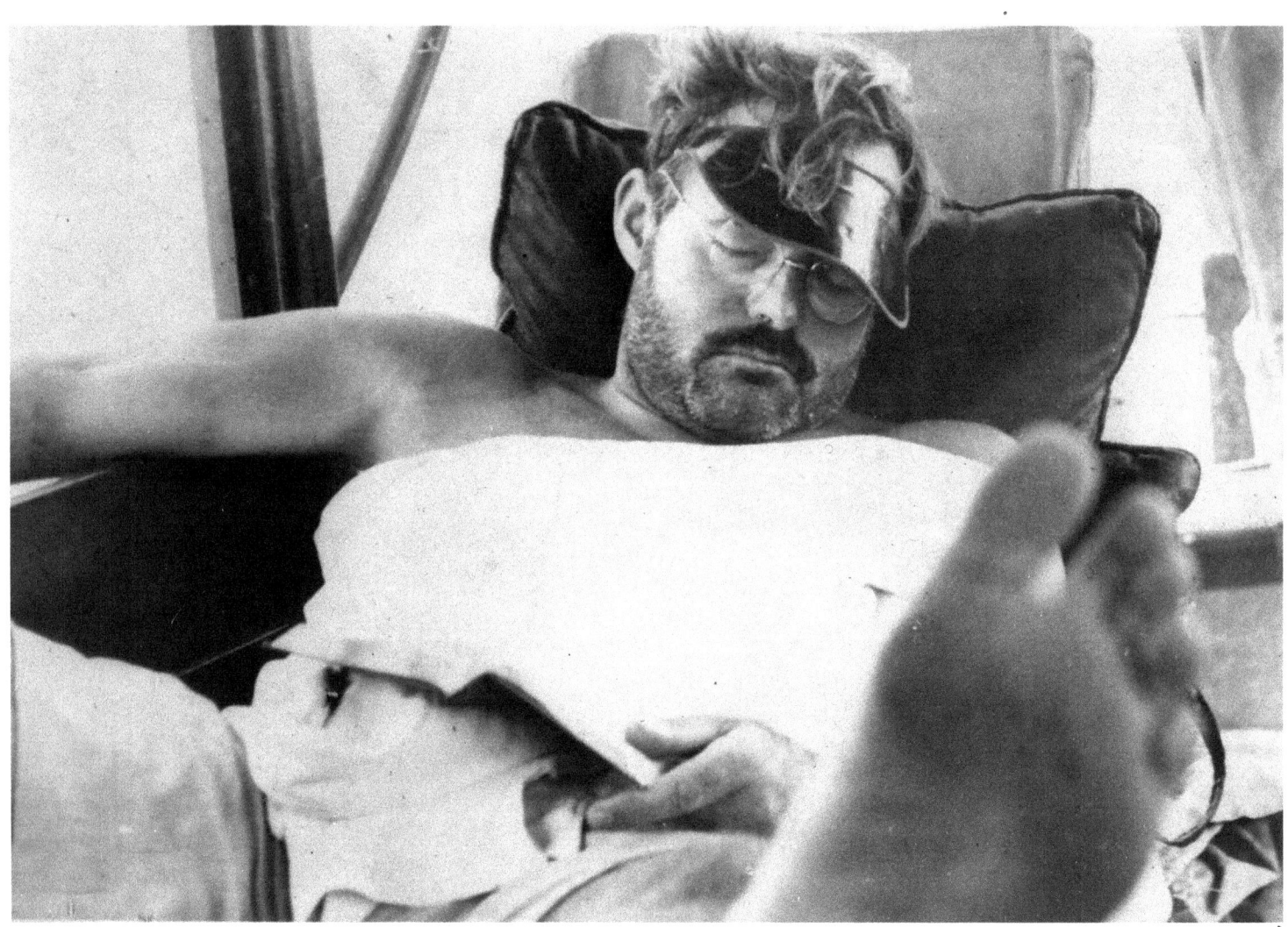

Like the other men, Hemingway shaved infrequently or stopped altogether when he got to Bimini. Here, dozing, he looks harmless enough, but Hemingway could be an S.O.B. He broke poet Wallace Stevens' jaw, marooned poet Archibald MacLeish on an abandoned cay after an argument, threatened to thrash numerous writers and editors, and got sore at Fitzgerald when he messed up on timekeeping in a supposedly friendly boxing match.

Sharks were so plentiful and aggressive in Bimini that they commonly "apple-cored" a fish before it could be brought to boat. Here, Ernest poses with Henry "Mike" Strater, an artist friend, with one that the sharks got to. This trip Hemingway perfected a technique of using brute strength to reel the big fish in quickly before the sharks could ruin it, and it made him the talk of international sport fishing.

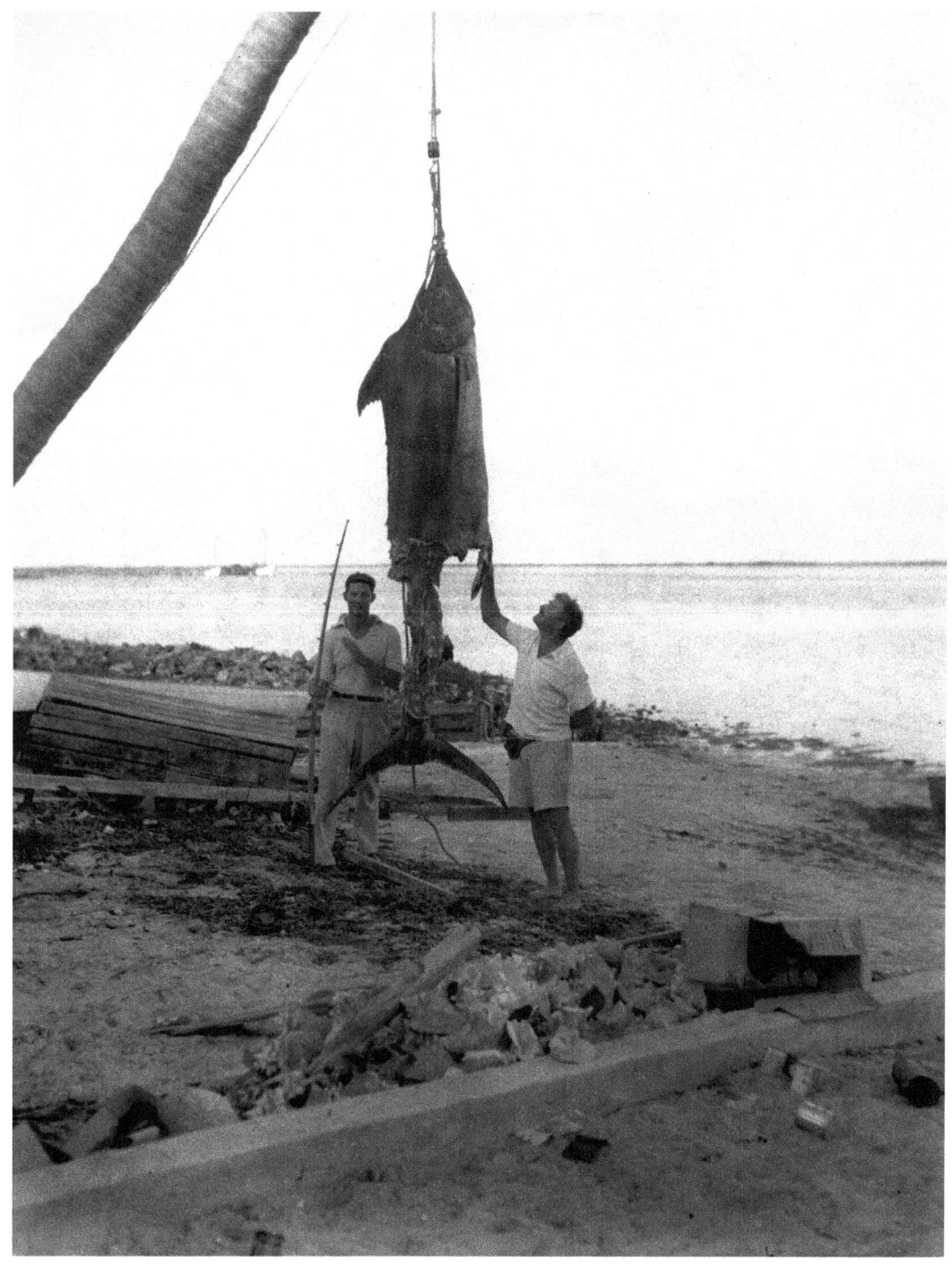

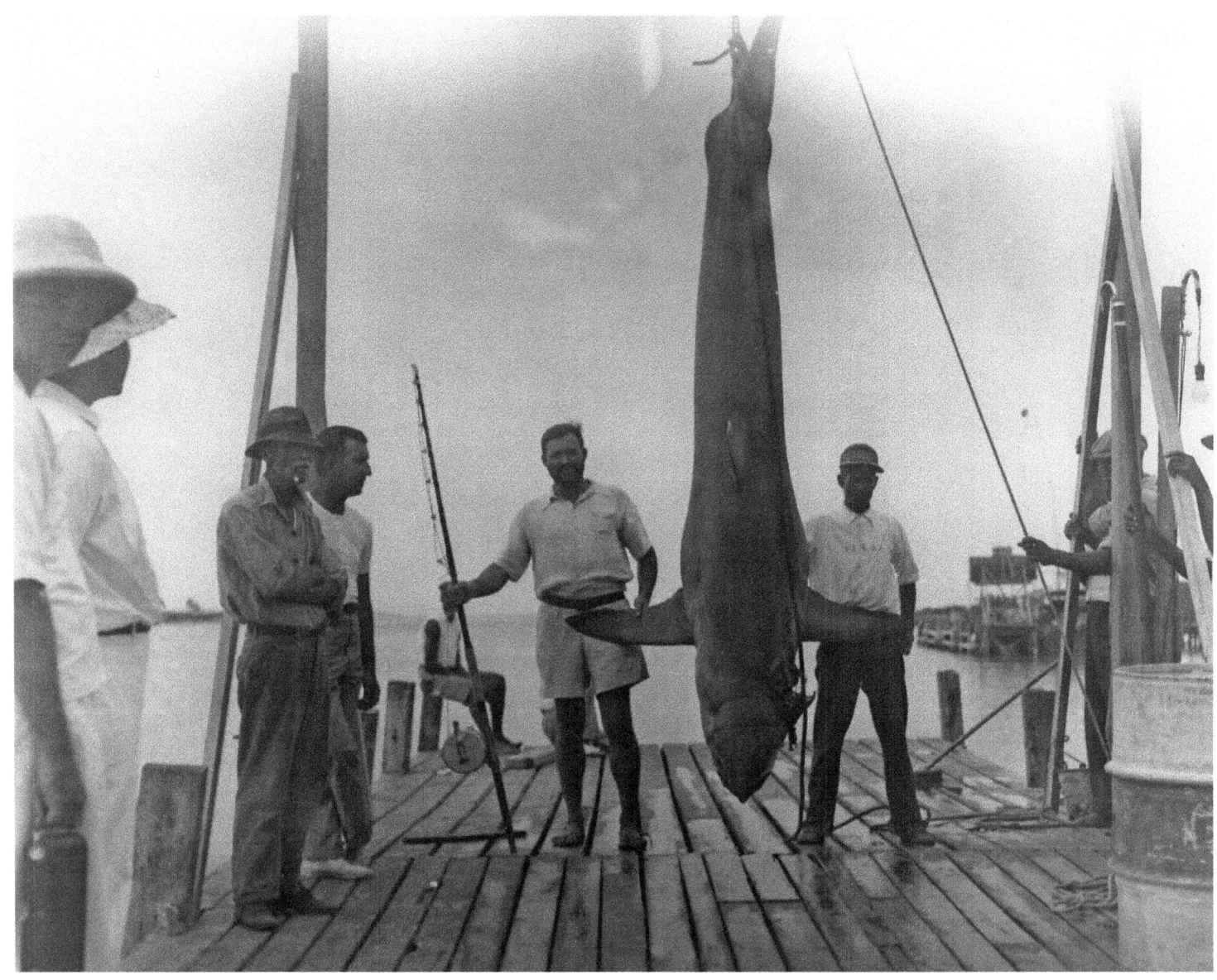

Hemingway was the first to land an unmutilated tuna in Bimini, using his quick-reel method that was touted in *Yachting* magazine. That summer he boated two whole tuna weighing 514 and 610 pounds. But those were topped by a monstrous 786-pound mako shark (pictured here), which Hemingway also caught on sporting tackle. *Outdoor Life* reported it was just 12 pounds shy of the Atlantic record.

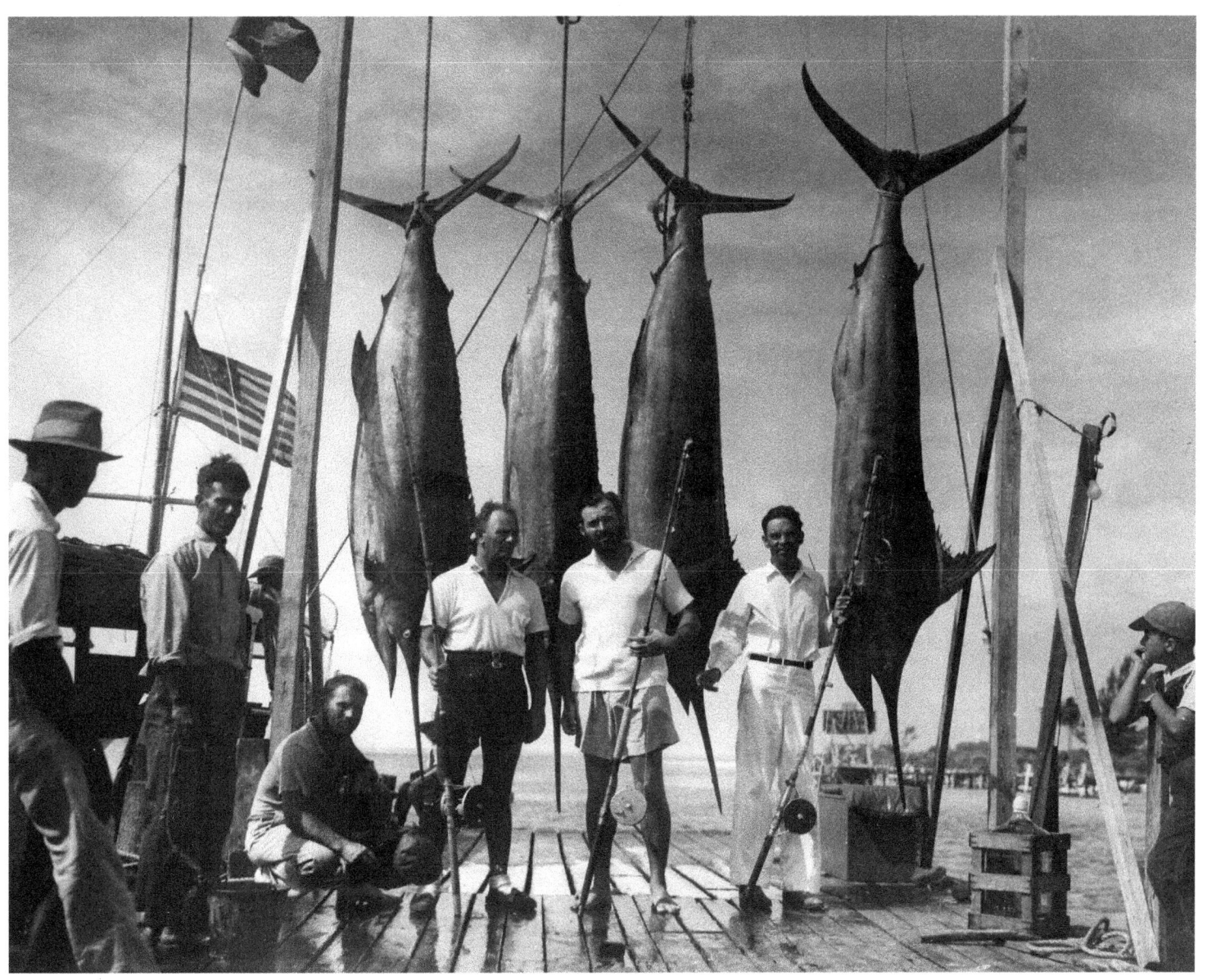

In July 1935, Hemingway hooked up with renowned saltwater angler Michael Lerner (left) and Julio Sanchez (right), with a catch of four marlin among them. Four years later Lerner would become a founder of the International Game Fish Association, and Hemingway would be named vice-president, a position he would hold until his death. Hemingway was inducted into the IGFA Hall of Fame in 1998. Were officers allowed to hold world records, Hemingway would be in the books for most marlin caught in a day.

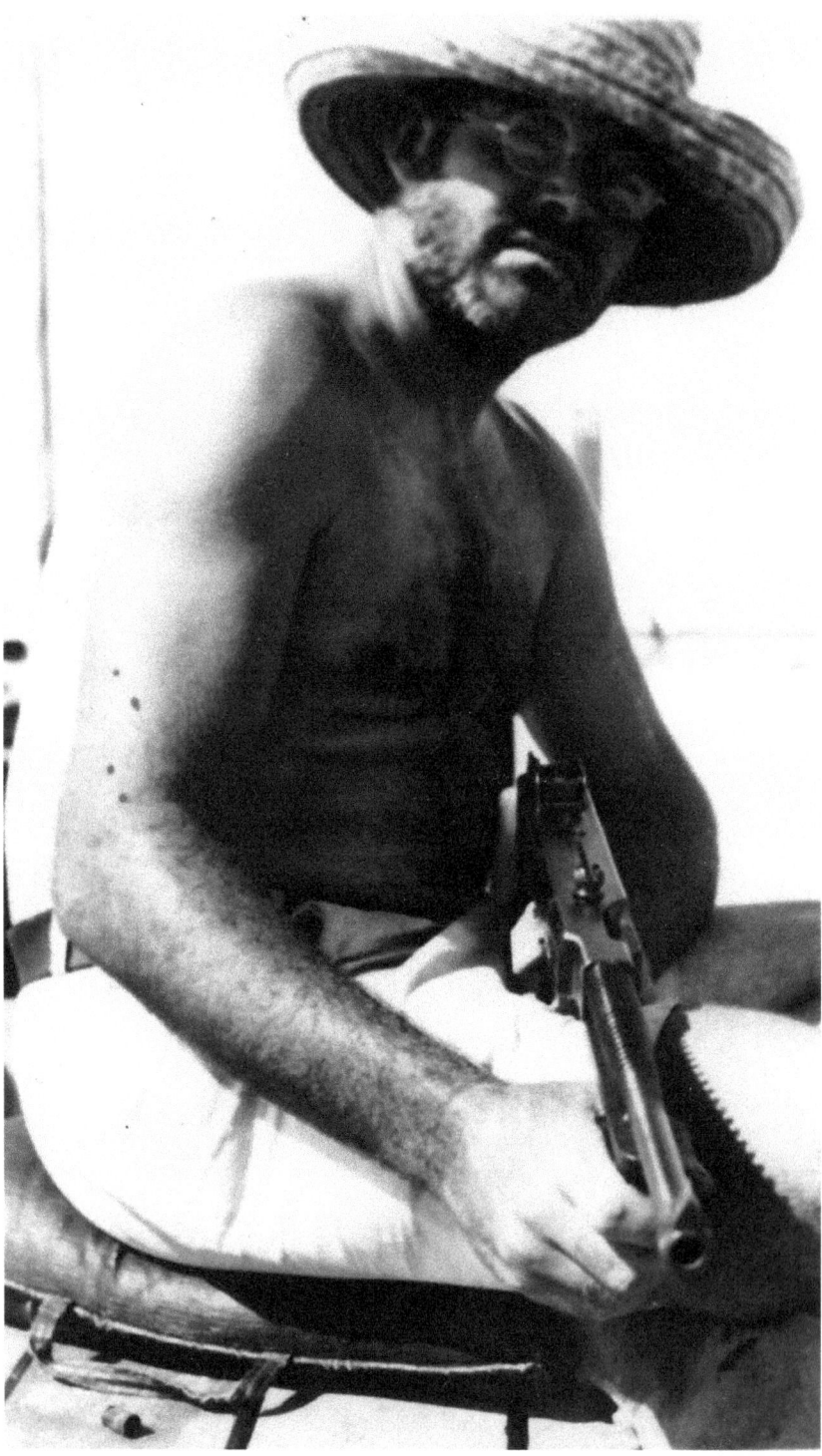

Of all the highlights in Bimini during the 1935 season, perhaps the biggest, for Hemingway, was his acquisition of a new Thompson submachine gun. While Hemingway was trying to land one of his tuna, millionaire fisherman Bill Leeds opened fire on sharks from his nearby yacht. Hemingway admired the gun so much that Leeds later made him a present of it.

Hemingway often practiced his shooting from piers, and he enjoyed firing his new weapon. From that point on, he called it his favorite gun and used the "Tommy" to shoot sharks with the same reckless abandon as he shot hyenas on his safari.

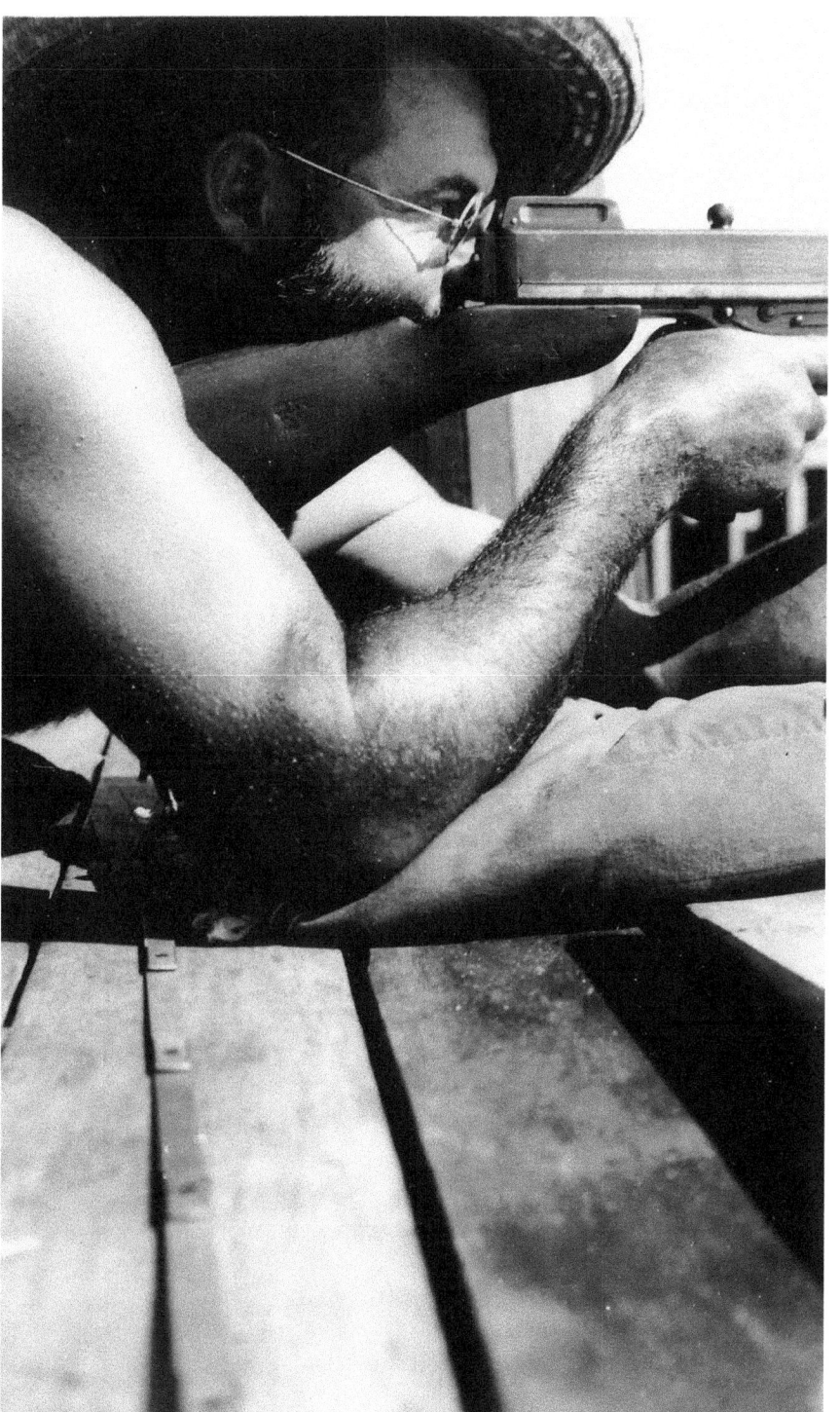

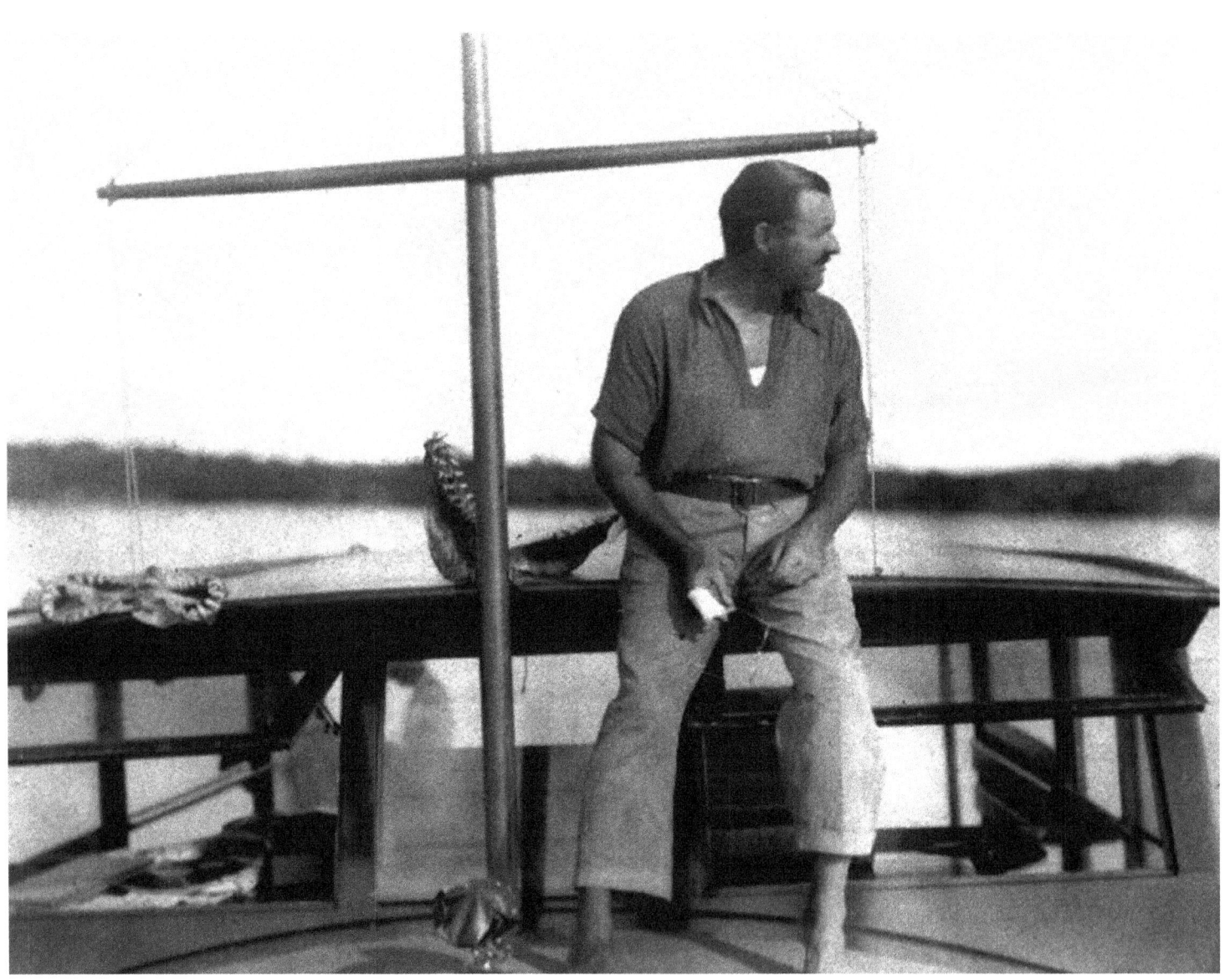

Hemingway aboard the *Pilar* with shark jaws, more trophies to be brought home. He had a collector's impulse, saving things rather than throwing them away—even a grammar school doodle book and his World War I pants that are riddled with holes, both of which are now in the collection of the East Martello Museum in Key West.

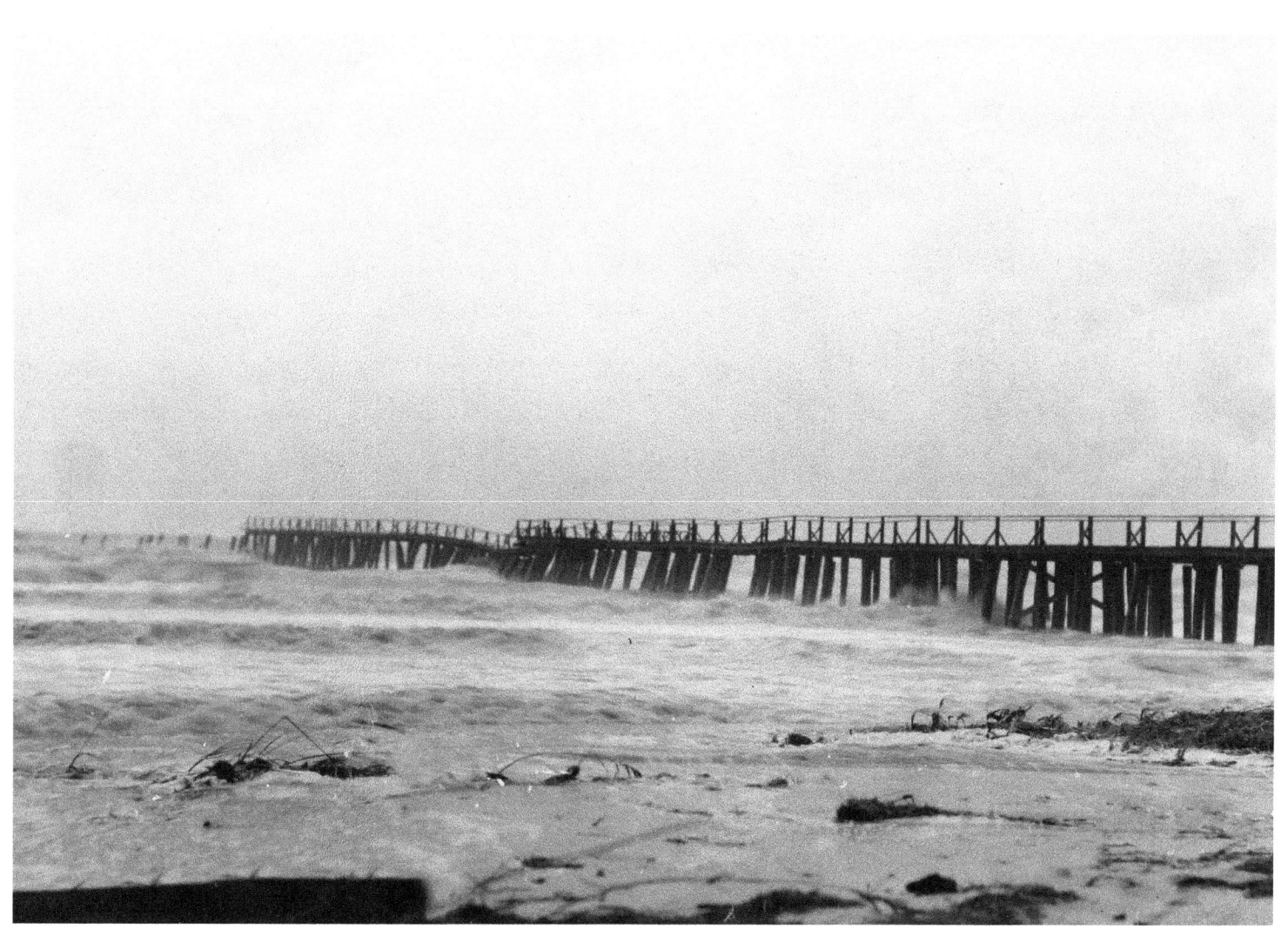

Hemingway's "man Friday," Toby Bruce, finished a brick wall to keep tourists off the grounds of the Hemingway house just before the Labor Day hurricane hit, missing Key West but killing many of the 650 war veterans who were constructing the Overseas Highway. Hemingway, who blamed bureaucrats for not evacuating the workers, responded with "Who Murdered the Vets?" for the left-wing *New Masses*. He also went to Lower Matecumbe the next day to help, and donated money for relief.

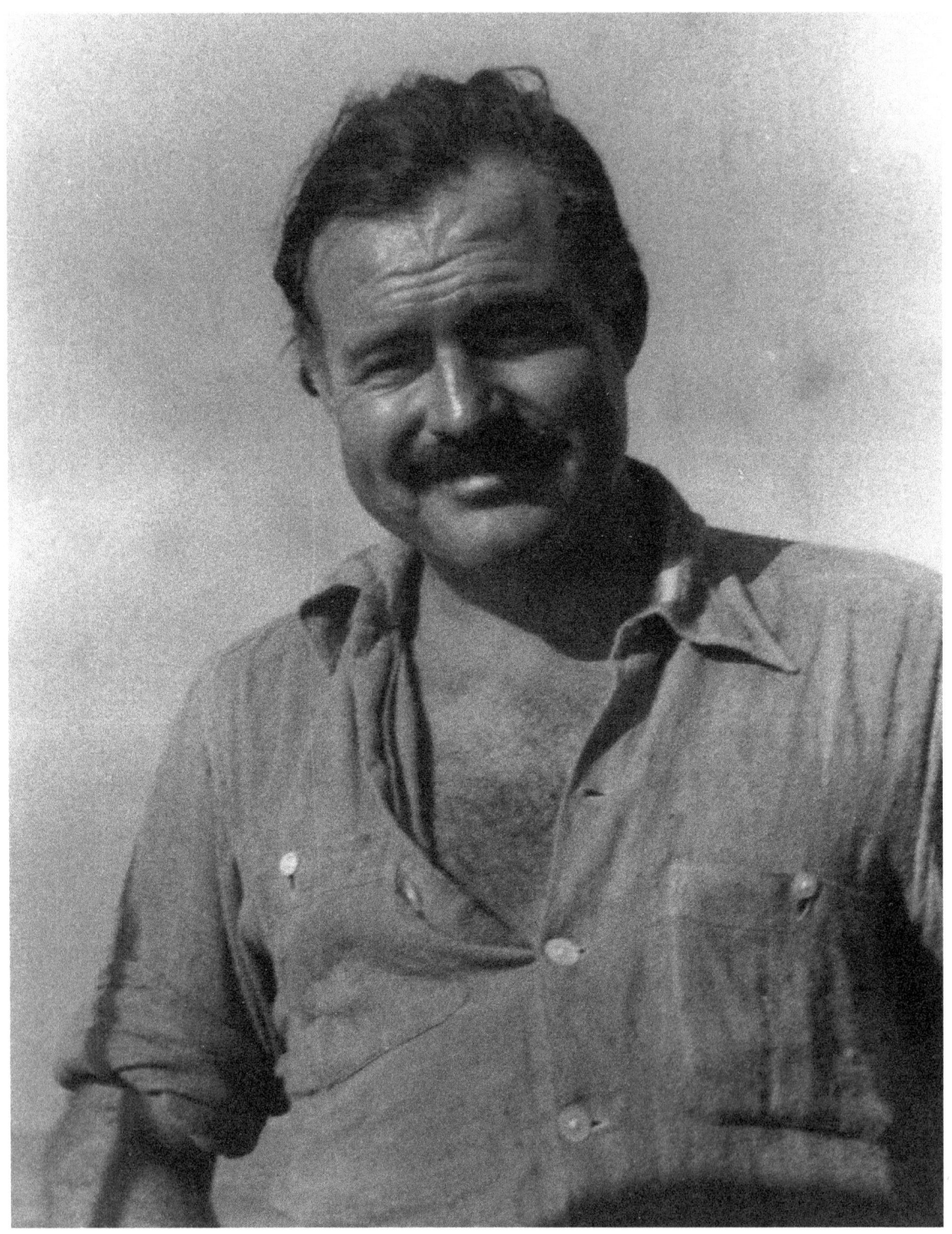

Ernest sometimes wrote on the *Pilar,* and he always had books onboard. It was the combination of ruggedness and intellectualism that made him attractive to women. In December 1936, after Jane Mason had moved on without him, Ernest met an attractive young writer-journalist named Martha Gellhorn in Sloppy Joe's. Martha was on vacation with her mother and brother, and though Hemingway was scruffy and overweight, she too would warm to him.

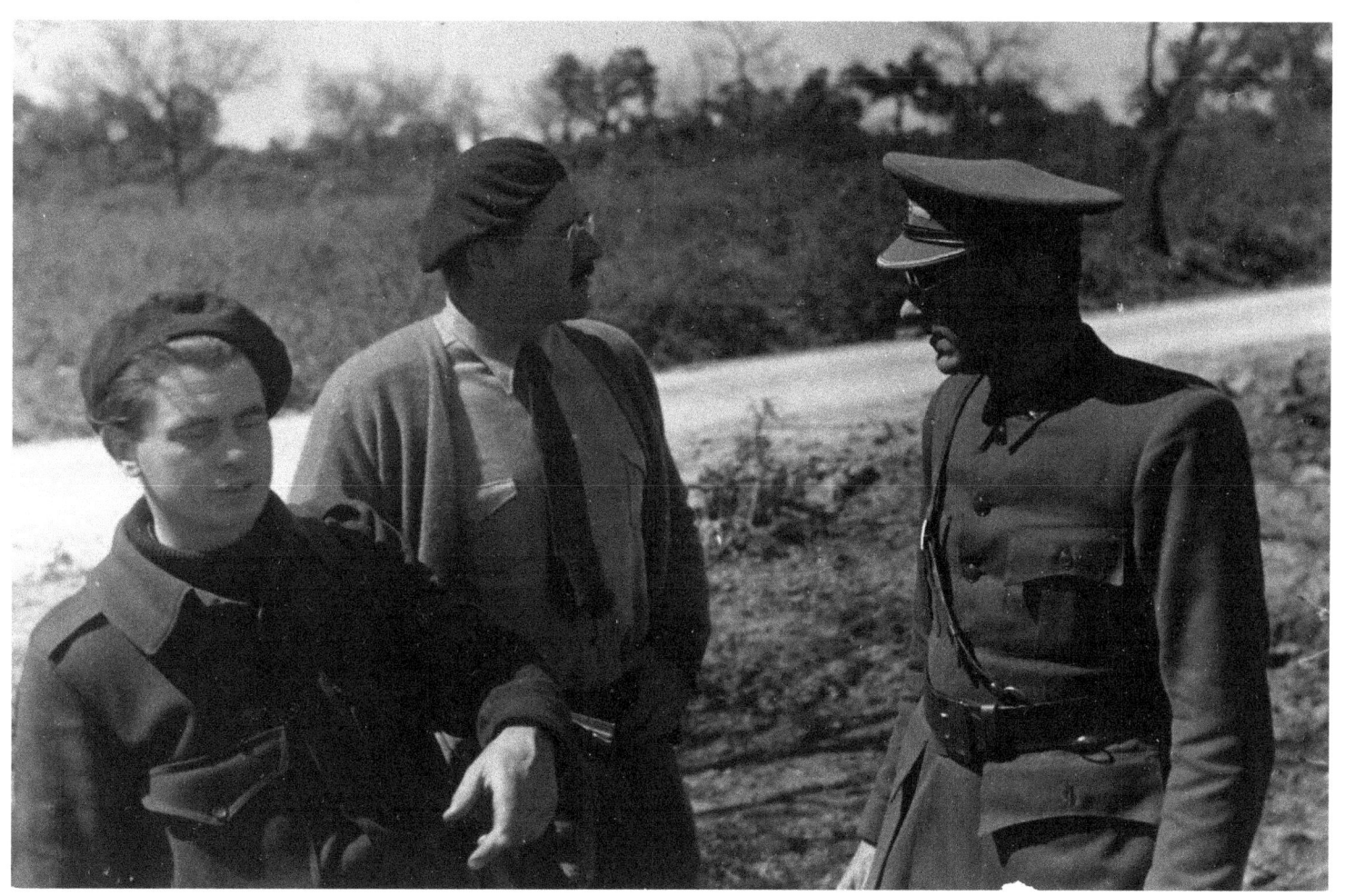

Hemingway was still working on *To Have and Have Not*, his most political novel and the only one set in America, when the Spanish civil war began. When gossip columnist Walter Winchell reported Hemingway was "on his way," the North American Newspaper Alliance asked Hemingway to be their correspondent. In spring 1937, he talked with writer Ludwig Renn (right) and filmmaker Joris Ivens (left), with whom he would collaborate on *The Spanish Earth*, a propaganda film about the war narrated by Hemingway.

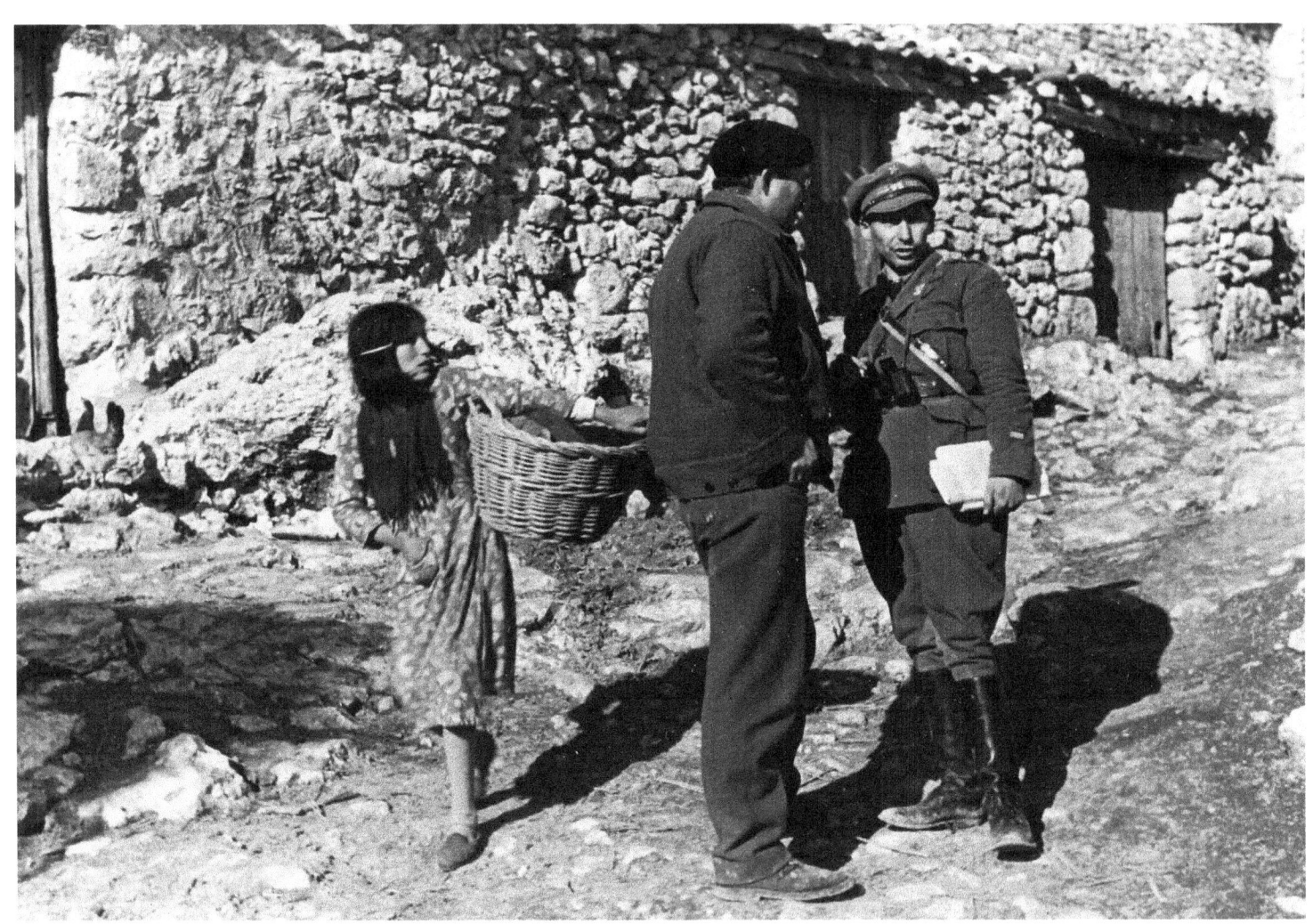

With the Loyalists in Spain, Hemingway speaks to Lieutenant Alexis Eisner. In the field Ernest used raw onions and cognac to stave off hunger, and he never failed to offer his flask to soldiers he met. But his mind was on another meeting. Martha Gellhorn, who wrote for *Collier's*, had also been sent to cover the war. She and Ernest stayed with journalists at the Hotel Florida during the siege of Madrid and were exposed as lovers when a direct hit sent everyone scurrying for cover.

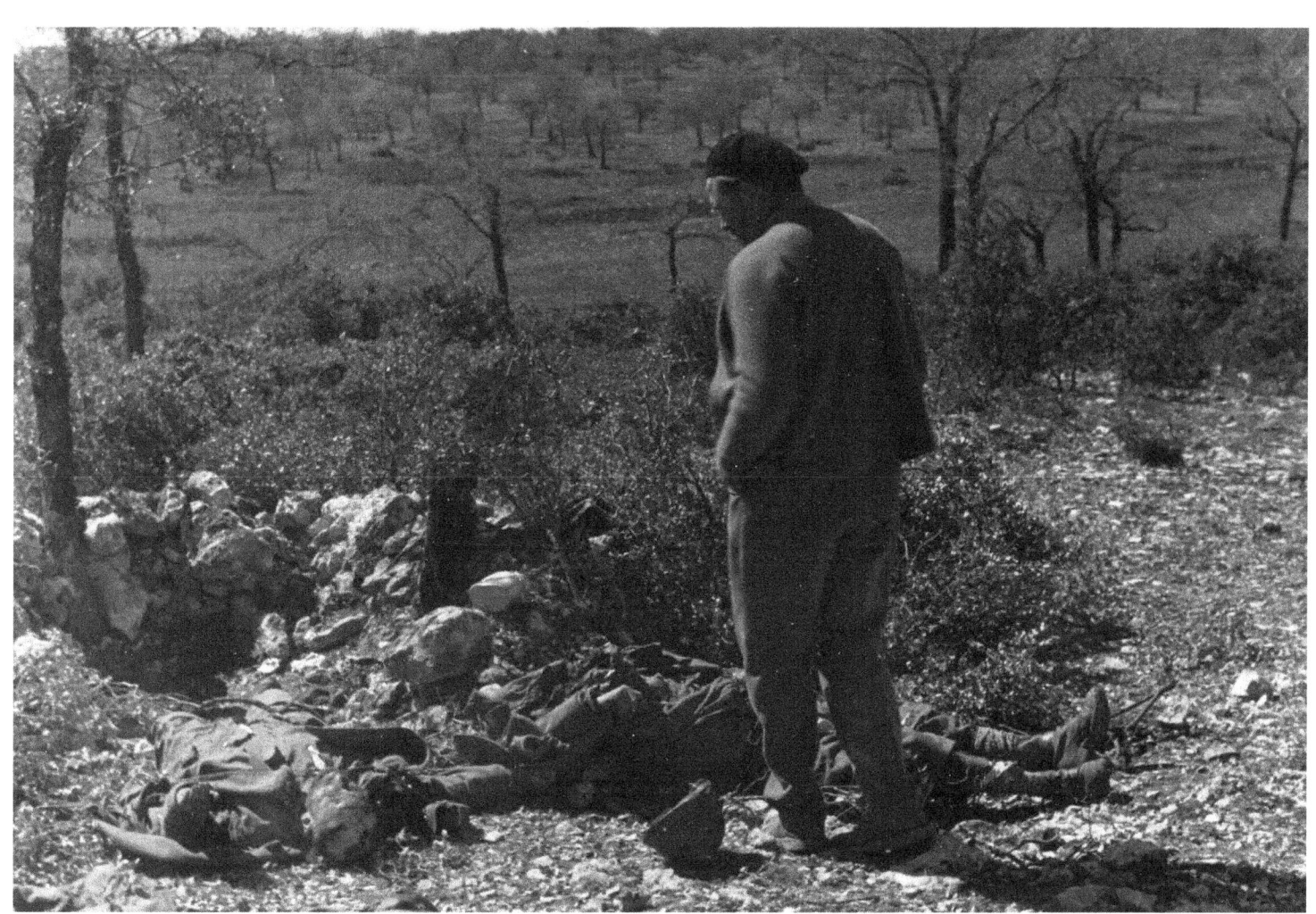

The day after the Labor Day hurricane, Hemingway said he hadn't seen so many dead bodies in one place since World War I, but he seems just as affected by two corpses in a field near Madrid. Hemingway taught Loyalist soldiers how to shoot and filed 31 dispatches during three trips to Spain in 1937-38. In addition, a mediocre play *(The Fifth Column),* six respectable short stories, and a new wife would come out of the experience.

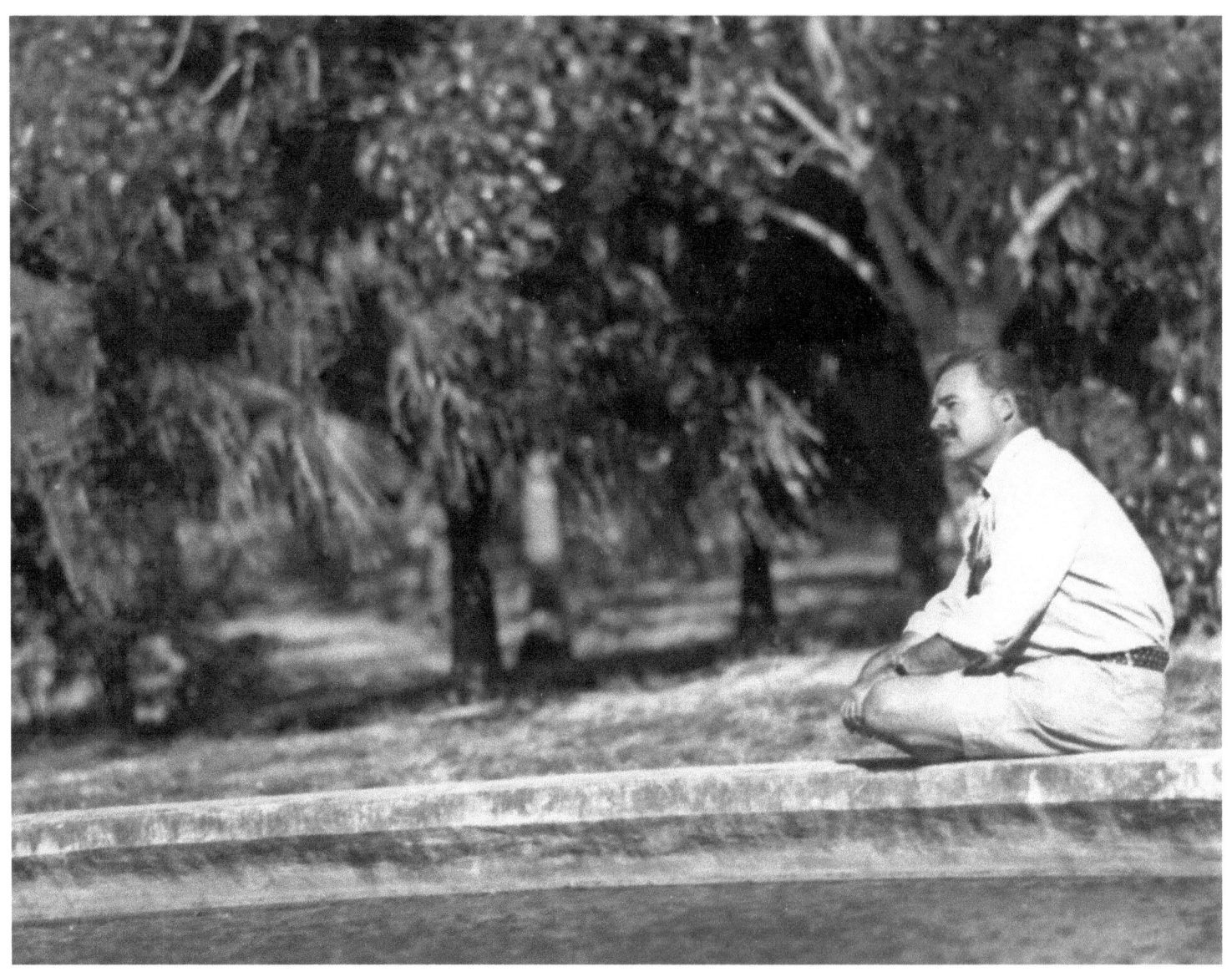

A posed shot at the edge of the pool, around 1939. Hemingway's preferred exercise routines were boxing and swimming. The Finca had a large pool with an equally large pergola at one end, which also made the area perfect for entertaining. One of the things that impressed Ernest early in their relationship was that Martha would dive right in and come up, as he did, wanting a drink. Later, actress Ava Gardner would swim here nude when she visited.

One Hundred Percent Papa

(1939–1951)

It's hard to pinpoint exactly when Ernest Hemingway became "his own worst invented character," as critic Edmund Wilson charged, or if he ever did. But it must have been increasingly difficult for Hemingway to live up to the expectations created by his public persona. Being "Papa" from 1939 to 1951 became a full-time job that encroached upon Hemingway's writing time and his own sense of himself.

As early as 1927, writer Virginia Woolf complained that Ernest Hemingway was "too self-consciously virile," but Ernest was just being Ernest. His personality led him to play to the cameras and sometimes seek the limelight as much as he craved adventure. But while he started referring to himself as "Papa" soon after the 1933-34 African safari, in the forties Hemingway would become Papa. He took to calling young women he liked "daughter" and often behaved as if he were an actor and Papa was his role. When, for example, his new secretary swam from the *Pilar* to shore and was afraid to swim back because of a five-foot shark in the shallows, Hemingway made a show of diving in to "save" her with a knife clenched between his teeth—though he knew it was only a cat shark and not inclined to attack swimmers. Likewise, there was a little more swagger when he covered the war in China and Europe, more readiness to take on challengers than in the past, and activities that could only be described as "grandstanding." Only Papa would race to become one of the first to liberate Paris, or outfit his boat with explosives to patrol the Caribbean looking for Nazi submarines.

It didn't help that the last book Hemingway wrote to critical acclaim was *For Whom the Bell Tolls* (1940). Other than editing and writing a preface for *Men at War* (1942), Hemingway's only significant literary production was *Across the River and Into the Trees* (1950), a disappointing book about an old man's crush on an Italian teenager. But Malcolm Cowley came to Havana to write an article for *Life* magazine called "A Portrait of Mr. Papa," and readers still cared about what Hemingway was doing because, as writer Anthony Burgess suggested, even at his worst Hemingway "reminds us that to engage literature one first has to engage life."

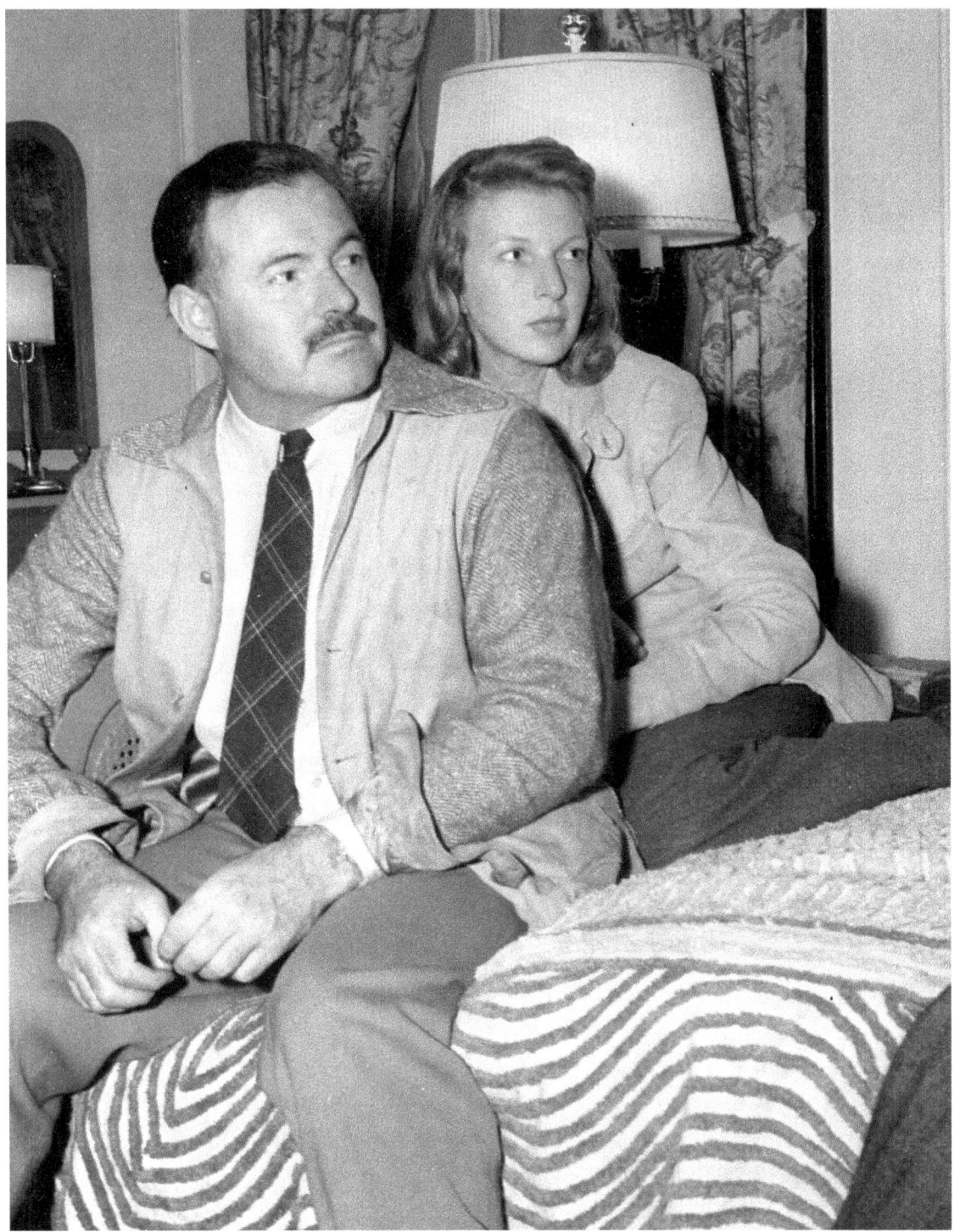

Sun Valley Lodge was America's first European-style ski resort, the brainchild of Union Pacific Railroad chairman Averell Harriman. To lure tourists, the Lodge invited celebrities like Ernest Hemingway and Gary Cooper to stay there, gratis. Though Hemingway was still married to Pauline, he and Martha checked into Suite 206 in the Main Lodge, which they dubbed "Glamour House," on September 19, 1939. Ernest let himself be photographed, and the couple got to play tennis, ride horses, swim, and shoot trap.

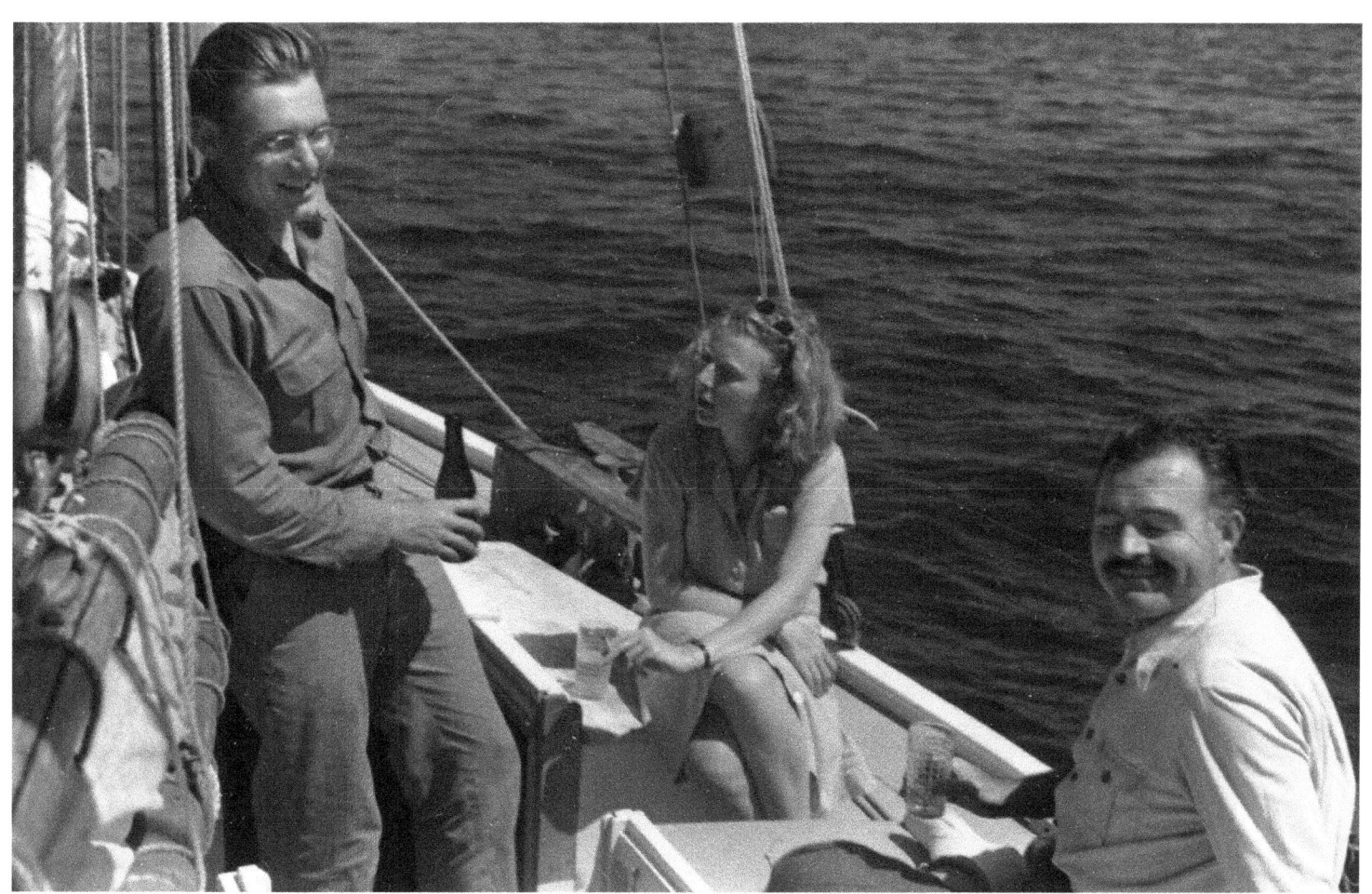

Les Hemingway came to visit his older brother in Havana in March 1940, while Ernest was still finishing his big book about the Spanish civil war. He sailed his schooner into Havana harbor, and Ernest and Martha joined him onboard. "Baron," as Ernest had nicknamed his brother, found Martha "enchanting" and would later pronounce her his favorite sister-in-law, though he also thought highly of Hadley and Pauline. What impressed him as much were the pelota and jai-alai players that his big brother knew.

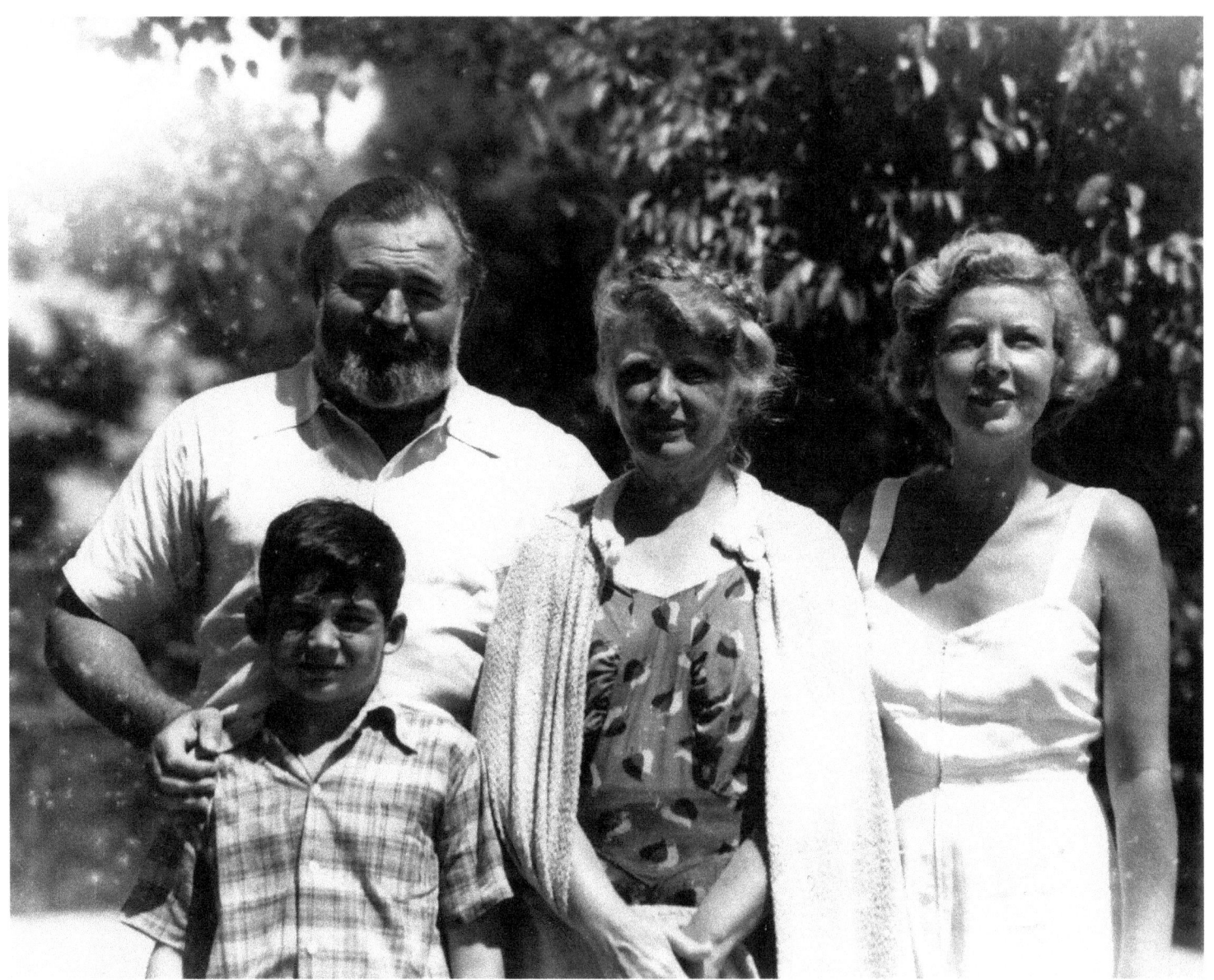

In July 1940, Martha's mother, Edna (center, beside Gregory), came to the Finca for an extended visit. She warned her daughter not to marry Hemingway, whom she said she "felt sorry for," though *For Whom the Bell Tolls* became the blockbuster book of his career, with a circulation of 360,000 copies and a $150,000 movie deal from Paramount. (By comparison, *The Sun Also Rises* had a print run of just 5,090 and *A Farewell to Arms* 31,000.) But she and the burly writer got along so well that Martha began wondering if he liked her mother better. Needless to say, Mother's cautions had just the opposite effect.

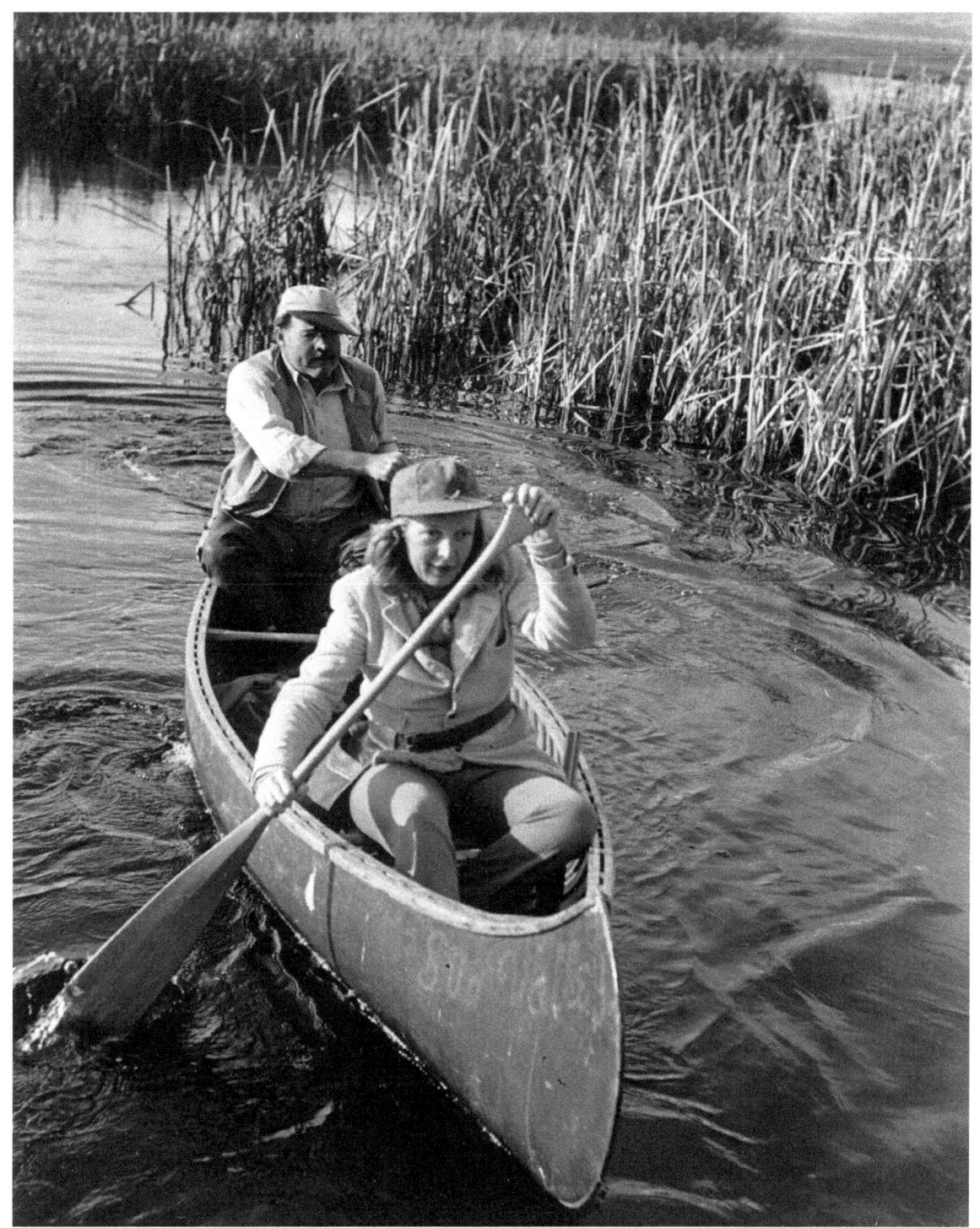

The lure of the West was strong, and in September 1940 Ernest and Martha returned to Sun Valley Lodge, this time with Hemingway's three sons in a kind of reverse honeymoon. Soon after his divorce was finalized, he and "Marty" would leave for Cheyenne, Wyoming, where they were married on November 21, 1940. Here they paddle Silver Creek. Like Hemingway's first two wives, Martha was willing to try the things that mattered most to him.

Lloyd Arnold was assigned to take photos of Ernest Hemingway while the author was in Sun Valley, and that meant going along on the trail, too. A happy Hemingway poses with his first Idaho big game—a pronghorn antelope. According to Arnold, Hemingway could jump off a horse, run up a hill, and crouch in firing position faster than most men. And he was an excellent shot, though not as gifted as the eagle-eyed Dr. Hemingway.

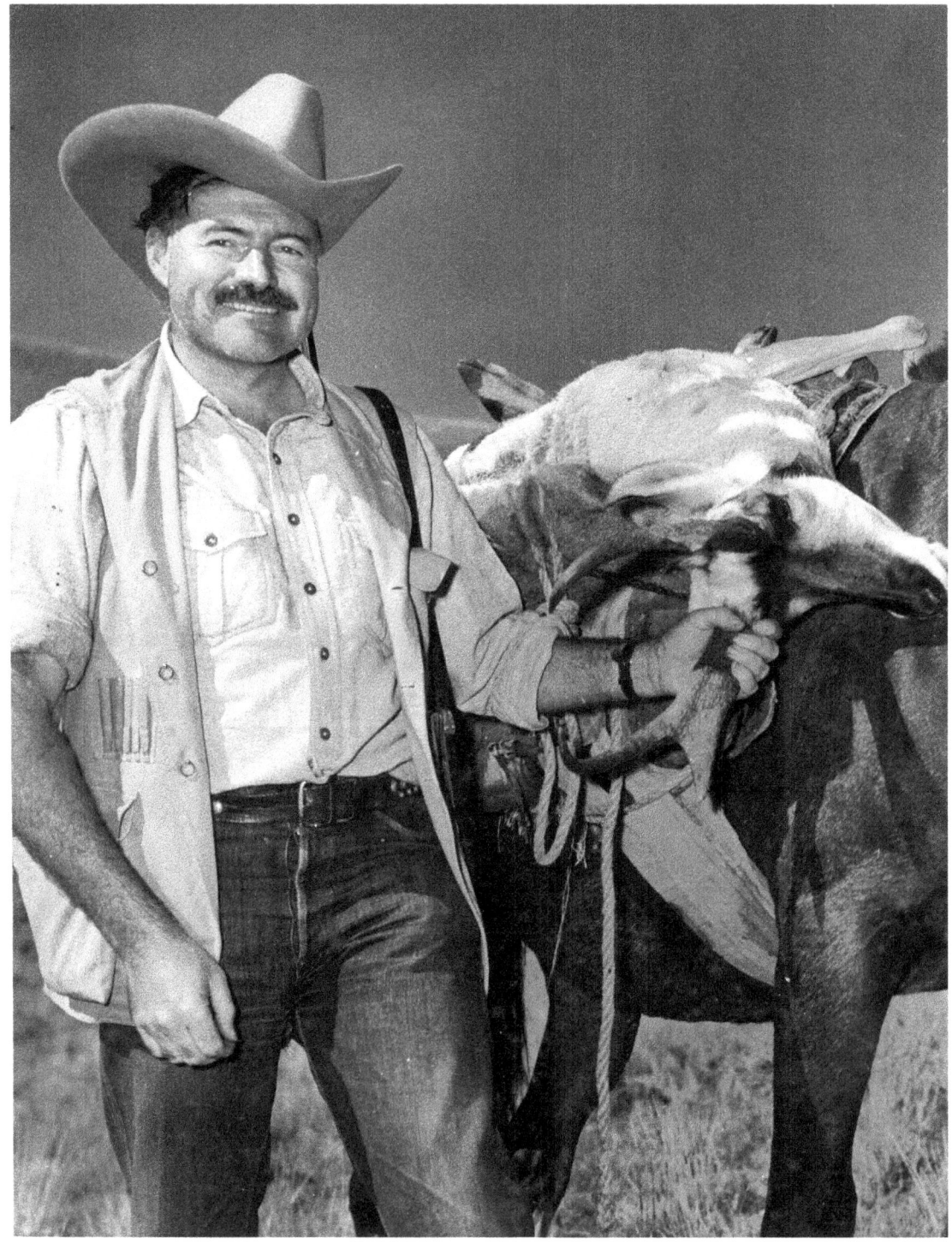

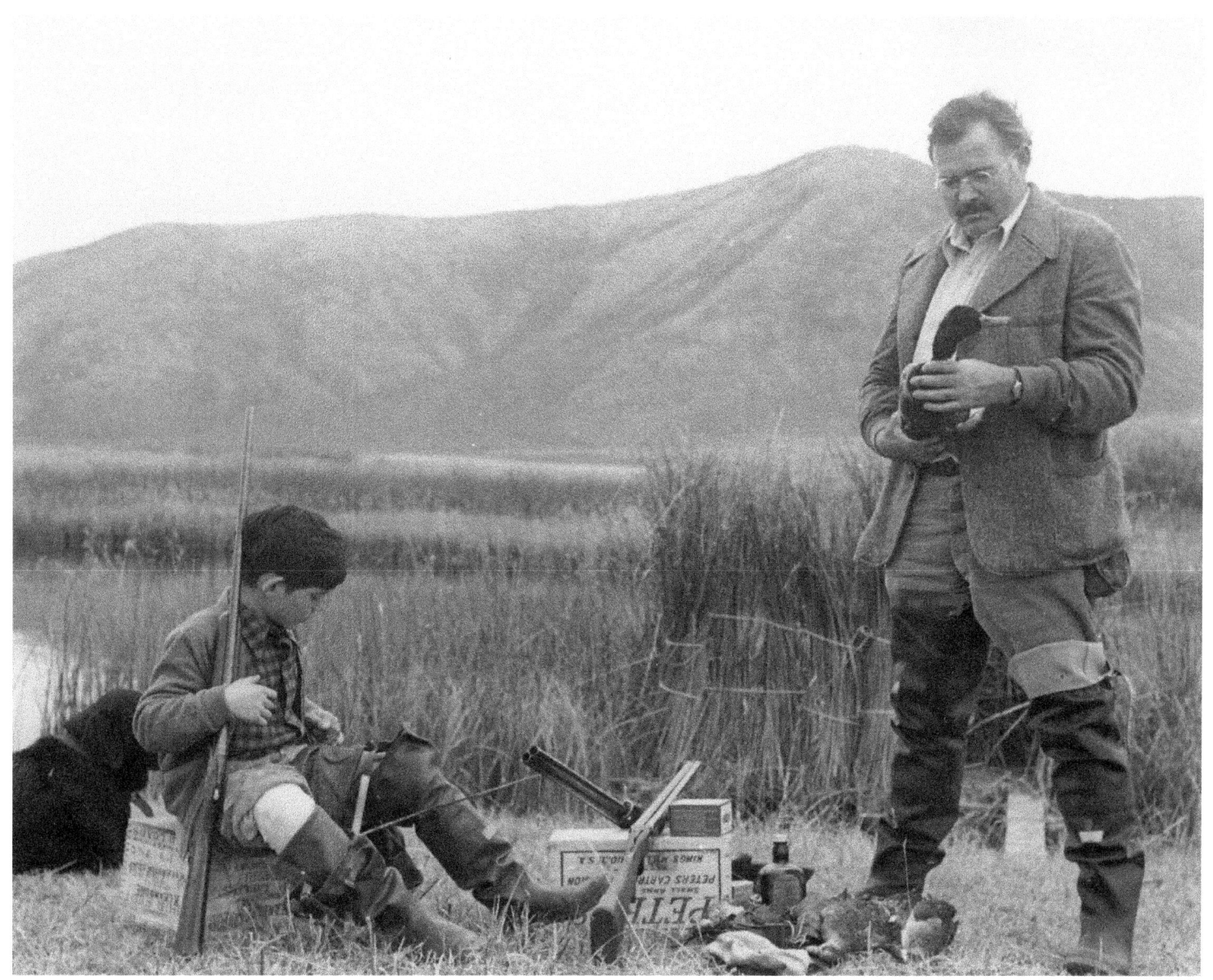

At Sun Valley, the boys stayed in smaller, inexpensive lodging while "Papa" and Marty enjoyed Glamour House. Hemingway had called Pauline P.O.M. (for "Poor Old Mama") in *Green Hills of Africa* and gradually took to calling himself "Papa," encouraging others to do the same. Hemingway was big on nicknames. Here he and "Gigi," as he called son Gregory, take a break from shooting ducks in the Silver Creek area, fall 1940. "He was an excellent father," Gregory would later write. "He just wasn't there."

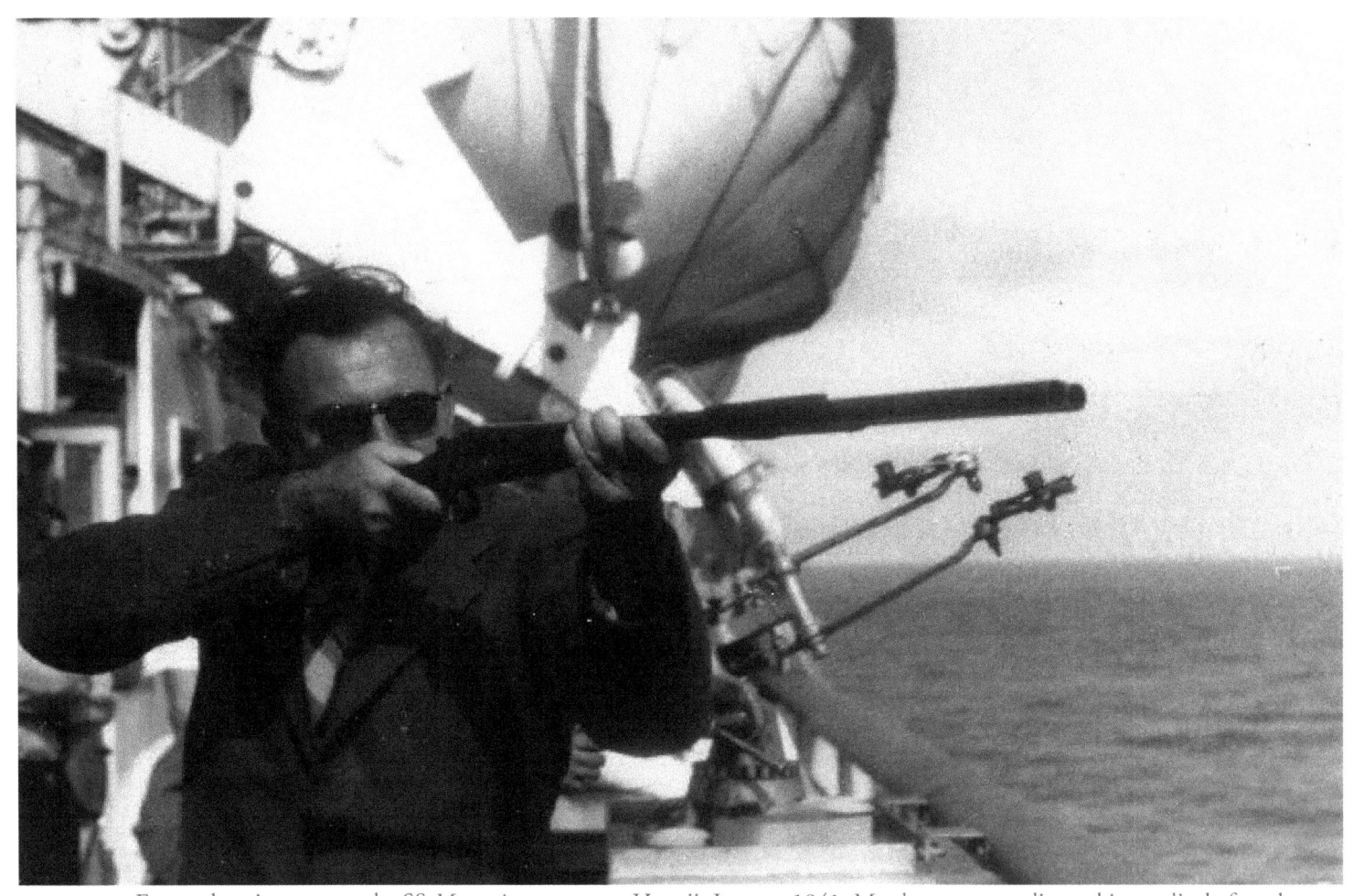

Ernest shooting trap on the SS *Matsonia* en route to Hawaii, January 1941. Martha was a novelist and journalist before she met Hemingway, and she had no intention of giving that up. When Collier's assigned her to go to China to cover the war with Japan, Ernest complained that instead of a honeymoon this was "her idea of fun." He responded by getting an assignment from *PM* magazine to go with her.

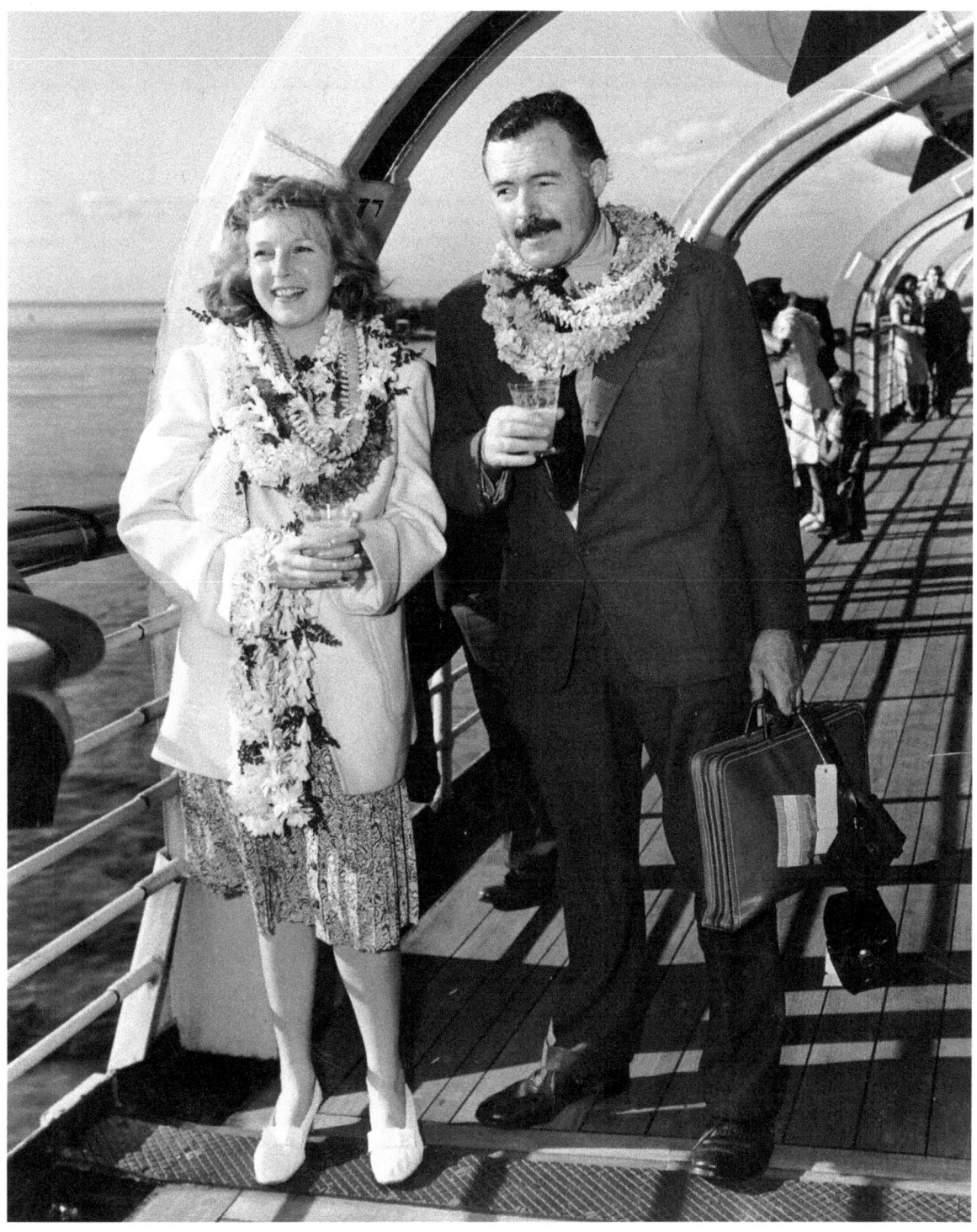

In Honolulu, Ernest drank too much at a luau in his honor and embarrassed Marty by challenging a trash-talking writer to a fight. Later, back in Cuba, he would ignore her pleas to enter the "real" war as a correspondent, instead outfitting the *Pilar* with a flying bridge, arming the boat with grenades, and recruiting Cuban irregulars to chase Nazi submarines in the Caribbean in a U.S.-sanctioned operation he called the "Crook Factory."

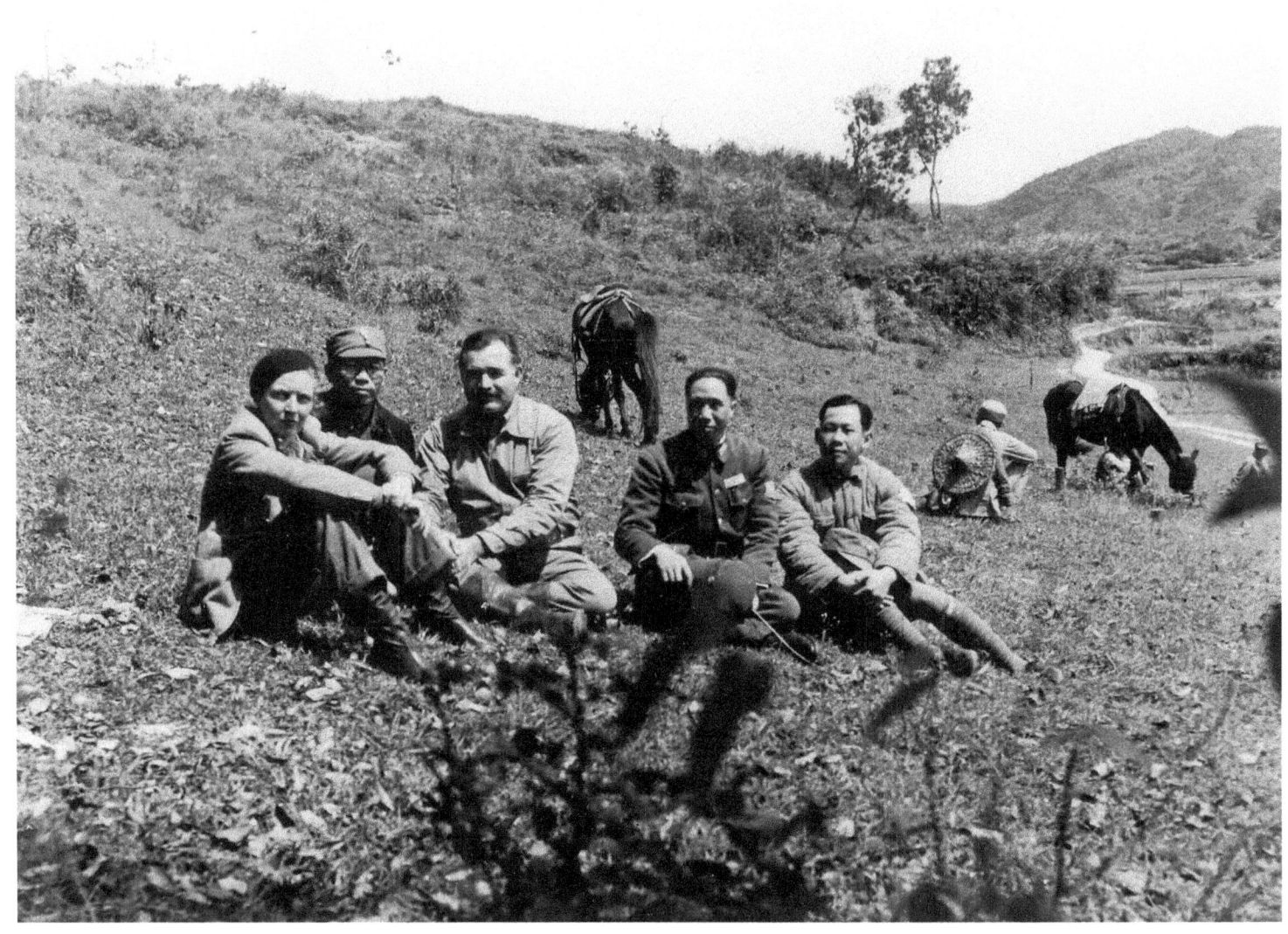

Ernest and Martha (far left) sit with Chinese regulars in the Army of the Kuomintang. Marty covered the Burma road alone, then she and Ernest went together in March 1941 to visit the Seventh War Zone, which was then occupied by 150,000 Chinese soldiers.

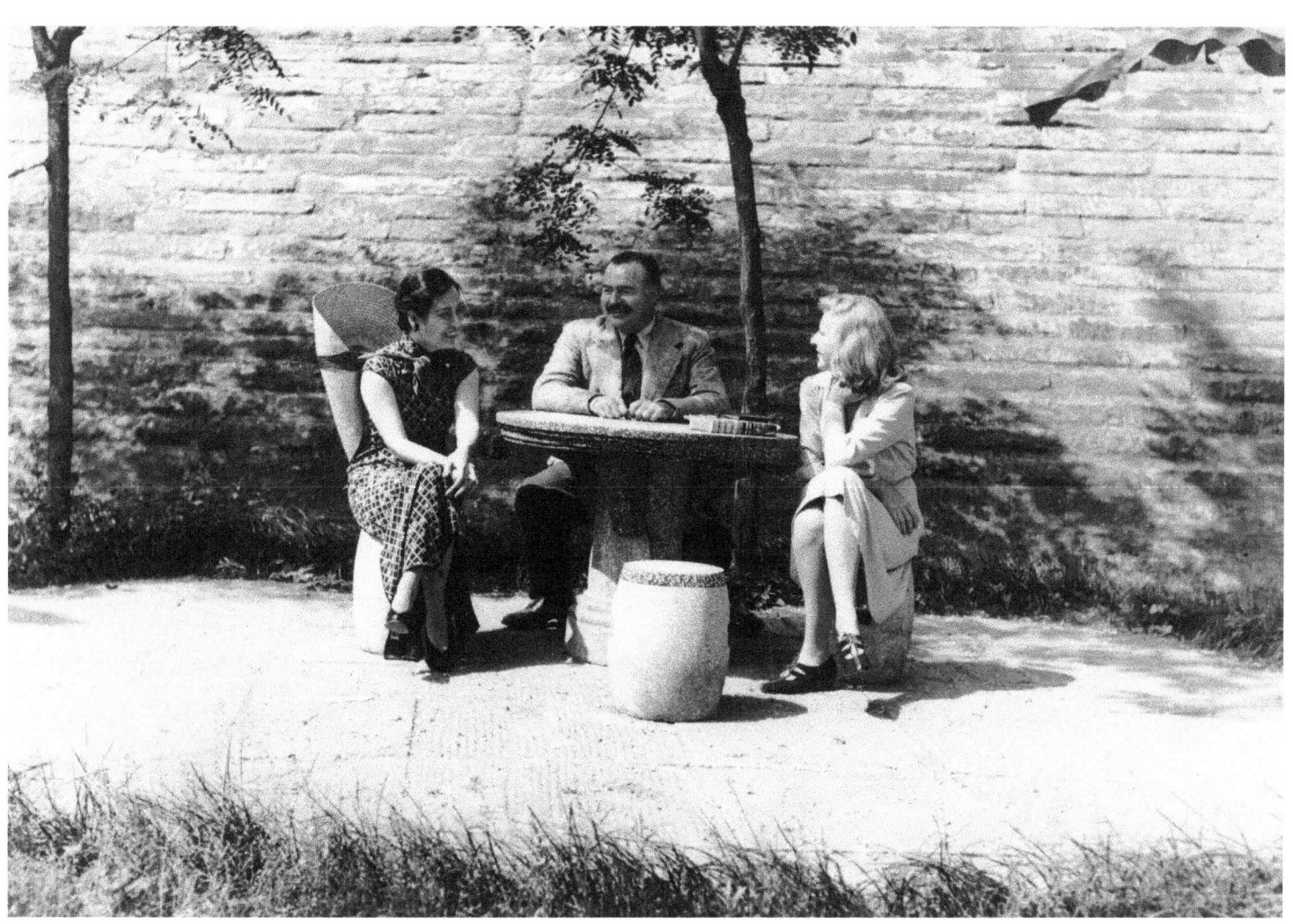

Marty and Ernest met with Chinese Nationalist leader Chiang Kai-shek in April 1941 and afterward talked with Mdme. Chiang Kai-shek, who had served as interpreter. Hemingway basked in the exotica of China, fascinated by such things as snake wine and talking in pidgin English with the peasants and peddlers, while Marty was bothered by the filthy conditions and contracted "China rot," which made her skin peel.

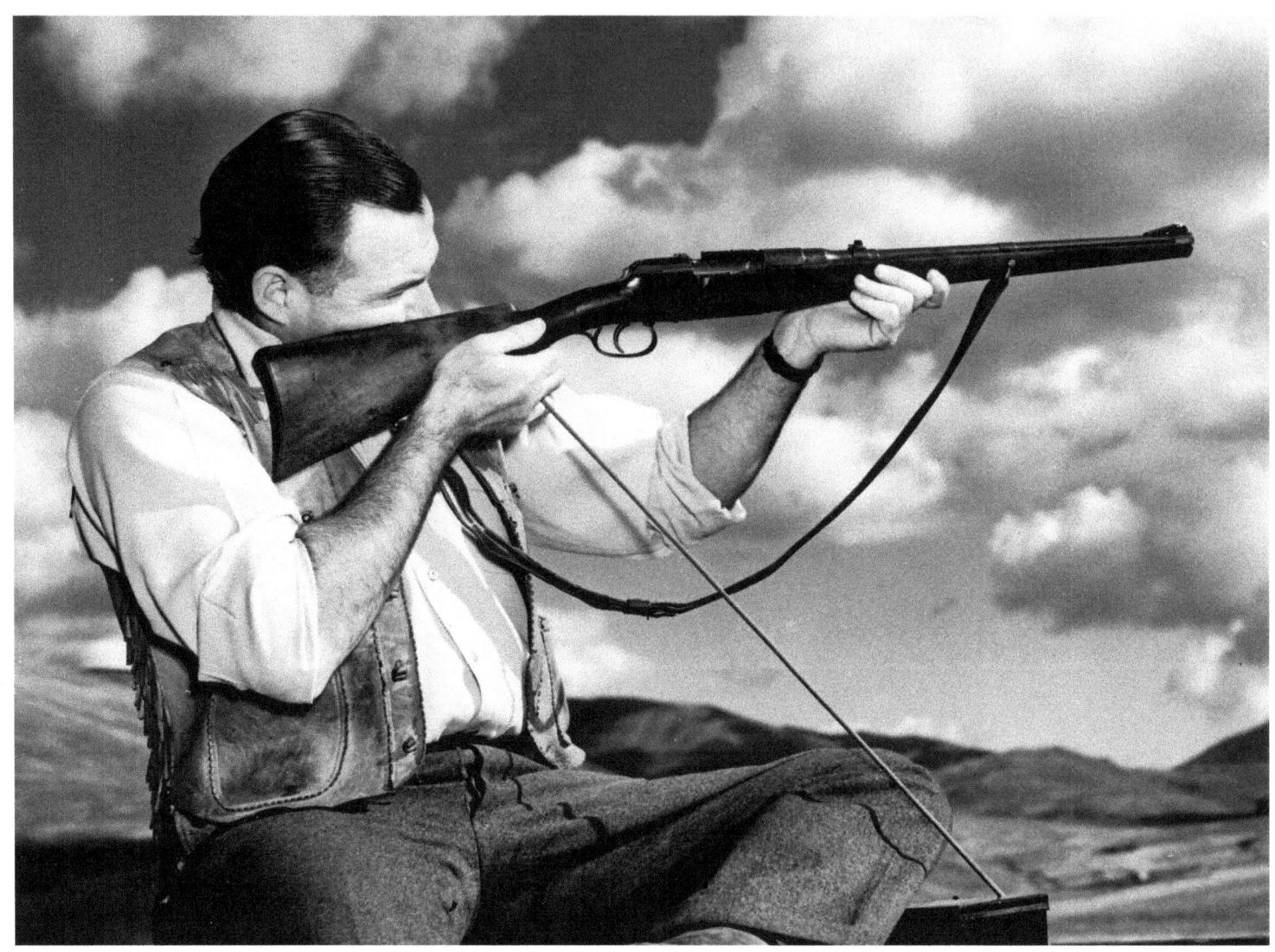

In September 1941, the Hemingways were back at Sun Valley again. Ernest's *For Whom the Bell Tolls* had been published the previous fall, and now Martha's novel, *The Heart of Another,* was scheduled for October release. In Sun Valley they were still no-pay tourist attractions, and part of Hemingway's responsibility was to be visible. Here, on the lodge deck, he cleans his favorite Mannlicher rifle.

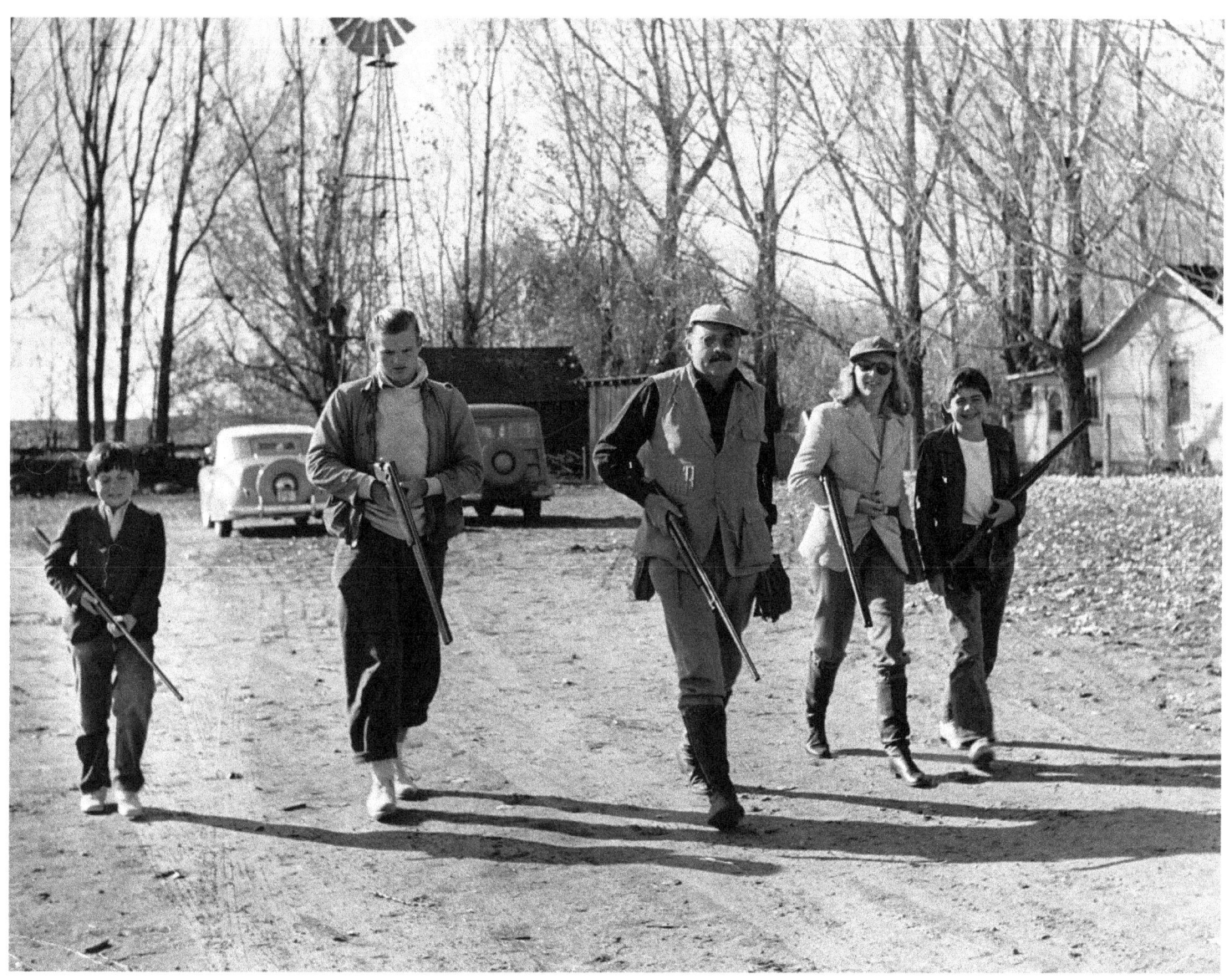

Heading out to jump-shoot ducks (left to right), Gregory, John, and Patrick join their famous father and his new wife, who was just learning to shoot. The sons approved of Martha, admiring the way she stood up to Papa. They also related to her because she was a young 33-year-old who could talk about anything but also listened. Gregory would later remark that Martha was a better mother than his own, who left the raising of children to a nurse named Ada.

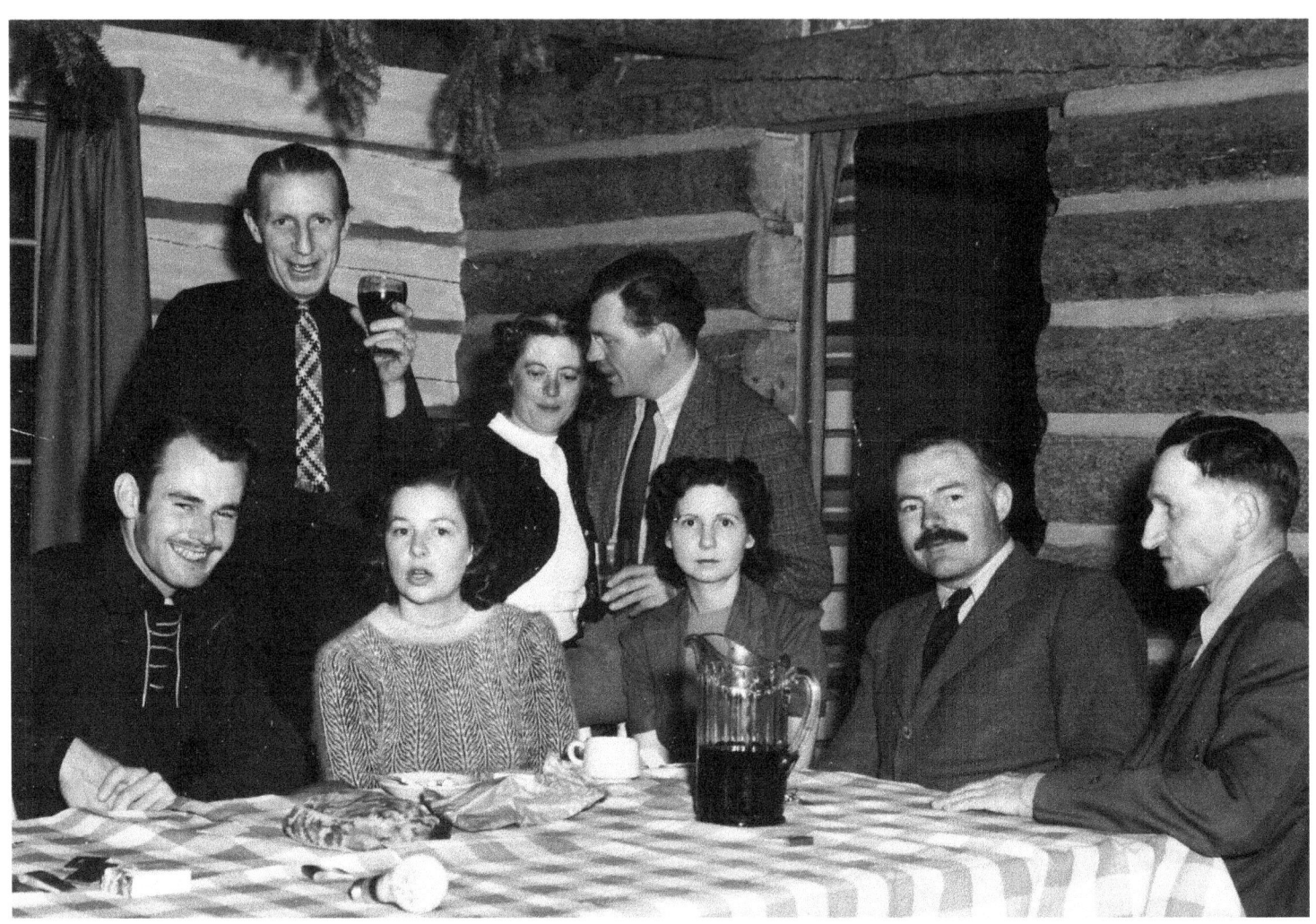

It never took Ernest long to find genuine friends. In Key West and Cuba he had his "mobs," but the Idaho friends he called his "family," and friends of family were also welcome. Here they enjoy one of many parties at Trail Creek Cabin, site of Hemingway's New Year's Eve parties. Photographer Lloyd Arnold raises his glass while Tillie Arnold, of whom Hemingway was quite fond, sits beside Papa. Taylor Williams, a veteran outdoorsman Hemingway took a shine to, is on his left.

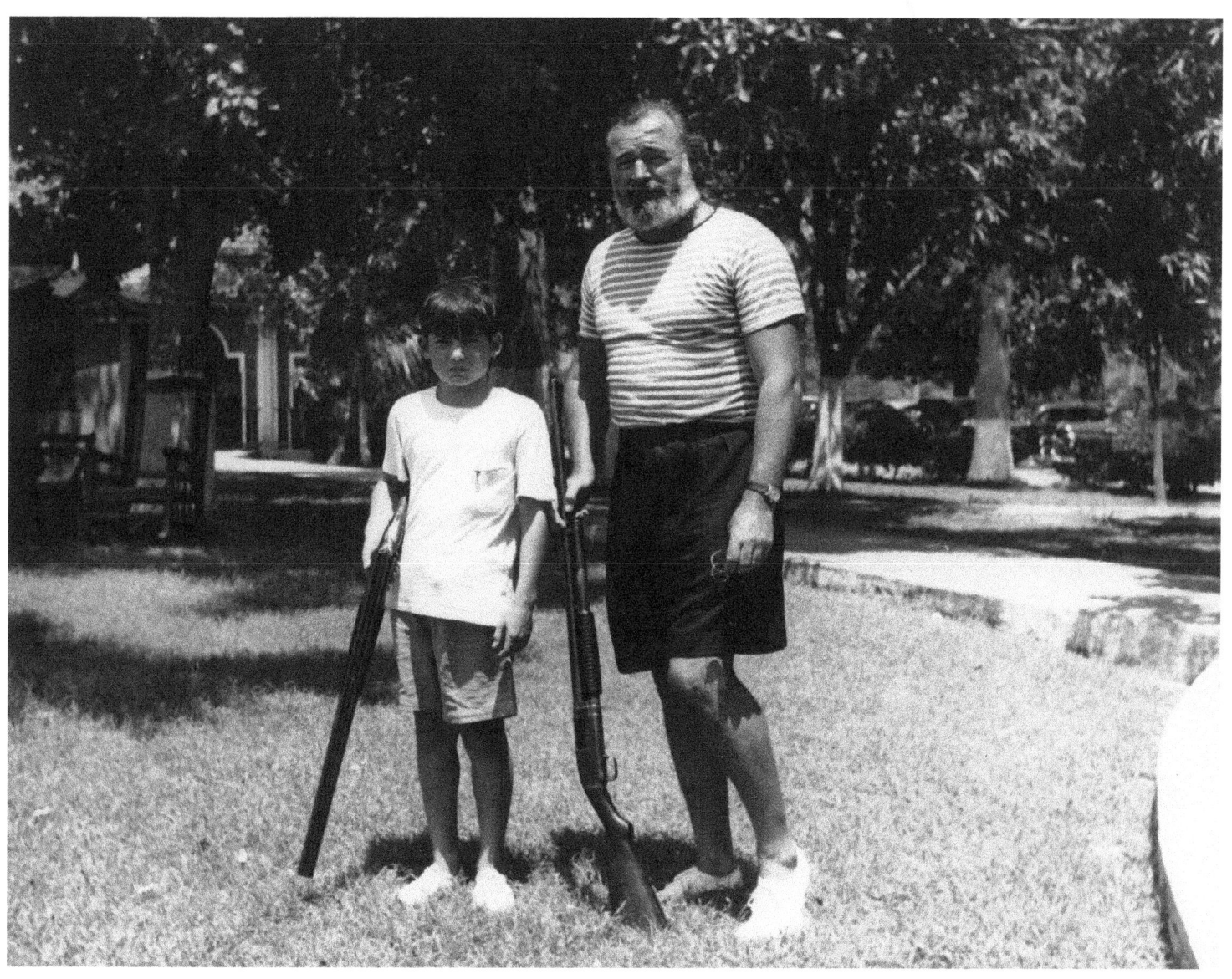

In August 1942, young Gregory finished runner-up at the Cuban pigeon-shooting championships, which were held at the exclusive Club de Cazadores del Cerro in Havana. Papa was a member and went there often to shoot trap, skeet, and live pigeons. He coached Gigi, who competed against close to 40 men in the tournament. Shooting was the one area in which Gregory would not disappoint his father.

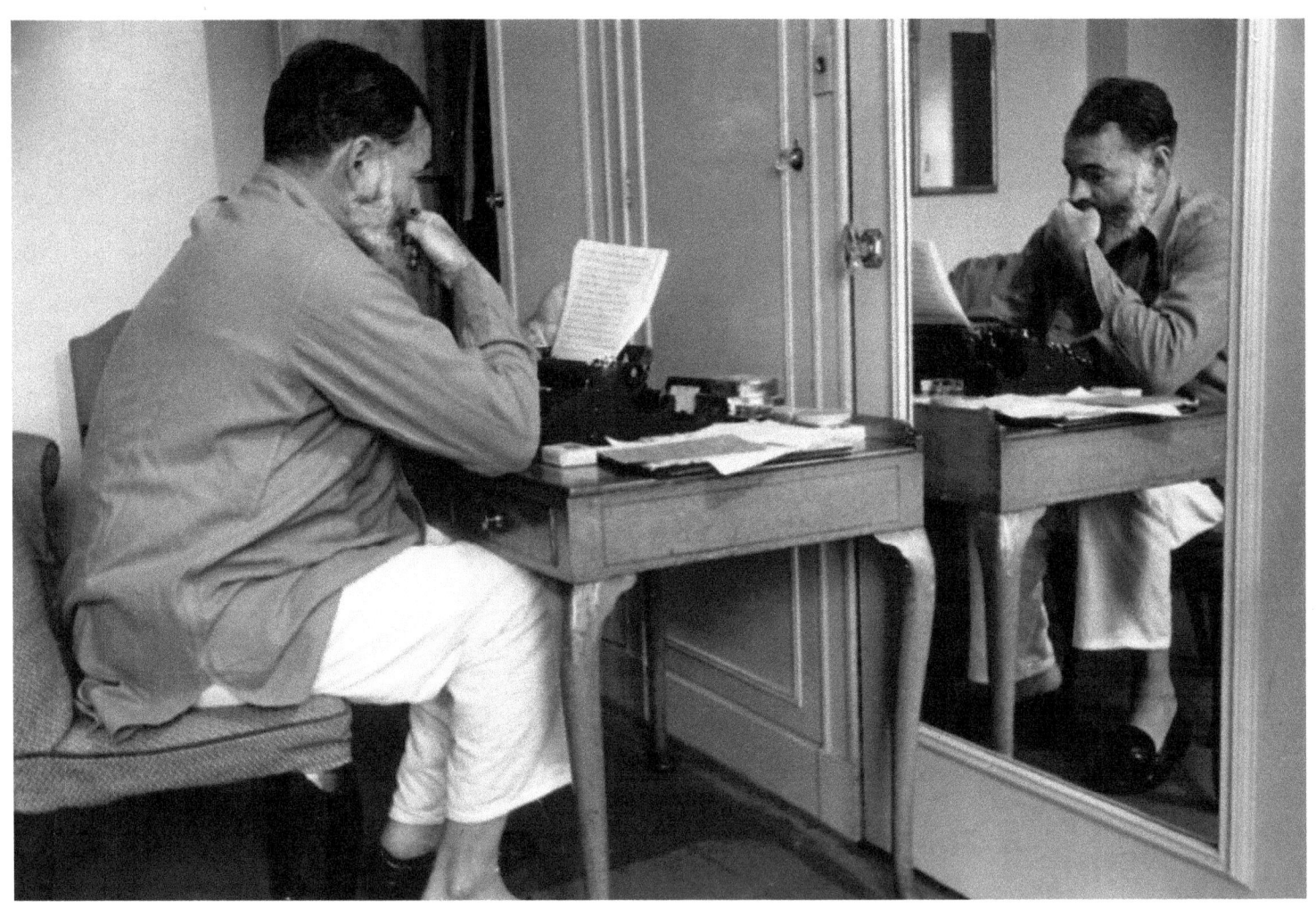

London, spring 1944. Ernest wanted Martha to stay in Cuba and be Mrs. Hemingway, but she had gone to Haiti to write about poverty, then angered Ernest when she had all his male cats neutered while he was away fishing. The tension between them came to a boil when Martha announced she was going to Europe to cover the war for Collier's and urged him to do the same. Hemingway responded by phoning Collier's and offering his services—in effect, taking her spot.

In London at the Dorchester hotel, the famous Ernest Hemingway entertained a constant stream of visitors. Even breakfast (which included whiskey) became a "Meet the Press" event. Shortly after this picture was taken he would be in a car crash and receive another concussion—following an all-night party. When Martha arrived at the hospital and heard how it happened, she had no sympathy. Lacking credentials, she had just traveled to Europe as the only passenger aboard a shipload of explosives.

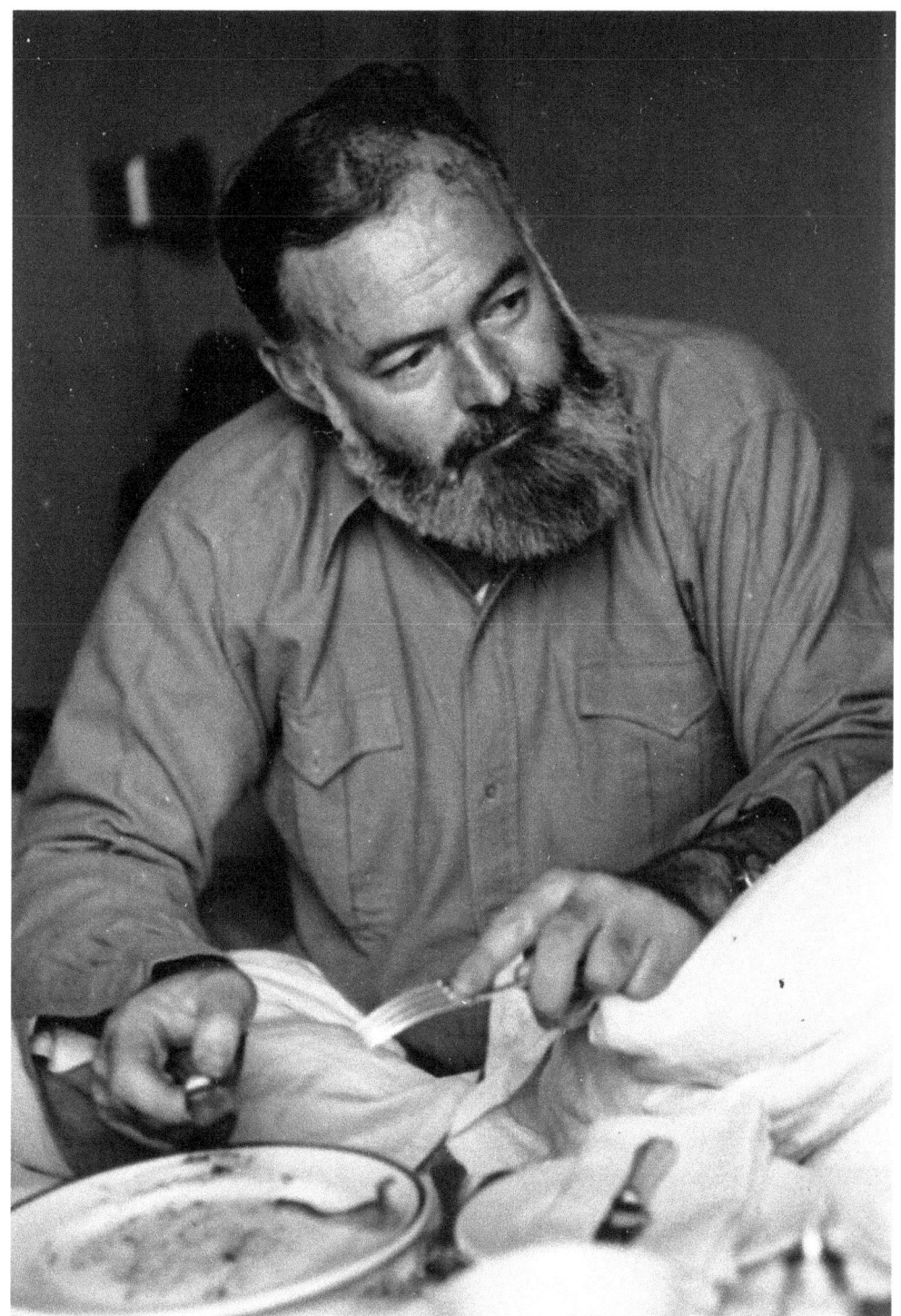

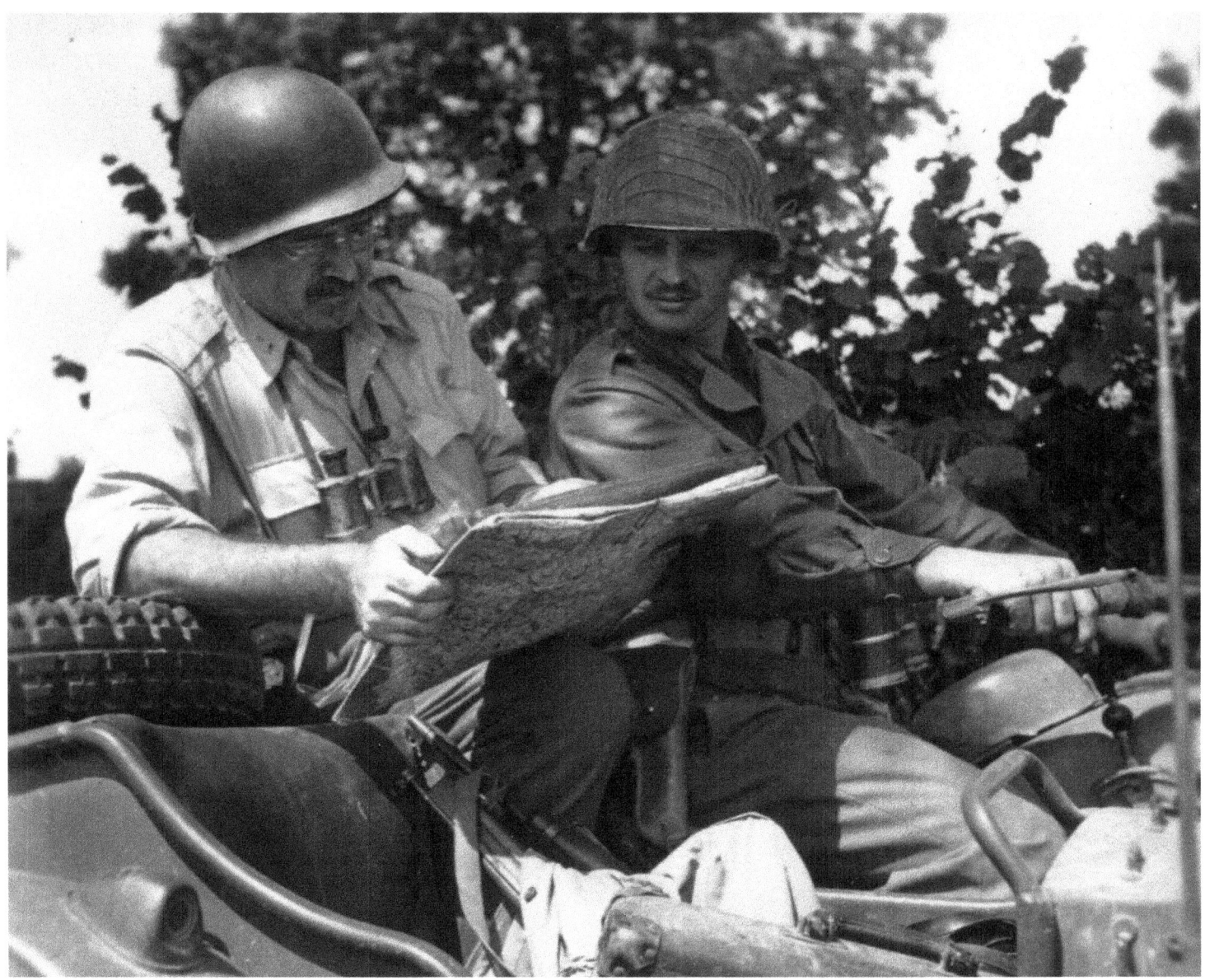

In London, Hemingway met and began courting *Time* magazine's Mary Welsh. Soon afterward he covered D-Day from a landing craft off the coast of Normandy (while Martha hid in a hospital ship, landed, was caught, and sent back), then he attached himself to the Fourth Infantry Division and directed a bunch of French irregulars at Rambouillet. Here, in August 1944, he's reading a map en route to "liberate" Paris—or at least the Traveller's Club and the bar at the Ritz Hotel.

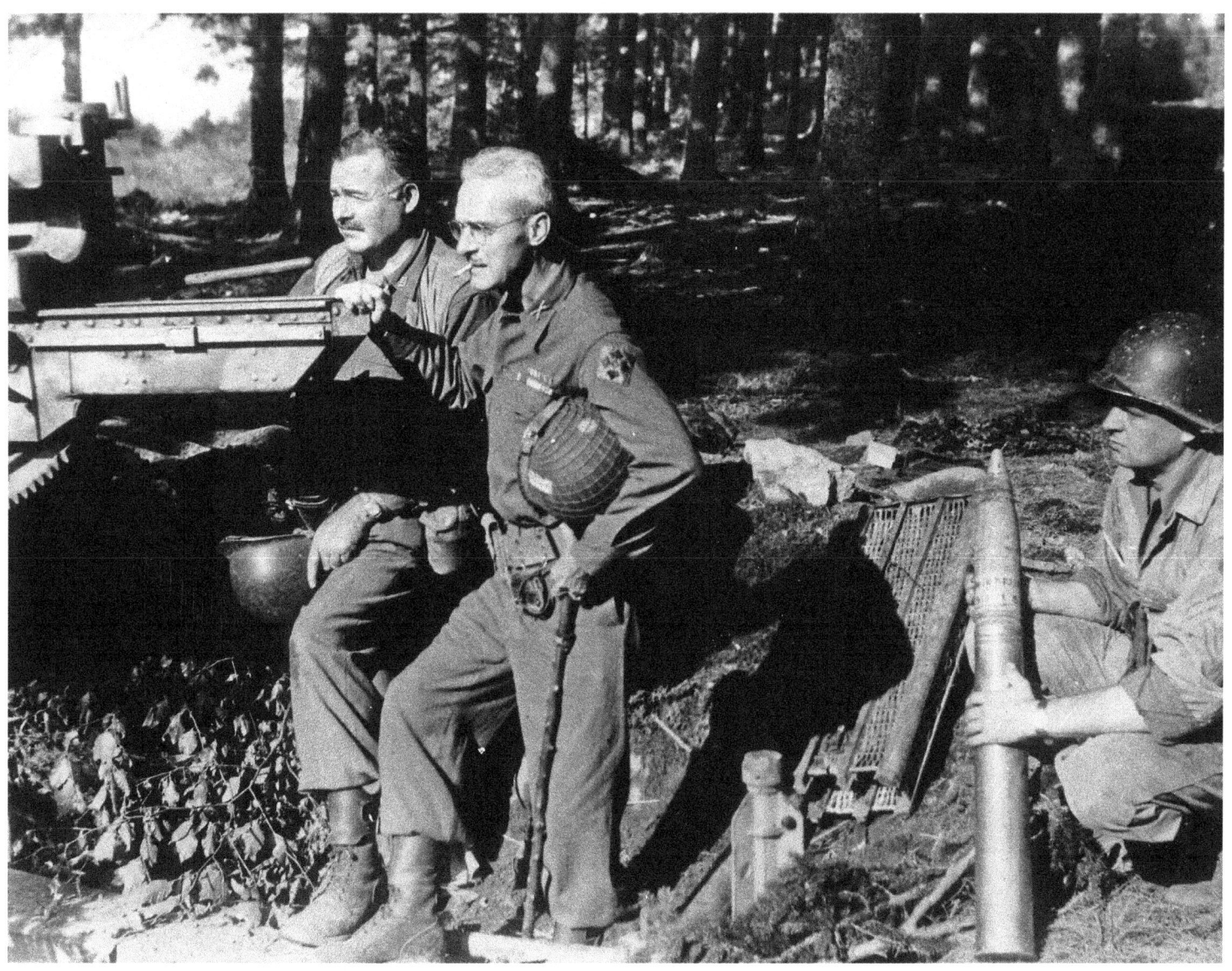

Ernest and Colonel Buck Lanham stand beside a captured German 88 mm anti-aircraft and anti-tank gun somewhere on the Siegfried Line, while a soldier hefts one of the shells. The two men would become fast friends, with Lanham visiting Cuba and Idaho, and even joining Hemingway in 1959 for his last bullfighting circuit tour.

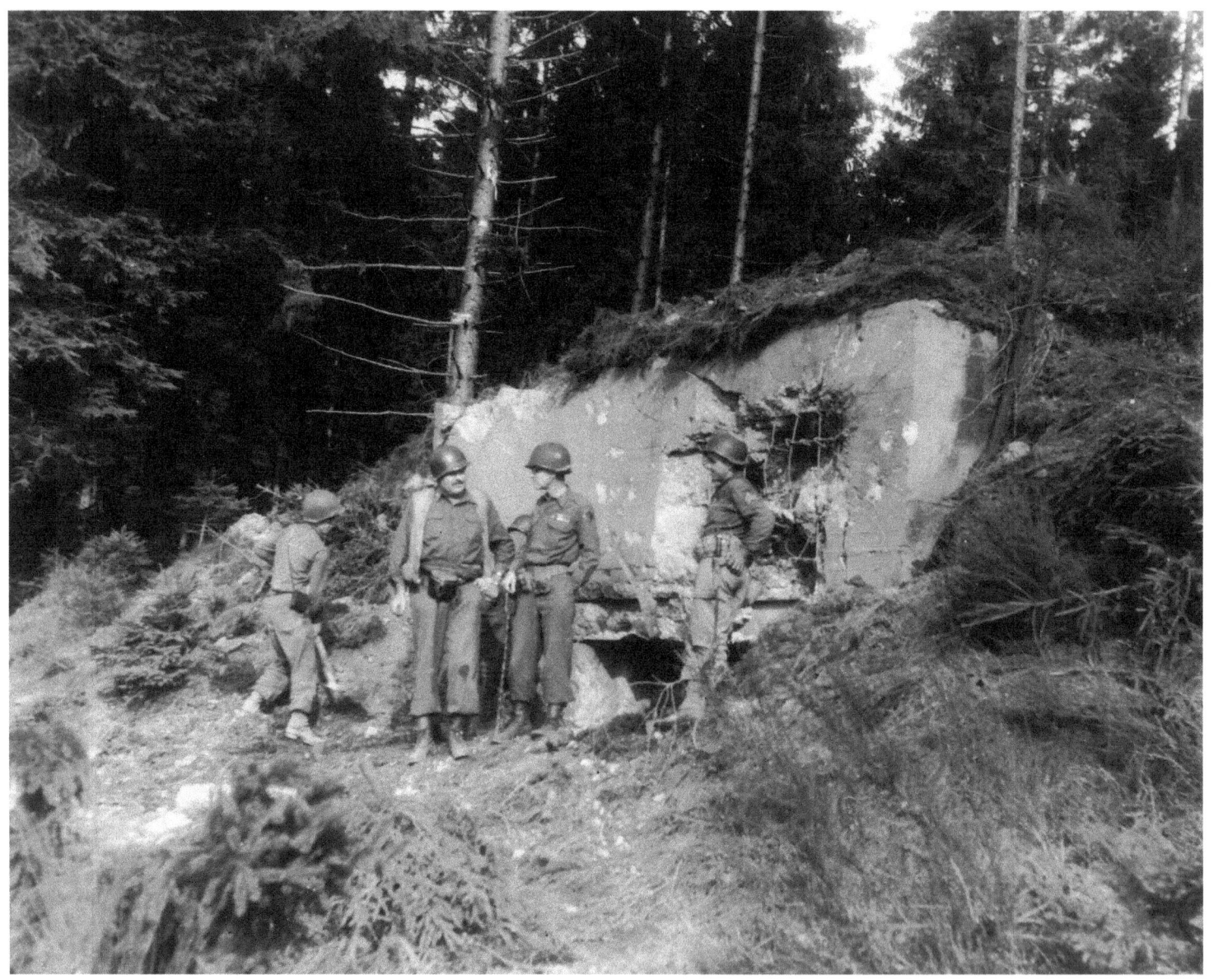

Hemingway and soldiers beside a bunker on the Siegfried Line, a defense system in eastern Germany that included more than 18,000 bunkers and traps. Later, Hemingway would follow Colonel Lanham's 22nd Infantry Regiment through one of the bloodiest engagements of the war: Hürtgen Forest, which was fought between September 1944 and February 1945, resulting in 32,000 American casualties. The battle would later be referenced in Hemingway's 1949 novel, *Across the River and Into the Trees*.

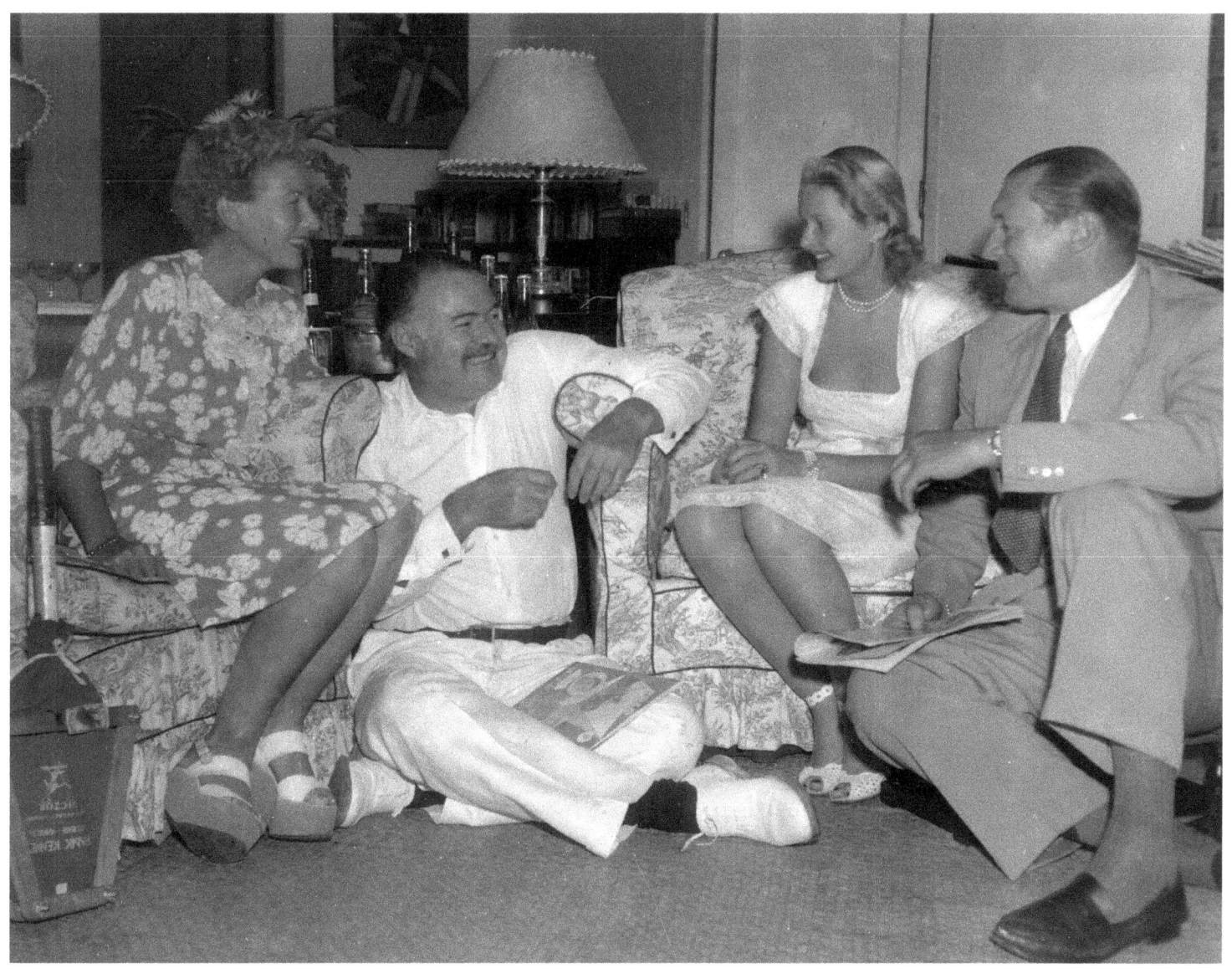

On the grounds that she had abandoned him, Ernest filed for a divorce from Martha and married Mary Welsh on March 18, 1946. Almost instantly the couple settled into Ernest's routines in Havana, which included frequent guests at the Finca. Here they spend time with Cuban heiress Graciela Sánchez, whom Ernest knew from the Club de Cazadores, and eventual hall-of-fame polo player Winston Guest, who was Ernest's second-in-command aboard the *Pilar* during Crook Factory operations.

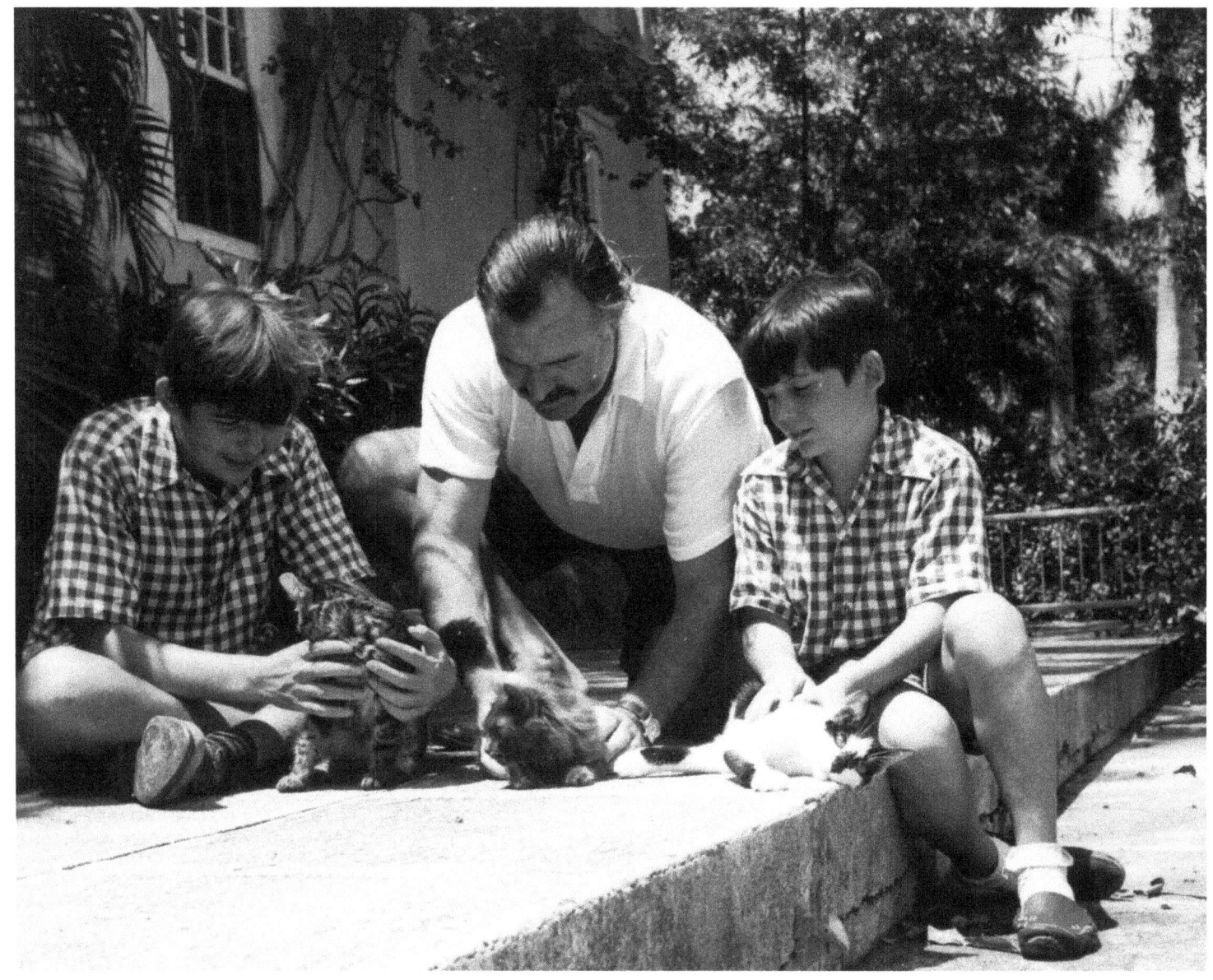

Papa, with visiting sons Patrick and Gregory in 1946, was a cat lover who had 57 at one point. Martha had hated the way the cats "owned" the place, but Mary quickly found a solution to the feline problem. She had built what would become known as the White Tower, which permitted the cats the first floor and Ernest the top overlook for working on revisions.

Sun Valley, October 1947. Ernest and Mary had come a long way. The preceding year he thought Mary, who had become pregnant, might die when she had to have emergency surgery for a burst fallopian tube. Then this past summer they were forced to leave Cuba because soldiers from the camp at Columbia had invaded the Finca looking for a member of "the opposition" and had killed one of his dogs. It was why Hemingway would welcome the Castro revolution when it finally came.

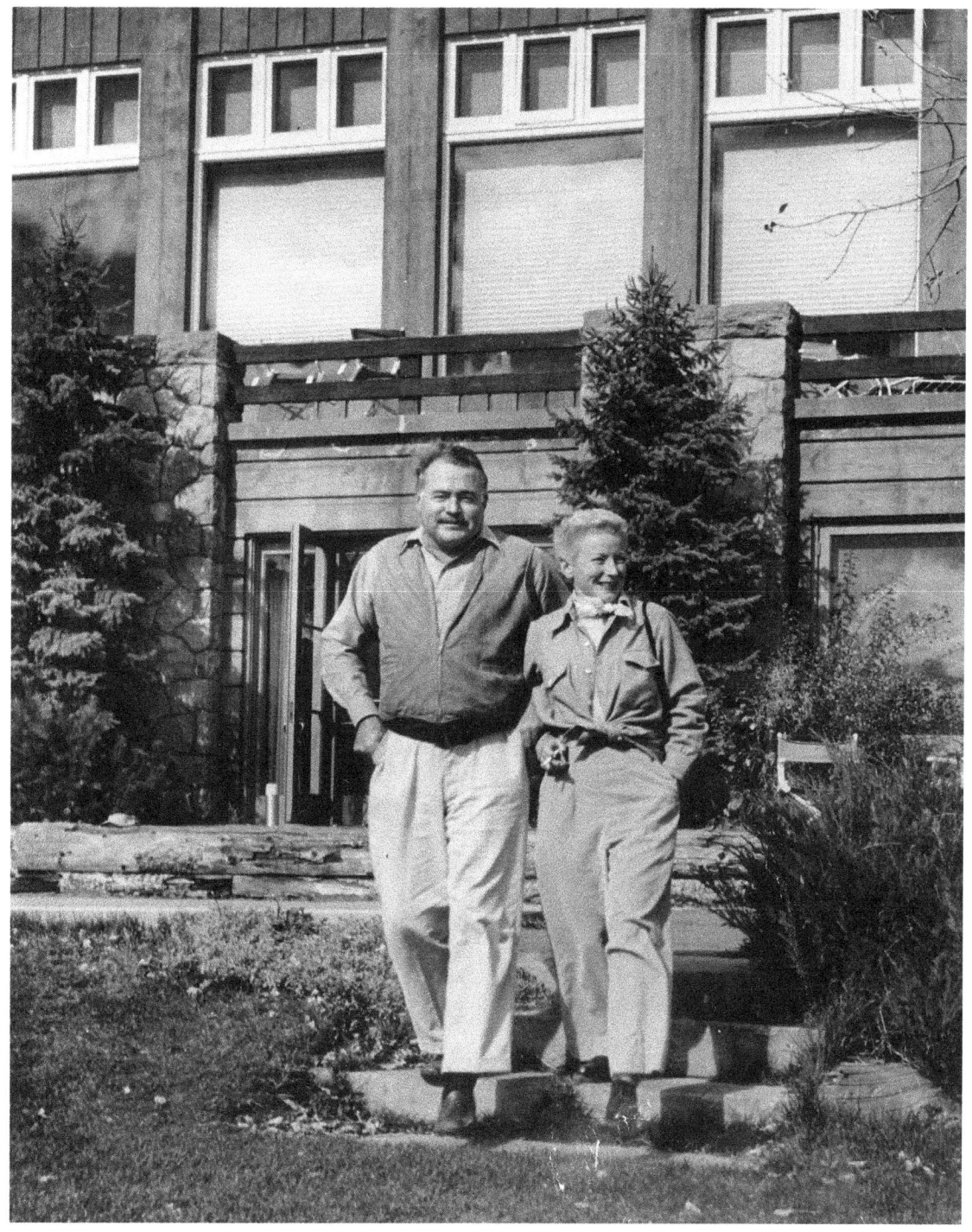

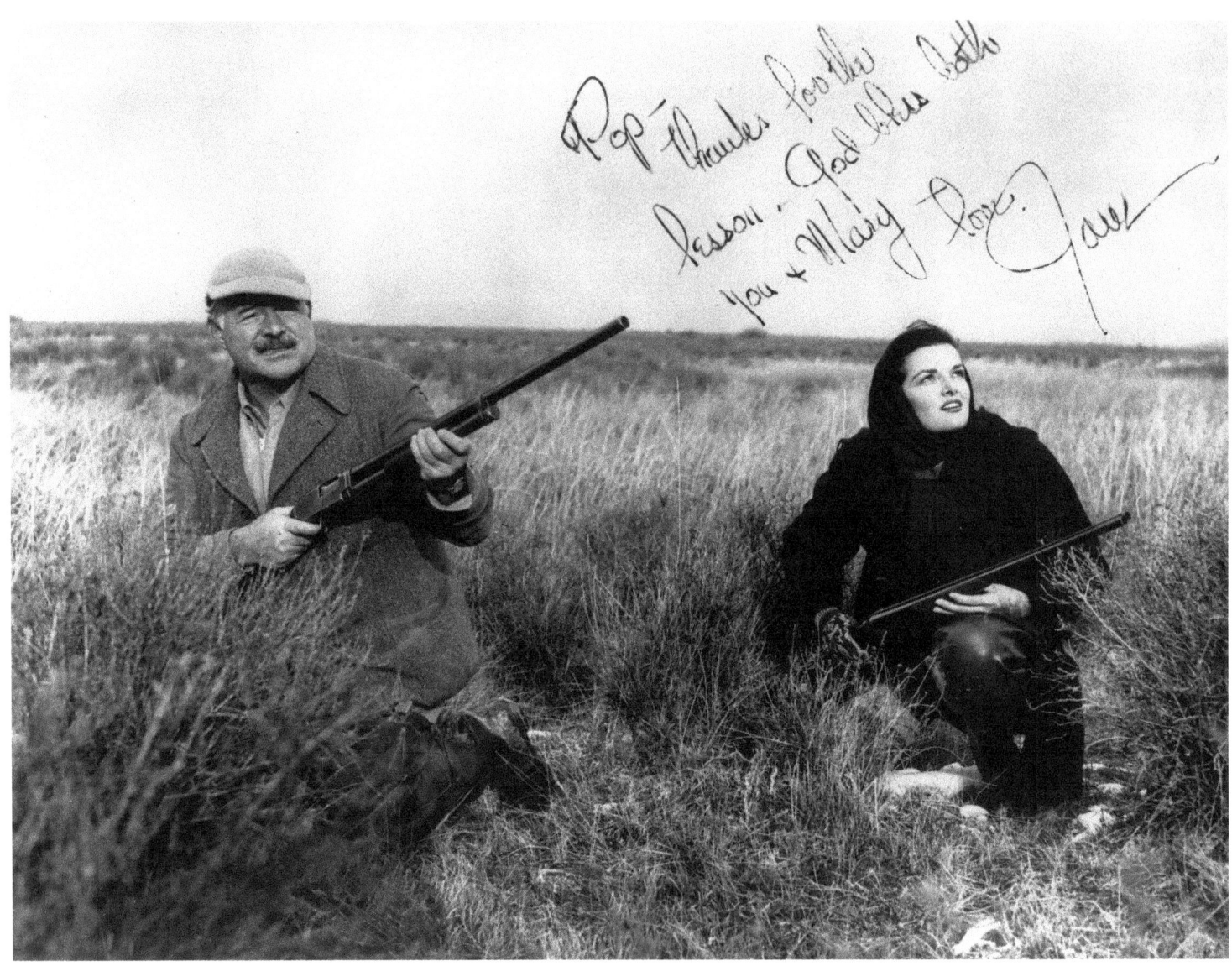

Hemingway attracted celebrities. He was good friends with Marlene Dietrich, Gary Cooper, Ingrid Bergman, and countless other actors, directors, bullfighters, boxers, sportsmen, and writers. That's because in conversation he was an interesting and entertaining man whose exploits sounded even better over drinks. As this "thank-you" photo of actress Jane Russell illustrates, he also loved to share his knowledge of the outdoors with whoever would listen.

Ernest at the Club de Cazadores del Cerro in Havana. Ernest and his sons won a great many tournaments at the club—so many that one of the local sportswriters wrote that "there aren't four shooters on the island who could beat Papa and his three sons."

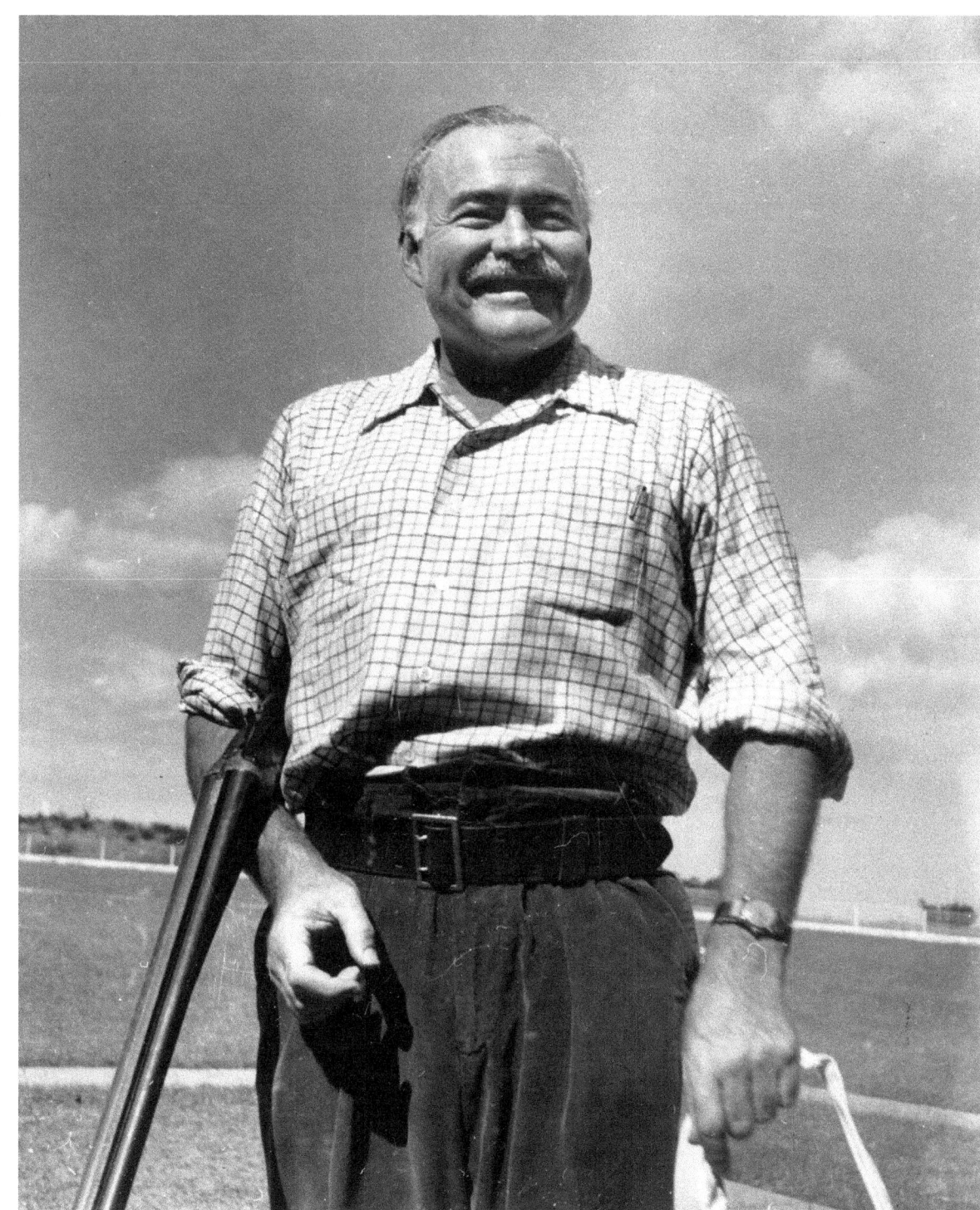

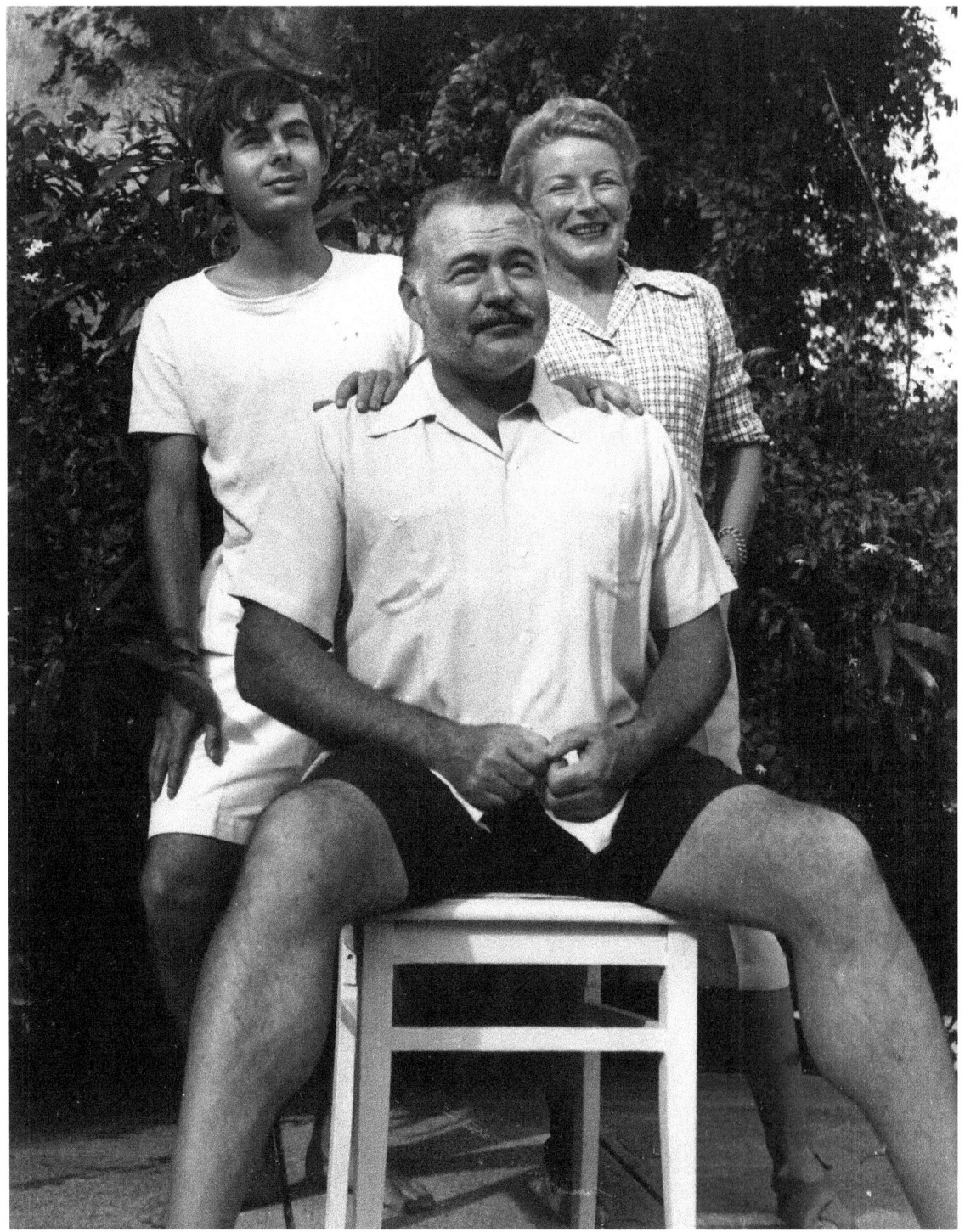

Son Patrick poses with his father and new stepmother, around spring 1948. About this time, Malcolm Cowley came to Havana to spend several weeks with the Hemingways in order to write his *Life* magazine profile, "A Portrait of Mr. Papa." That cover story all but confirmed that the myth of Papa was now and forever intertwined with Ernest Hemingway the writer.

The Hemingways in 1948 with Black Dog, a stray Ernest adopted after he found it wandering around town. It would become his favorite, one who would lie at his feet as he stood on the kudu skin in his bedroom to write. Black Dog died at the Finca in December 1956 while his master was in Europe. He's buried on the grounds of the estate with Hemingway's other favorite pets, his grave marked by a tombstone.

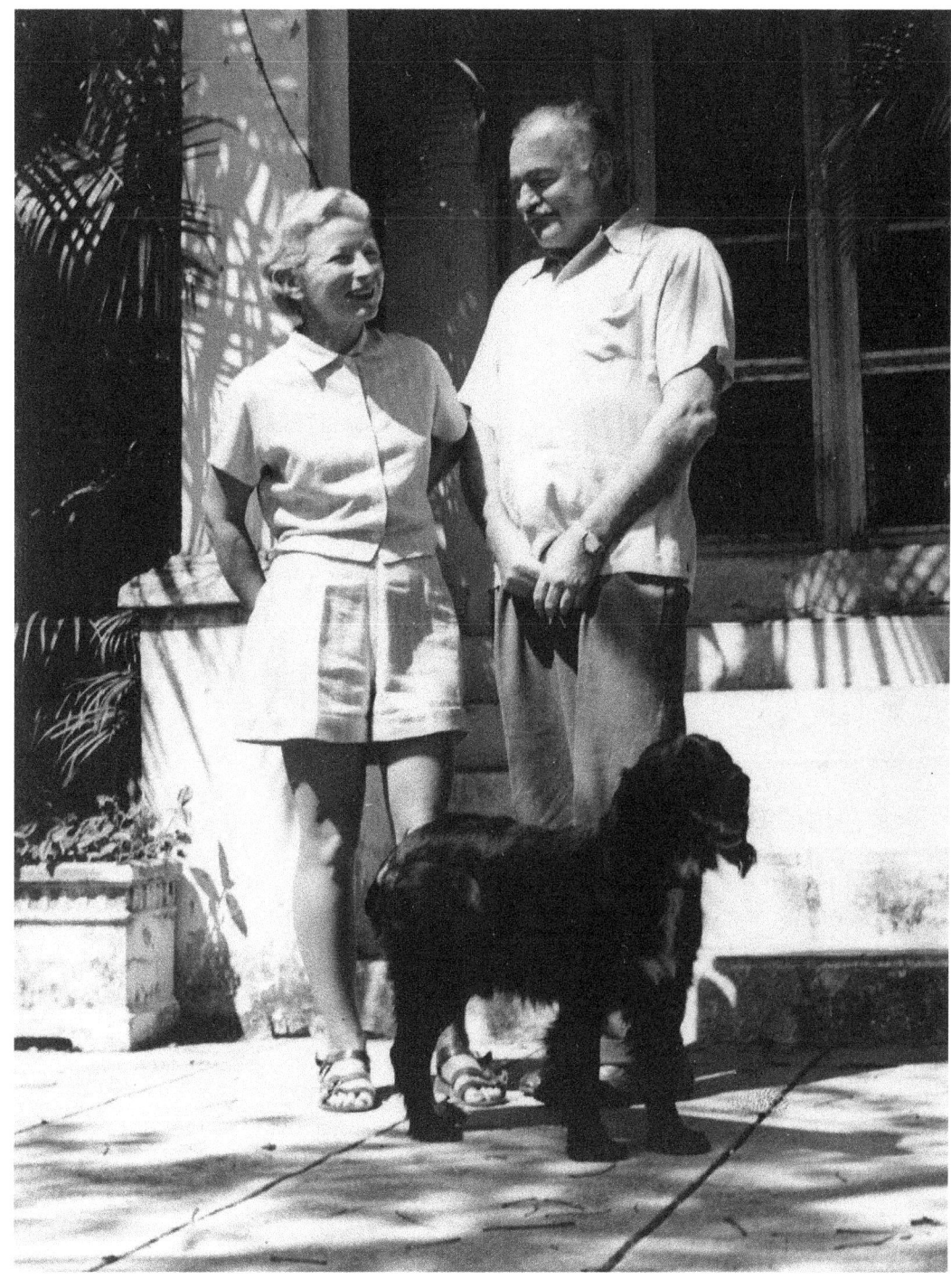

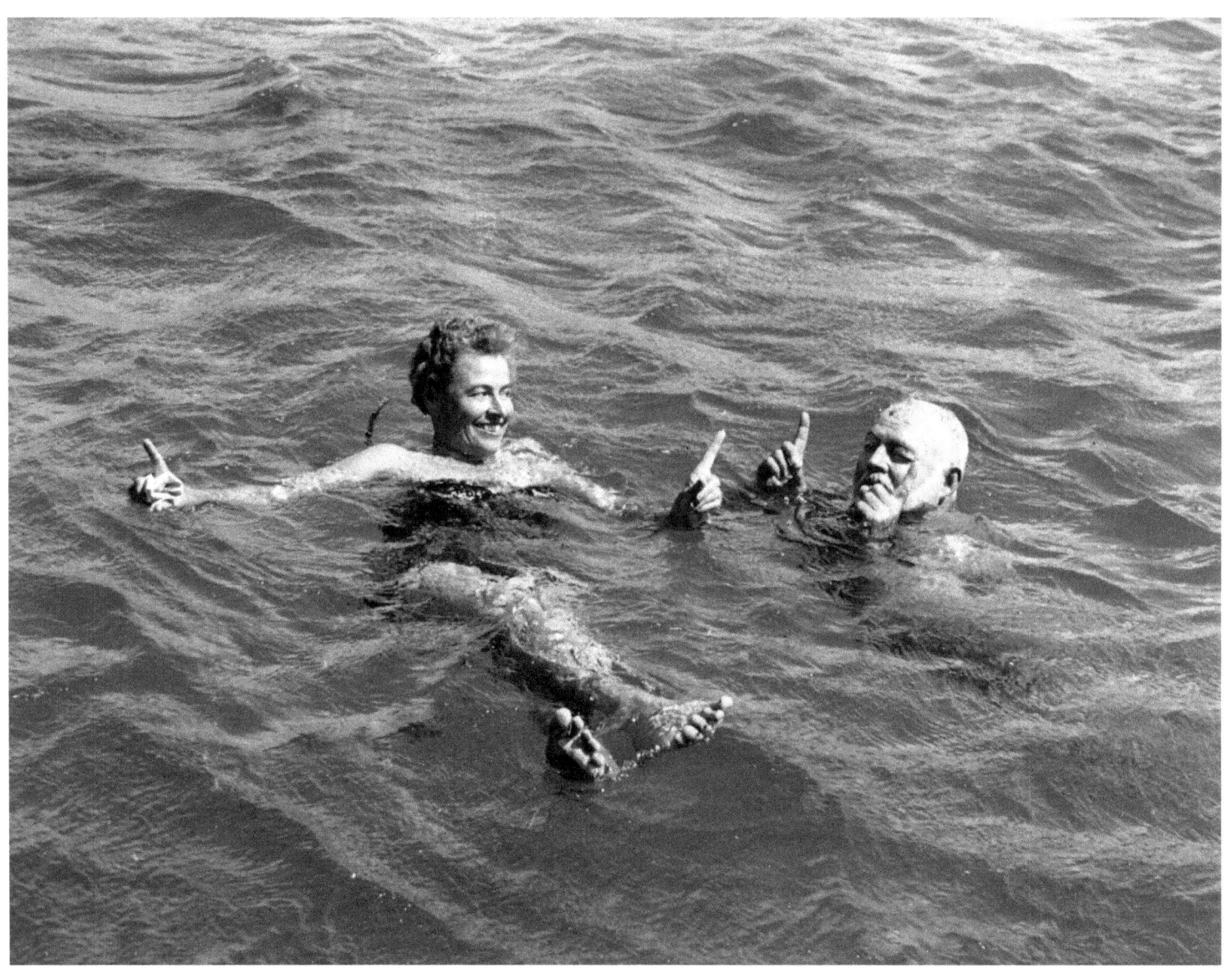

In December 1948 Ernest's sister Sunny came for a visit, and they enjoyed swimming off the *Pilar* at Cayo Parsíso, where Hemingway often went. It was a world apart from the midnight skinny-dipping swims they had taken at Windemere with their parents' blessings. Hemingway trusted his sister, whom he had paid years before to type the manuscript of *A Farewell to Arms*. And he enjoyed meeting his nephew. Since the boy called him "Uncle Ernie," he took to calling him "Little Uncle Ernie."

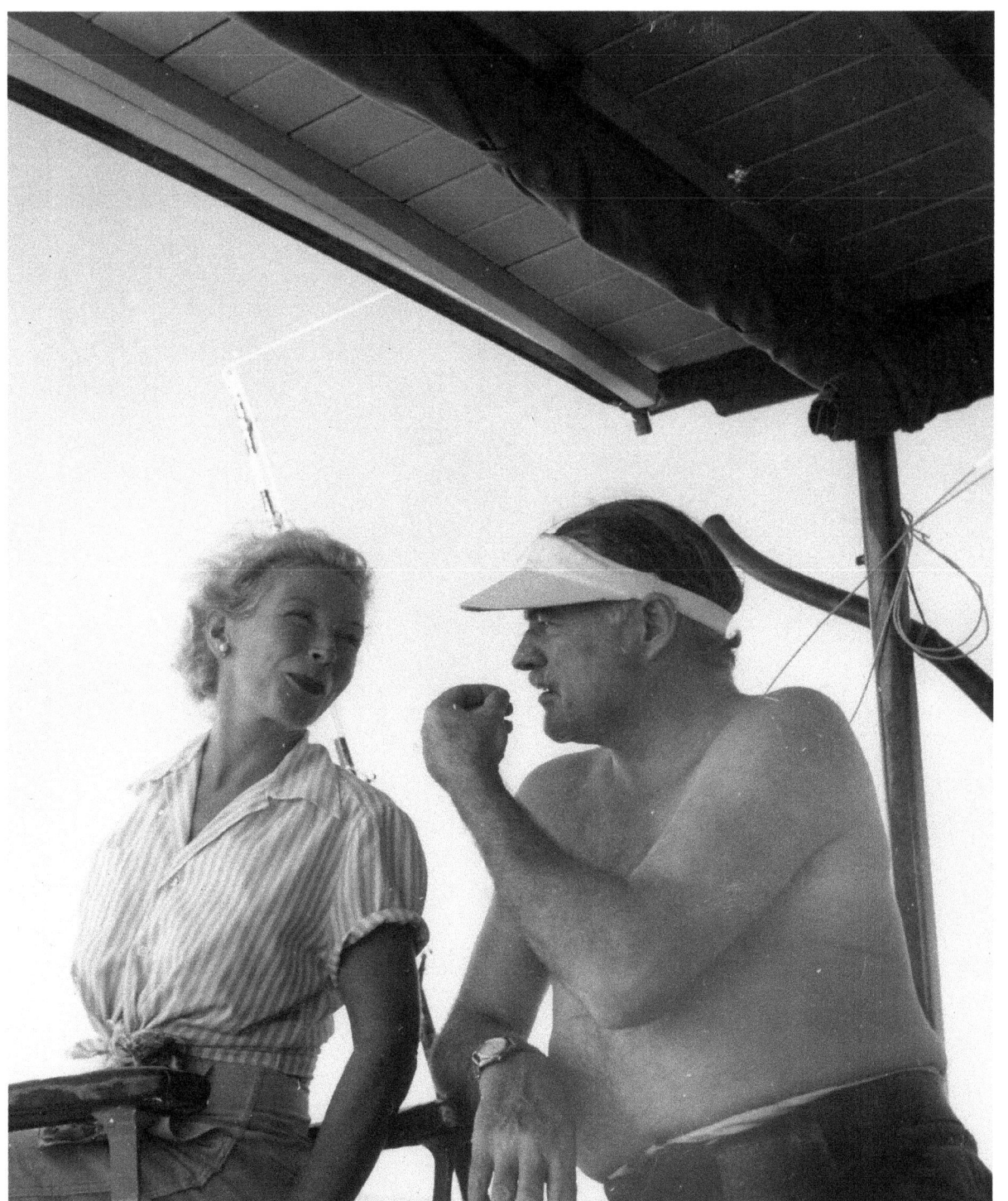

Ernest with his true love—the *Pilar*. His marriage to Mary would contain as many fights as tender moments. They even fought on their wedding day, but Hemingway could be a difficult man. Son Jack would later remark that if Papa was treating Mary poorly to make her leave, she wasn't rising to the bait. She loved him, and she intended to stay. Had he treated the others this poorly, Jack said they most certainly would have left him.

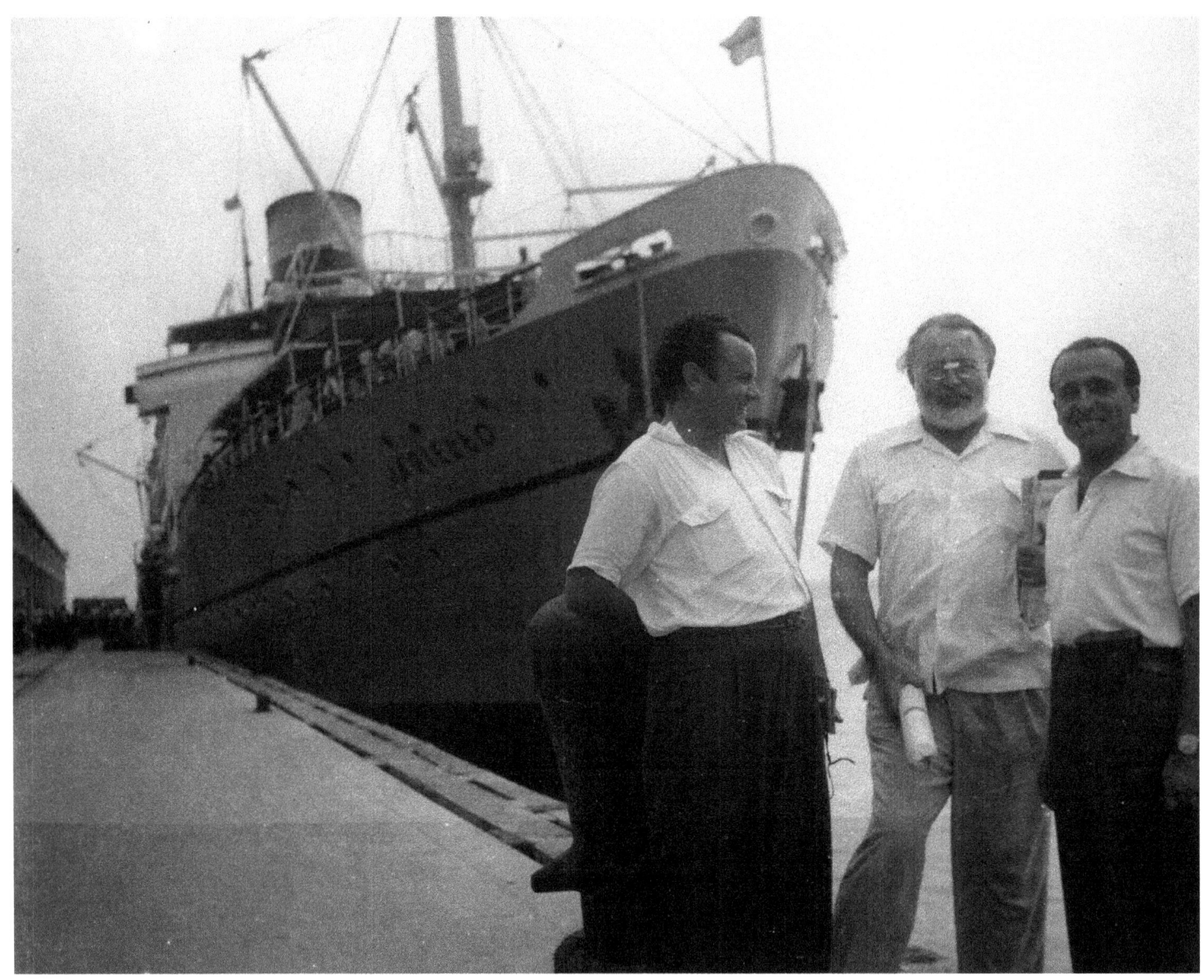

After working on an introduction to a new edition of *A Farewell to Arms*, Hemingway grew nostalgic and wanted to travel to Italy again and show Mary places that were important to him. In fall 1948 they booked passage on the SS *Jagiello*, a steamer bound for Genoa that moved slowly enough for Ernest to troll along the way. Gregorio Fuentes, who had replaced Carlos Gutiérrez on the *Pilar*, had found a special extra-sturdy rod for him to use.

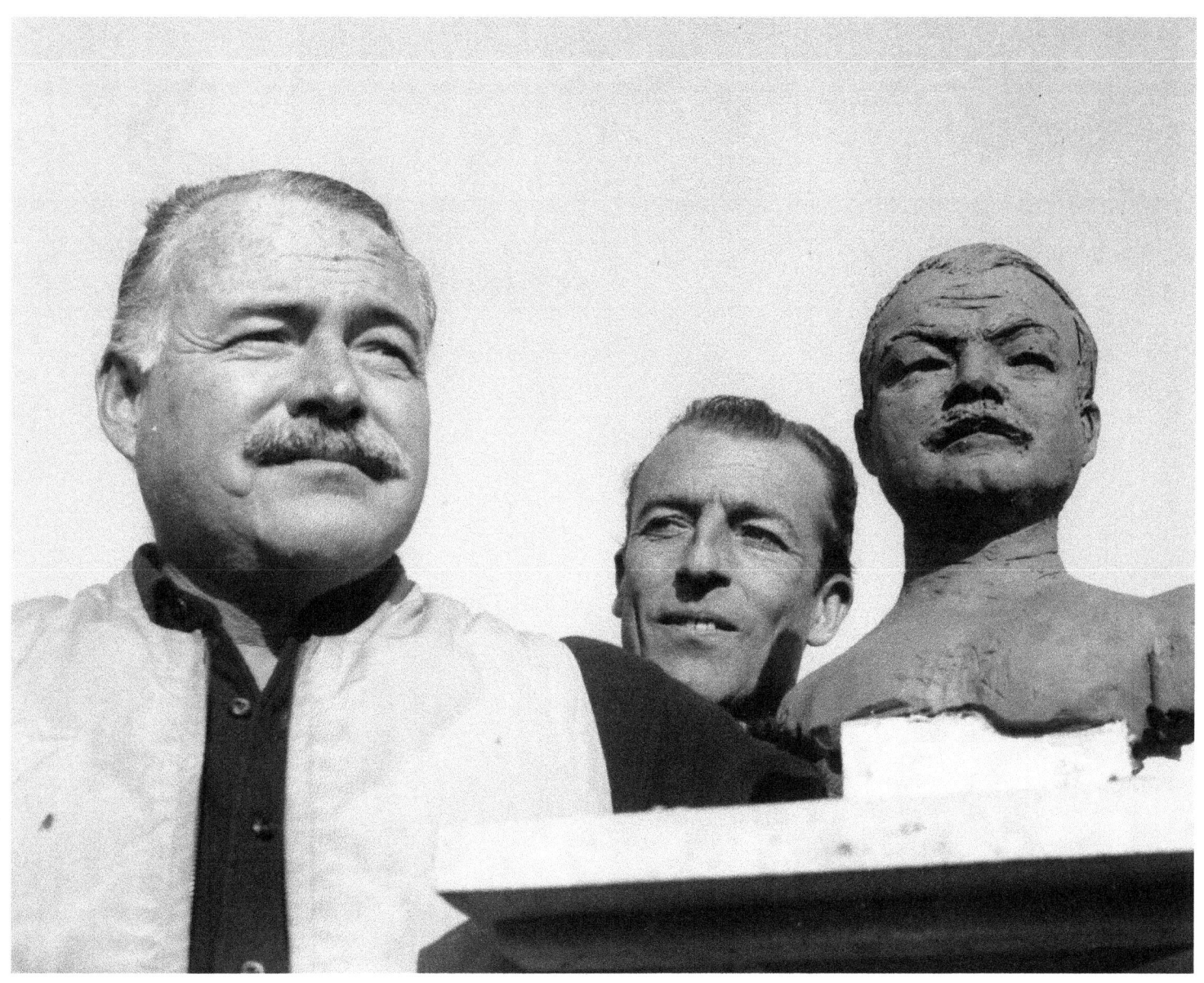

In Italy, Venetian sculptor Tony Lucarda got Hemingway to pose for him. Mary's assessment was that the mouth was not wide enough and "with that sour puss he should wear a pince-nez and be a Republican banker."

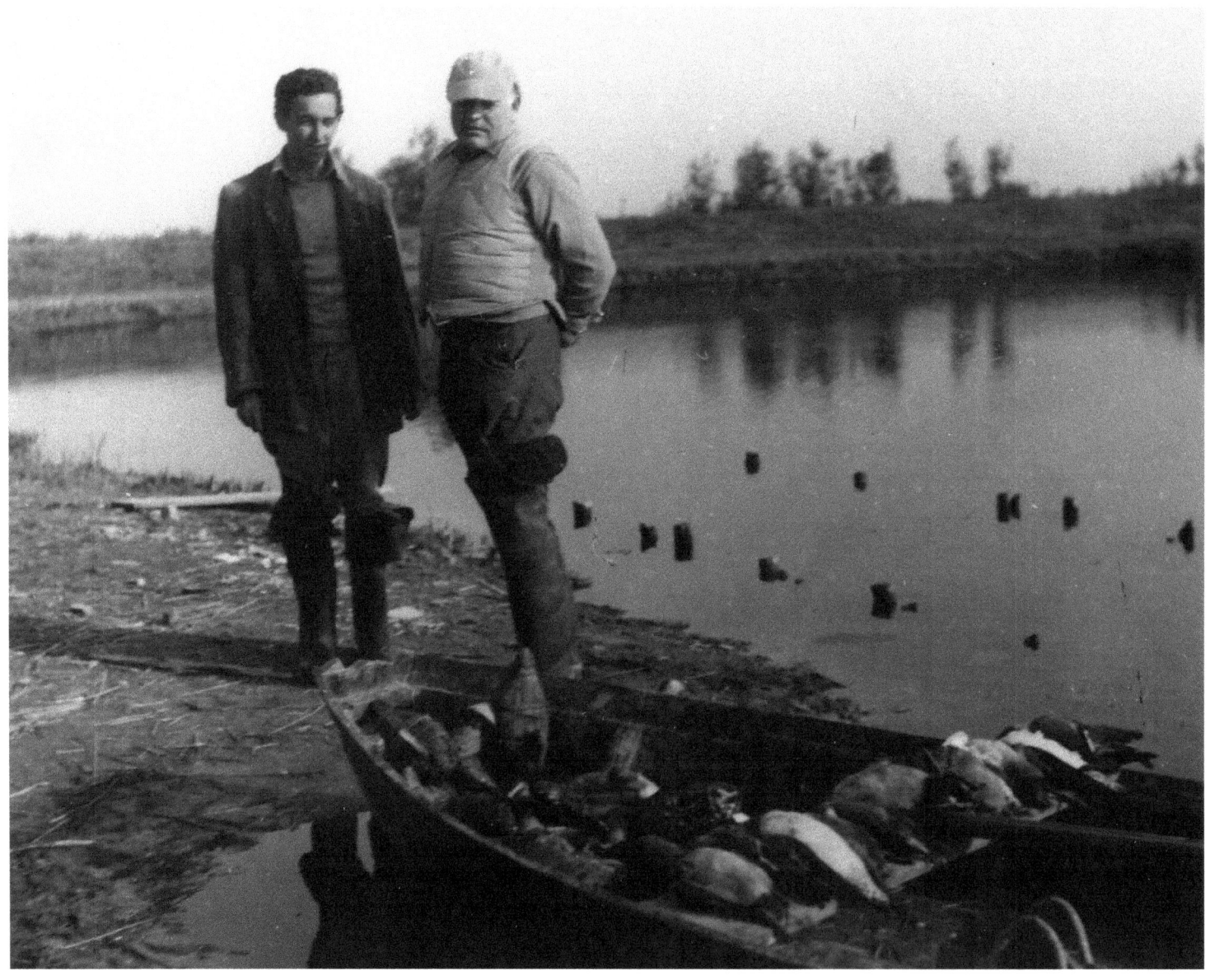

Celebrity trumps royalty. In Venice, Ernest was invited to go fishing with Count Kechler and shoot ducks with a baron named Nanyuki Franchetti. After a day out on the water, Ernest joked with Mary that he'd been "shooting in a Venetian blind."

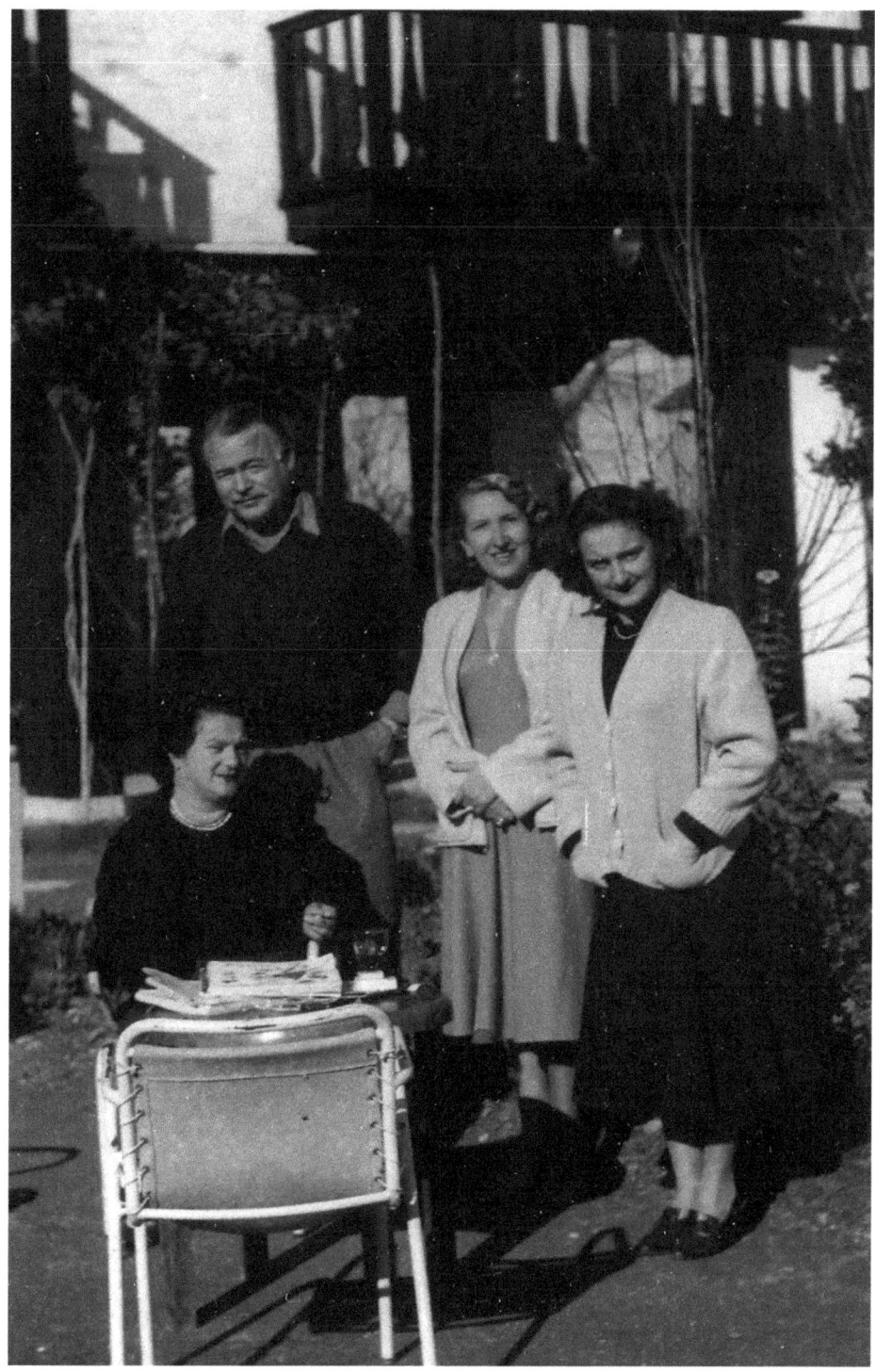

That season in Italy, by far the biggest attraction for Ernest was an 18-year-old aristocratic Italian woman named Adriana Ivancich (right). She was a dark-haired beauty who had gone shooting with Franchetti and grew frustrated afterward when her hair was in a tangle and she had no comb. Like an Elizabethan gentleman spreading his cape across a mud puddle, Ernest broke his comb in two and gave her half. Here, they're having lunch in Cortina.

Gut sucked in, Ernest leaves a ristorante with new bounce in his step. He was in Italy and he was in love again. Adriana found Hemingway's doe-eyed fawning flattering but amusing, while her mother was apparently of the opinion that it wouldn't hurt to infuse the family title with a little American cash. The first fiction Adriana inspired was a thinly disguised (and melodramatically bad) version of Hemingway's male fantasy for her. *Across the River and Into the Trees* was roundly booed by critics.

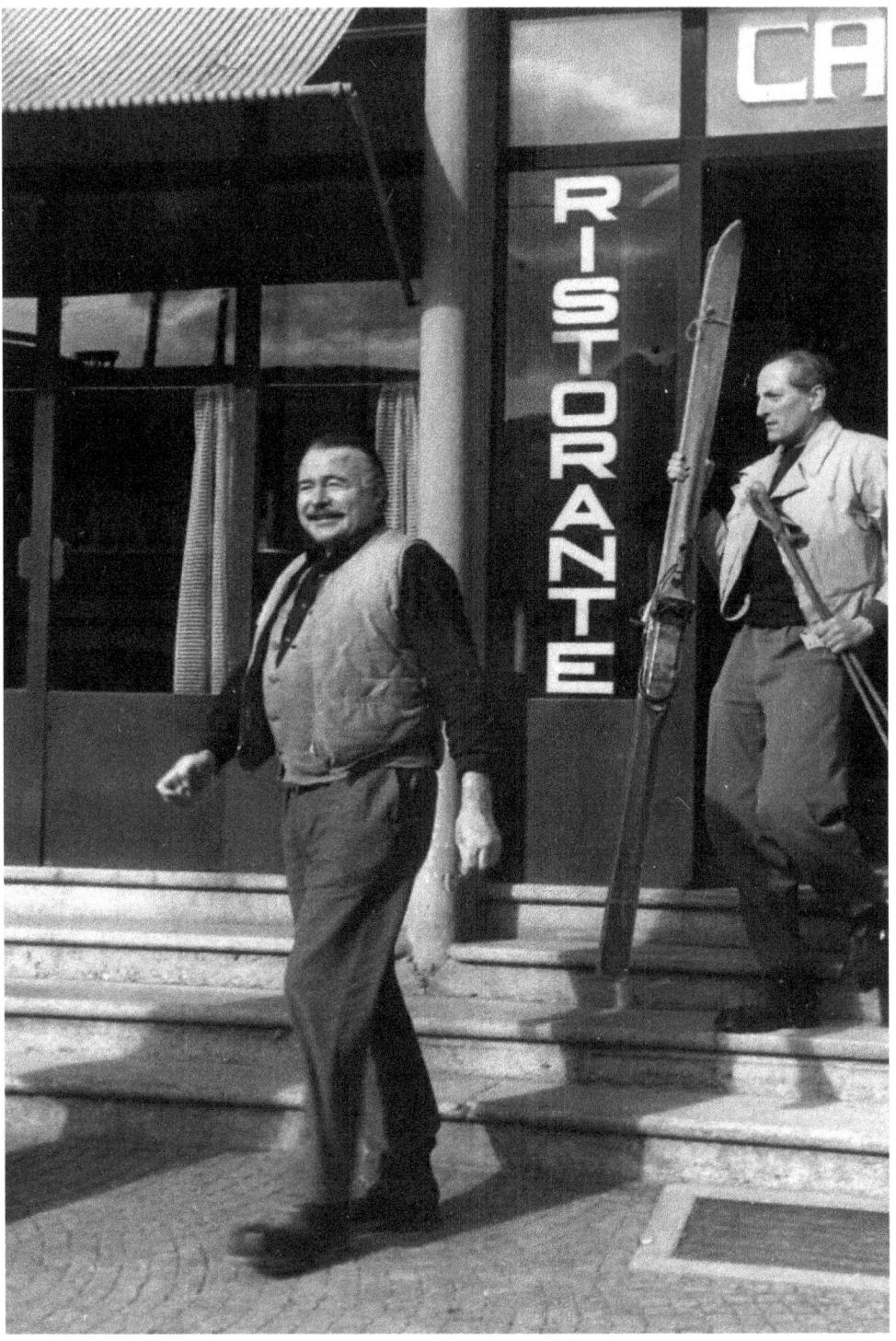

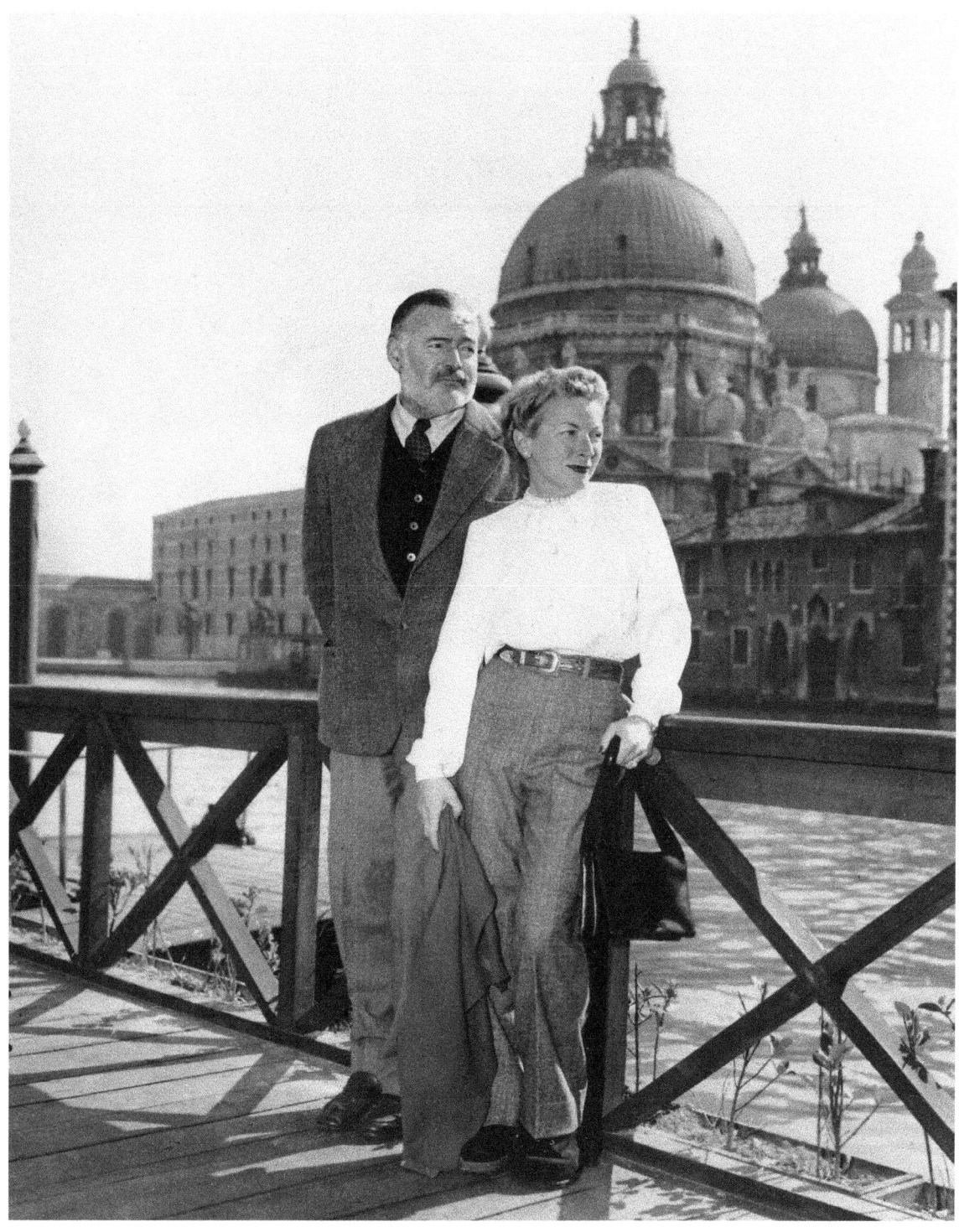

In March 1949 the Hemingways were back in Venice again, where they met writer Sinclair Lewis. In a three-hour lunch, Ernest tired of listening to the Nobel laureate flatter him but suggest, in a backhanded compliment, that if he were to win the big prize he might not write another good thing afterward. This trip Ernest also developed an eye infection serious enough to require hospitalization.

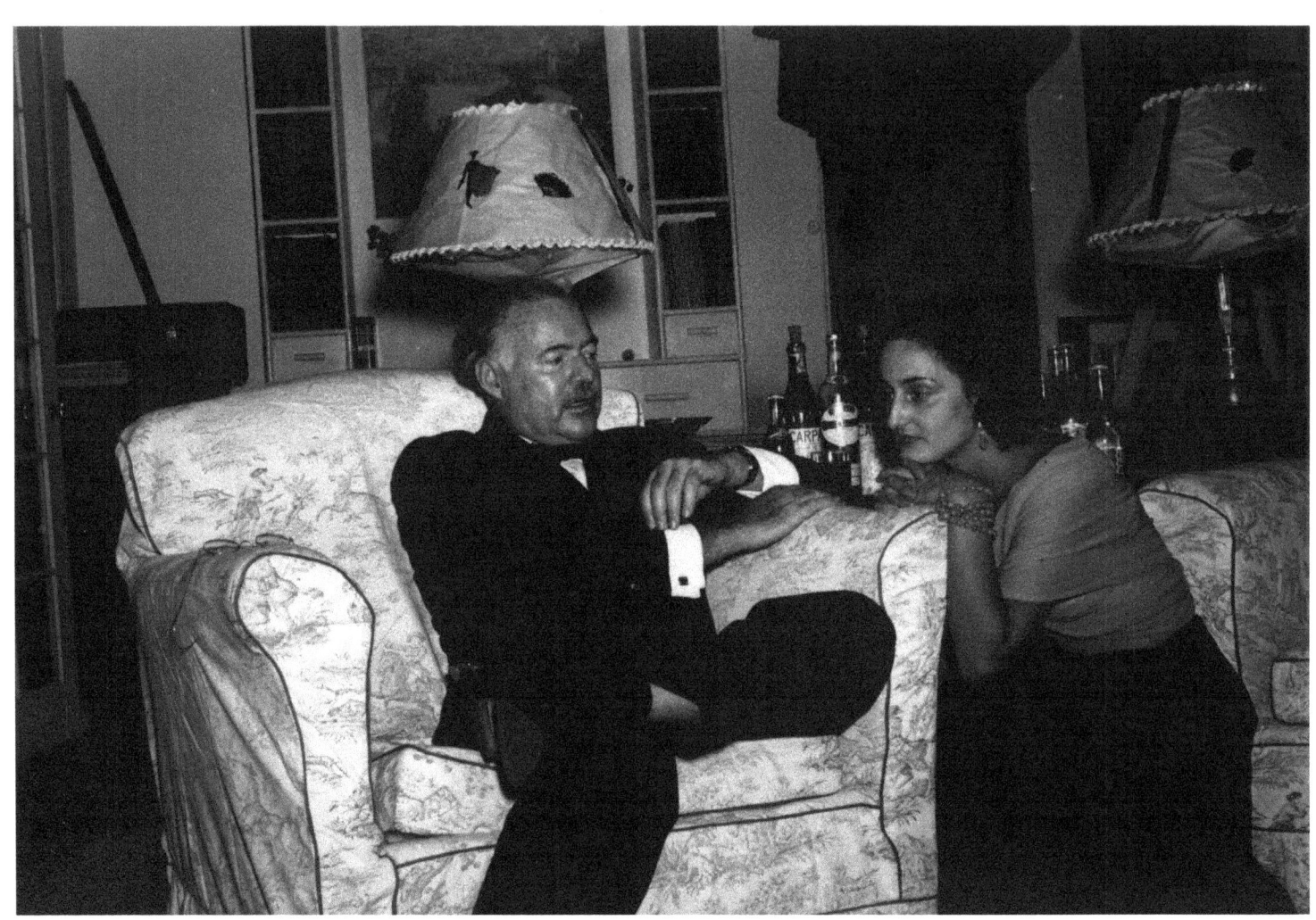

In October 1950, the Hemingways played host to Adriana and her mother, whom Ernest had invited for a visit. They stayed in Havana until the first week of February 1951. During that time, the love-struck Hemingway wrote the first draft of *The Old Man and the Sea*, a book that would prove to critics that he wasn't all washed up, and whose dust jacket he let Adriana design.

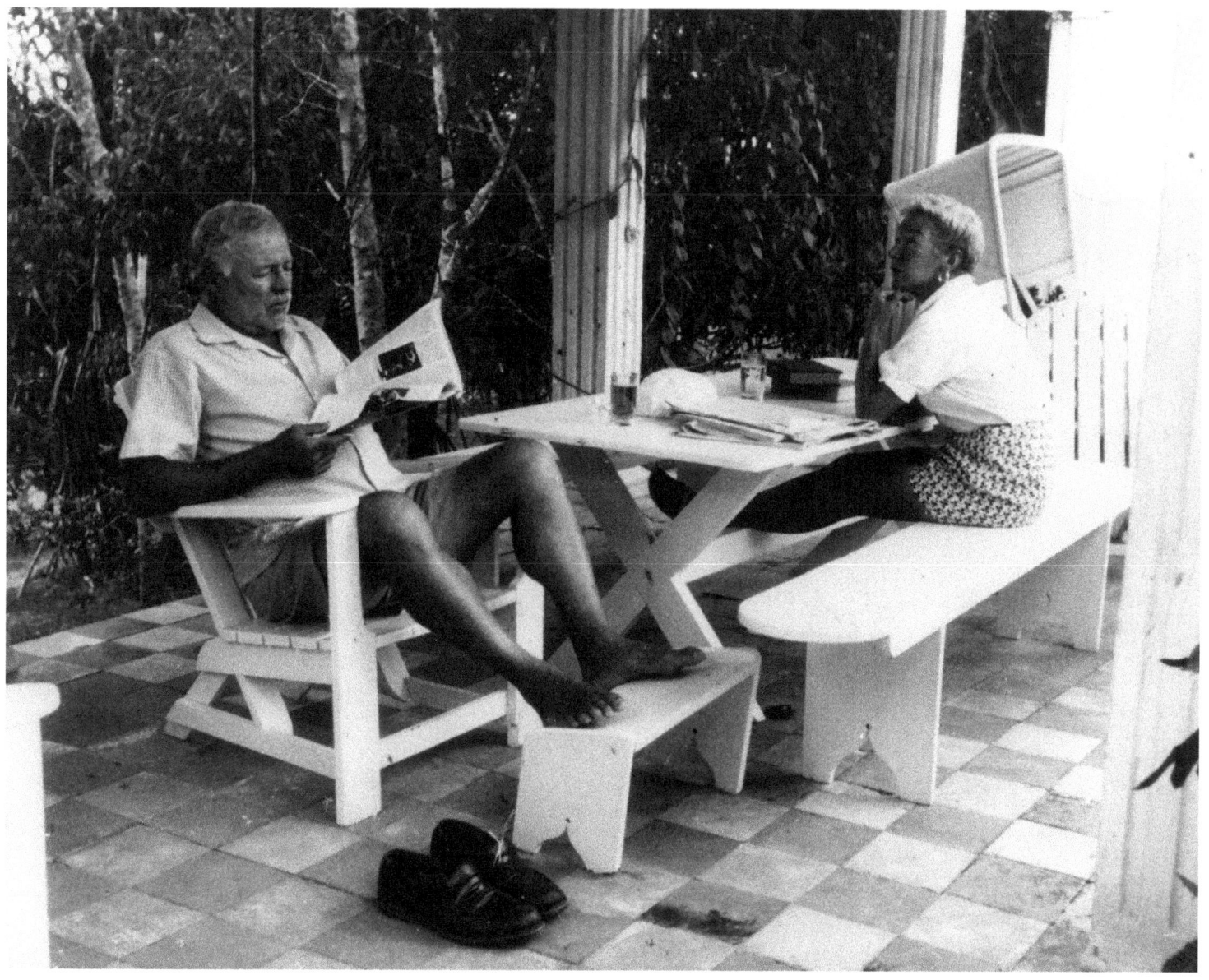

Under the pergola by the Finca pool, Mary and Ernest seem to be in their own separate worlds. Her husband was embarrassing himself by fawning all over a teenager, but Mary was confident the flirtation would stay platonic . . . and it did. But she had the advantage of knowing Ernest needed a companion, someone to take care of him in his old age, which he hinted at when he first met her in London.

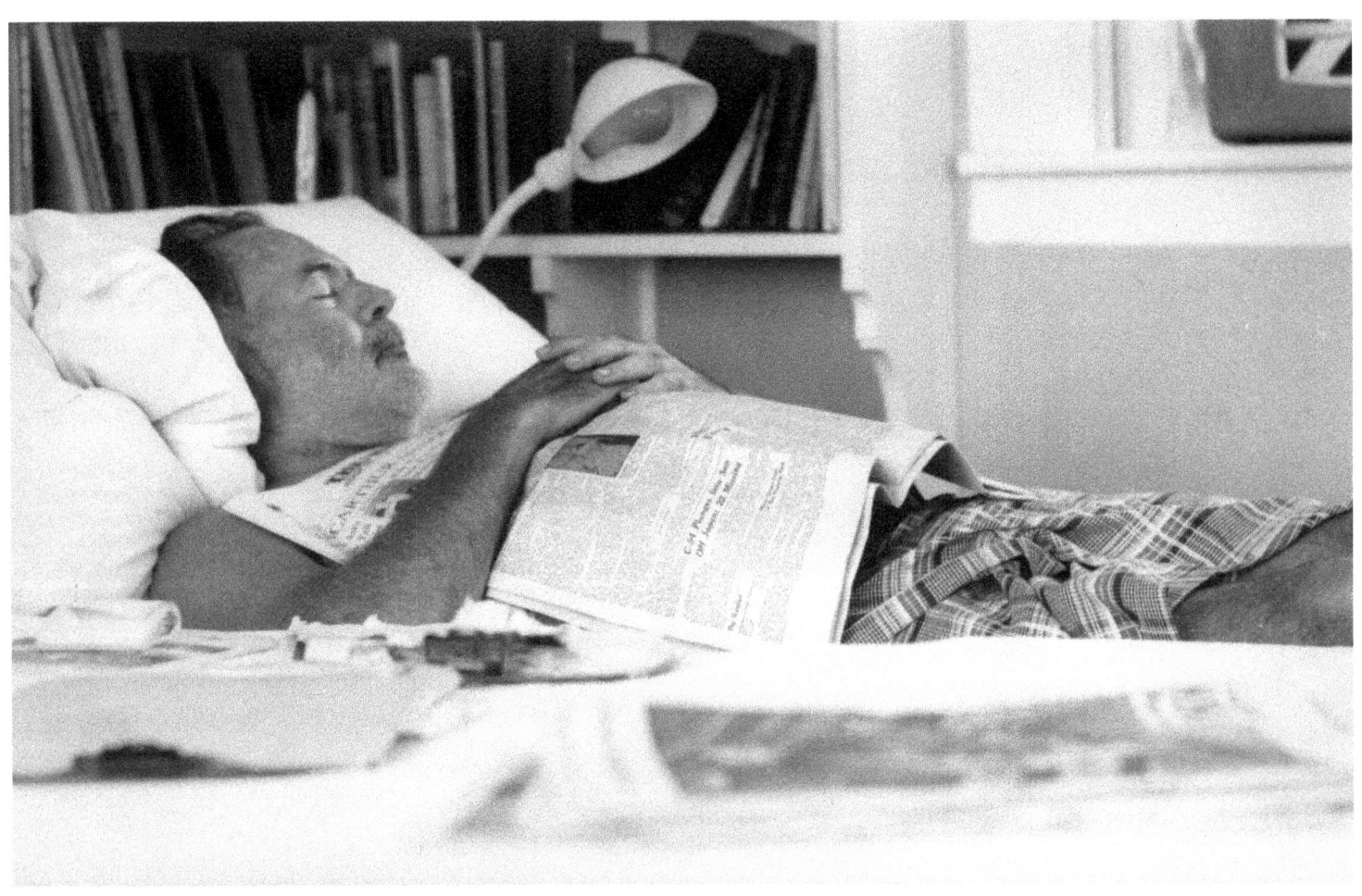

Santiago in *The Old Man and the Sea* dreams of lions. One wonders what Hemingway dreamed of when he dozed after reading newspapers or books, as he often did. This photo was taken during the time he was still smitten with Adriana.

LIFE TAKES ITS TOLL

(1952–1961)

One couldn't conceive of a better metaphor for Ernest Hemingway late in his career than the Cuban fisherman he wrote about in *The Old Man and the Sea* (1952). Like Santiago, Hemingway had fallen on hard times. The critics were saying he was through, and Hemingway's writing drought was as painfully obvious as the old fisherman's 84 days without catching a fish. Santiago had a bad back and hands that hurt him just to grip the tools of his trade, and Hemingway had his own ailments. His blood pressure was so high at times that it alarmed doctors, he had early symptoms of diabetes, liver and kidney problems from years of hard drinking, and encroaching dementia. He had been in rapid decline since the African plane crashes, but like Santiago, Papa hung in there until his luck changed . . . at least for a time.

There was no way to reverse the years of hard living that had taken its toll, but it was gratifying for Hemingway to finally receive recognition for his work—both a Pulitzer and a Nobel Prize. This last decade of his life was spent looking backward and revisiting old places that were special to him: Venice, Pamplona, Paris—even Africa. But his celebrity continued to be a constant drain, with journalists, editors, and now biographers and scholars wanting some of his time. In what would turn out to be a last hurrah, Ernest would follow two matadors he admired on a 1959 tour of Spain, which he would write about for *Life* magazine. That summer, he also had a most memorable 60th birthday party in Málaga, Spain.

This last decade, Papa still hunted and fished, but the zest just wasn't there. First and foremost always a writer, he worked on his memoir of Paris in the twenties, along with an expanded version of "The Dangerous Summer" and two books which incorporated his African adventures, *The Garden of Eden* (1986) and *True at First Light* (1999). He wrote even after he was in severe pain following the plane crashes. That's how dedicated he was to his craft. Hemingway lived on his own terms, and in the end he would die on his own terms.

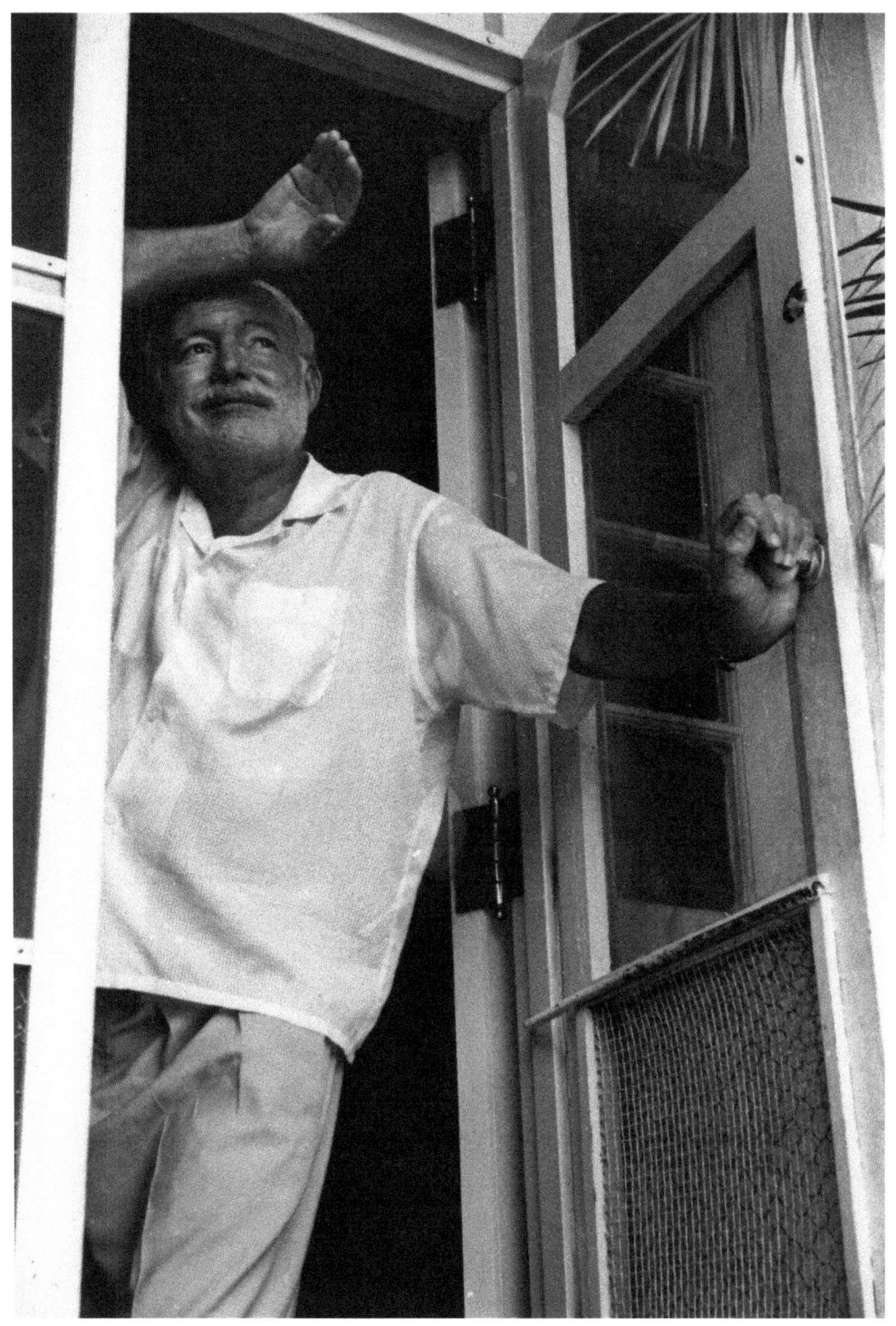

Ernest, standing at the door of the Finca, early fifties. Though Hemingway traveled so much every year it's hard to think of him as having a home, Cuba certainly came closest. He began *For Whom the Bell Tolls* in Havana, and also wrote *Across the River and Into the Trees*, *The Old Man and the Sea*, *A Moveable Feast*, *Islands in the Stream*, and *The Dangerous Summer* while living here. Hemingway finished *The Old Man and the Sea* in February 1951 and *Life* magazine published the entire novella on September 1, 1952. Some five million copies were sold in just two days. When the book appeared one week later, critics raved about this spare novel about a Cuban fisherman—even Hemingway's rival, William Faulkner. Fittingly, Hemingway was out on the *Pilar* when he heard on the radio the novel had won the Pulitzer Prize.

Hemingway was not above using his fame to make a few extra dollars. Here, he poses for a two-page Ballantine Ale ad that would run in a 1952 issue of *Life* magazine. In it, he wrote how good a Ballantine tastes after fighting a big fish. He also endorsed a number of other products and businesses, including Parker Pens and Pan American Airways.

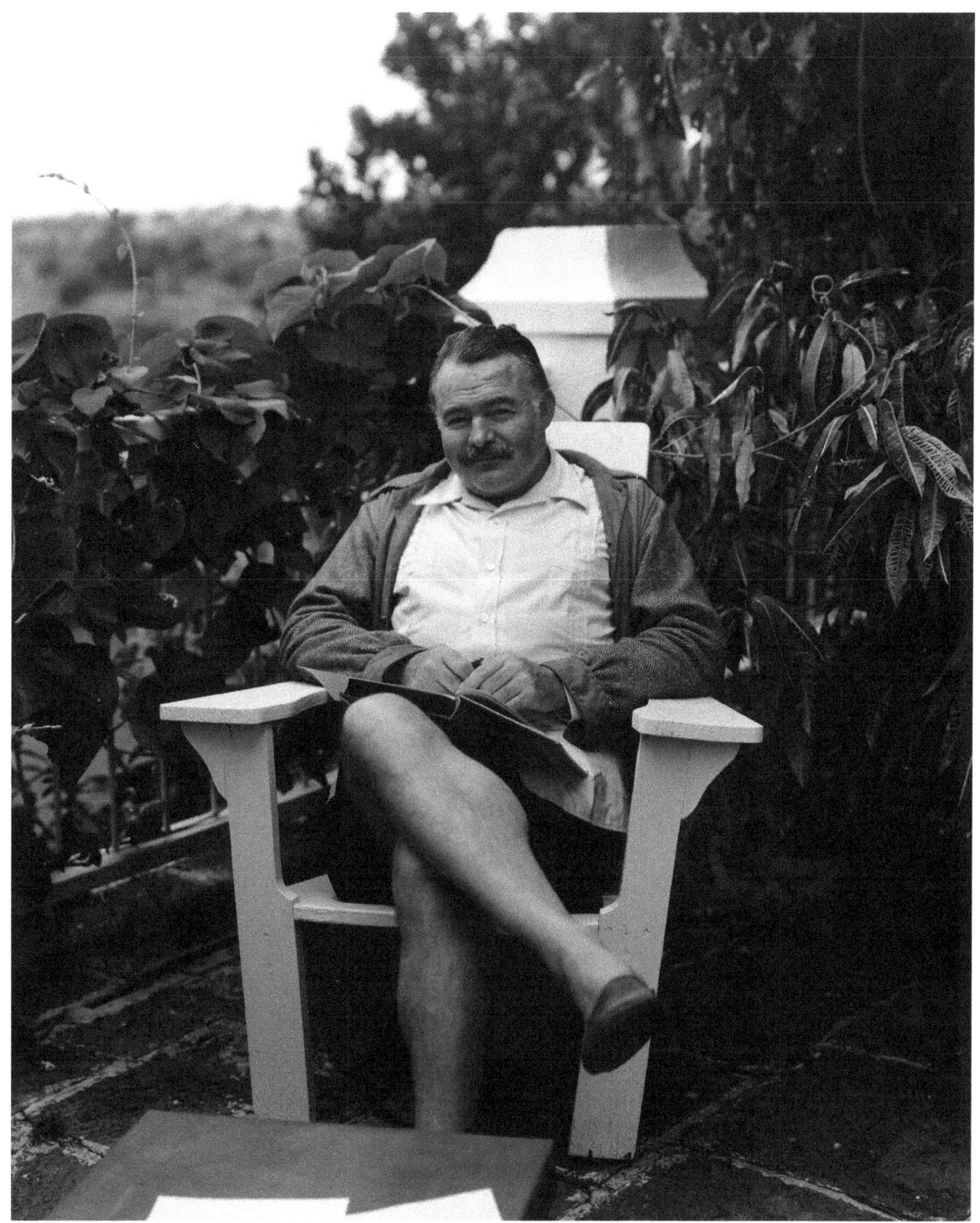

Before guests arrive, Mary gets Ernest to try an olive. Ernest was an extrovert who needed people around him to recharge his battery. When you married Hemingway, you were married to his "mob." The liquor was always at arm's reach between two stuffed easy chairs, where the couple would also read and relax when they were alone. Mary observed that, not including servant salaries, more than half the money spent was on liquor.

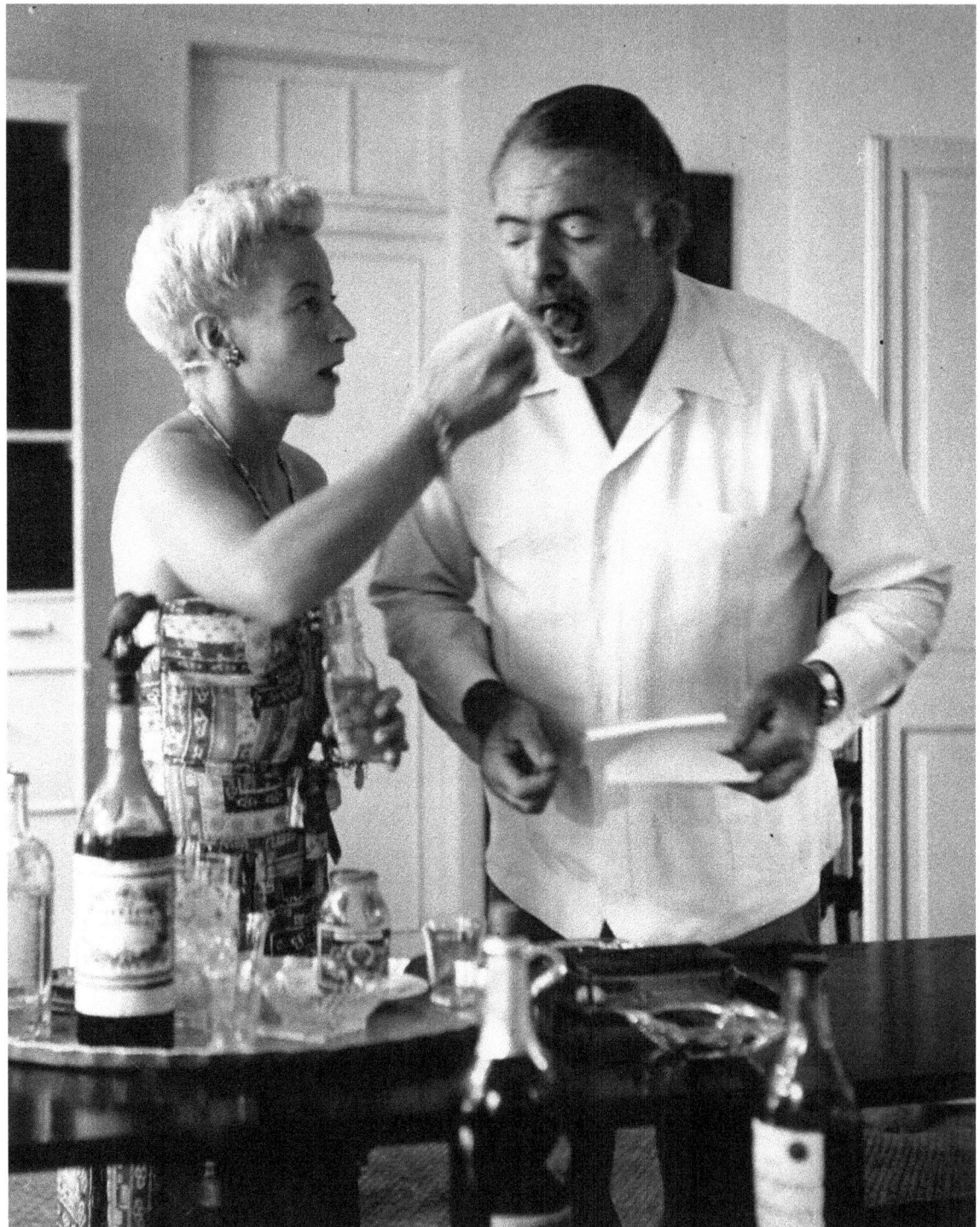

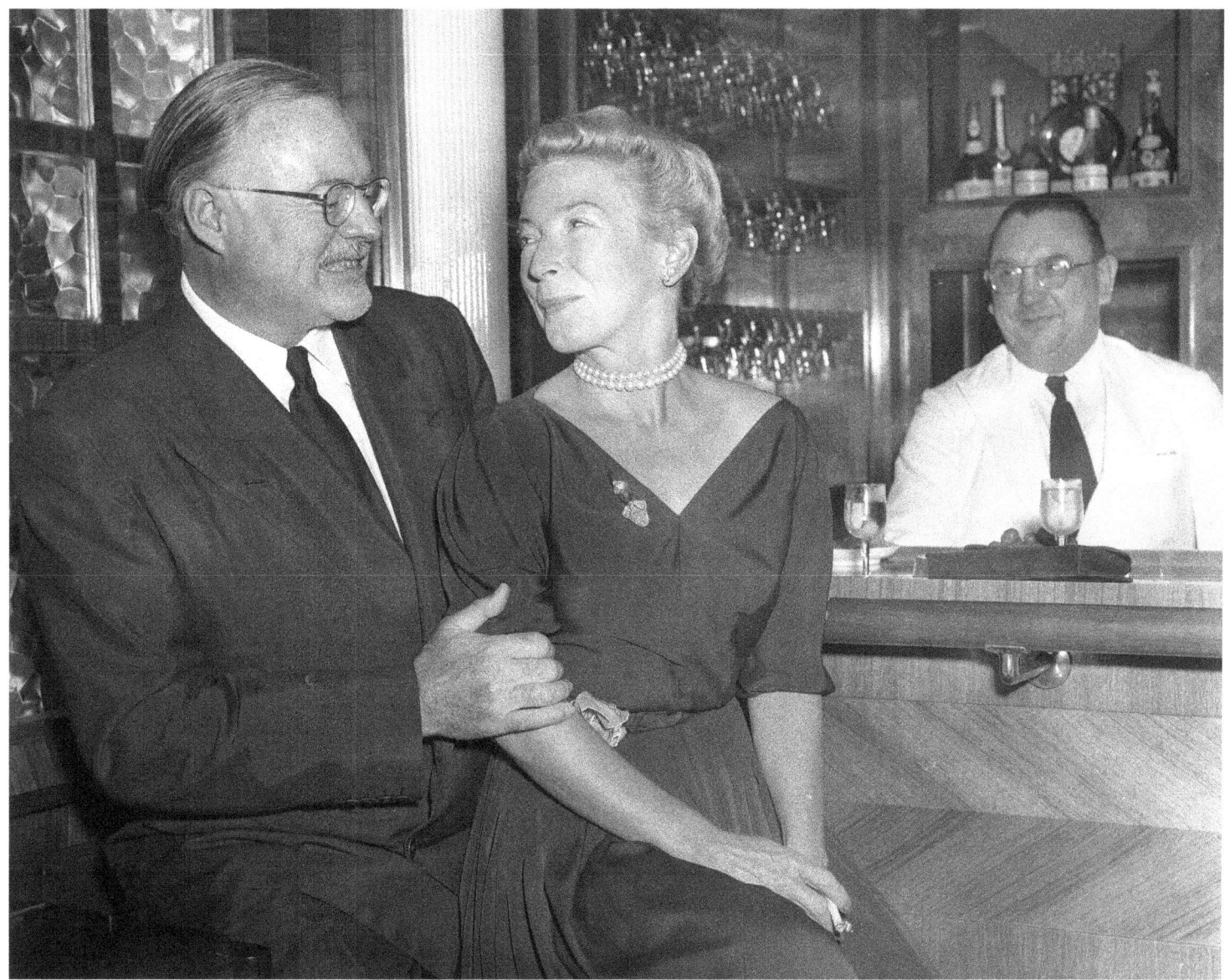

In June 1953, after the award and the windfall $150,000 he got from selling the movie rights to *The Old Man and the Sea,* Hemingway had an urge to revisit old haunts. Aboard the SS *Flandre* en route to Spain, their recent good times have clearly had a positive effect on their relationship. Soon Ernest would take her to Pamplona—his first visit since 1931—and show her some of the sites he'd written about.

Near Burgos, Spain, in July 1953, Ernest enjoys one of the locations described in *For Whom the Bell Tolls* with his chauffeur, Adamo Simon. Ernest's weight was down again, and so was his blood pressure—which had gotten dangerously high the past few years.

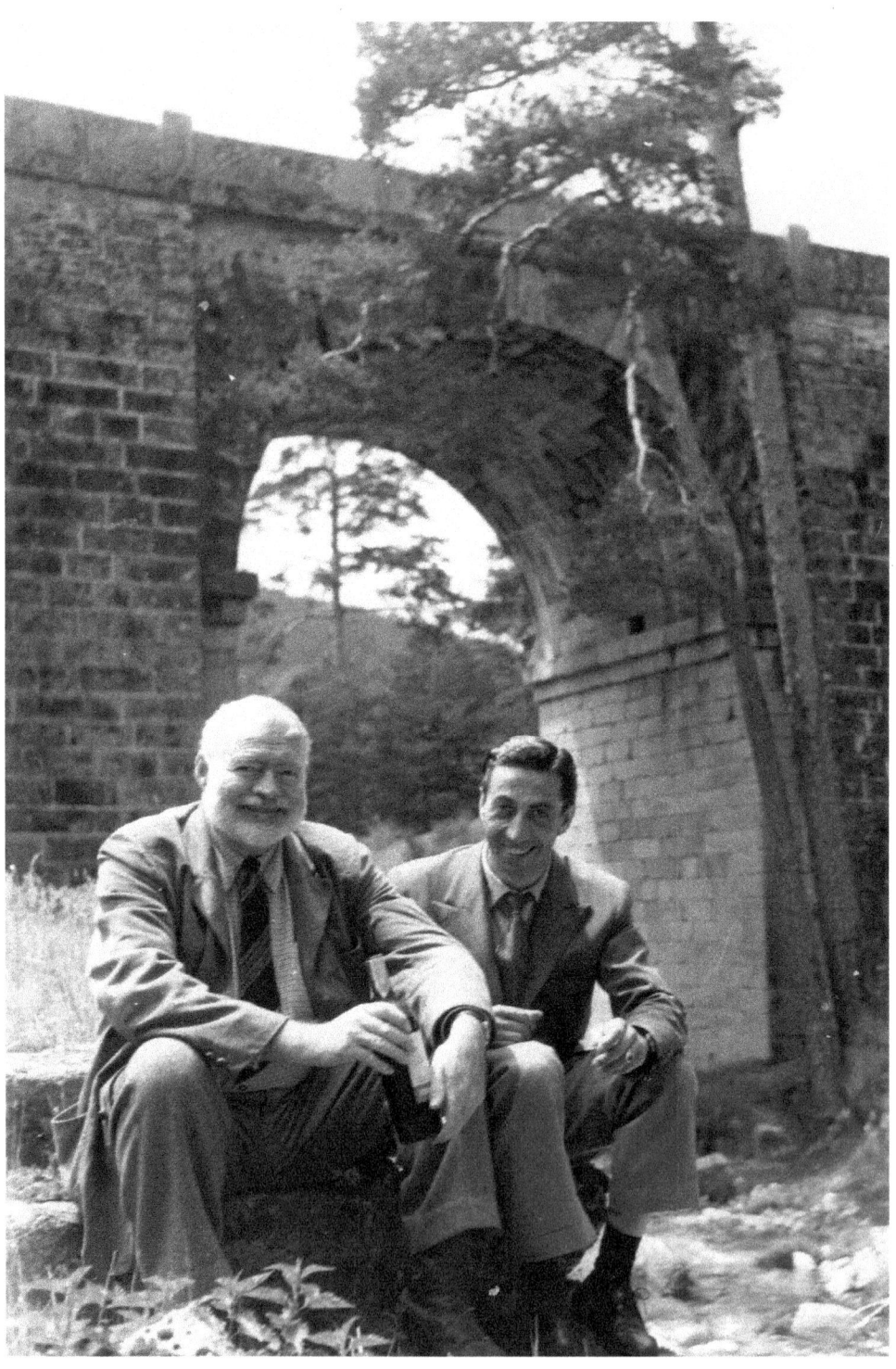

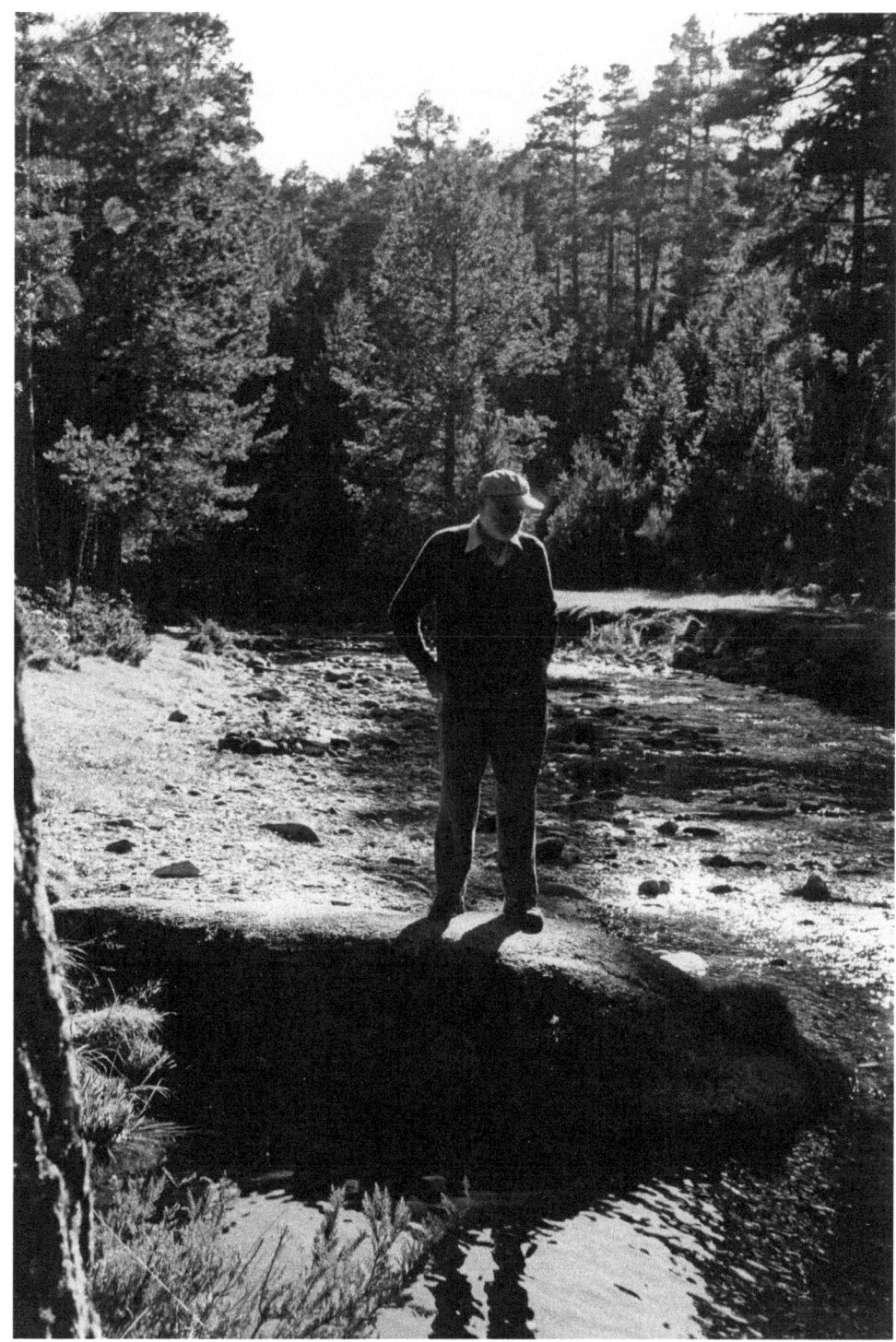

Although there were parts of Spain that still felt as fresh as when he first visited, Hemingway was as much an adventurer as he was a writer. A part of him had to have been thinking his time was quickly passing. Here he was nostalgically revisiting a place, when two months earlier Edmund Hillary and Tenzing Norgay made headlines as the first climbers to reach the top of Mount Everest.

Hemingway's desire to recapture the past and convince himself that he was still virile and capable included plans to take Mary on safari with him to Africa—to re-travel old steps and renew old acquaintances, including his friendship with hunting guide Philip Percival. *Look* magazine came along to chronicle Papa's second safari, with Earl Theisen taking the photographs.

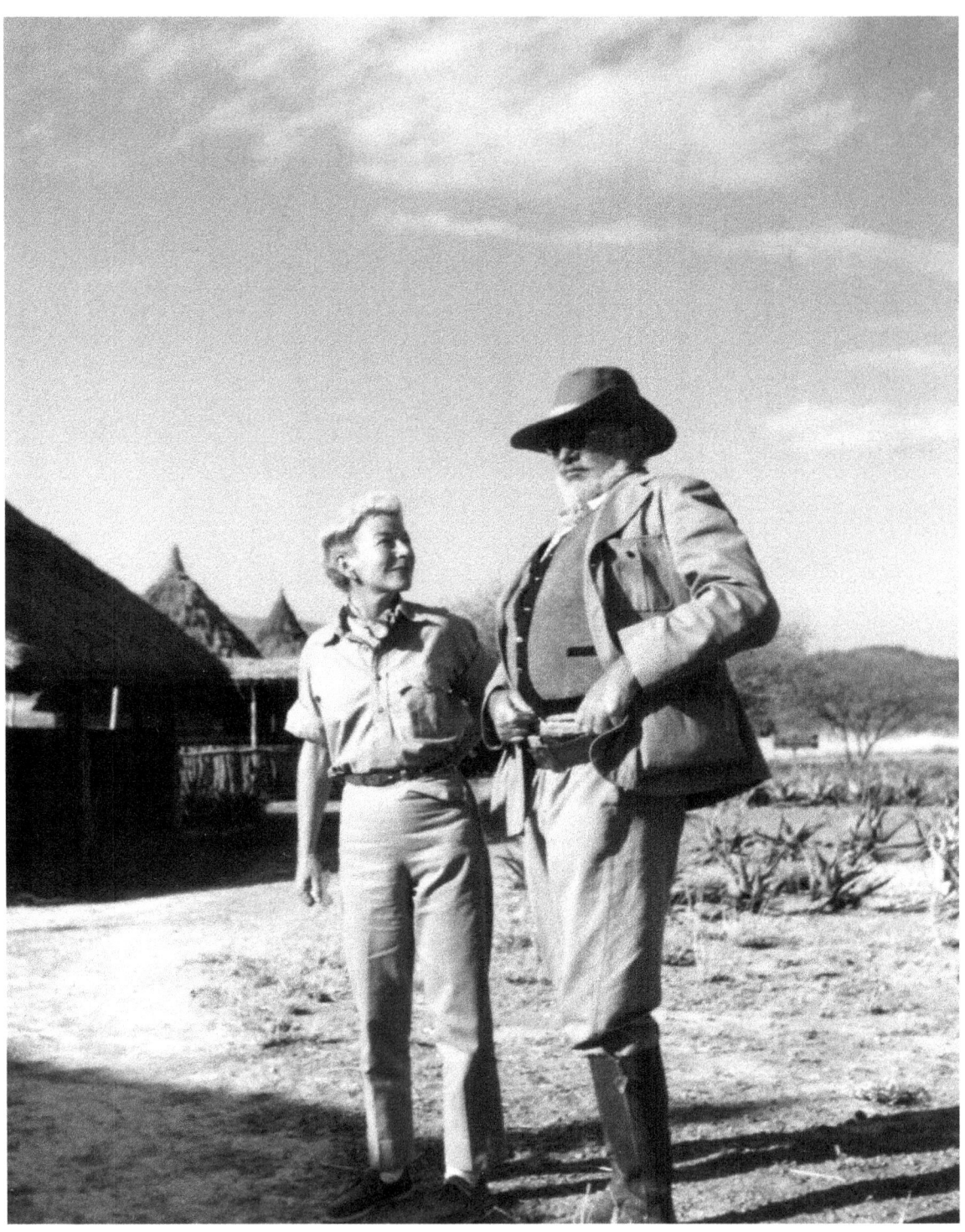

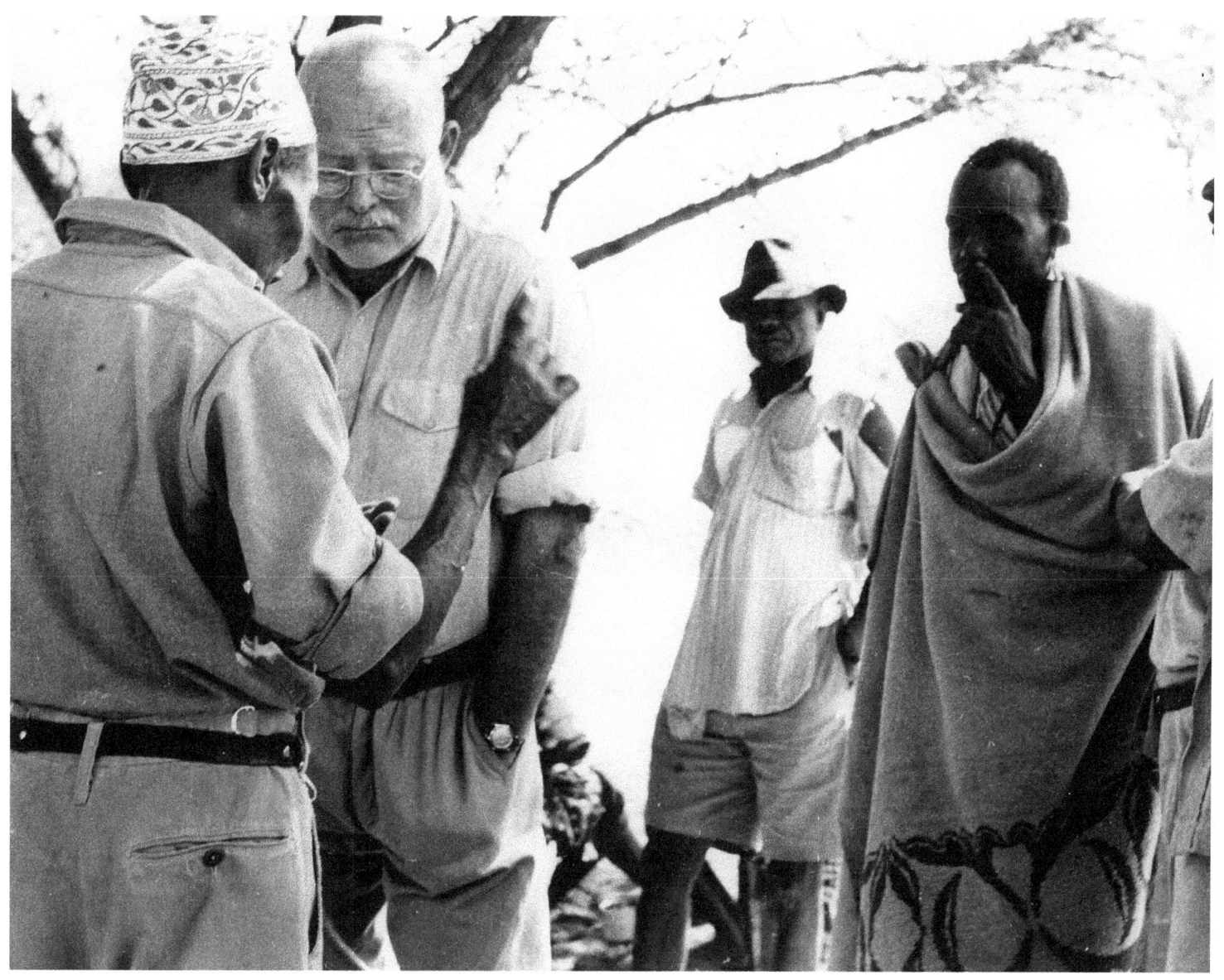

This safari, Hemingway was obsessed with native culture. He learned how to hunt with a Masai spear, dyed his clothes to match Masai colors, and "married" a Wakamba girl named Debba—much to the bemusement of Mary.

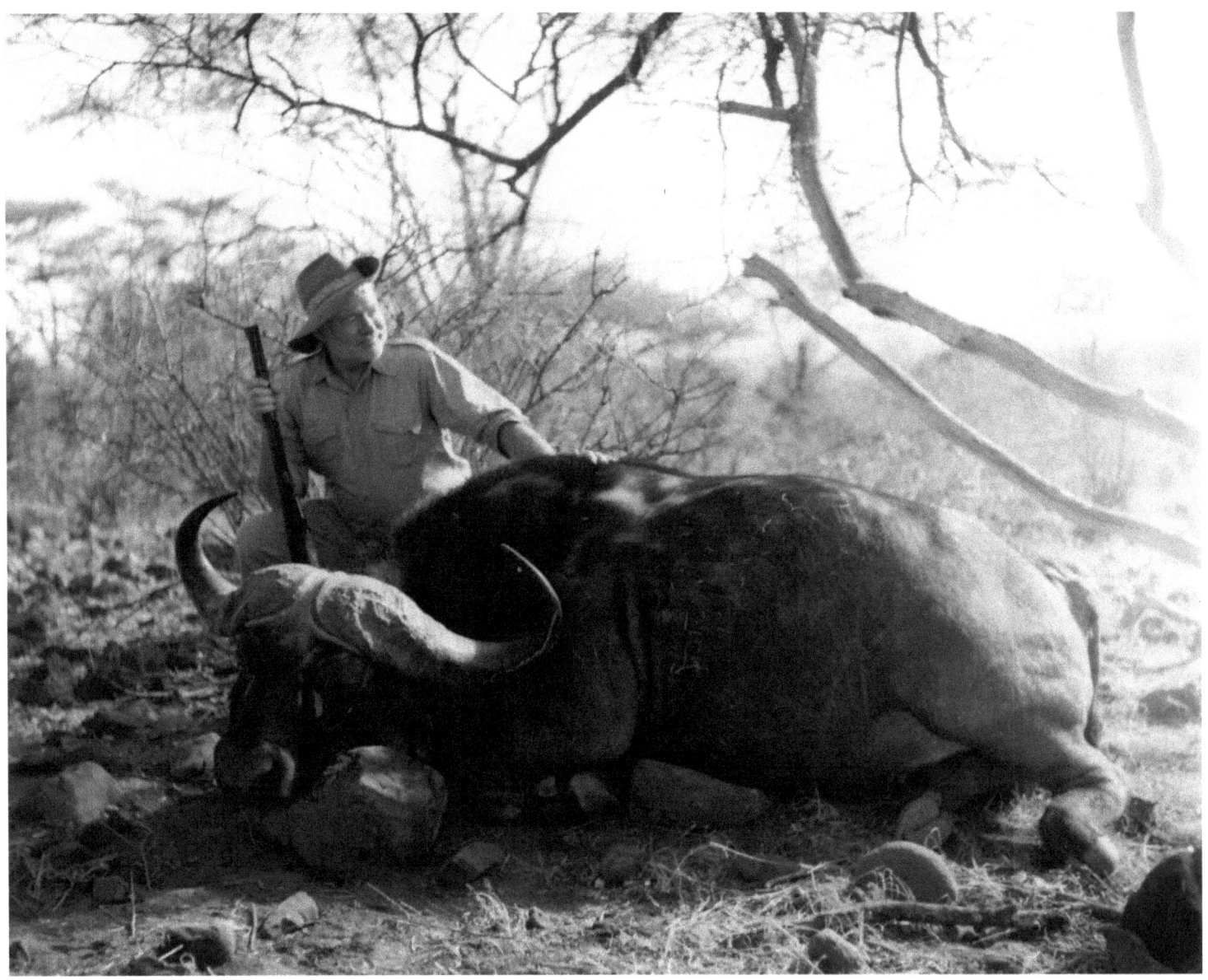

Ernest with a cape buffalo. Later, since it was shot in a Masai-controlled area, he would receive a bill for 15 shillings. He and Mary were also billed for two lions, two oryx, one leopard, two Grant's gazelles, one lesser kudu, six wildebeest, eight Grant's zebra, eleven Thompson's gazelles, two gerenuk, seven impala, and one Coke's hartebeest. And outside Masai land, Ernest would shoot a charging rhino.

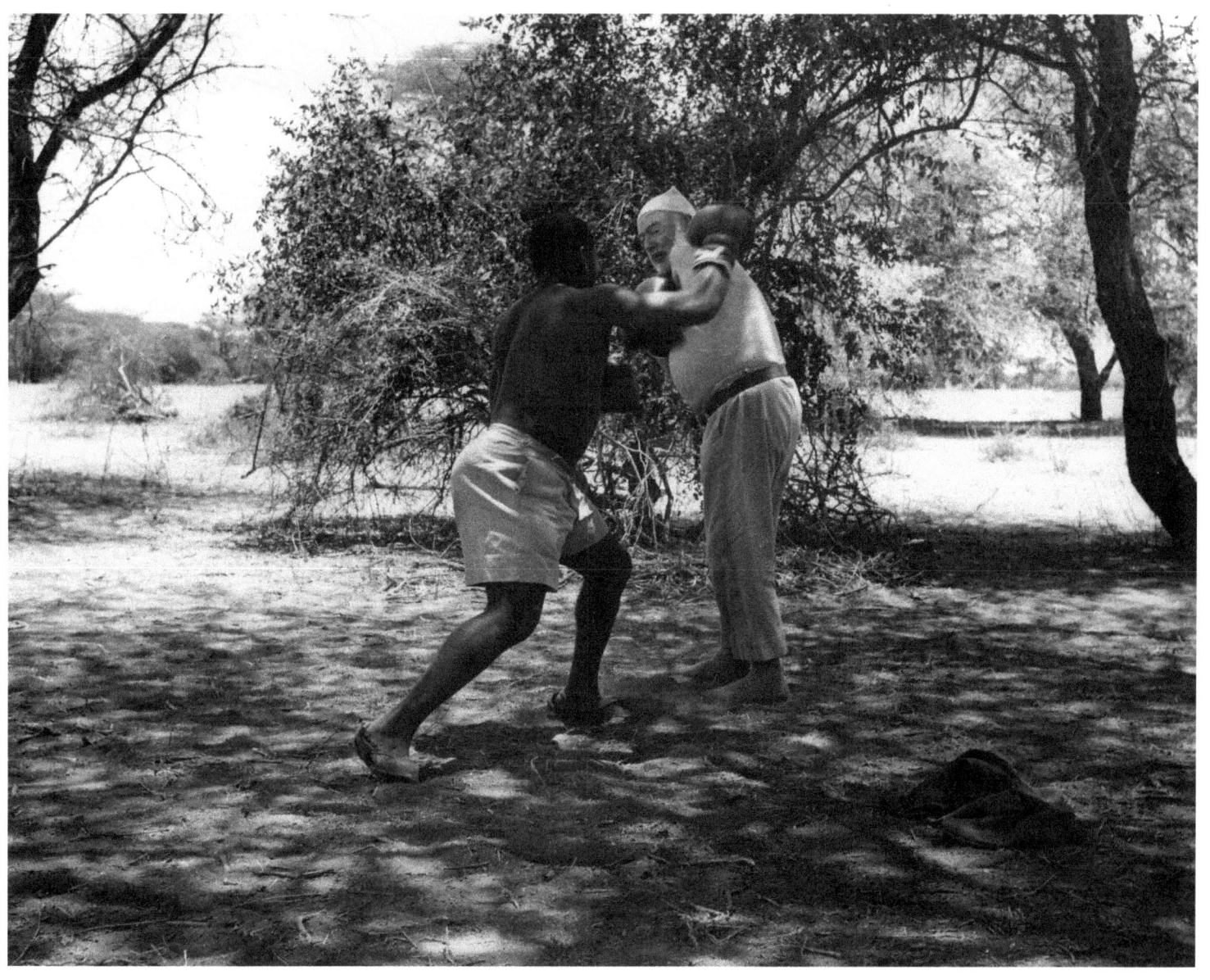

In camp, Ernest tried to make time for a boxing workout. He would write and read on safari, too, maintaining his customary routines. In many respects, the second safari was a rousing success, and Hemingway was working hard to deliver the 15,000-word article that *Look* magazine had contracted him to write, for which he would be paid $10,000 plus expenses.

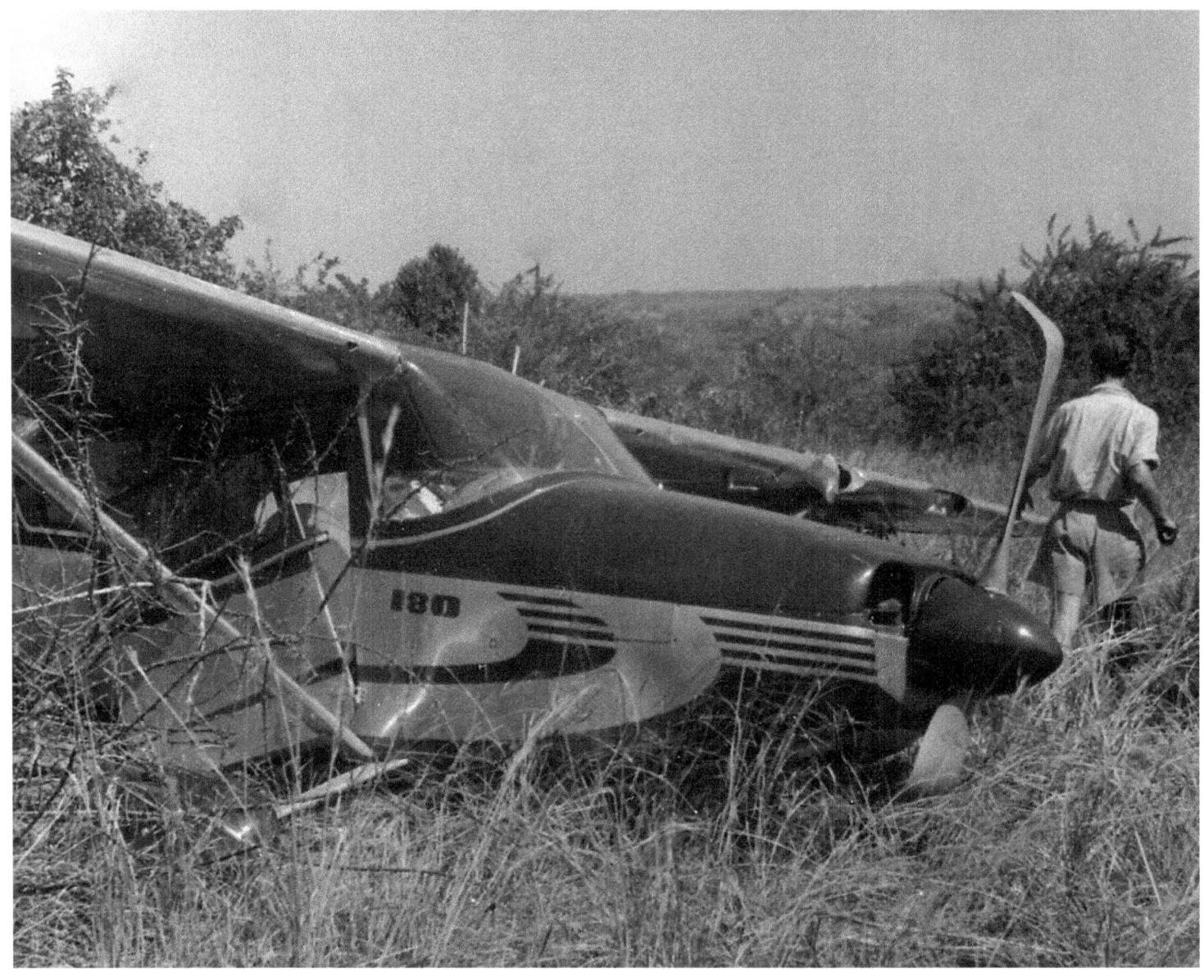

On January 23, the Hemingways took off in a chartered Cessna 180 for a scenic flight over Murchison Falls, but the plane clipped an old telegraph wire and crash-landed (pictured). They were badly shaken. A second plane came to rescue them, but that plane crashed on take-off and caught fire. Mary and the pilot got out through a window that was too small for Ernest, who had to use his head for a battering ram to escape.

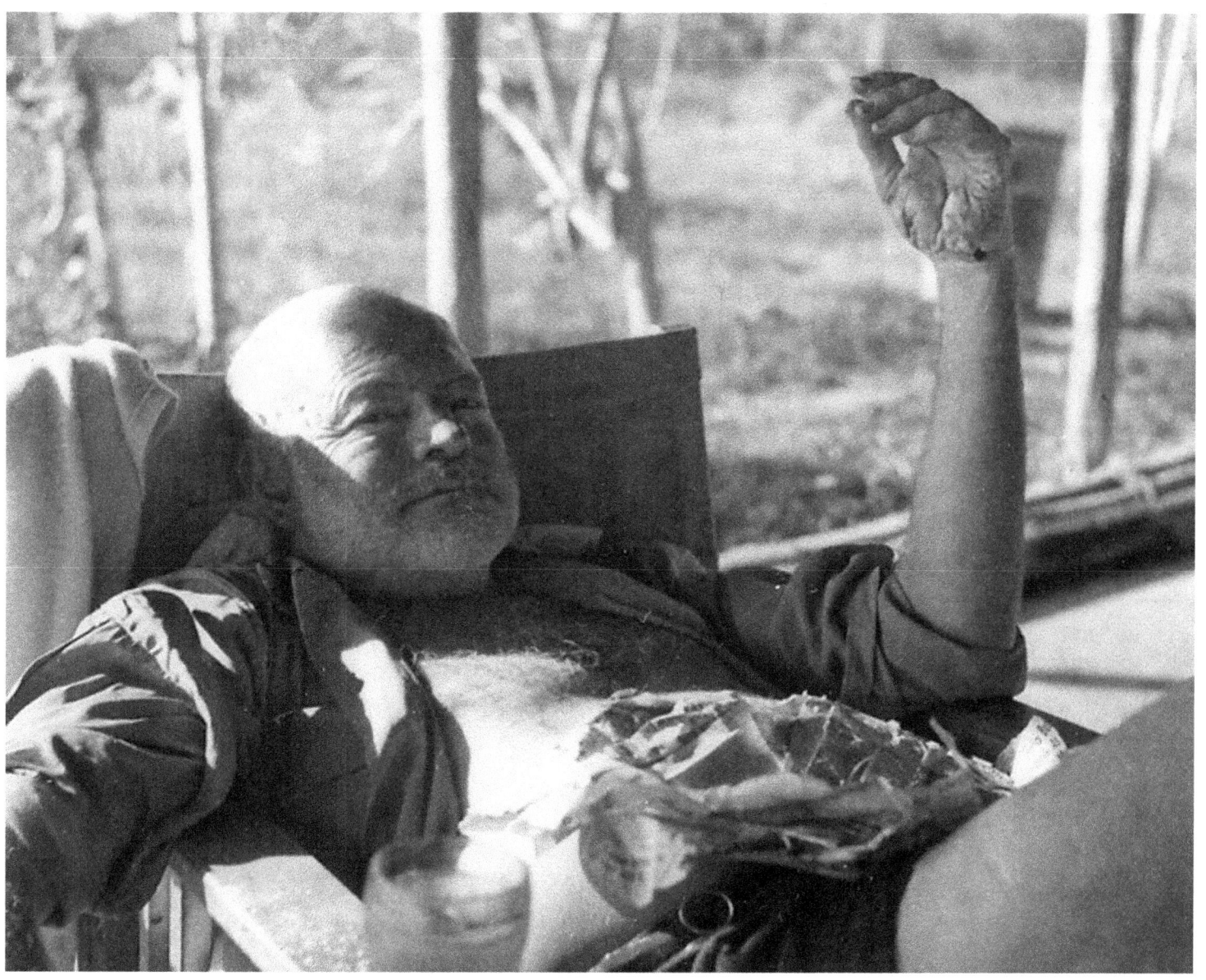

The *New York Herald Tribune* and London's *Daily Mirror* ran Hemingway's obituary on page one, and when the news proved premature the *Post* called him "invulnerable Papa," while *Newsweek* trumpeted, "You can't kill 'Papa.'" But Hemingway had life-threatening injuries, including a concussion, three ruptured organs, loss of vision and hearing, a crushed vertebra, sprains, and burns. Then, still on the mend, he fell into a brush fire at Shimoni camp—where he recuperates in this photograph from late January 1954.

Hemingway bounced back. He wrote while still recovering in Nairobi, then sailed for Venice in March 1954, as planned. Ernest had a soft spot for animals. In Africa, he and Mary adopted a baby Grant's gazelle, and here on a square in Venice he seems wholly at ease playing "statue" for pigeons. At the Finca he had hundreds of them—ironic, considering he killed them for sport at the Club de Cazadores. But Hemingway was a man of many contradictions.

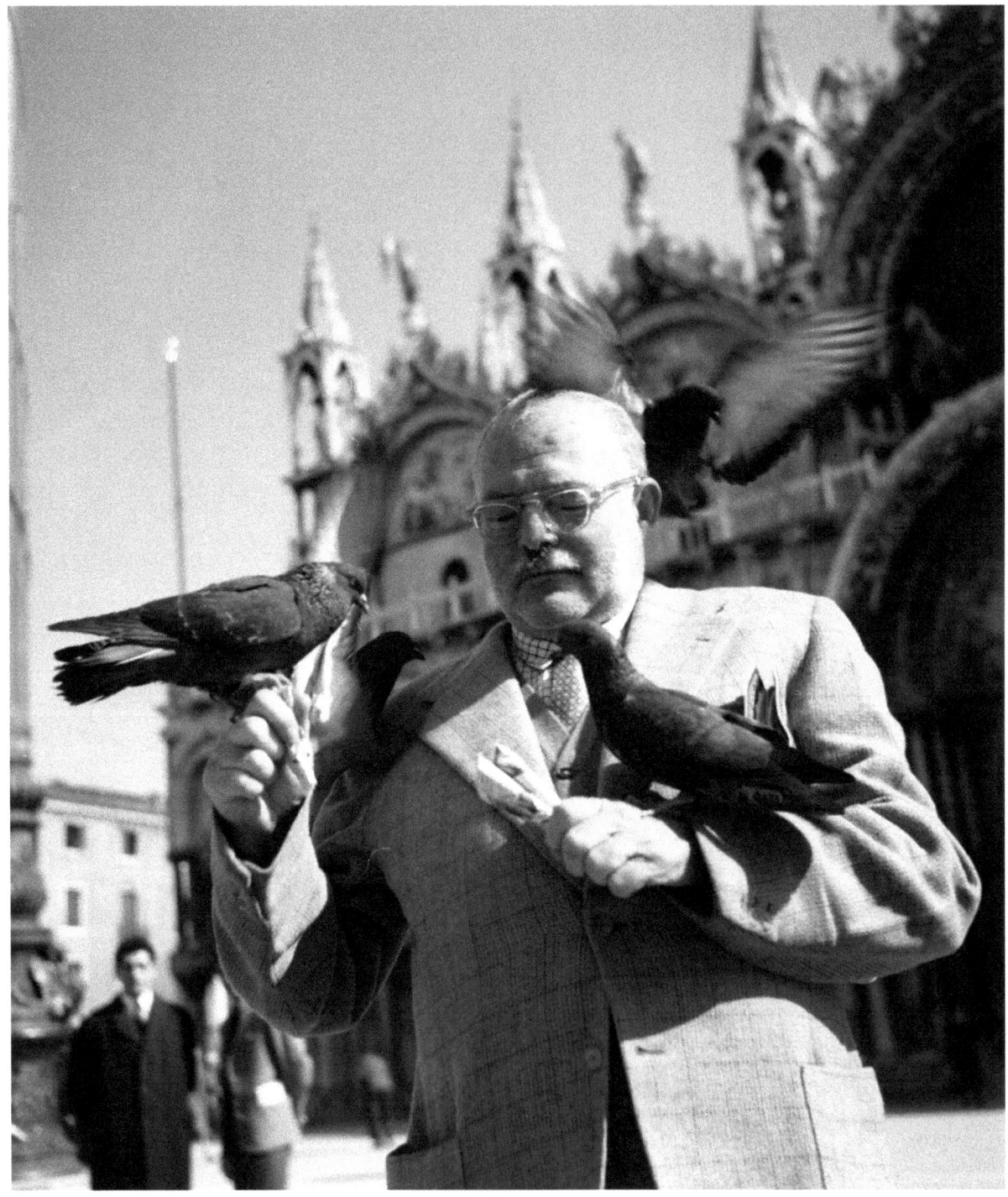

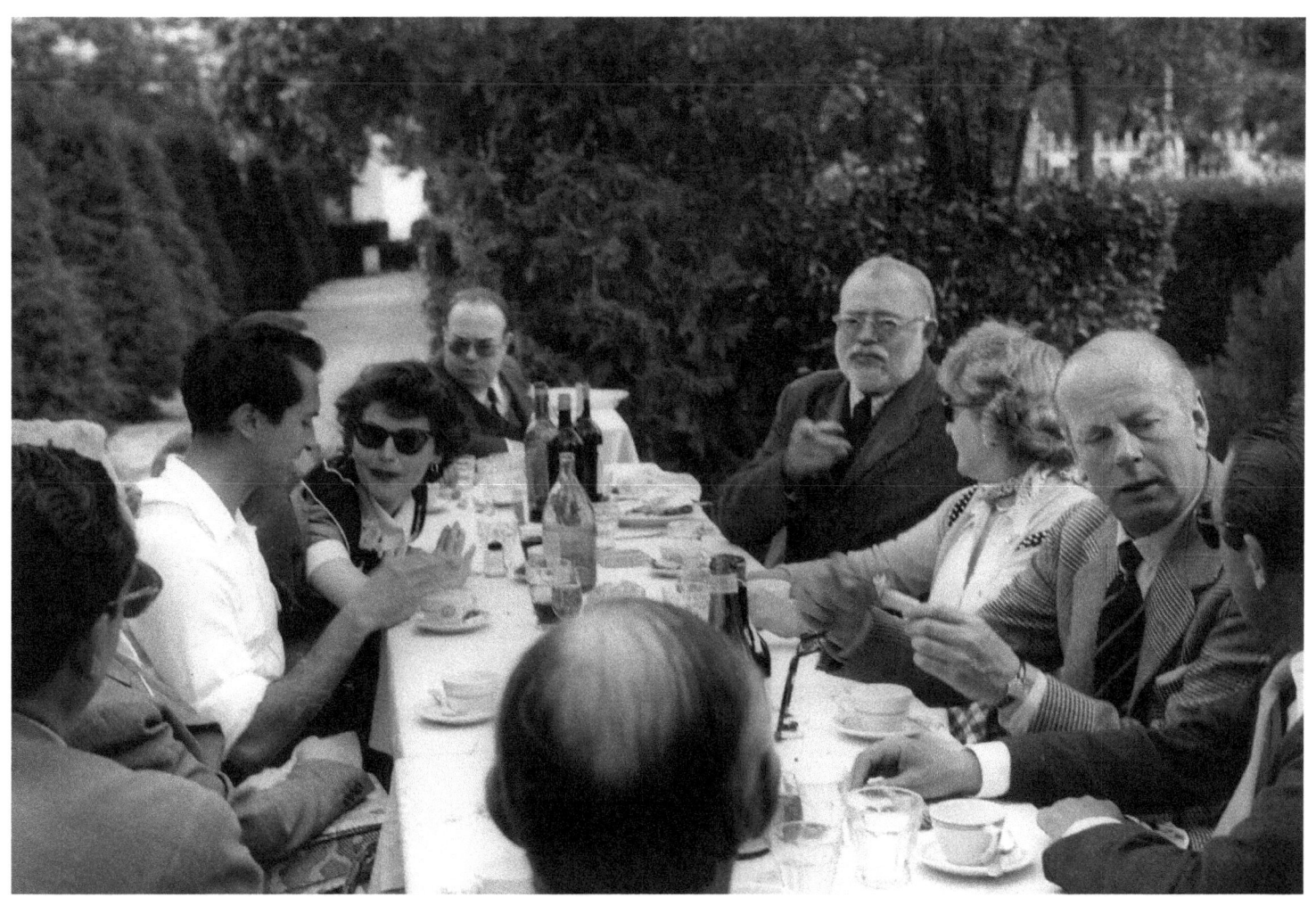

Before long, it was business as usual, with Hemingway attracting an entourage that would tour together, eat together, and drink together. Here, in May 1954, they enjoy an outdoor luncheon on the Costa del Sol, where earlier they visited a bull-breeding ranch at El Escorial and watched bullfighter Luis Miguel Dominguin handle yearlings. The woman in dark glasses talking to Dominguin is actress Ava Gardner.

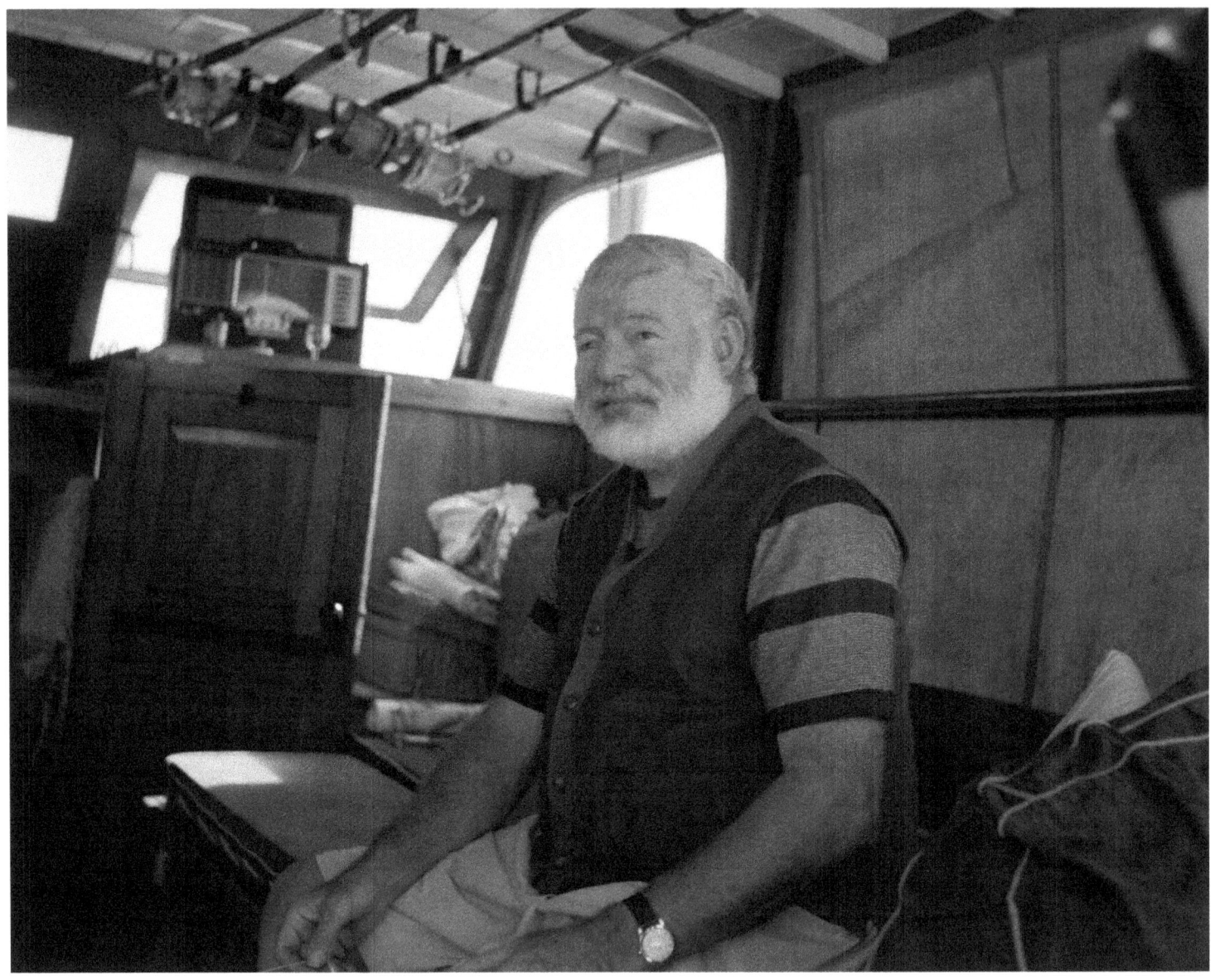

Inside the *Pilar*, an older Papa was content to rest when the younger Ernest Hemingway would have stood. But he could still land a big fish. Hemingway loved grilled fish steaks almost as much as he enjoyed elk steaks, his favorite game meat.

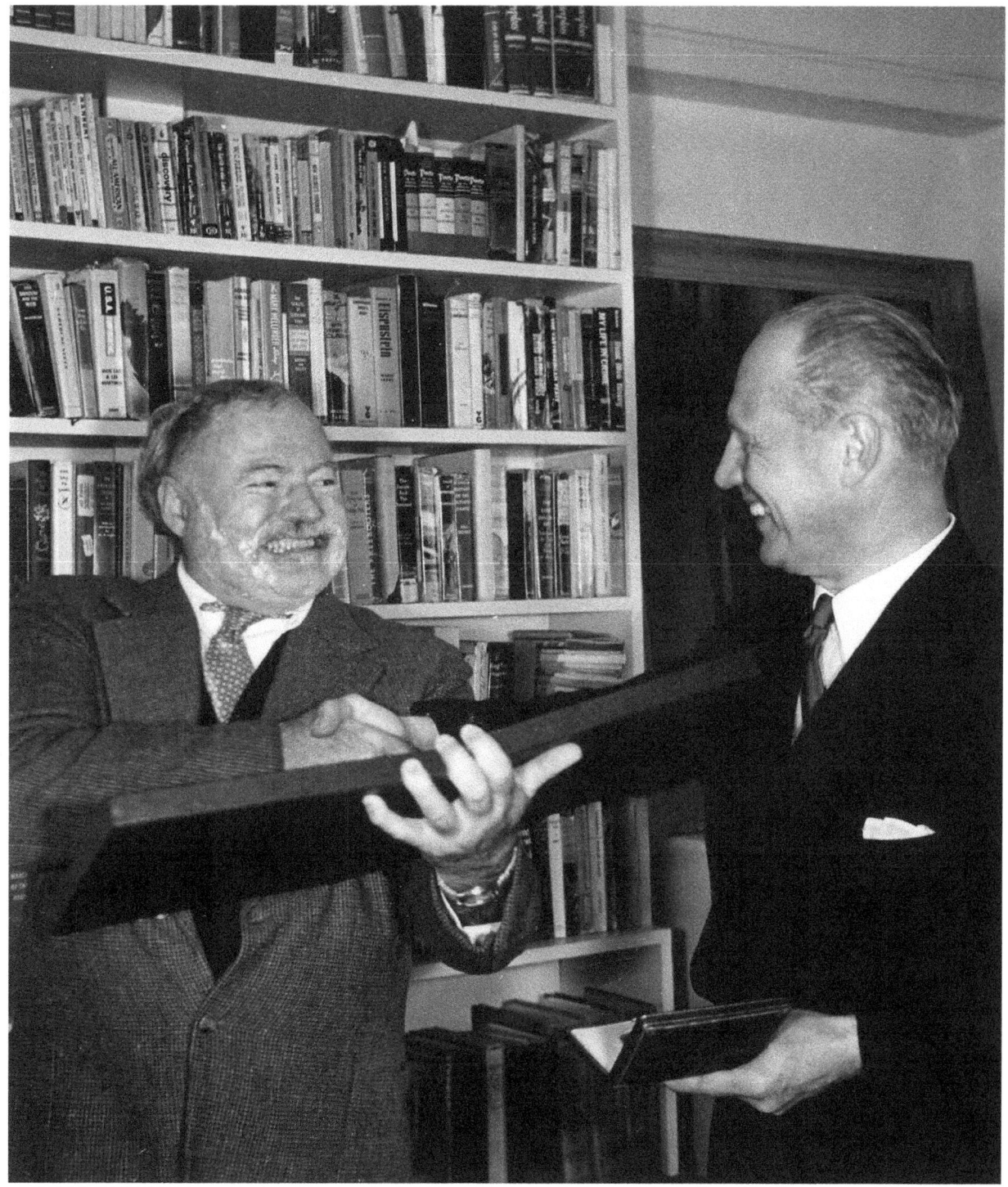

Big news came on October 28, when Hemingway was announced as winner of the Nobel Prize. In December 1954, he received the award at the Finca from the Swedish Ambassador to Cuba. Too frail to accept in Stockholm, his remarks were read by U.S. Ambassador John C. Cabot. Hemingway kept the tax-free $35,000, but dedicated the gold medal to the Cuban people and presented it to the Virgen de Cobre, Cuba's national saint.

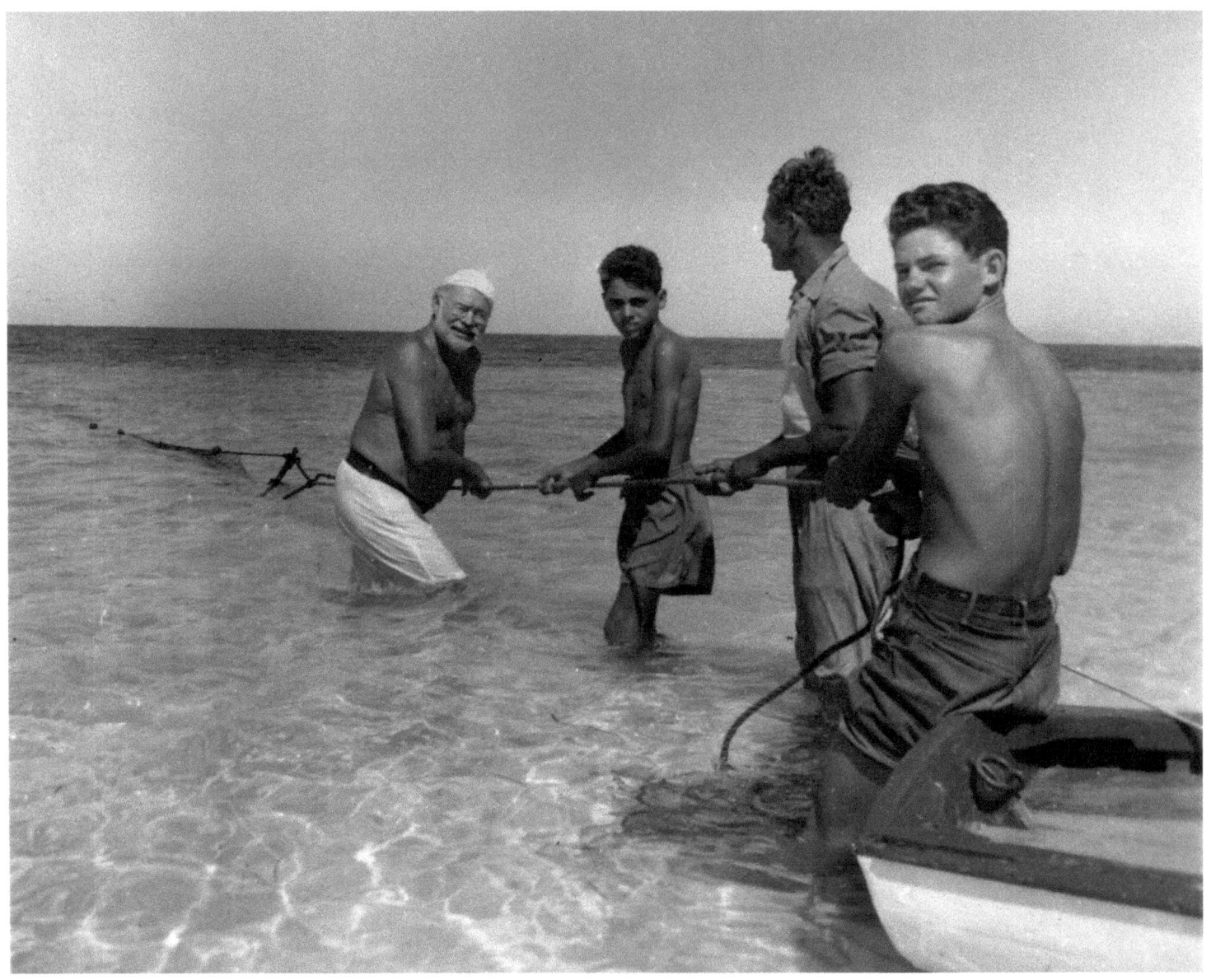

Cojímar, around 1955. Despite his international celebrity, Ernest still relished being an insider and loved spending time with everyday people. He admired the local fishermen, many of whom still had to row out to try for the big fish. Here he helps young Cubans haul in their net, all hoping it will contain enough bait fish to use for their marlin fishing.

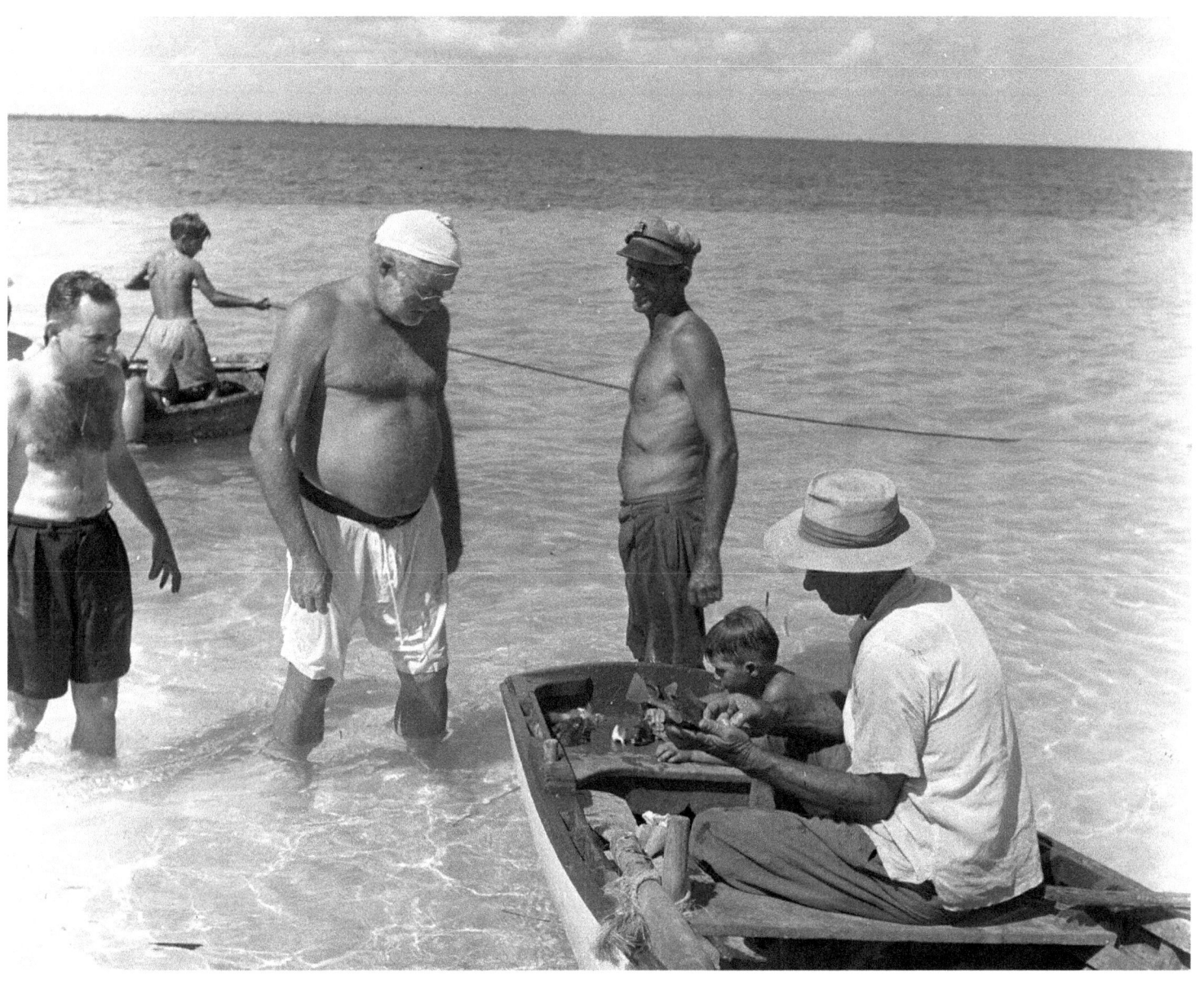

Checking the catch. Hemingway wasn't just a writer who was constantly looking for material. He had a great curiosity and he was able to empathize with people and put himself in their shoes—two qualities at least as important as the "built-in, shock-proof shit detector" he felt all writers needed (and which he himself lacked late in life).

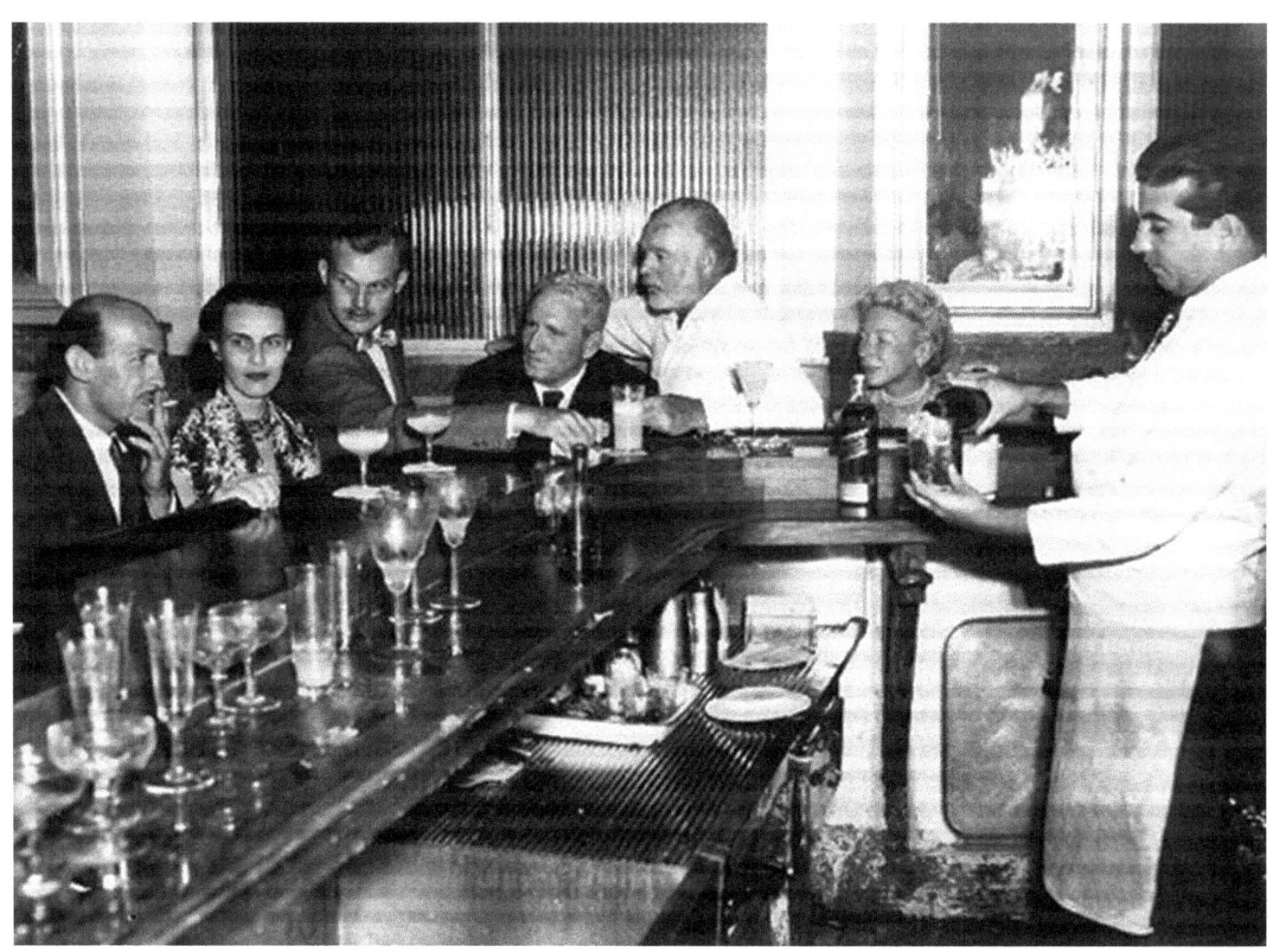

At the Floridita in Havana, the end of the bar was known as "Hemingway's corner," where the writer would be joined by his "mob" and any visitors wanting to pay their respects. The place of honor was always to Hemingway's right, and today it was Spencer Tracy, who in 1955 was in Havana for the start of the filming of *The Old Man and the Sea*. Far left is Roberto Herrera, Hemingway's longtime secretary and one of his "Crook Factory" crew members.

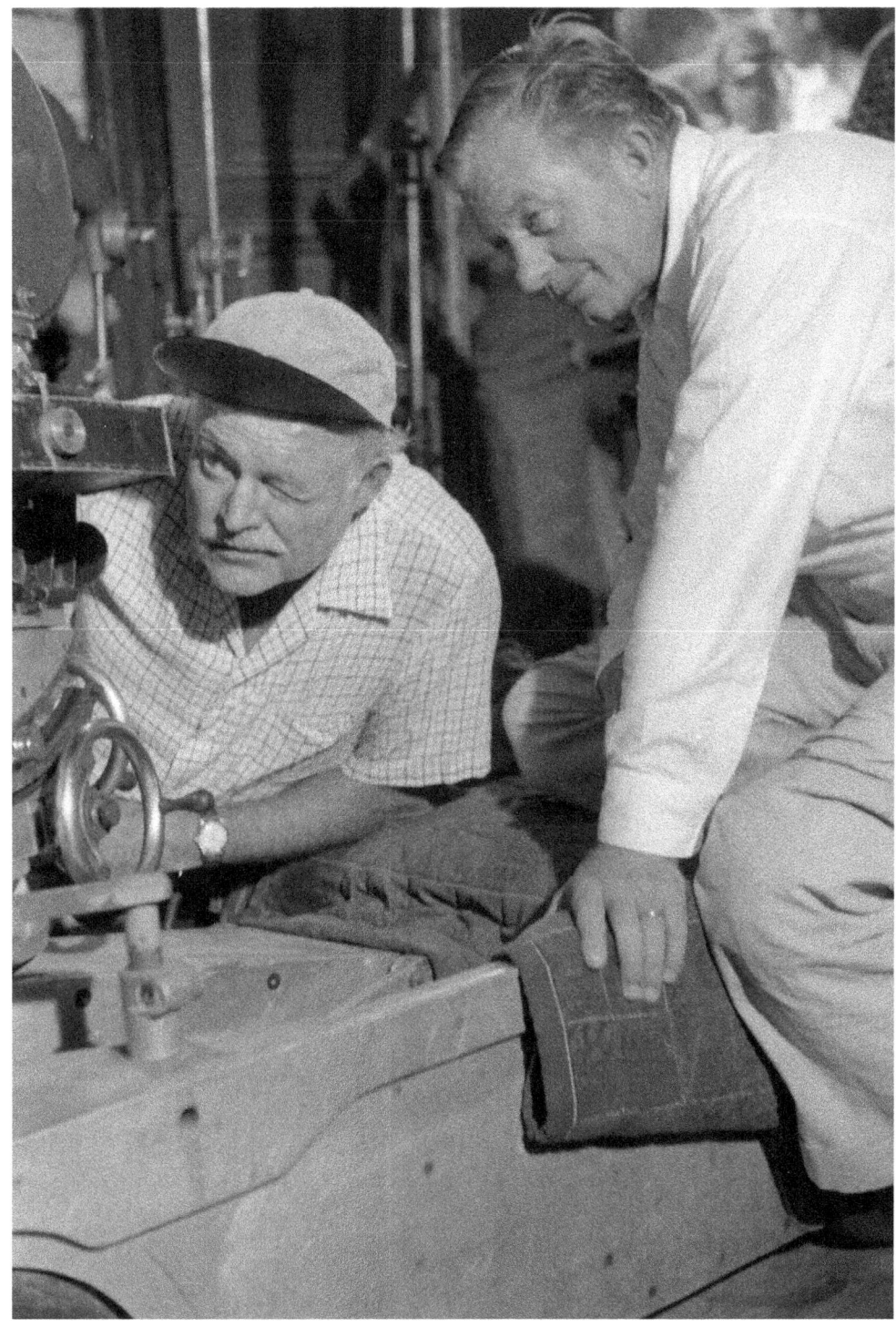

As with *For Whom the Bell Tolls*, Hemingway received $150,000 for the movie rights to *The Old Man and the Sea*, for which he was also asked to serve as technical advisor. The movie was partially filmed in Cojímar Bay, Havana, and Boca de Jaruco, Cuba. Here, in February or March 1956, Hemingway visits the set. Though Tracy was a teetotaler, Hemingway liked him well enough at first, but afterward complained he looked like a rich, fat, white actor instead of a poor Cuban fisherman.

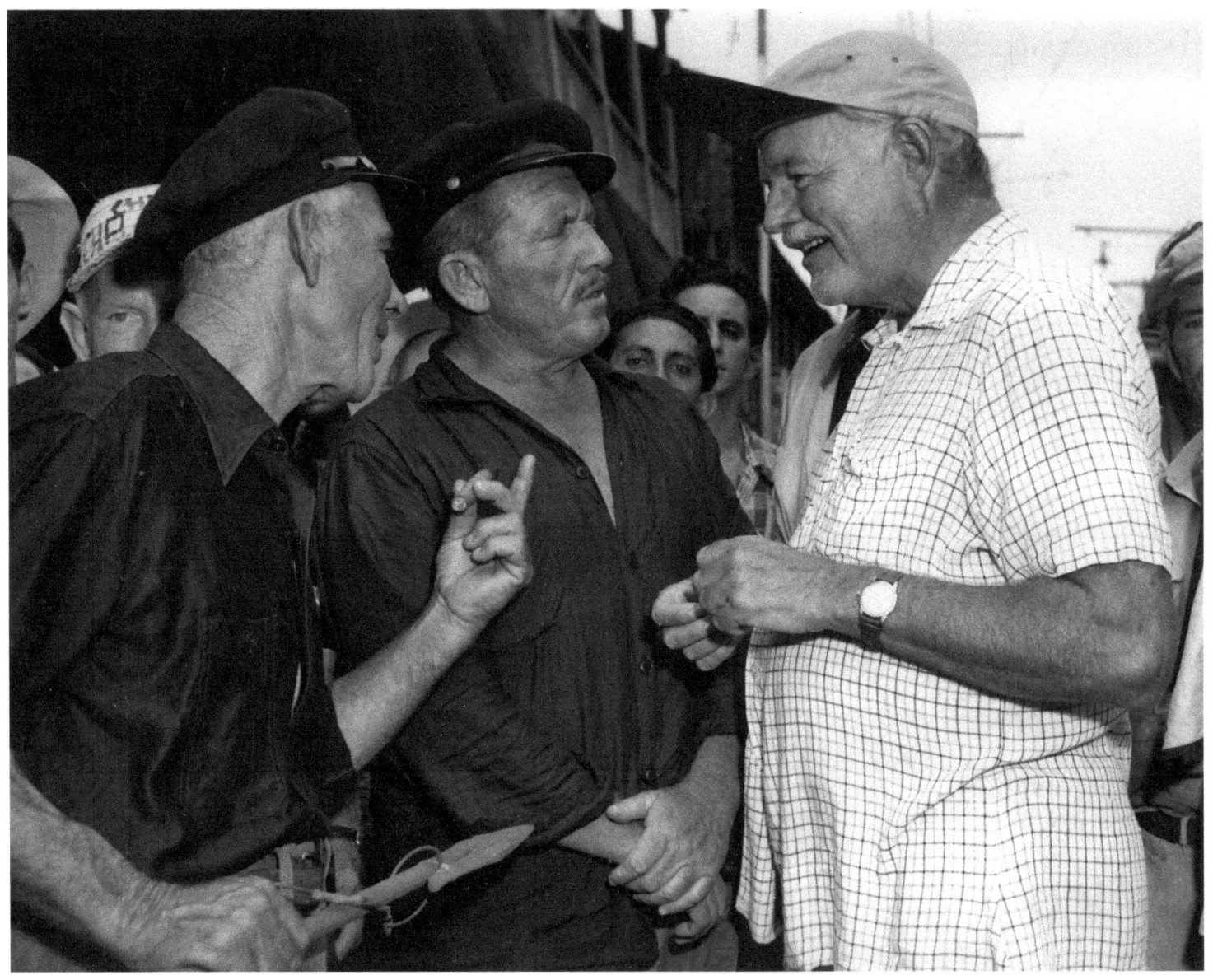

Trying to get a word in edgewise to Spencer Tracy's right is Gregorio Fuentes, who took over as mate of the *Pilar* after Carlos Gutiérrez was hired away while Hemingway covered the war in Spain. Hemingway bequeathed the boat to Fuentes, who, with Gutiérrez, was one of the models for Santiago. Because Fuentes thought Papa and the *Pilar* belonged to all Cubans (and ownership of property was not allowed in a socialist system), he donated it to the government.

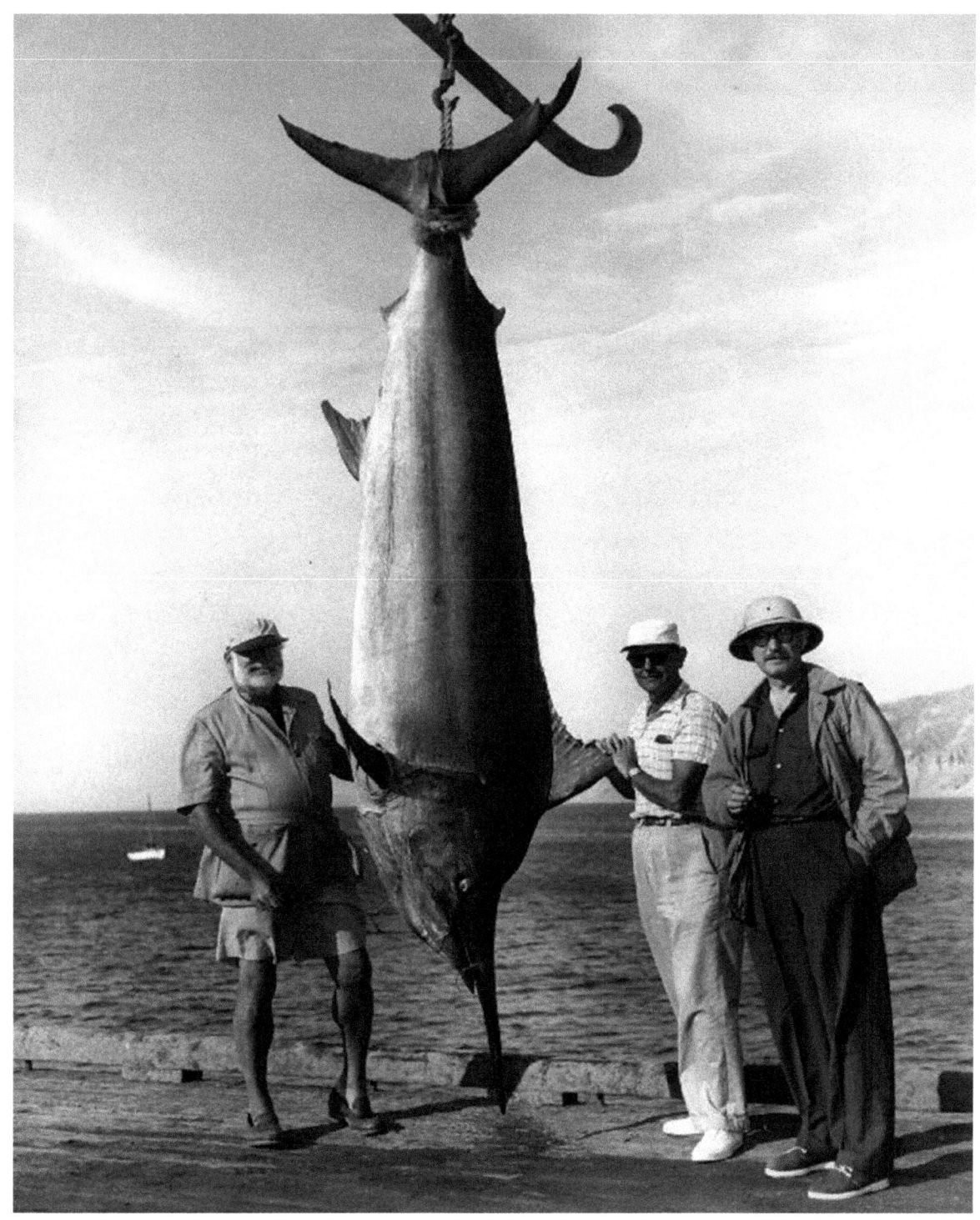

In April 1956 Hemingway went with top Cuban fisherman Elicio Argüelles and outdoorsman Ellis Briggs to Cabo Blanco, Peru. Hemingway had been enlisted to catch a marlin so director John Sturges could get footage for the film, but none of the fish he caught in the Gulf were big enough. In Peru, Hemingway caught a 680-pounder and let it jump for the camera. But to Hemingway's annoyance, Sturges finally chose to use a rubber marlin for close-ups and stock footage of marlin fishing.

The safari and fishing whittled pounds away, and Hemingway was down to 217. Just as he kept track of his daily word count, Hemingway kept a scale in his bathroom at the Finca and wrote his daily weight on the wall in pencil. Here on the flying bridge of the *Pilar* he looks healthy enough, but years of hard drinking, two plane crashes, five automobile accidents, and hereditary medical conditions have taken a toll.

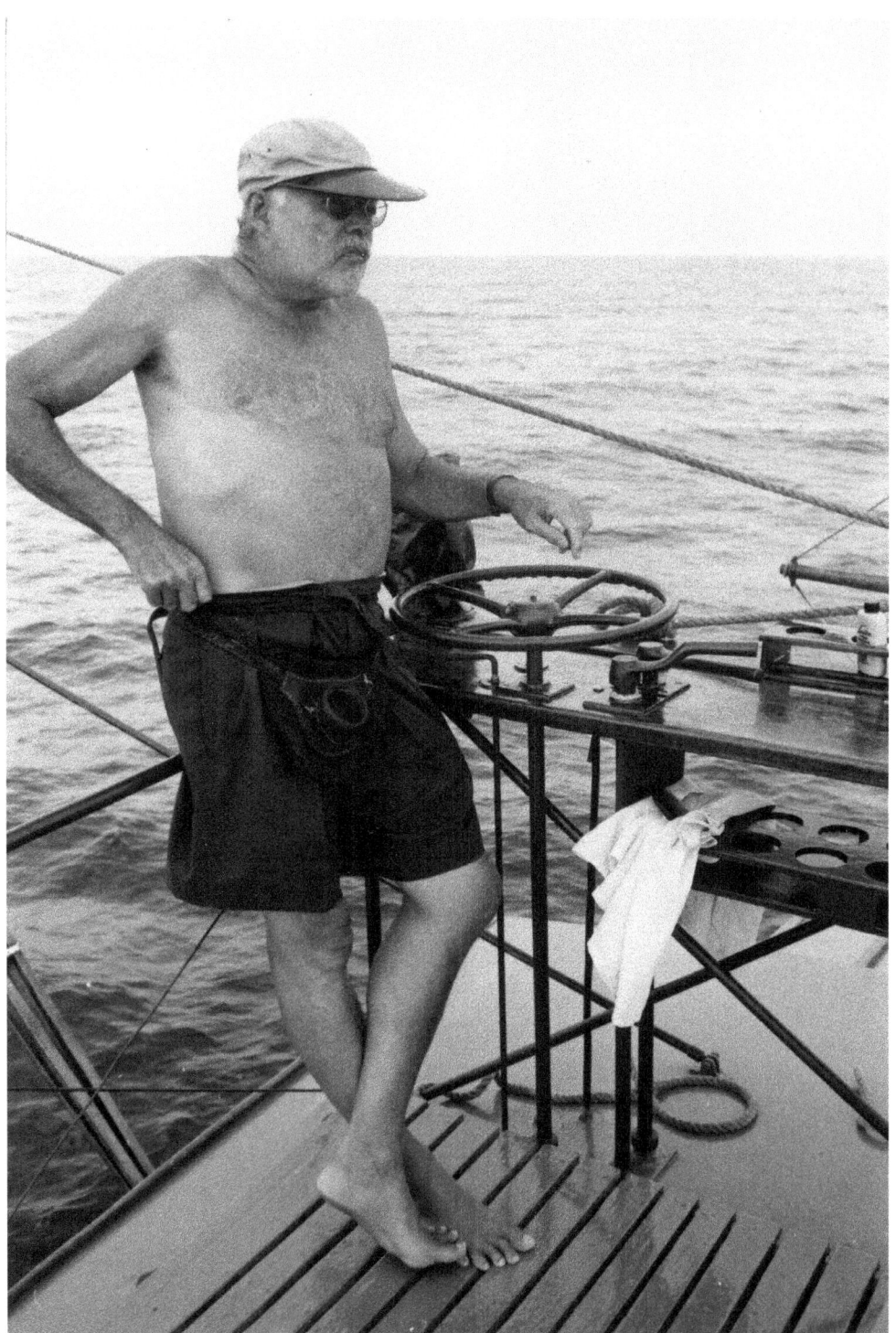

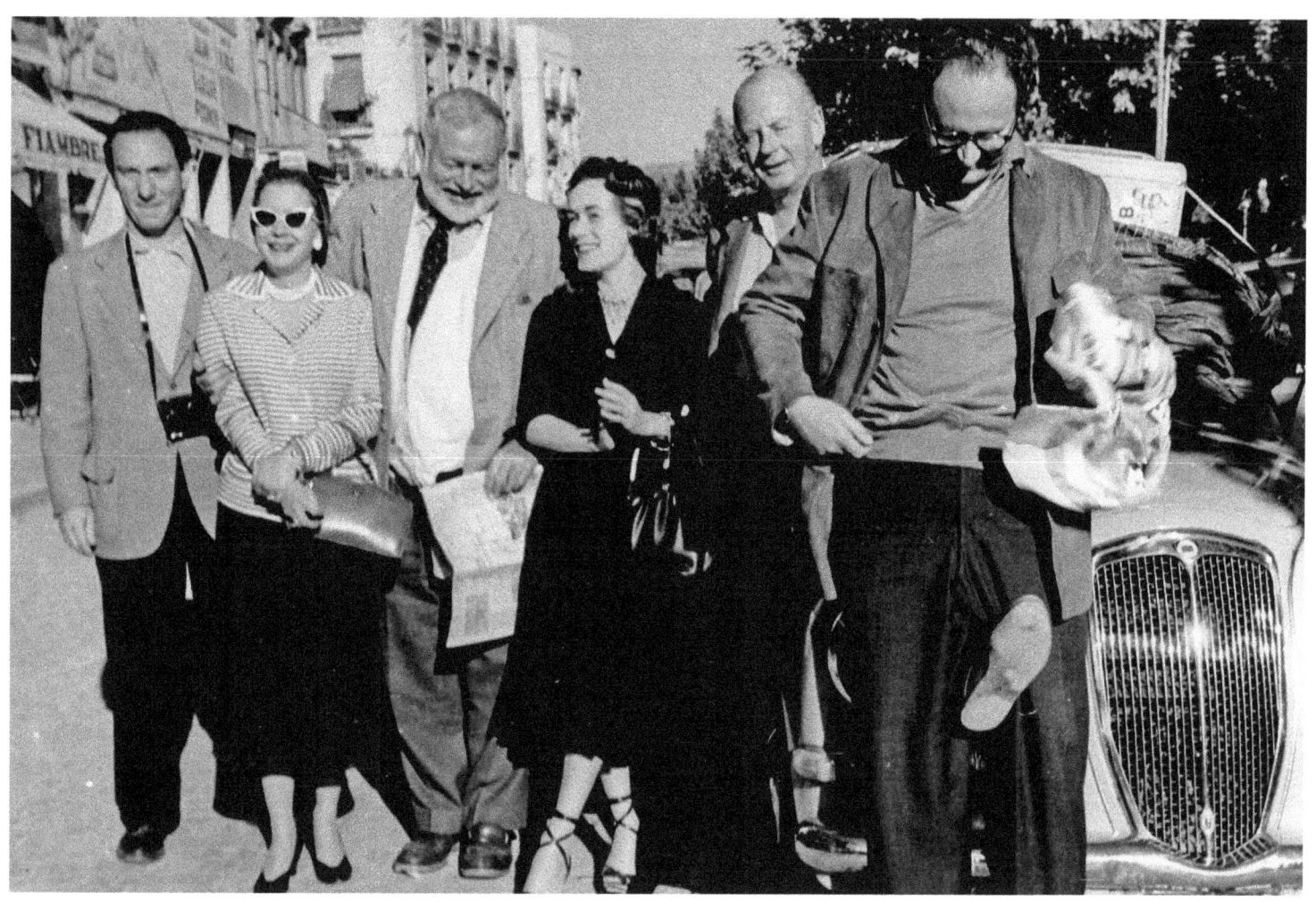

In the fifties, journalist A. E. Hotchner (left) became part of Hemingway's inner circle. "Hotch" had come to Cuba in 1949 to write a profile for *Cosmopolitan,* but soon afterward persuaded Cosmo to pay Hemingway $15,000 to write his own article. Instead, Hemingway would use the opportunity to get the magazine to publish the serialized version of *Across the River and Into the Trees.* Here, in Calatayud, Spain, sometime in October 1956, the group du jour has a laugh after lunch.

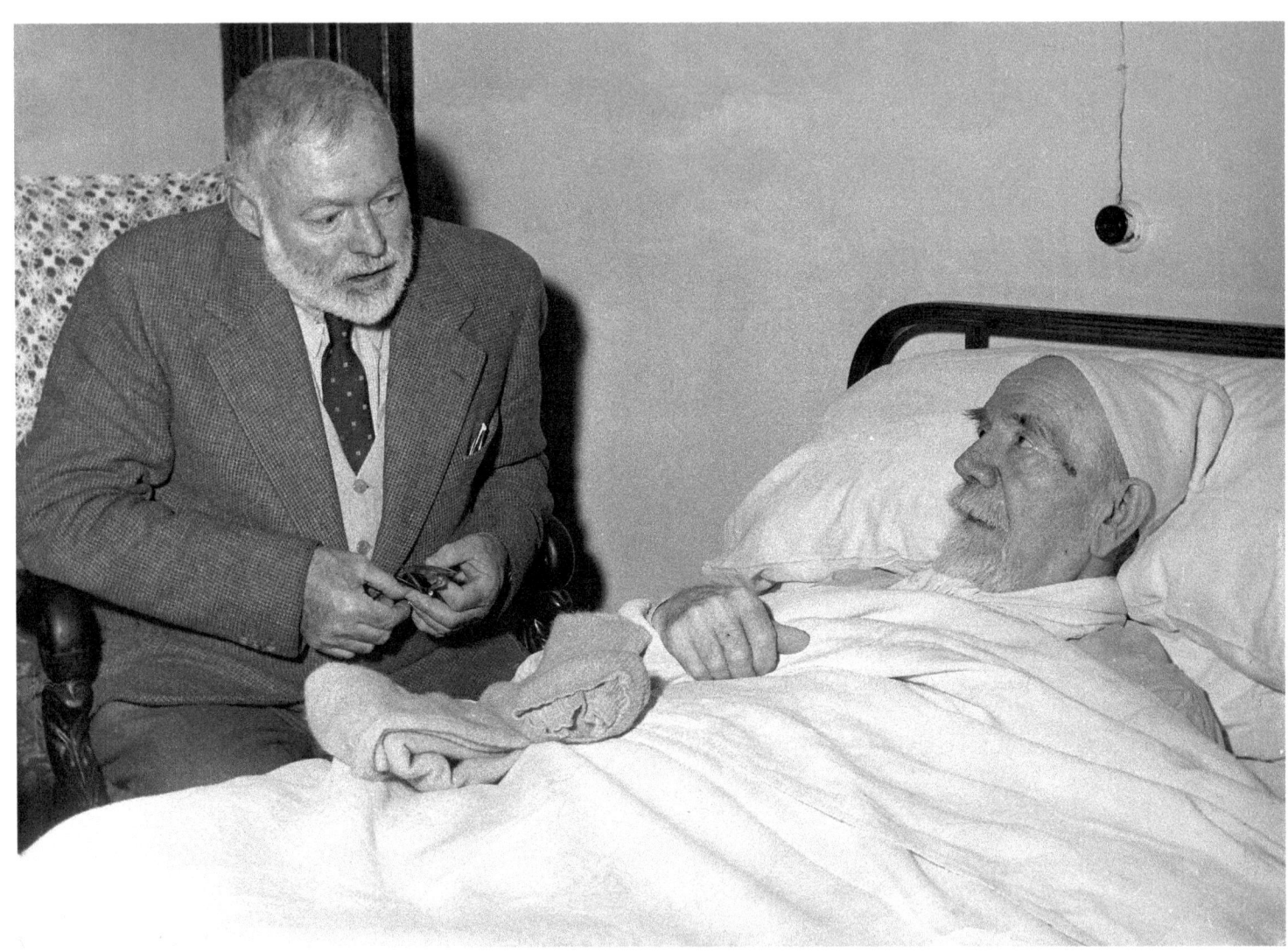

While in Spain, Hemingway attended bullfights as usual, but upon learning that Basque writer Pío Baroja y Nessi was on his deathbed, Ernest donned a suit and paid his respects, bringing with him a bottle of Scotch and generous words. Ernest told Baroja that he was the one who should have won the Nobel prize. Later, he was among the handful of mourners at Baroja's funeral.

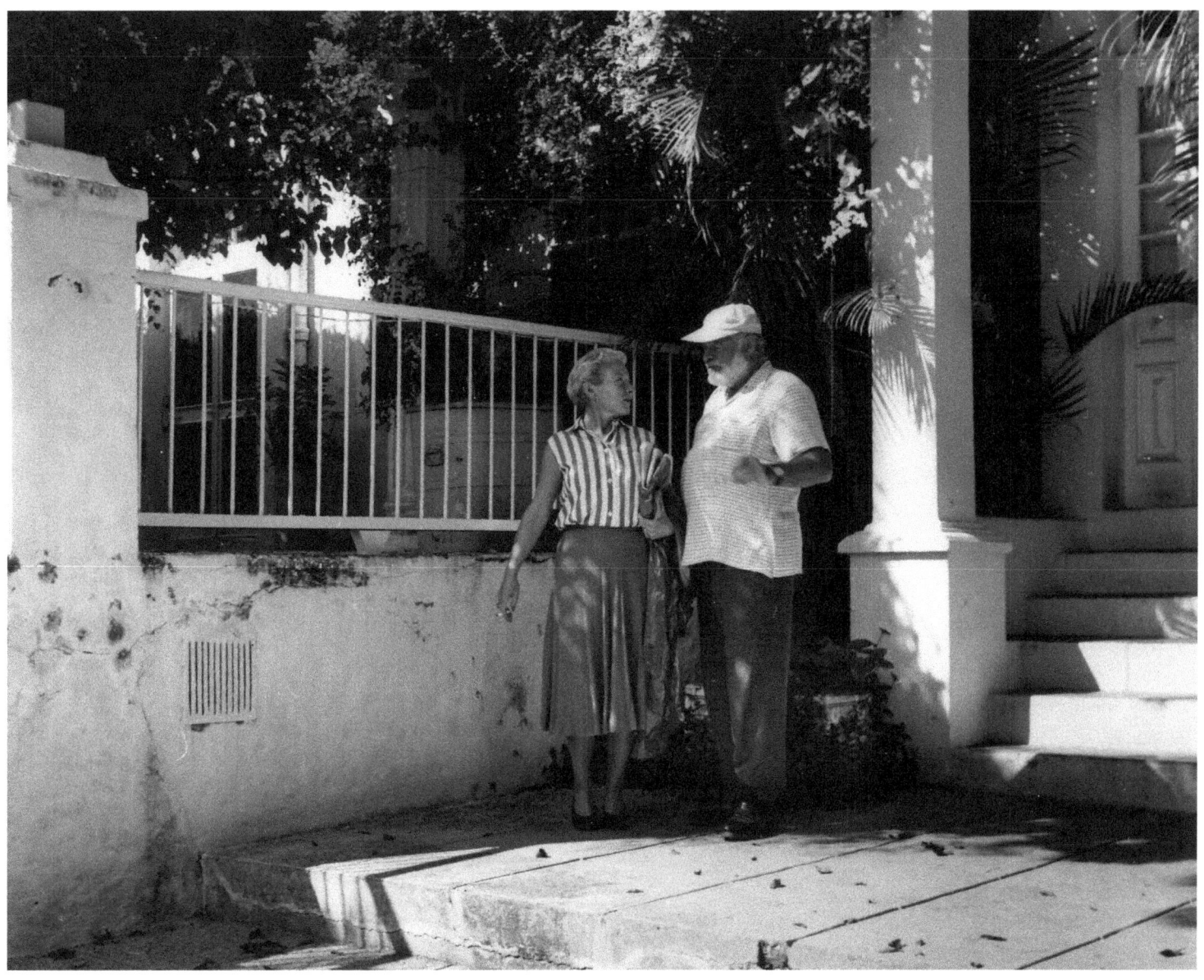

Ernest and Mary on the front porch of the Finca. When they returned from their 1956 trip to Europe, they brought back two trunks that were discovered in the basement of the Ritz Hotel, where Hemingway had left them in 1928. Reams of fiction and notebooks, all in Hemingway's own hand, included reminiscences of his early years in Paris. Hemingway found new energy and enthusiasm to write, and set to work on what would be published after his death as *A Moveable Feast*.

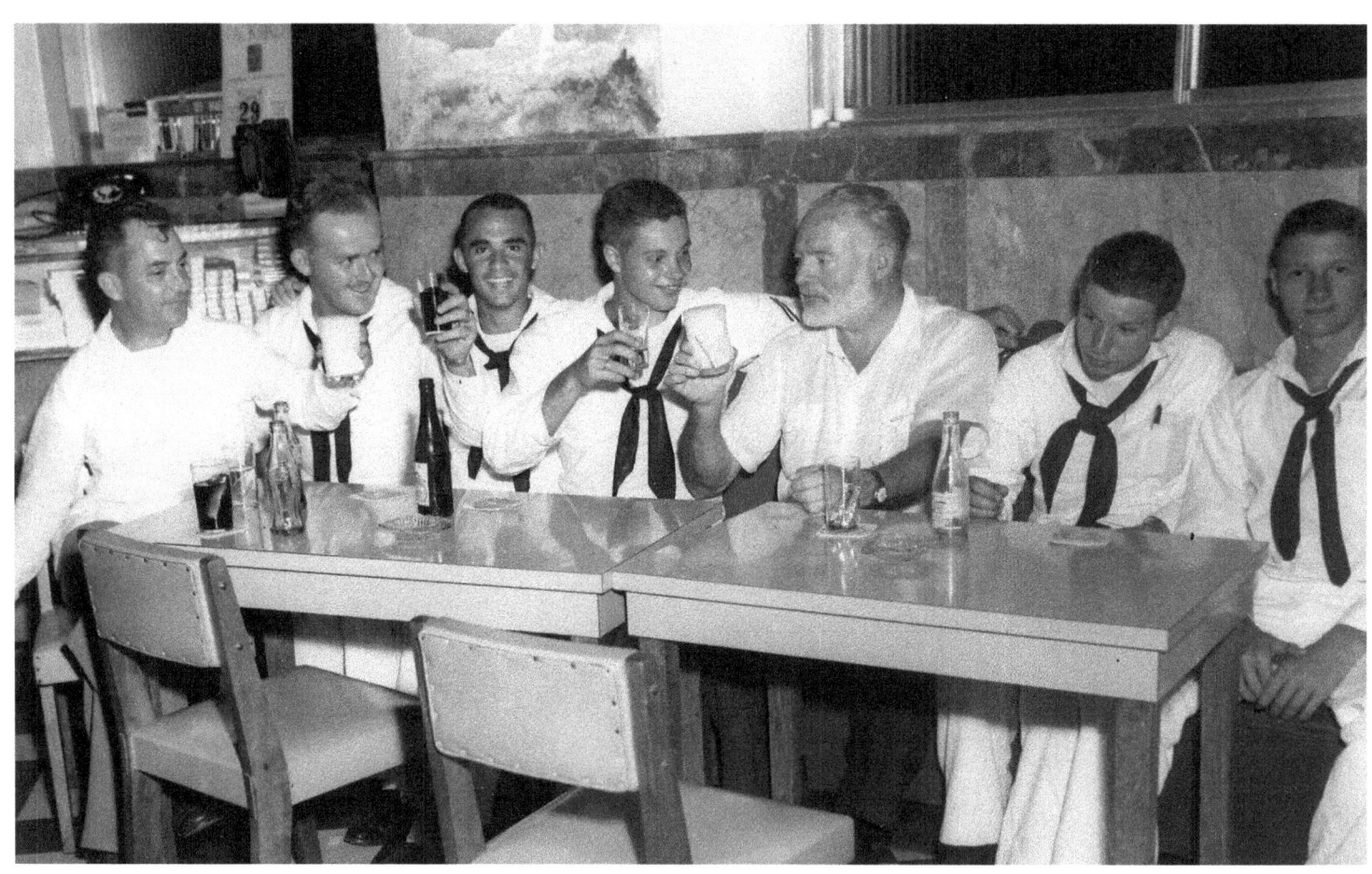

With Batista finally gone from power, the Hemingways were free to stay in Havana. Years after he was a tourist attraction in Sun Valley, Hemingway was an attraction in Cuba as well. The Air Force and Navy rewarded personnel for good behavior by sending them in groups to visit the famous author at his home or to have drinks with him at La Terraza. Hemingway, who always admired servicemen, happily obliged.

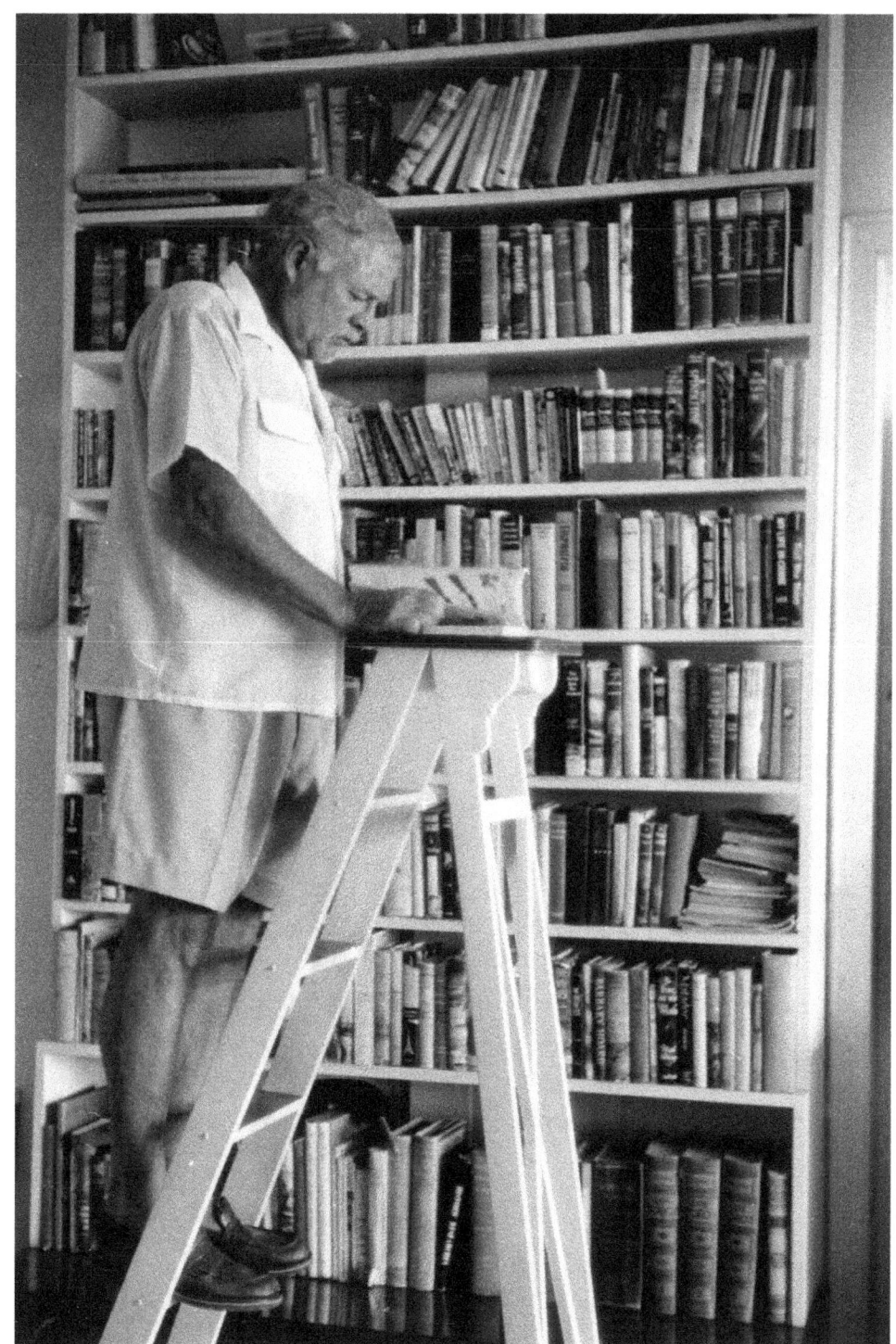

In his library at the Finca in the late fifties. Hemingway read daily throughout his life, even while on safari or on the *Pilar*. Sometimes he read two books a day, and often he made notes in the books. A quick reader with a photographic memory, Hemingway left behind a library at the Finca containing roughly 8,000 volumes—both fiction and nonfiction—all of which remain as part of the museum.

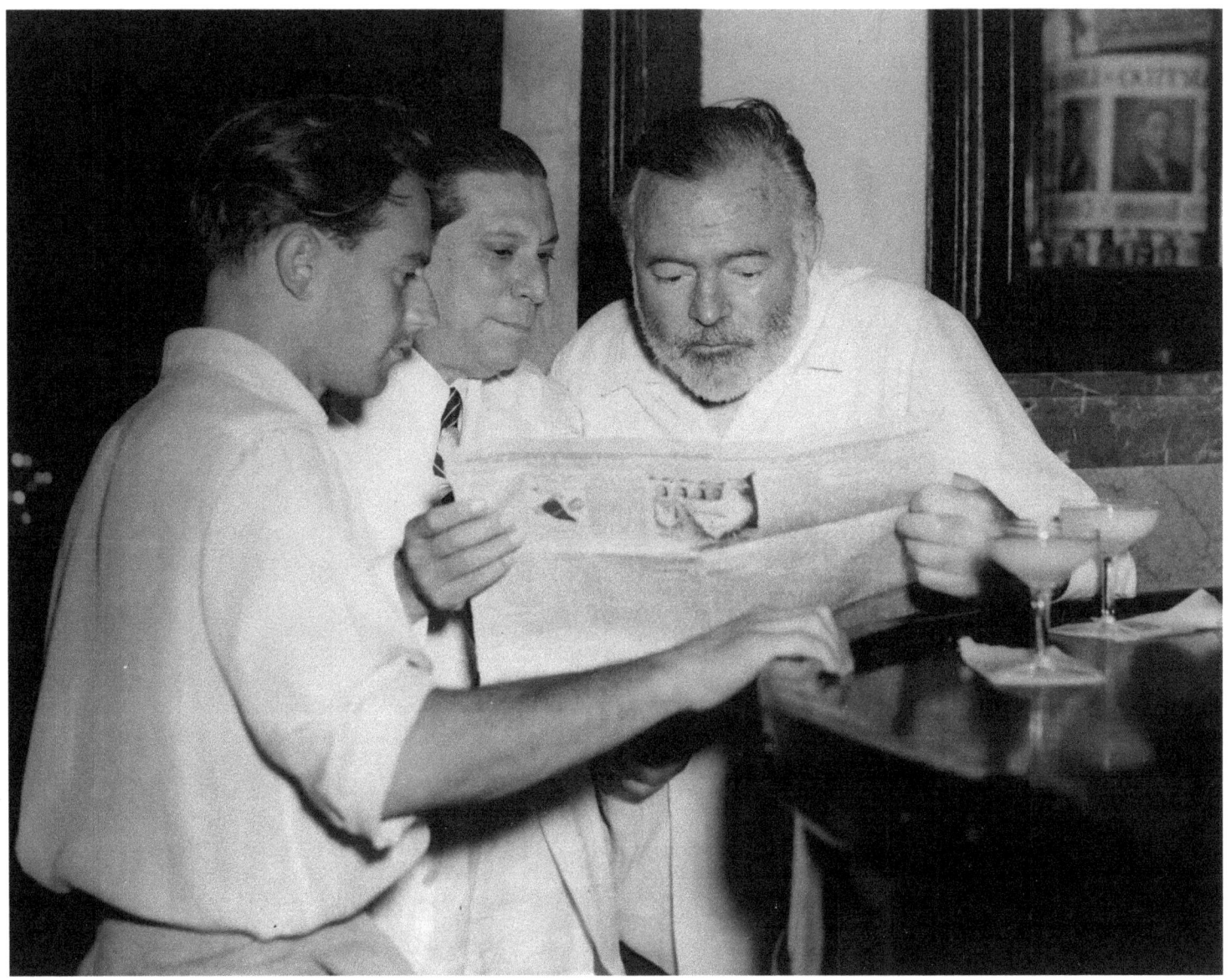

Checking the pelota and jai-alai results at the Floridita. Hemingway drank his daiquiris at the Floridita, where the frozen daiquiri was born, and his mojito where they were invented at La Bodeguita del Medio. At the Floridita, it was Papa Dobles, a double frozen drink made according to Hemingway's tastes. Legend has it that Papa once downed a dozen at a sitting.

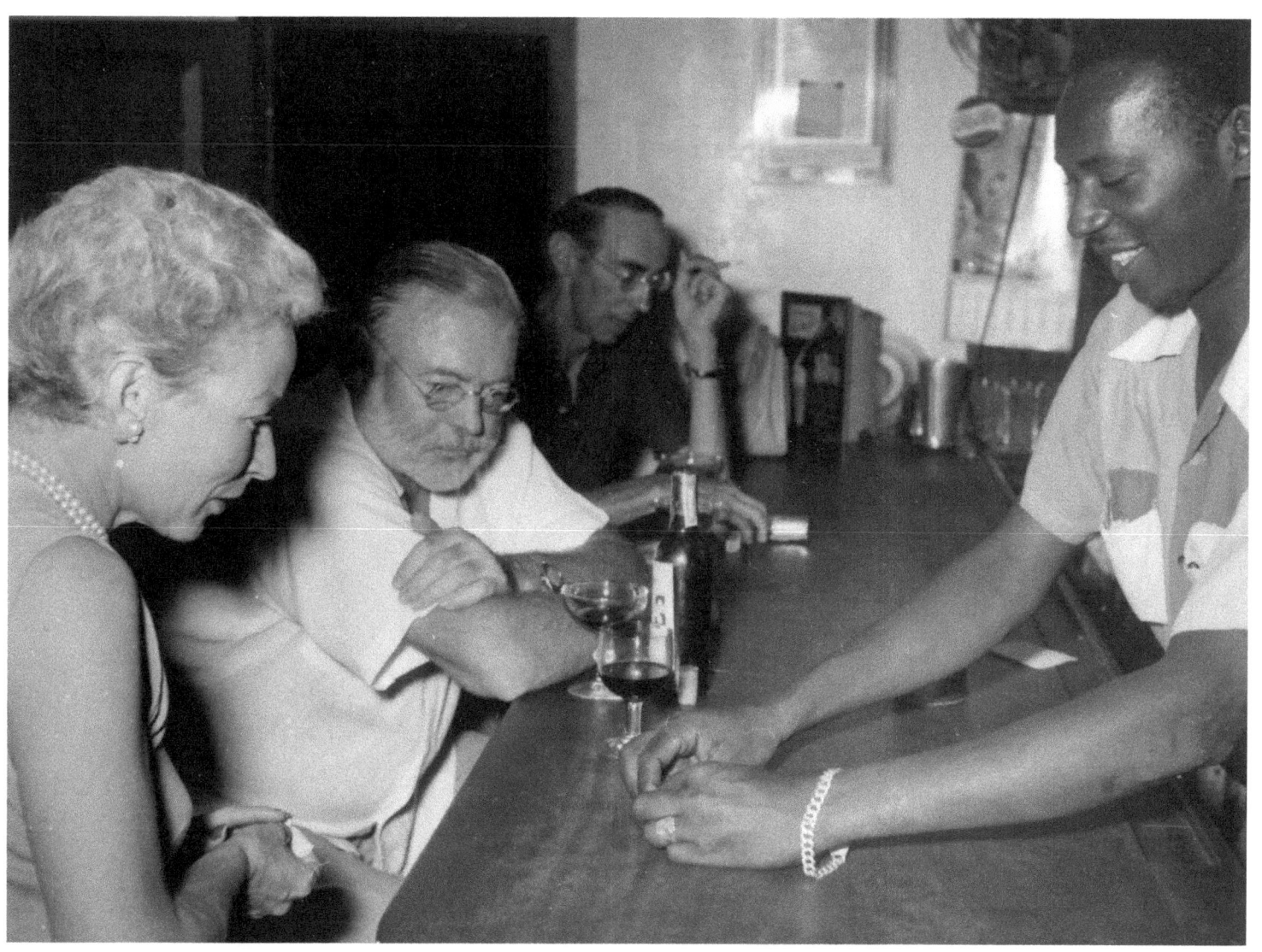

Dressed for a social event, Ernest and Mary stop at another Havana bodega, around the late fifties. The Hemingways moved freely all over Havana, and Ernest was never class-conscious. During this time, Papa continued to look back to his Paris years, working on the book that would be published after his death as *A Moveable Feast*.

In Idaho again, fall 1958. Ernest had promised his Polish translator, Bron Zielinski, some good hunting. They went on a chukar hunt with Hemingway's doctor, George Saviers, and John Powell, owner of the property. As this photo illustrates, Hemingway did all right, which was fine by Mary. Chukar was the tastiest upland game bird.

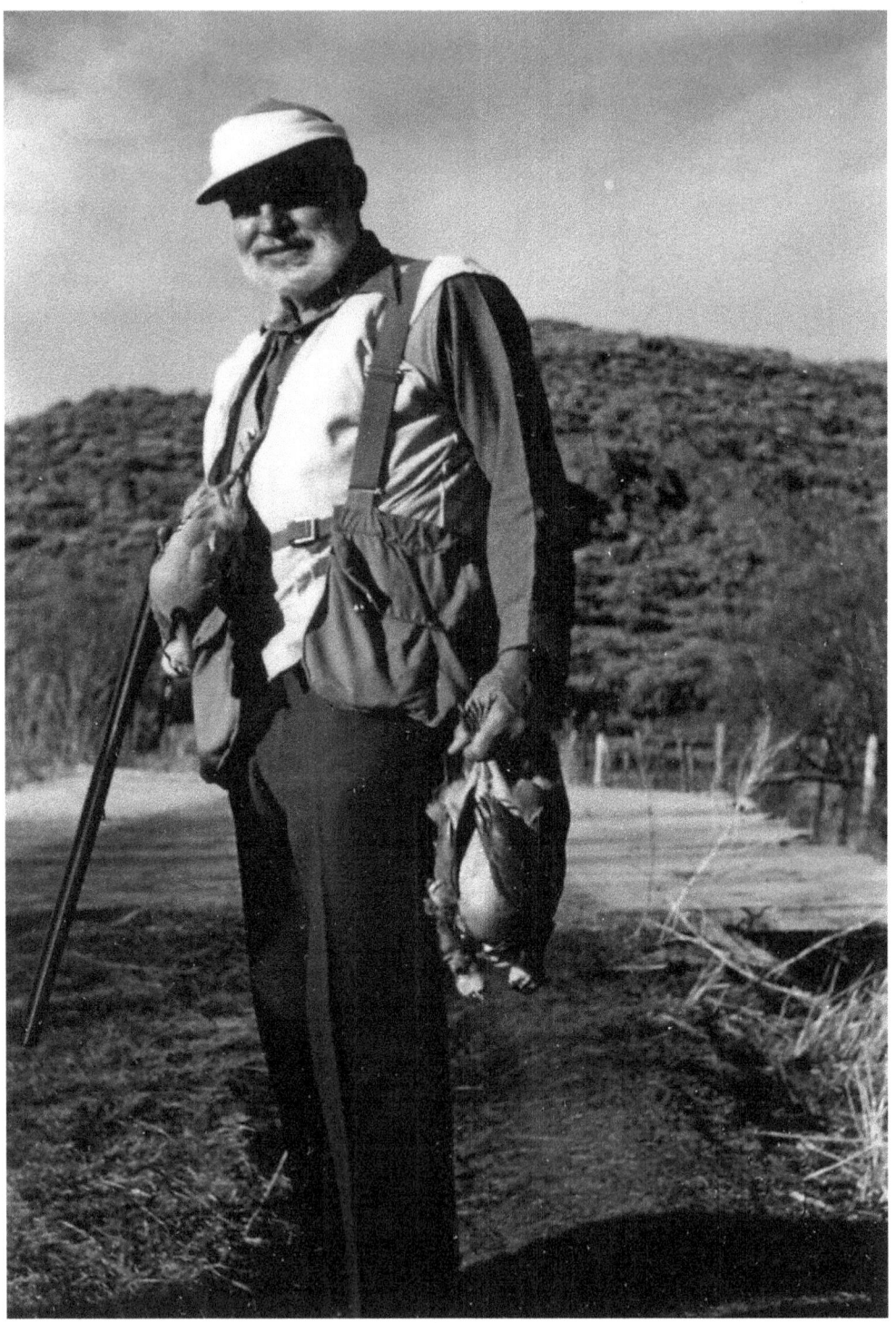

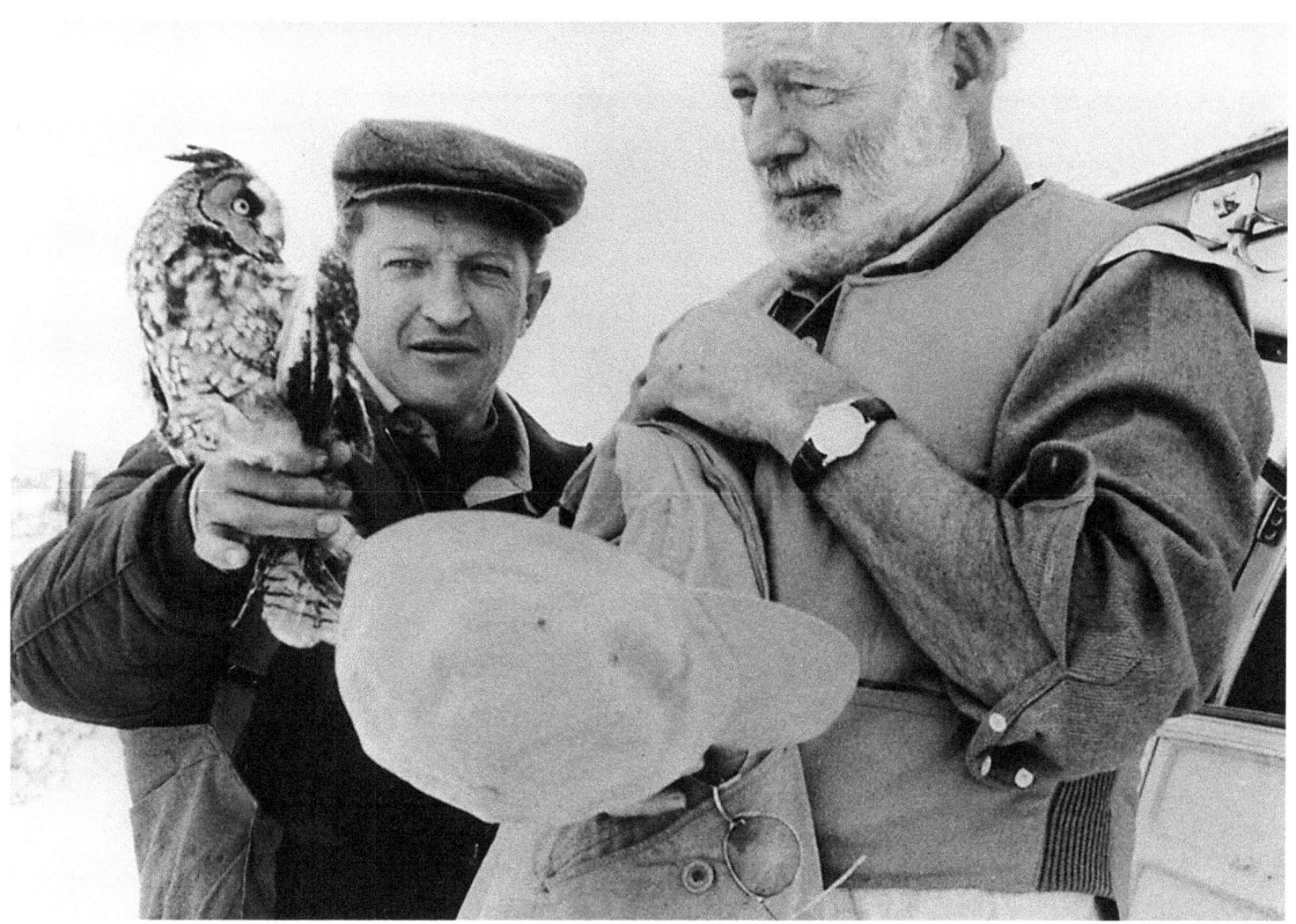

Ernest with Forrest MacMullen and "Mister Owl." According to MacMullen, no matter how cold it got, Hemingway always liked to drive with his window down and used to make up songs about things he saw along the way—like Mister Magpie, Mister Crow, or Mister Owl. But in fall 1958, Papa, the best shot, deliberately winged an owl to use as a live decoy for crow hunting, then released him after he was nursed back to health.

The Hemingways rented a house in Ketchum for the winter of 1958. A year later they would buy the Topping house, with its large picture windows that overlooked the Wood River Valley and a pair of kingbirds that Ernest would watch from the window as he wrote.

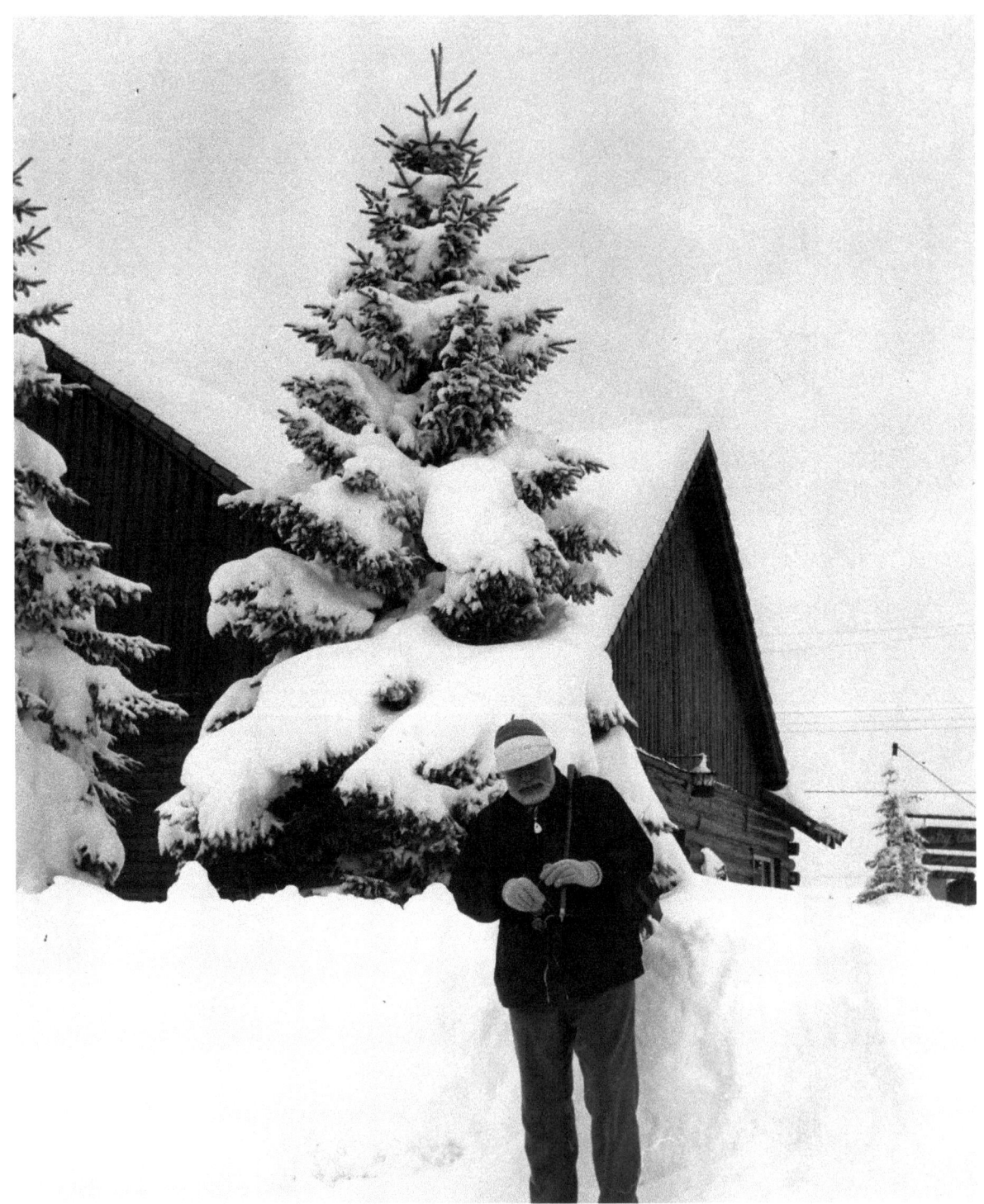

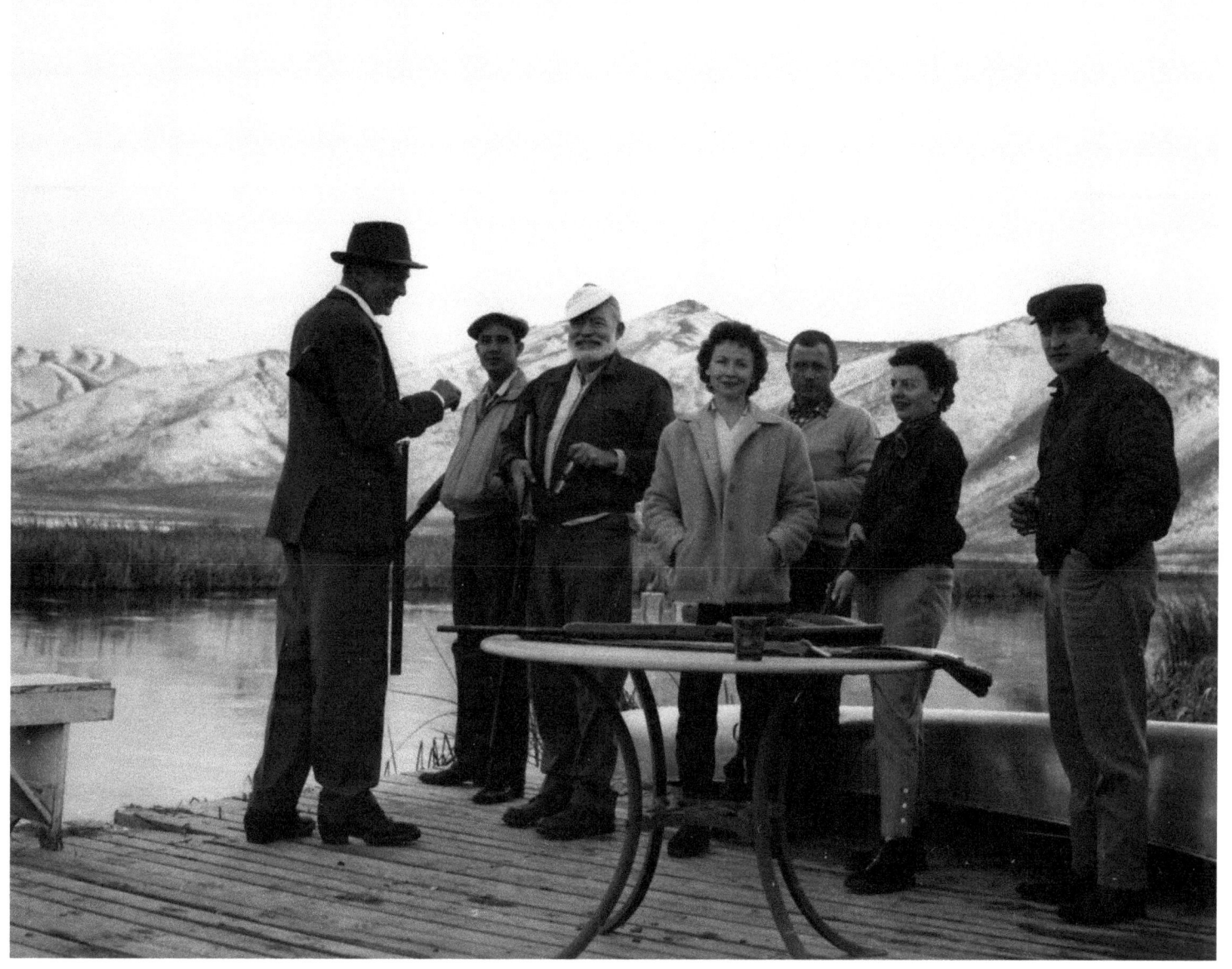

Hemingway often hunted with Idaho friends Forrest "Duke" MacMullen (right) and Bud Purdy (to the left of Hemingway), a rancher whose property was adjacent Silver Creek. In January 1959, Gary Cooper and his wife, Rocky, arrived for what would turn out to be their last visit to Idaho. Here "Coop" (far left) enjoys a magpie shoot on the deck of a private gun club near the Purdy ranch.

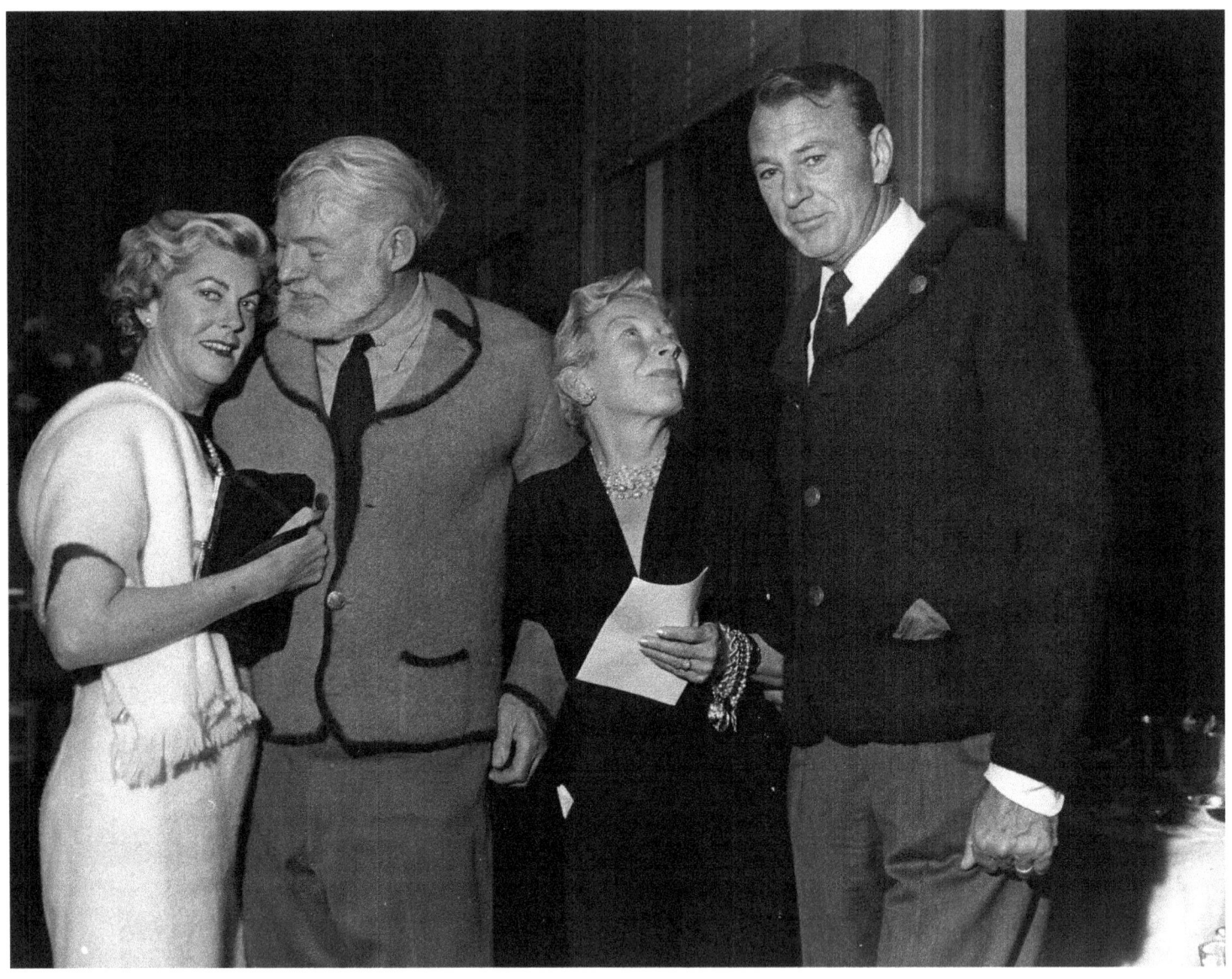

The Hemingways with Gary and Rocky Cooper, January 1959, at the home of Lloyd and Tillie Arnold. Cooper was a Montana boy who, despite his celebrity, liked to spend time with regular people as much as Hemingway, and they had a long history together. "Coop" starred in two Hemingway film adaptations—*A Farewell to Arms* (1932) and *For Whom the Bell Tolls* (1943)—and they had hunted together since a first shared autumn in Idaho, 1940. They would also die within months of each other.

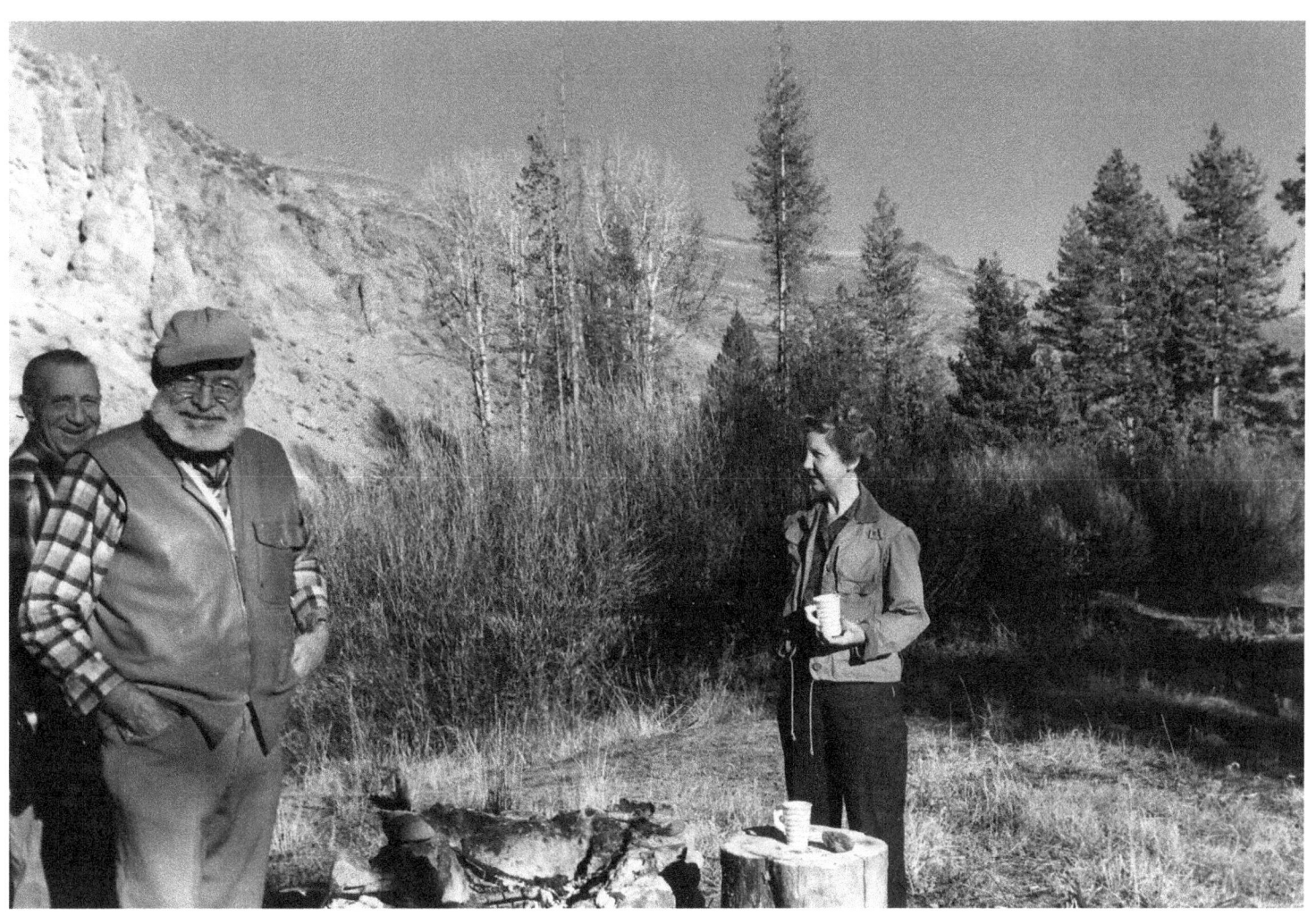

In the foothills with Lloyd and Tillie Arnold, 1959. There were always picnics and outings with the "family" in Idaho. And there was always wine. For years Hemingway's doctors had been telling him to stop drinking, but the best he could muster was a year without hard liquor.

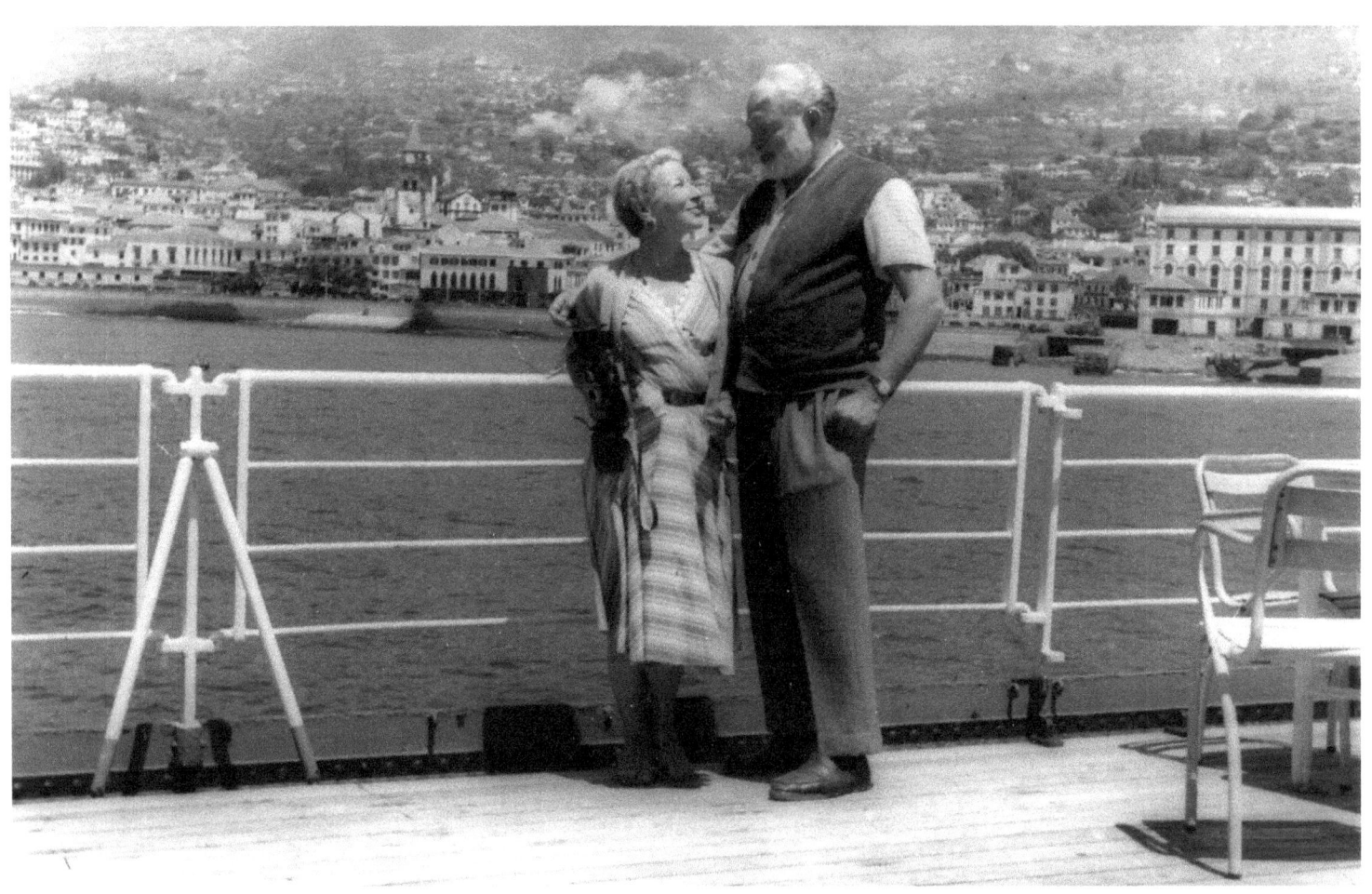

Whether coincidence or a reaction to putting down roots, shortly after buying the house in Ketchum, Mary and Ernest boarded a steamer for Spain. He had been planning to chronicle a summer of bullfighting. In April 1959 in the harbor at Algeciras, Mary and Ernest enjoy a moment before embarking on the "dangerous summer," which would see them following the mano a mano Ordóñez-Dominguín corridas across Spain.

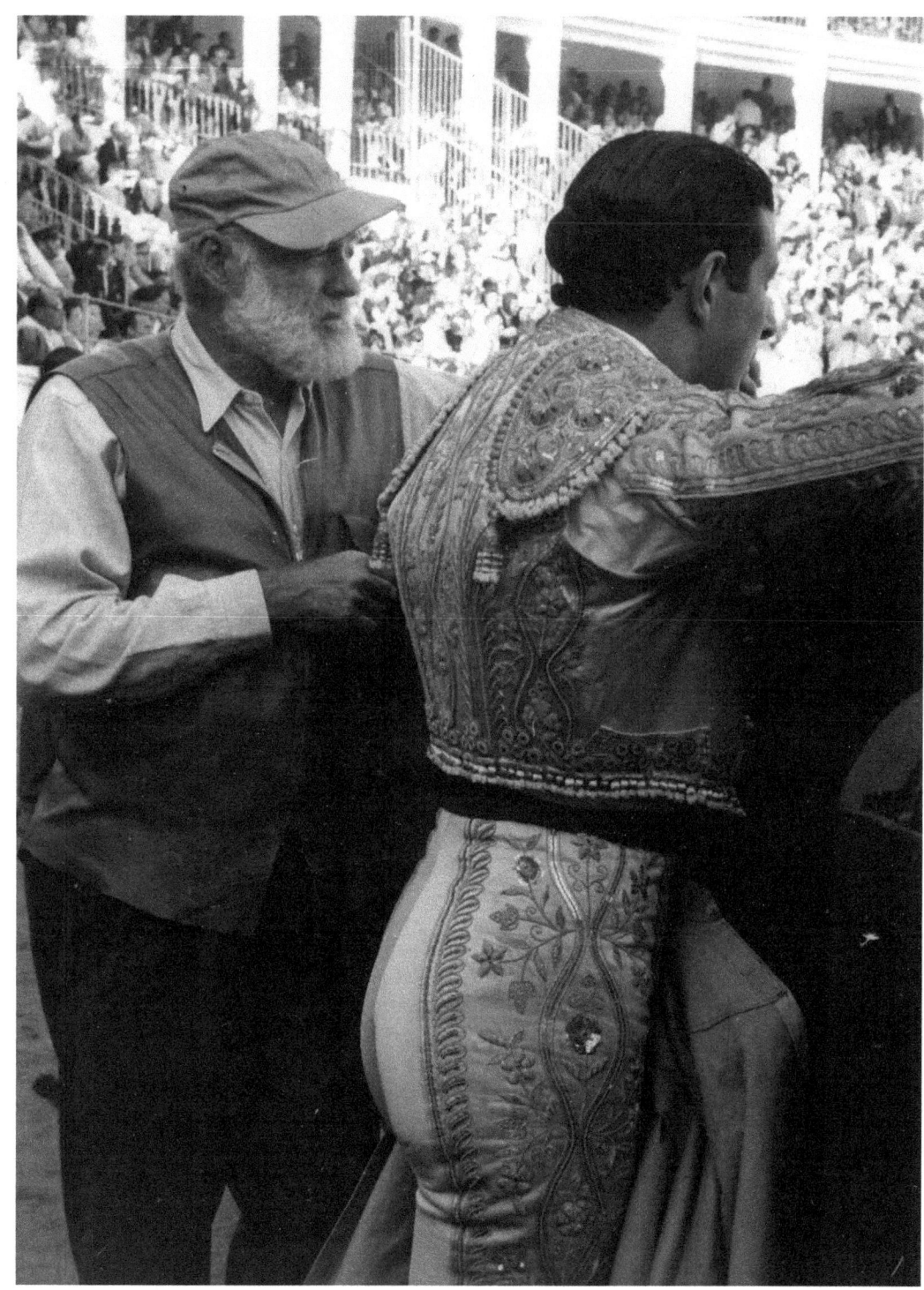

Ernest watches from behind the barrera with Antonio Ordóñez, son of the bullfighter whom Hemingway used as the model for Pedro Romero in *The Sun Also Rises.* Ordóñez was 27 the year he competed against his brother-in-law, Luis Miguel Domínguín, who was coaxed out of retirement at age 33 to travel from bullring to bullring in summer 1959. Hemingway wrote about their exploits in an article for *Life* magazine, and his expanded account would be published in book form 25 years later (1985). When Domínguín was gored in Valencia, Ernest was among those who first attended to him. Antonio Ordóñez won the summer-long competition.

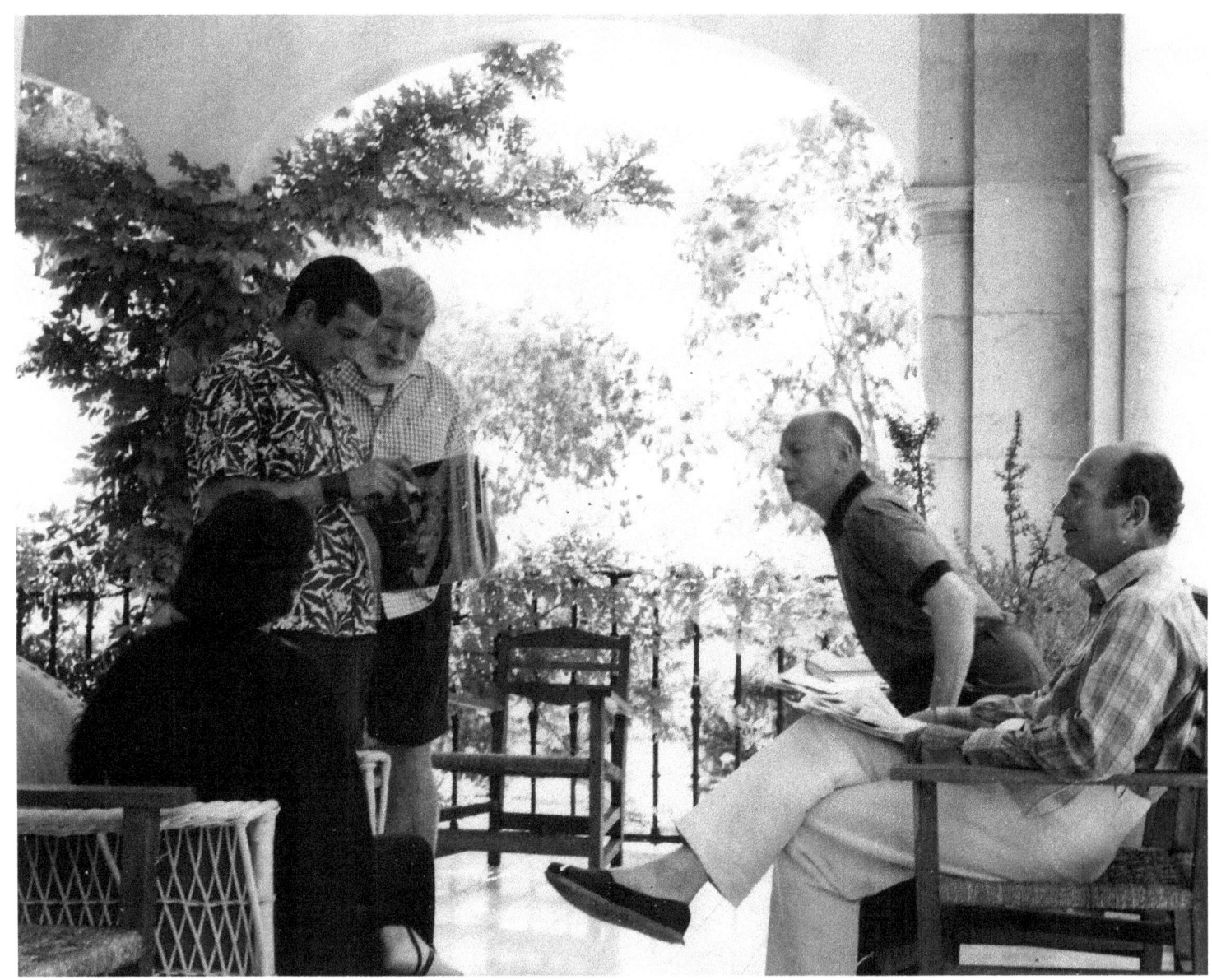

In Spain, the Hemingways stayed with their good friends Annie and Bill Davis at their estate, La Consula, in Málaga. When "The Dangerous Summer" was published in magazine form, Hemingway took some criticism for being biased toward Ordóñez. And he did spend more time with him. Here at La Consula they consult while Bill Davis, their host, watches from far-right.

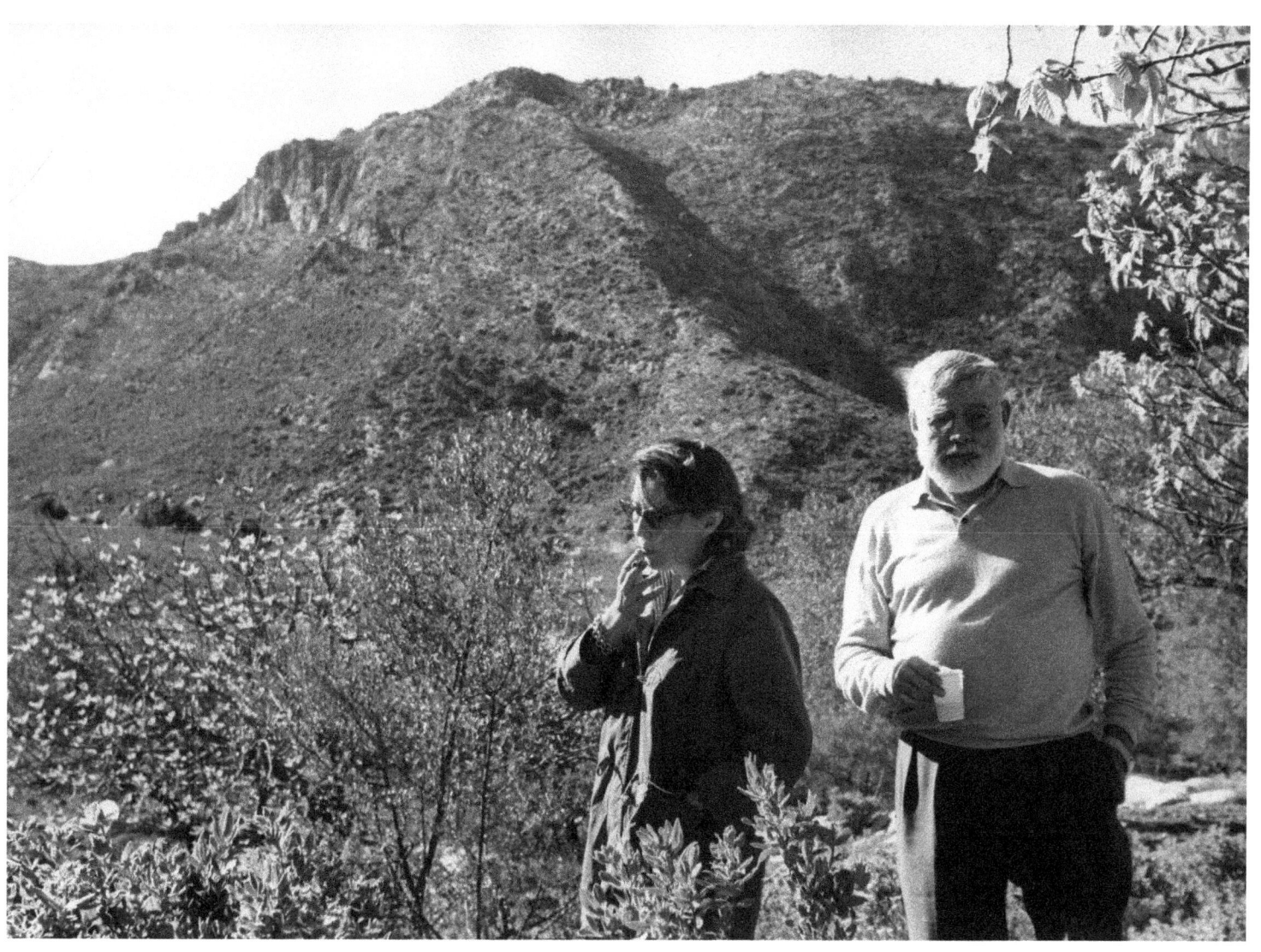

In Málaga, with Annie Davis, Ernest enjoyed just being back in Spain again. But Mary felt he was treating her like a "non-person" and would threaten to leave him when the trip finally ended.

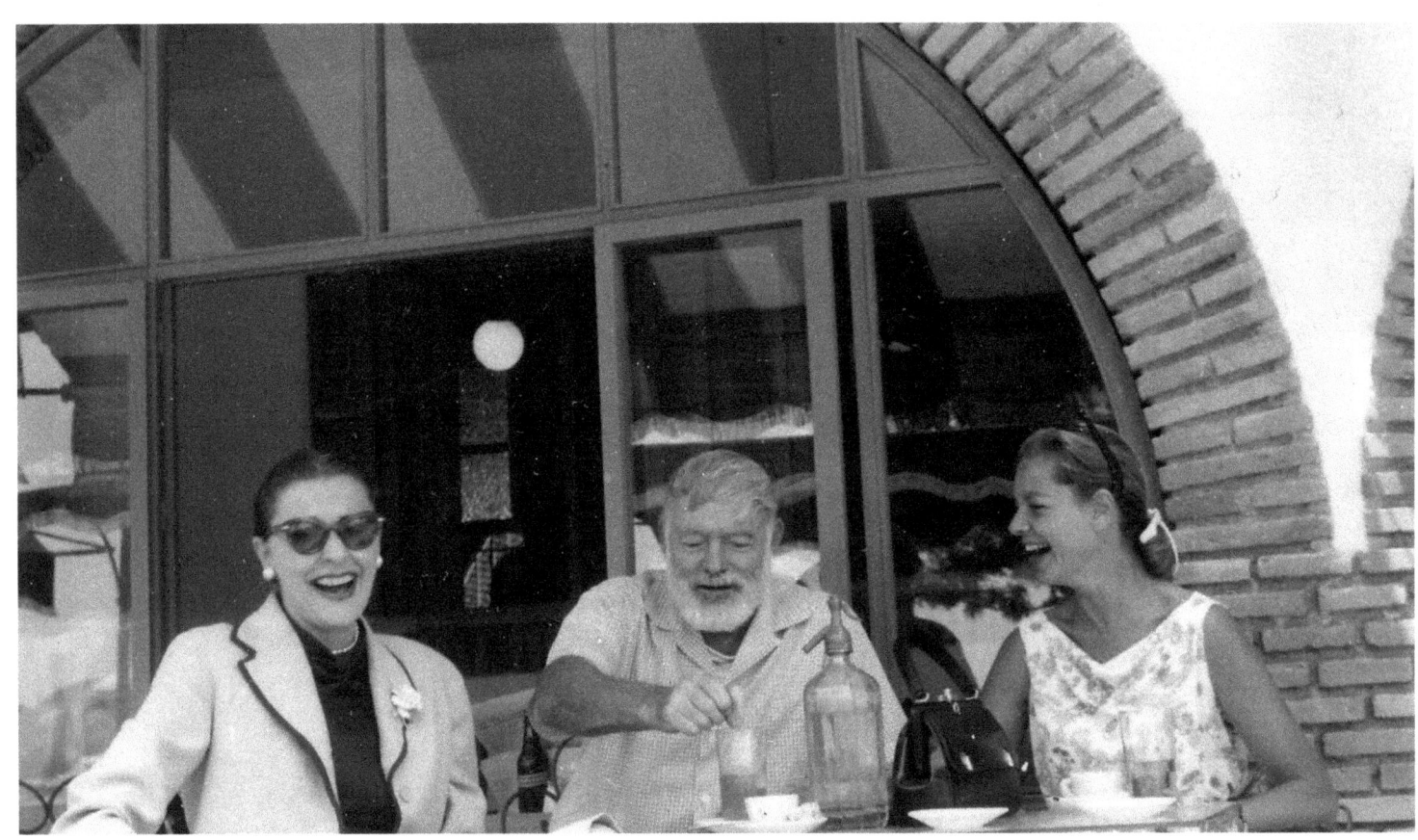

Lauren Bacall (right), who starred with Humphrey Bogart in the film adaptation of Hemingway's *To Have and Have Not,* enjoys a three-hour lunch with Papa and her friend Nancy "Slim" Hayward at a Málaga café, July 1959. Years had passed since Slim almost accidentally blew Ernest's head off when she and husband Howard Hawks hunted with him in Idaho. Bacall wanted to finally meet the famous writer, and later said that Hemingway "turned on the charm" and told her the way she tended to Bogie during his illness made her "okay in his book."

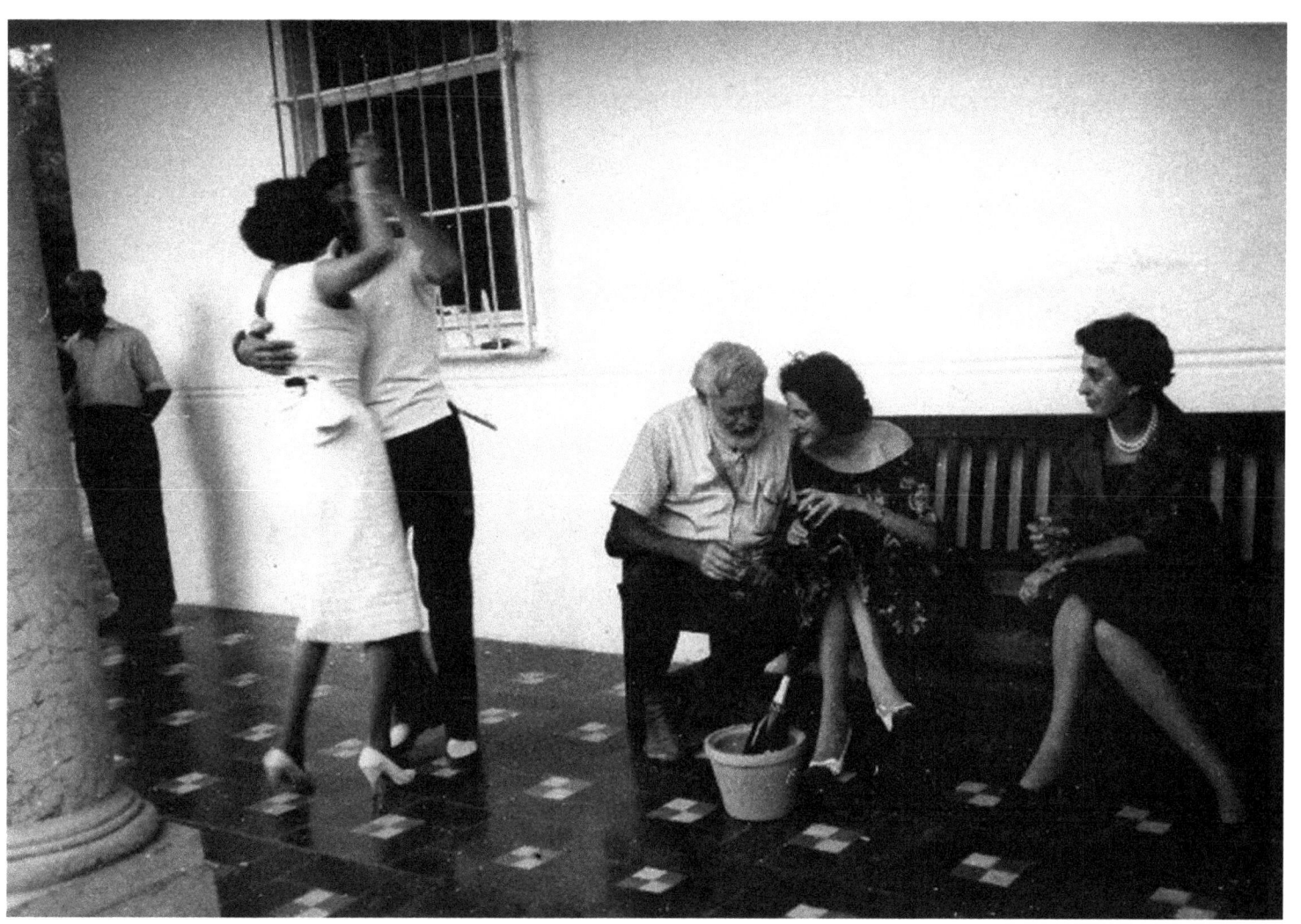

Ernest's 60th birthday party was quite the blow-out affair at La Consula. At one point he repeated his old trick of shooting a cigarette out of the mouth of a volunteer, and here spends time with new secretary Valerie Danby-Smith while Antonio Ordóñez and his wife, Carmen, dance.

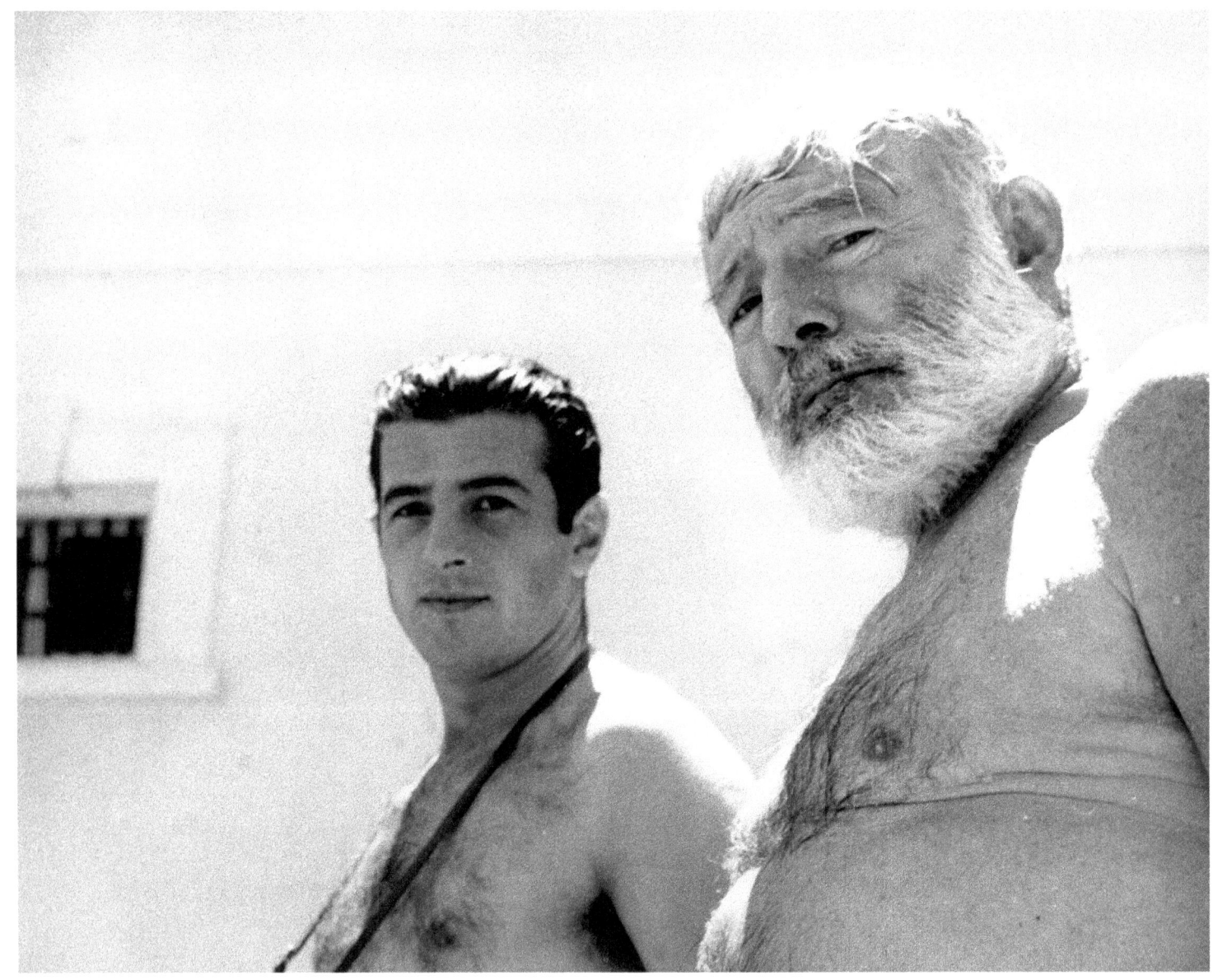

Pecho a pecho with Antonio Ordóñez. Chest hair or not, at moments like these, Hemingway had to be conscious of his own dwindling powers.

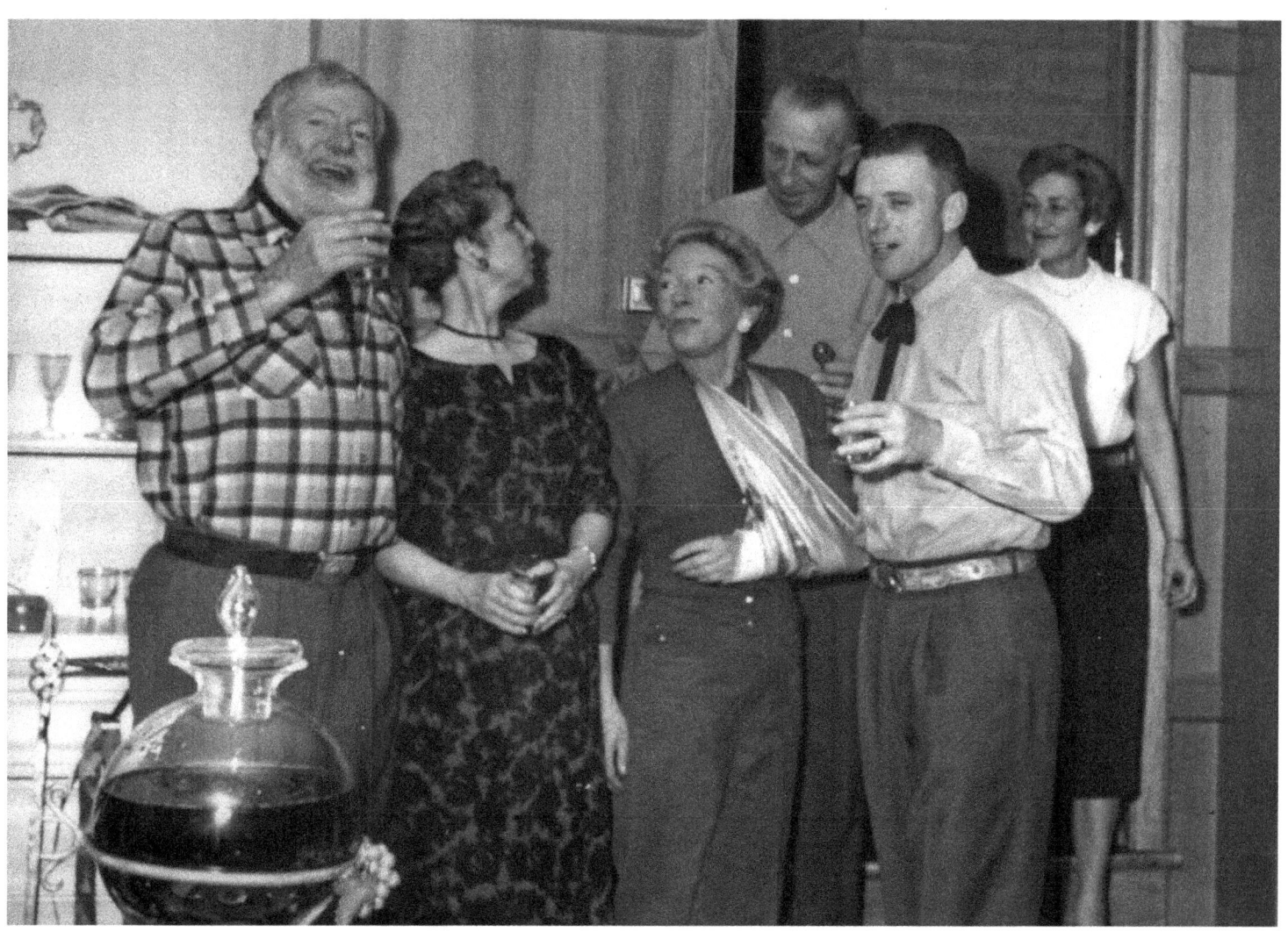

Christmas, 1959. Mary had fallen on the frozen ground while they were hunting and shattered her elbow. What was worse, Ernest, who had not been himself since the plane crashes, had grown more paranoid, thinking the FBI was after him because of his Cuban exploits. His health was also rapidly deteriorating.

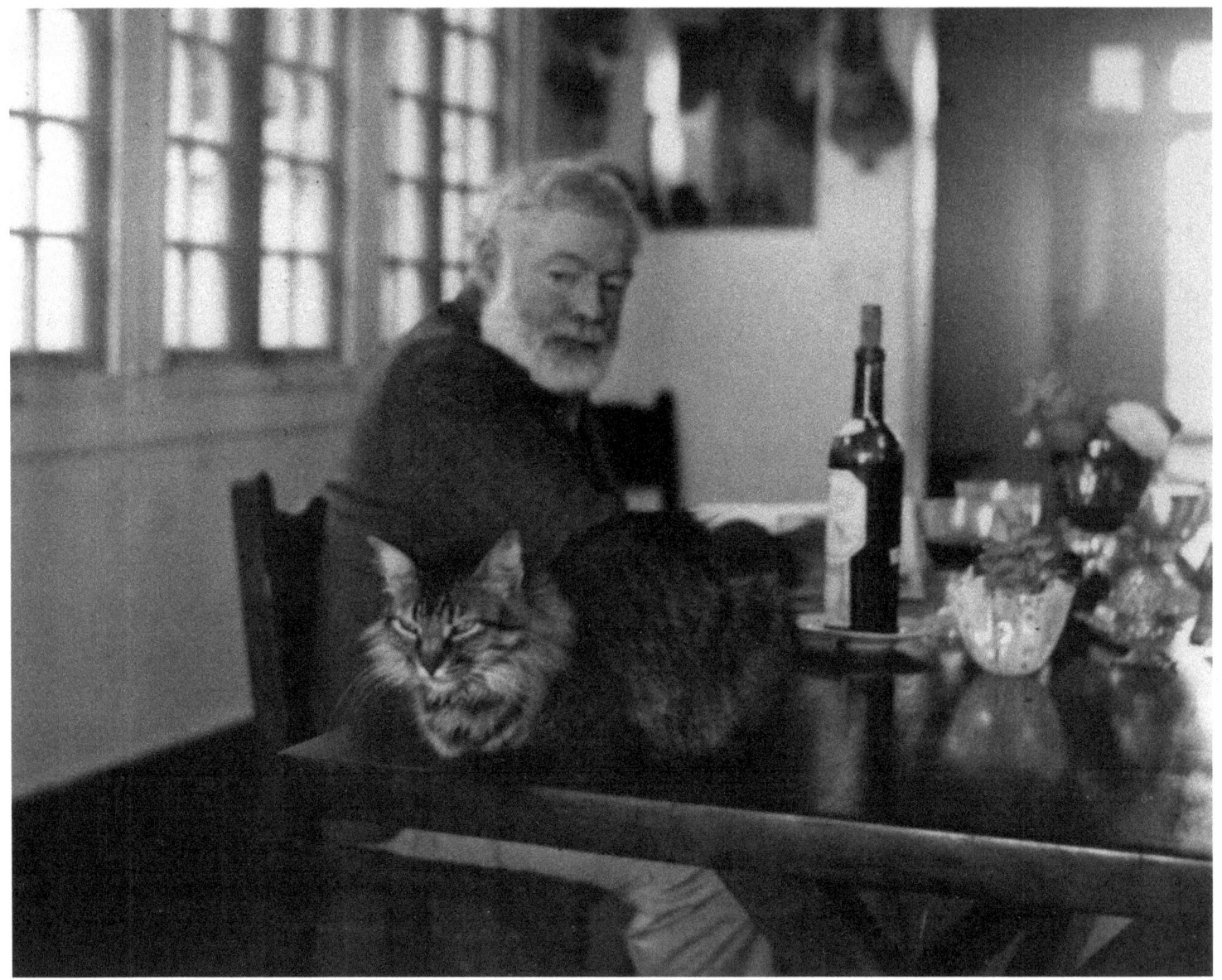

Back in Cuba, Ernest had been asked if he publicly supported the revolution, and he told reporters that he was "Cuban"—meaning, he supported what was good for the people. He and Mary spent January through July 1960 in Havana, where he worked hard on *The Dangerous Summer*, though he seemed to grow more frail by the day.

In later years, Hemingway let the cats roam again wherever they wanted. He coached one named Friendless to drink with him, pouring whiskey into his milk, grateful, it seems, for the company. By now, the writing was not going well, and Hemingway was seriously depressed on top of all his other medical problems.

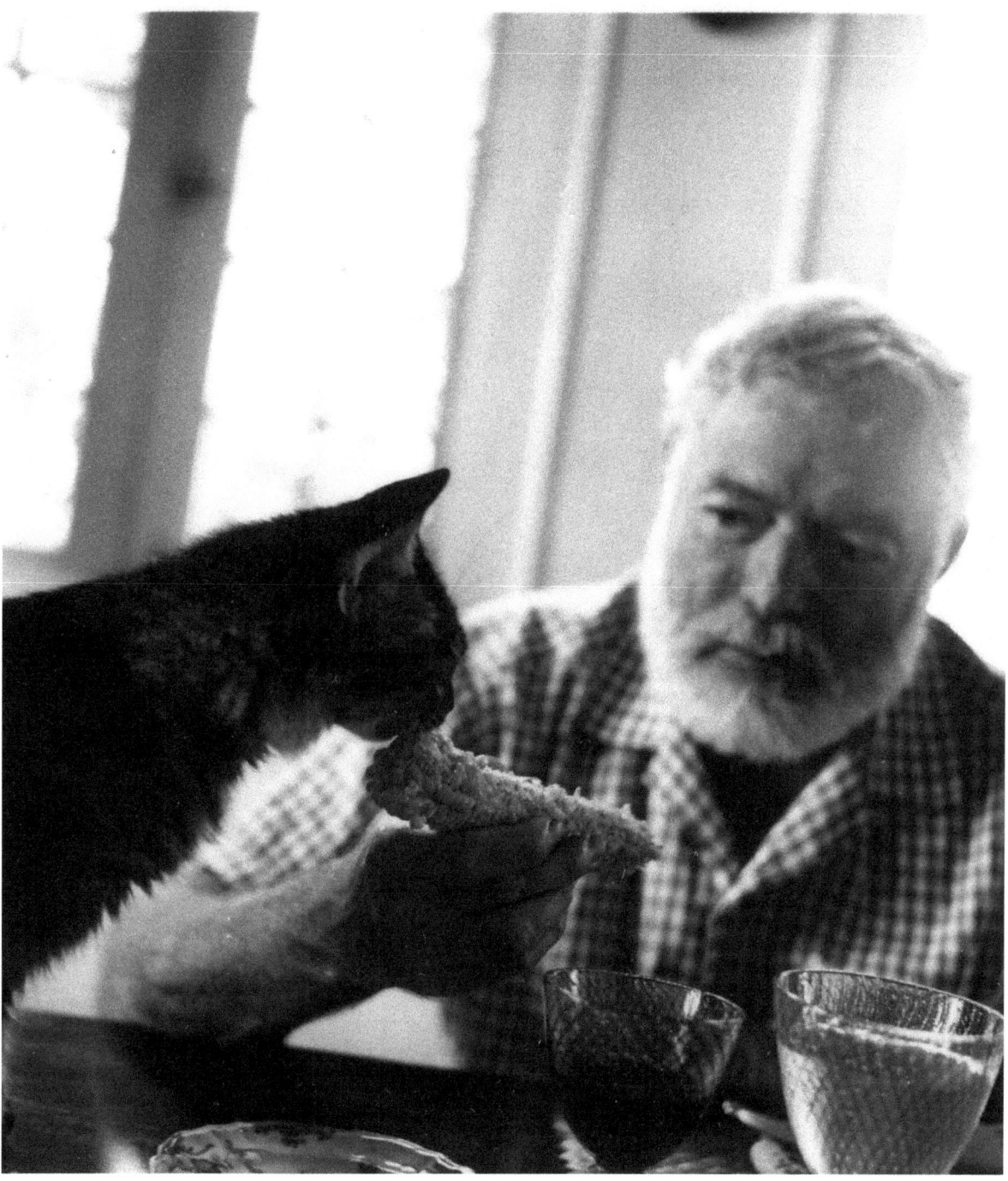

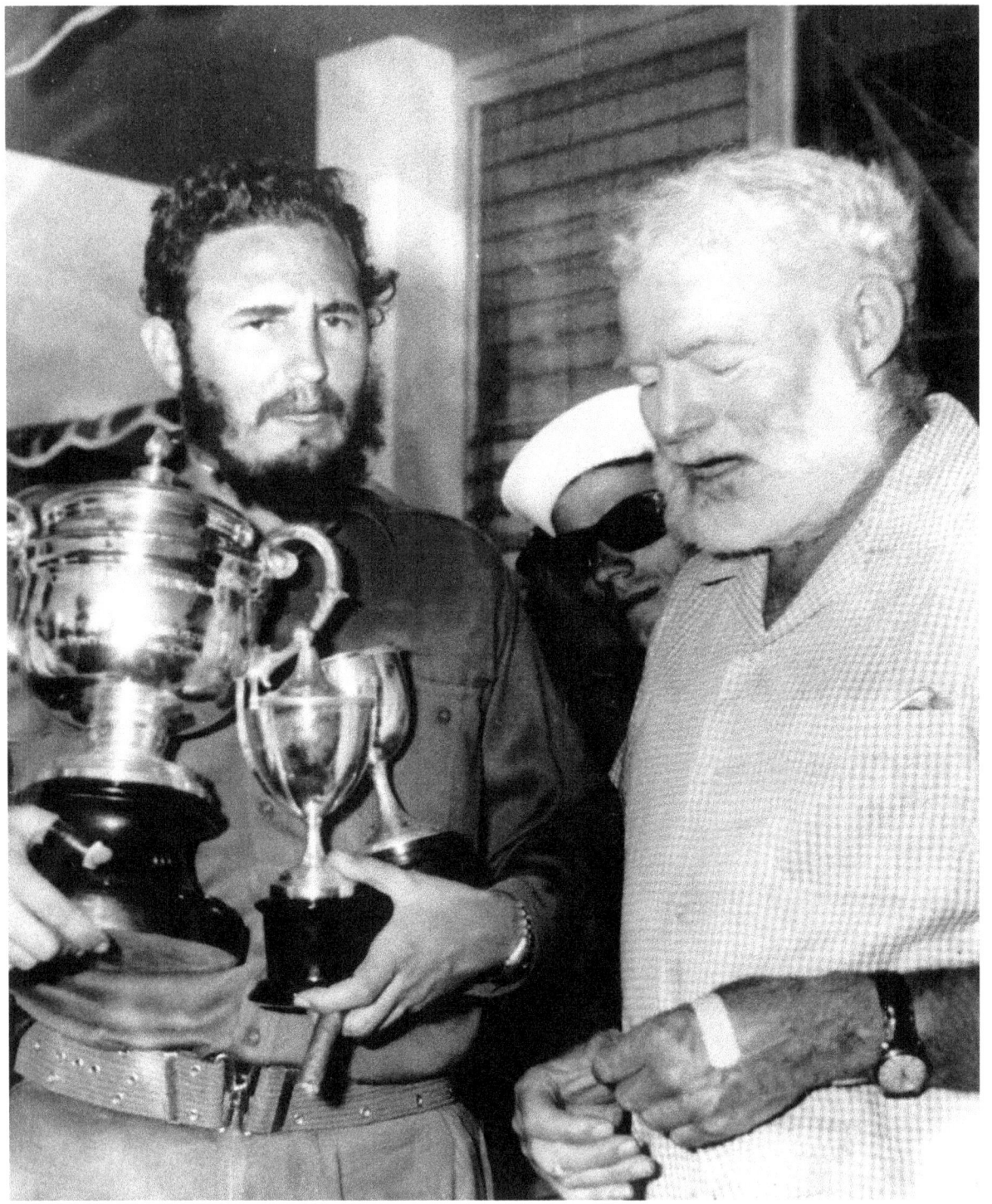

On May 15, 1960, Ernest Hemingway and Fidel Castro met for the only time at a fishing tournament named in Hemingway's honor. After Hemingway's death, Mary donated the Finca Vigía to the Cuban government. It is now the Museo Ernest Hemingway, and Ernest's beloved *Pilar* rests in permanent dry-dock exhibit on the property. Everything in the Finca is just as Mary and Ernest left it, not knowing if they would ever return.

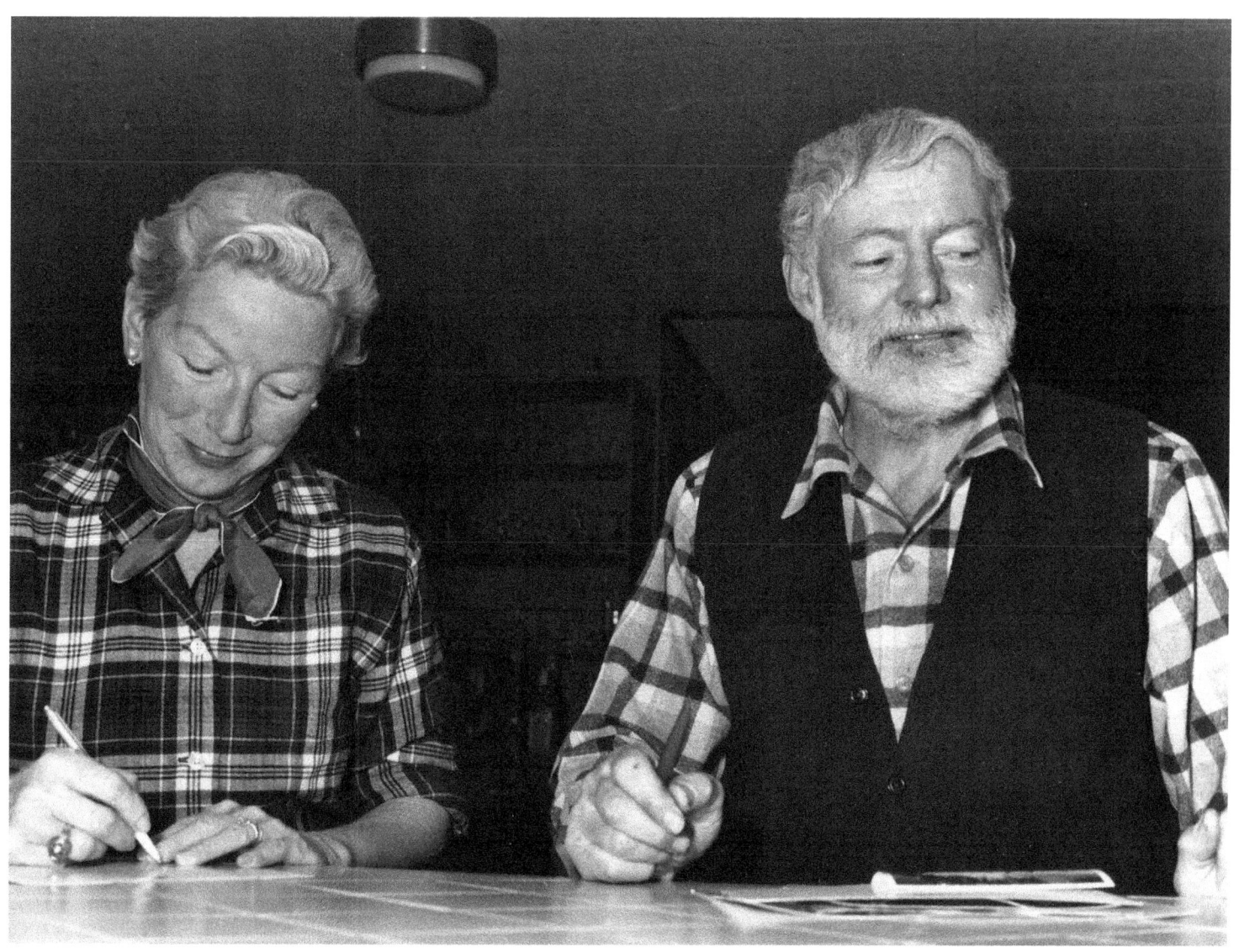

Near the end, Ernest had both mental and physical problems. He underwent electroshock treatments for depression twice at the Mayo Clinic, he was losing weight, unable to write, and like his father before him, feeling as if his body had turned on him. On July 2, nineteen days before his 62nd birthday, Hemingway killed himself with his shotgun in the entryway to his Idaho home. His friends, loyal to the end, cut the gun into pieces and buried it somewhere. They buried Ernest Hemingway in Ketchum Cemetery on July 5, 1961.

Notes on the Photographs

These notes, listed by page number, attempt to include all aspects known of the photographs. Each of the photographs is identified by the page number, photograph's title or description, photographer and collection, archive, and call or box number when applicable. Although every attempt was made to collect all data, in some cases complete data may be unavailable due to the age and condition of some of the photographs and records.

Cover **Hemingway at Work**
Ernest Hemingway Collection/
John F. Kennedy Presidential
Library and Museum, Boston
CUBAEH-P5647.tif

II **With Sheep Trophy**
Ernest Hemingway Collection/
John F. Kennedy Presidential
Library and Museum, Boston
IDAHOEH-P4537.tif

VI **Cojímar**
Ernest Hemingway Collection/
John F. Kennedy Presidential
Library and Museum, Boston
COJIMAREH-P4487.tif

X **Infancy**
Ernest Hemingway Collection/
John F. Kennedy Presidential
Library and Museum, Boston
EH-4889P.tif

2 **439 N. Oak Park**
Ernest Hemingway Collection/
John F. Kennedy Presidential
Library and Museum, Boston
EH6157P.tif

3 **At Bear Lake**
Ernest Hemingway Collection/
John F. Kennedy Presidential
Library and Museum, Boston
SB1 page 16-17 crop.tif

4 **In Baby Carriage**
Ernest Hemingway Collection/
John F. Kennedy Presidential
Library and Museum, Boston
EH-G031.tif

5 **With Marcelline**
Ernest Hemingway Collection/
John F. Kennedy Presidential
Library and Museum, Boston
EH-N558.tif

6 **The Family and Neighbors**
Ernest Hemingway Collection/
John F. Kennedy Presidential
Library and Museum, Boston
EH.N611.tif

7 **At Age Two**
Ernest Hemingway Collection/
John F. Kennedy Presidential
Library and Museum, Boston
EH-P4876.tif

8 **Fishing at Horton's Creek**
Ernest Hemingway Collection/
John F. Kennedy Presidential
Library and Museum, Boston
EH5516P.tif

9 **Grace and Children**
Ernest Hemingway Collection/
John F. Kennedy Presidential
Library and Museum, Boston
SB2 page 82-83 crop.tif

10 **Memorial Day 1907**
Ernest Hemingway Collection/
John F. Kennedy Presidential
Library and Museum, Boston
EH9986P.tif

11 **600 N. Kenilworth**
Ernest Hemingway Collection/
John F. Kennedy Presidential
Library and Museum, Boston
EH-N1136.tif

12 **16th Anniversary**
Ernest Hemingway Collection/
John F. Kennedy Presidential
Library and Museum, Boston
EH-P4871.tif

13 **With Gun and Grouse**
Ernest Hemingway Collection/
John F. Kennedy Presidential
Library and Museum, Boston
1913EH-N783.tif

14 **Petoskey Bound, 1915**
Ernest Hemingway Collection/
John F. Kennedy Presidential
Library and Museum, Boston
1916EH-N785.tif

15 **Catching a Fish**
Ernest Hemingway Collection/
John F. Kennedy Presidential
Library and Museum, Boston
EH746N.tif

16 **With Boyhood Friends**
Ernest Hemingway Collection/
John F. Kennedy Presidential
Library and Museum, Boston
CAMPINGTRIPEH-N750.tif

17 **Lakeside near Windemere**
Ernest Hemingway Collection/
John F. Kennedy Presidential
Library and Museum, Boston
EH-P7813.tif

18 **Taking Notes**
Ernest Hemingway Collection/
John F. Kennedy Presidential
Library and Museum, Boston
EH784N.tif

19 **Walloon Lake**
Ernest Hemingway Collection/
John F. Kennedy Presidential
Library and Museum, Boston
WALLOONLAKEEH-N579.tif

20 **With String of Trout**
Ernest Hemingway Collection/
John F. Kennedy Presidential
Library and Museum, Boston
EH-7813P.tif

21 **1917 Trapeze Staff**
Courtesy of Oak Park and
River Forest High School
Class of 1917.tif

22 **Freight Train Pose**
Ernest Hemingway Collection/
John F. Kennedy Presidential
Library and Museum, Boston
CAMPINGTRIPEH-N753.tif

23 **In Italy, 1918**
Ernest Hemingway Collection/
John F. Kennedy Presidential
Library and Museum, Boston
WWIEH-P10042.tif

24 **War Injuries**
Ernest Hemingway Collection/
John F. Kennedy Presidential
Library and Museum, Boston
WWIEH-P2679.tif

25 **At Red Cross Hospital**
Ernest Hemingway Collection/
John F. Kennedy Presidential
Library and Museum, Boston
WWIEH-P2526.tif

26 **Posing with Rifle**
Ernest Hemingway Collection/
John F. Kennedy Presidential
Library and Museum, Boston
EH2525P.tif

27 **At San Siro Track**
Ernest Hemingway Collection/
John F. Kennedy Presidential
Library and Museum, Boston
WWIEH-P2665.tif

28 **With Agnes von Kurowsky**
Ernest Hemingway Collection/
John F. Kennedy Presidential
Library and Museum, Boston
EH2528P.tif

29 **Home from the War**
Ernest Hemingway Collection/
John F. Kennedy Presidential
Library and Museum, Boston
EH-P8068.tif

30 **TOASTING ERNESTO**
Ernest Hemingway Collection/
John F. Kennedy Presidential
Library and Museum, Boston
EH-P9570.tif

31 **BACKYARD SPORT**
Ernest Hemingway Collection/
John F. Kennedy Presidential
Library and Museum, Boston
EH-P8070.tif

32 **BACK TO HORTON BAY**
Ernest Hemingway Collection/
John F. Kennedy Presidential
Library and Museum, Boston
1919EH-P2616.tif

33 **BANISHED FROM WINDEMERE**
Ernest Hemingway Collection/
John F. Kennedy Presidential
Library and Museum, Boston
EH5529P.tif

34 **AT SMITH APARTMENT**
Ernest Hemingway Collection/
John F. Kennedy Presidential
Library and Museum, Boston
CHICAGOEH-P6947.tif

35 **BOXING PRACTICE**
Ernest Hemingway Collection/
John F. Kennedy Presidential
Library and Museum, Boston
EH-P9583.tif

36 **WITH HADLEY RICHARDSON**
Ernest Hemingway Collection/
John F. Kennedy Presidential
Library and Museum, Boston
HADLEYCOURTSHIPEH-
P5010.tif

37 **WITH GROOMSMEN**
Ernest Hemingway Collection/
John F. Kennedy Presidential
Library and Museum, Boston
HADLEYMARRIAGEEH-
N613.tif

38 **BRIDE AND GROOM**
Ernest Hemingway Collection/
John F. Kennedy Presidential
Library and Museum, Boston
HADLEYMARRIAGEEH-
P5746.tif

39 **NEWLYWEDS AND FAMILY**
Ernest Hemingway Collection/
John F. Kennedy Presidential
Library and Museum, Boston
FAMILYEH-N1133.tif

40 **BELATED HONEYMOON**
Ernest Hemingway Collection/
John F. Kennedy Presidential
Library and Museum, Boston
SWITZERLANDEH-
P8095.tif

41 **WITH LEICESTER**
Ernest Hemingway Collection/
John F. Kennedy Presidential
Library and Museum, Boston
EH-N1103.tif

42 **ARRIVED IN PARIS**
Ernest Hemingway Collection/
John F. Kennedy Presidential
Library and Museum, Boston
PARISEH-P7987.tif

43 **WITH BUMBY**
Ernest Hemingway Collection/
John F. Kennedy Presidential
Library and Museum, Boston
PARISEH-P5180.tif

44 **GERTRUDE STEIN**
Ernest Hemingway Collection/
John F. Kennedy Presidential
Library and Museum, Boston
EH5134P.tif

45 **WITH FRIENDS AT CAFE**
Ernest Hemingway Collection/
John F. Kennedy Presidential
Library and Museum, Boston
EH5734P.tif

46 **RUNNING THE BULLS**
Ernest Hemingway Collection/
John F. Kennedy Presidential
Library and Museum, Boston
PAMPLONAEH-P9807.tif

47 **SAN FERMIN REVELERS**
Ernest Hemingway Collection/
John F. Kennedy Presidential
Library and Museum, Boston
PAMPLONA1927EH-P6258.
tif

48 **CONFRONTING THE BULL**
Ernest Hemingway Collection/
John F. Kennedy Presidential
Library and Museum, Boston
EH7891P.tif

49 **BULLFIGHT**
Ernest Hemingway Collection/
John F. Kennedy Presidential
Library and Museum, Boston
PAMPLONA1925EH-P7112.
tif

50 **THE FITZGERALDS, CHRISTMAS 1925**
Courtesy of Princeton
University Library

51 **WITH GERALD MURPHY AND JOHN DOS PASSOS**
Ernest Hemingway Collection/
John F. Kennedy Presidential
Library and Museum, Boston
EH7281N.tif

52 **ON THE SLOPES NEAR SCHRUNS**
Ernest Hemingway Collection/
John F. Kennedy Presidential
Library and Museum, Boston
AUSTRIA1925EH-P7962.tif

53 **ON SKIS WITH BUMBY**
Ernest Hemingway Collection/
John F. Kennedy Presidential
Library and Museum, Boston
AUSTRIA1925EH-P8094.tif

54 **ON HOTEL BALCONY**
Ernest Hemingway Collection/
John F. Kennedy Presidential
Library and Museum, Boston
AUSTRIA1925EH-P7956.tif

55 **WITH HADLEY AND BUMBY IN SCHRUNS**
Ernest Hemingway Collection/
John F. Kennedy Presidential
Library and Museum, Boston
AUSTRIA1926EH-P7276.tif

56 **WITH PAULINE PFEIFFER**
Ernest Hemingway Collection/
John F. Kennedy Presidential
Library and Museum, Boston
PAULINEEH-P6978.tif

58 **AT SAN FERMIN, 1926**
Ernest Hemingway Collection/
John F. Kennedy Presidential
Library and Museum, Boston
EH6949P.tif

59 **AT THE CORRIDA**
Ernest Hemingway Collection/
John F. Kennedy Presidential
Library and Museum, Boston
EH8726P.tif

60 **SKIING AT GSTAAD**
Ernest Hemingway Collection/
John F. Kennedy Presidential
Library and Museum, Boston
SWITZERLAND1927EH-
P4497.tif

61 **ON THE BEACH AT SAN SEBASTIAN**
Ernest Hemingway Collection/
John F. Kennedy Presidential
Library and Museum, Boston
EH6896P.tif

62 **SITTING WITH OXEN**
Ernest Hemingway Collection/
John F. Kennedy Presidential
Library and Museum, Boston
SPAIN1927EH-P7976.tif

63 **DRAWN TO THE RING**
Ernest Hemingway Collection/
John F. Kennedy Presidential
Library and Museum, Boston
SPAINEH-P7982.tif

64 **SKYLIGHT INJURY**
Ernest Hemingway Collection/
John F. Kennedy Presidential
Library and Museum, Boston
ALONEH-P6078.tif

65 **AT SHAKESPEARE AND COMPANY**
Courtesy of Princeton
University Library

66 **ARRIVED AT KEY WEST**
Ernest Hemingway Collection/
John F. Kennedy Presidential
Library and Museum, Boston
PORTRAITEH-N7249.tif

67 **UNPLANNED VISIT**
Ernest Hemingway Collection/
John F. Kennedy Presidential
Library and Museum, Boston
BRENTSEH-P8096.tif

68 **A DOUBLE PARADISE**
Ernest Hemingway Collection/
John F. Kennedy Presidential
Library and Museum, Boston
KEYWEST1928EH-N7244.tif

69 **KEY CROSSING**
Ernest Hemingway Collection/
John F. Kennedy Presidential
Library and Museum, Boston
KEYWEST1928EH-N7251.tif

70 **OUT ON THE DOCKS**
Ernest Hemingway Collection/
John F. Kennedy Presidential
Library and Museum, Boston
EH8124P.tif

71 **PAULINE WITH PATRICK AND BUMBY**
Ernest Hemingway Collection/
John F. Kennedy Presidential
Library and Museum, Boston
SONSEH-N7303686.tif

72 **WITH DOS AND TARPON**
Ernest Hemingway Collection/
John F. Kennedy Presidential
Library and Museum, Boston
EH8128P.tif

73 HAVANA
Ernest Hemingway Collection/
John F. Kennedy Presidential
Library and Museum, Boston
CUBAEH-N1877.tif

74 WITH SIDNEY FRANKLIN
IN SPAIN
Ernest Hemingway Collection/
John F. Kennedy Presidential
Library and Museum, Boston
SPAIN1929EH-P4212.tif

75 WITH PAULINE AT 907
WHITEHEAD
Ernest Hemingway Collection/
John F. Kennedy Presidential
Library and Museum, Boston
KEYWESTEH-P5702.tif

76 ON THE ANITA AT SAN
FRANCISCO DOCKS
Ernest Hemingway Collection/
John F. Kennedy Presidential
Library and Museum, Boston
HAVANAEH-N1355.tif

77 NORDQUIST L-BAR-T ON
THE YELLOWSTONE
Ernest Hemingway Collection/
John F. Kennedy Presidential
Library and Museum, Boston
WYOMING1932EH-N1253.
tif

78 ELK HUNT RACKS
Ernest Hemingway Collection/
John F. Kennedy Presidential
Library and Museum, Boston
WYOMING1932EH-N5593.
tif

79 FISHING ABOARD THE
ANITA
Ernest Hemingway Collection/
John F. Kennedy Presidential
Library and Museum, Boston
ANITAEH-P9463.tif

80 WITH CHARLES
THOMPSON
Ernest Hemingway Collection/
John F. Kennedy Presidential
Library and Museum, Boston
HAVANAEH-P1350.tif

81 AT CASABLANCA DOCKS
Ernest Hemingway Collection/
John F. Kennedy Presidential
Library and Museum, Boston
HAVANAEH-N1302.tif

82 PAULINE'S RHINO KILL
Ernest Hemingway Collection/
John F. Kennedy Presidential
Library and Museum, Boston
EH7417P.tif

83 KUDU AND ORYX RACKS
Ernest Hemingway Collection/
John F. Kennedy Presidential
Library and Museum, Boston
EH6941P.tif

84 THE PILAR
Ernest Hemingway Collection/
John F. Kennedy Presidential
Library and Museum, Boston
PILAREH-P8300.tif

85 WITH PAULINE AND
ARNOLD SAMUELSON
Ernest Hemingway Collection/
John F. Kennedy Presidential
Library and Museum, Boston
HAVANAEH-P4532.tif

86 RECLASSIFYING MARLIN
Ernest Hemingway Collection/
John F. Kennedy Presidential
Library and Museum, Boston
PILAREH-N1331.tif

87 LUNCHEON ON THE PILAR
Ernest Hemingway Collection/
John F. Kennedy Presidential
Library and Museum, Boston
PILAREH-N1773.tif

88 WHALING
Ernest Hemingway Collection/
John F. Kennedy Presidential
Library and Museum, Boston
PILAREH-P8298.tif

89 PERFECTING TECHNIQUE
Ernest Hemingway Collection/
John F. Kennedy Presidential
Library and Museum, Boston
HAVANAEH-N1892.tif

90 WITH JANE MASON
Ernest Hemingway Collection/
John F. Kennedy Presidential
Library and Museum, Boston
EH1785N.tif

91 PILAR DOCKED
Ernest Hemingway Collection/
John F. Kennedy Presidential
Library and Museum, Boston
HAVANAEH-N1908.tif

92 FATHER-SON MOMENT
Ernest Hemingway Collection/
John F. Kennedy Presidential
Library and Museum, Boston
PILAREH-N1539.tif

93 WITH FRANKLIN AND
BLUE MARLIN TROPHY
Ernest Hemingway Collection/
John F. Kennedy Presidential
Library and Museum, Boston
HAVANAEH-N1893.tif

94 PILAR BELOW DECK
Ernest Hemingway Collection/
John F. Kennedy Presidential
Library and Museum, Boston
PILAREH-N1388.tif

95 CUBA
Ernest Hemingway Collection/
John F. Kennedy Presidential
Library and Museum, Boston
CUBAEH-N1881.tif

96 PILAR AND CROWD
Ernest Hemingway Collection/
John F. Kennedy Presidential
Library and Museum, Boston
HAVANAEH-N1888.tif

97 BIMINI BOUND
Ernest Hemingway Collection/
John F. Kennedy Presidential
Library and Museum, Boston
BIMINI1935EH-P8267.tif

98 REPUTED BRAWLER
Ernest Hemingway Collection/
John F. Kennedy Presidential
Library and Museum, Boston
BIMINI1935EH-P6942.tif

99 BOXING AFICIONADO
Ernest Hemingway Collection/
John F. Kennedy Presidential
Library and Museum, Boston
EH-3333P.tif

100 CAT CAY ARRIVAL
Ernest Hemingway Collection/
John F. Kennedy Presidential
Library and Museum, Boston
BIMINIEH-N1592.tif

101 SITTING FOR HAIRCUT
Ernest Hemingway Collection/
John F. Kennedy Presidential
Library and Museum, Boston
BIMINIEH-N5685.tif

102 DOZING
Ernest Hemingway Collection/
John F. Kennedy Presidential
Library and Museum, Boston
PILAREH-P6906.tif

103 WITH HENRY STRATER
Ernest Hemingway Collection/
John F. Kennedy Presidential
Library and Museum, Boston
EH8264P.tif

104 MAKO SHARK CATCH
Ernest Hemingway Collection/
John F. Kennedy Presidential
Library and Museum, Boston
BIMINI1935EH-N1570.tif

105 WITH MICHAEL LERNER
Ernest Hemingway Collection/
John F. Kennedy Presidential
Library and Museum, Boston
BIMINI1935EH-P7066.tif

106 AND NEW TOMMY GUN
Ernest Hemingway Collection/
John F. Kennedy Presidential
Library and Museum, Boston
BIMINI1935EH-P4392.tif

107 GUNNING FOR SHARKS
Ernest Hemingway Collection/
John F. Kennedy Presidential
Library and Museum, Boston
BIMINI1935EH-P5709.tif

108 AND SHARK JAWS
Ernest Hemingway Collection/
John F. Kennedy Presidential
Library and Museum, Boston
EH 4506P.tif

109 LABOR DAY HURRICANE
Ernest Hemingway Collection/
John F. Kennedy Presidential
Library and Museum, Boston
KEYWESTEH-P51081.tif

110 PORTRAIT OF THE MAN
Ernest Hemingway Collection/
John F. Kennedy Presidential
Library and Museum, Boston
PILAREH-P2832.tif

111 SPANISH CIVIL WAR
Ernest Hemingway Collection/
John F. Kennedy Presidential
Library and Museum, Boston
SCIVILWAREH-P5387.tif

112 WITH LOYALISTS
Ernest Hemingway Collection/
John F. Kennedy Presidential
Library and Museum, Boston
SCIVILWAREH-P5380.tif

113 CASUALTIES OF WAR
Ernest Hemingway Collection/
John F. Kennedy Presidential
Library and Museum, Boston
SCIVILWAREH-P5381.tif

114 FINCA POOLSIDE
Ernest Hemingway Collection/
John F. Kennedy Presidential
Library and Museum, Boston
CUBAEH-N1025.tif

116 WITH MARTHA GELLHORN
Ernest Hemingway Collection/
John F. Kennedy Presidential
Library and Museum, Boston
IDAHO1940EH-P5640.tif

117 **WITH LES AND MARTHA**
Ernest Hemingway Collection/
John F. Kennedy Presidential
Library and Museum, Boston
HAVANAEH-P5628.tif

118 **SON GREGORY, EDNA, AND MARTHA**
Ernest Hemingway Collection/
John F. Kennedy Presidential
Library and Museum, Boston
EUROPEEH-N1023.tif

119 **PADDLING SILVER CREEK WITH MARTHA**
Ernest Hemingway Collection/
John F. Kennedy Presidential
Library and Museum, Boston
IDAHO1940EH-P4834.tif

120 **IDAHO ANTELOPE KILL**
Ernest Hemingway Collection/
John F. Kennedy Presidential
Library and Museum, Boston
EH5659P (c)Arnold.tif

121 **WITH GIGI AT SILVER CREEK**
Ernest Hemingway Collection/
John F. Kennedy Presidential
Library and Museum, Boston
IDAHOEH-P4798.tif

122 **EN ROUTE TO HAWAII**
Ernest Hemingway Collection/
John F. Kennedy Presidential
Library and Museum, Boston
SINOJAPANESEWAREH-P4687.tif

123 **IN HONOLULU**
Ernest Hemingway Collection/
John F. Kennedy Presidential
Library and Museum, Boston
EH5594P.tif

124 **THE SEVENTH WAR ZONE**
Ernest Hemingway Collection/
John F. Kennedy Presidential
Library and Museum, Boston
SINOJAPANESEWAREH-P4646.tif

125 **BASKING IN CHINA**
Ernest Hemingway Collection/
John F. Kennedy Presidential
Library and Museum, Boston
EH5540P.tif

126 **BACK IN SUN VALLEY**
Ernest Hemingway Collection/
John F. Kennedy Presidential
Library and Museum, Boston
Photo: Lloyd Arnold
IDAHOEH-P5114.tif

127 **DUCK SHOOT OUTING**
Ernest Hemingway Collection/
John F. Kennedy Presidential
Library and Museum, Boston
Photo: Lloyd Arnold
EH5102P (c)Arnold.tif

128 **AT TRAIL CREEK CABIN**
Ernest Hemingway Collection/
John F. Kennedy Presidential
Library and Museum, Boston
IDAHO1941EH-P4801.tif

129 **GREGORY AND PAPA**
Ernest Hemingway Collection/
John F. Kennedy Presidential
Library and Museum, Boston
EUROPEEH-P2949.tif

130 **WAR CORRESPONDENT**
Ernest Hemingway Collection/
John F. Kennedy Presidential
Library and Museum, Boston
EH4475P.tif

131 **AT LONDON'S DORCHESTER HOTEL**
Ernest Hemingway Collection/
John F. Kennedy Presidential
Library and Museum, Boston
ALONE1944EH-P4934.tif

132 **LIBERATING PARIS**
Ernest Hemingway Collection/
John F. Kennedy Presidential
Library and Museum, Boston
WWII1944EH-P10039.tif

133 **WITH COLONEL LANHAM**
Ernest Hemingway Collection/
John F. Kennedy Presidential
Library and Museum, Boston
EH3749P.tif

134 **ON THE SIEGFRIED LINE**
Ernest Hemingway Collection/
John F. Kennedy Presidential
Library and Museum, Boston
WWII1944EH-P3746.tif

135 **WITH MARY, GRACIELA SÁNCHEZ, AND WINSTON GUEST**
Ernest Hemingway Collection/
John F. Kennedy Presidential
Library and Museum, Boston
CUBAEH-P5686.tif

136 **WITH PATRICK AND GREGORY AT THE FINCA**
Ernest Hemingway Collection/
John F. Kennedy Presidential
Library and Museum, Boston
EH2871P.tif

137 **AT SUN VALLEY, 1947**
Ernest Hemingway Collection/
John F. Kennedy Presidential
Library and Museum, Boston
IDAHO1947EH-P4972.tif

138 **WITH JANE RUSSELL**
Ernest Hemingway Collection/
John F. Kennedy Presidential
Library and Museum, Boston
IDAHOEH-P4925.tif

139 **AT THE HAVANA CLUB**
Ernest Hemingway Collection/
John F. Kennedy Presidential
Library and Museum, Boston
cubaEH-P4192.tif

140 **WITH PATRICK AND MARY**
Ernest Hemingway Collection/
John F. Kennedy Presidential
Library and Museum, Boston
CUBAEH-P8516.tif

141 **BLACK DOG**
Ernest Hemingway Collection/
John F. Kennedy Presidential
Library and Museum, Boston
EH-10226P.tif

142 **SWIMMING WITH SUNNY**
Ernest Hemingway Collection/
John F. Kennedy Presidential
Library and Museum, Boston
PILAREH-P4659.tif

143 **A TRUE LOVE**
Ernest Hemingway Collection/
John F. Kennedy Presidential
Library and Museum, Boston
pilarEH-P3232.tif

144 **NOSTALGIA**
Ernest Hemingway Collection/
John F. Kennedy Presidential
Library and Museum, Boston
EUROPEEH-N1402.tif

145 **LUCARDA SCULPTURE**
Ernest Hemingway Collection/
John F. Kennedy Presidential
Library and Museum, Boston
EUROPE1948EH-N2029.tif

146 **VENETIAN DUCK SHOOT**
Ernest Hemingway Collection/
John F. Kennedy Presidential
Library and Museum, Boston
EUROPEEH-P4425.tif

147 **WITH ADRIANA IVANCICH**
Ernest Hemingway Collection/
John F. Kennedy Presidential
Library and Museum, Boston
EUROPEEH-P4932.tif

148 **RISTORANTE**
Ernest Hemingway Collection/
John F. Kennedy Presidential
Library and Museum, Boston
EUROPEEH-P4912.tif

149 **BACK IN VENICE**
Ernest Hemingway Collection/
John F. Kennedy Presidential
Library and Museum, Boston
EUROPE1955EH-P3462.tif

150 **HOSTING ADRIANA**
Ernest Hemingway Collection/
John F. Kennedy Presidential
Library and Museum, Boston
EH4183P.tif

151 **UNDER THE PERGOLA**
Ernest Hemingway Collection/
John F. Kennedy Presidential
Library and Museum, Boston
CUBAEH-P8511.tif

152 **DOZING DREAMER**
Ernest Hemingway Collection/
John F. Kennedy Presidential
Library and Museum, Boston
EH3984P.tif

154 **PULITZER PRIZE WINNER**
Ernest Hemingway Collection/
John F. Kennedy Presidential
Library and Museum, Boston
CUBAEH-P3070.tif

155 **ENDORSING ALE**
Ernest Hemingway Collection/
John F. Kennedy Presidential
Library and Museum, Boston
EH-C717T.tif

156 **LIQUOR AND OLIVES**
Ernest Hemingway Collection/
John F. Kennedy Presidential
Library and Museum, Boston
Photo: George Leavens
CUBAEH-P7040.tif

157 **EN ROUTE TO SPAIN**
Ernest Hemingway Collection/
John F. Kennedy Presidential
Library and Museum, Boston
EH3111P.tif

158 **NEAR BURGOS, SPAIN, WITH ADAMO SIMON**
Ernest Hemingway Collection/
John F. Kennedy Presidential
Library and Museum, Boston
EH3243P.tif

159 OLD SPANISH HAUNTS
Ernest Hemingway Collection/
John F. Kennedy Presidential
Library and Museum, Boston
SPAIN1953EH-S2440.tif

160 ANOTHER SAFARI
Ernest Hemingway Collection/
John F. Kennedy Presidential
Library and Museum, Boston
AFRICAEH-T542.tif

161 NATIVE OBSESSION
Ernest Hemingway Collection/
John F. Kennedy Presidential
Library and Museum, Boston
AFRICAEH-S7492.tif

162 CAPE BUFFALO KILL
Ernest Hemingway Collection/
John F. Kennedy Presidential
Library and Museum, Boston
EH-C266T.tif

163 BOXING IN CAMP
Ernest Hemingway Collection/
John F. Kennedy Presidential
Library and Museum, Boston
AFRICAEH-S7572.tif

164 TWO PLANE CRASHES
Ernest Hemingway Collection/
John F. Kennedy Presidential
Library and Museum, Boston
AFRICAEH-P4463.tif

165 INVULNERABLE PAPA
Ernest Hemingway Collection/
John F. Kennedy Presidential
Library and Museum, Boston
AFRICAEH-P3650.tif

166 BOUNCING BACK
Ernest Hemingway Collection/
John F. Kennedy Presidential
Library and Museum, Boston
EH-C355T.tif

167 COSTA DEL SOL LUNCH
Ernest Hemingway Collection/
John F. Kennedy Presidential
Library and Museum, Boston
EH8864P.tif

168 INSIDE THE PILAR
Ernest Hemingway Collection/
John F. Kennedy Presidential
Library and Museum, Boston
EH-C222T.tif

169 AWARDED NOBEL PRIZE
Ernest Hemingway Collection/
John F. Kennedy Presidential
Library and Museum, Boston
NOBELPRIZE1954EH-
P3987.tif

170 WITH CUBANS AT
COJÍMAR, 1955
Ernest Hemingway Collection/
John F. Kennedy Presidential
Library and Museum, Boston
EH7324P.tif

171 CHECKING THE CATCH
Ernest Hemingway Collection/
John F. Kennedy Presidential
Library and Museum, Boston
EH1015S.tif

172 AT THE FLORIDITA
Ernest Hemingway Collection/
John F. Kennedy Presidential
Library and Museum, Boston
EH5084P.tif

173 AS TECHNICAL ADVISOR
Ernest Hemingway Collection/
John F. Kennedy Presidential
Library and Museum, Boston
FILMINGEH-P3067.tif

174 WITH SPENCER TRACY
AND GREGORIO FUENTES
Ernest Hemingway Collection/
John F. Kennedy Presidential
Library and Museum, Boston
FILMINGEH-P3228.tif

175 IN PERU, WITH MARLIN
Ernest Hemingway Collection/
John F. Kennedy Presidential
Library and Museum, Boston
EH2732P.tif

176 ON THE BRIDGE
Ernest Hemingway Collection/
John F. Kennedy Presidential
Library and Museum, Boston
PILAREH-P3076.tif

177 IN CALATAYUD, SPAIN
Ernest Hemingway Collection/
John F. Kennedy Presidential
Library and Museum, Boston
EH2437S.tif

178 RESPECTS TO BAROJA
Ernest Hemingway Collection/
John F. Kennedy Presidential
Library and Museum, Boston
EH6412P.tif

179 WITH MARY, AT HOME
Ernest Hemingway Collection/
John F. Kennedy Presidential
Library and Museum, Boston
CUBAEH-P7035.tif

180 WITH SERVICEMEN
Ernest Hemingway Collection/
John F. Kennedy Presidential
Library and Museum, Boston
FINCAVIGIAEH-P6650.tif

181 IN HIS LIBRARY
Ernest Hemingway Collection/
John F. Kennedy Presidential
Library and Museum, Boston
CUBAEH-P3068.tif

182 FLORIDITA DAIQUIRIS
Ernest Hemingway Collection/
John F. Kennedy Presidential
Library and Museum, Boston
HAVANAEH-P4969.tif

183 AT HAVANA BODEGA
WITH MARY
Ernest Hemingway Collection/
John F. Kennedy Presidential
Library and Museum, Boston
HAVANAEH-P8616.tif

184 IDAHO CHUKAR HUNT
Ernest Hemingway Collection/
John F. Kennedy Presidential
Library and Museum, Boston
IDAHO1959EH-PC6576.tif

185 MISTER OWL
Courtesy of Forrest MacMullen
Photo: A. E. Hotchner

186 WINTER IN KETCHUM
Ernest Hemingway Collection/
John F. Kennedy Presidential
Library and Museum, Boston
IDAHOEH-2923.tif

187 MAGPIE SHOOT
Ernest Hemingway Collection/
John F. Kennedy Presidential
Library and Museum, Boston
Photo: Lloyd Arnold
IDAHO1959EH-S2284.tif

188 WITH THE COOPERS
Ernest Hemingway Collection/
John F. Kennedy Presidential
Library and Museum, Boston
Photo: Lloyd Arnold
IDAHOEH-P4958.tif

189 WITH THE ARNOLDS
Ernest Hemingway Collection/
John F. Kennedy Presidential
Library and Museum, Boston
IDAHO1959EH-P8377.tif

190 DANGEROUS SUMMER
Ernest Hemingway Collection/
John F. Kennedy Presidential
Library and Museum, Boston
EUROPE1959EH-P5001.tif

191 BEHIND THE BARRERA
Ernest Hemingway Collection/
John F. Kennedy Presidential
Library and Museum, Boston
SPAINEH-P8774.tif

192 WITH ANNIE AND BILL
DAVIS AT LA CONSULA
Ernest Hemingway Collection/
John F. Kennedy Presidential
Library and Museum, Boston
SPAINEH-S2381.tif

193 IN MÁLAGA
Ernest Hemingway Collection/
John F. Kennedy Presidential
Library and Museum, Boston
SPAINEH-P2915.tif

194 WITH LAUREN BACALL
AND NANCY HAYWARD,
1959
Ernest Hemingway Collection/
John F. Kennedy Presidential
Library and Museum, Boston
LAURENBACALEH-P4474.
tif

195 60TH BIRTHDAY PARTY
Ernest Hemingway Collection/
John F. Kennedy Presidential
Library and Museum, Boston
Photo: Paco Cano
EH5920P.tif

196 WITH ANTONIO ORDÓÑEZ
Ernest Hemingway Collection/
John F. Kennedy Presidential
Library and Museum, Boston
EH2401S.tif

197 CHRISTMAS 1959
Courtesy of Forrest MacMullen
Photo: Lloyd Arnold
Christmas 1959.tif

198 BACK IN CUBA
Ernest Hemingway Collection/
John F. Kennedy Presidential
Library and Museum, Boston
CUBAEH-P3941.tif

199 FRIENDLESS
Ernest Hemingway Collection/
John F. Kennedy Presidential
Library and Museum, Boston
EH8504P.tif

200 WITH CASTRO
Provided by Landov Media
Photo: dpa/Landov Media
6749876.tif

201 NEAR THE END
Ernest Hemingway Collection/
John F. Kennedy Presidential
Library and Museum, Boston

Photo: Lloyd Arnold

IDAHOEH-P8385.tif

HISTORIC PHOTOS OF
ERNEST HEMINGWAY

When Ernest Hemingway won the 1954 Nobel Prize for Literature, presenters called him "one of this epoch's great molders of style," praising his vivid dialogue and journalistic eye for "robust details to accumulate and take on momentous significance."

But even the Swedish Academy could not separate Hemingway the writer from Hemingway the adventurer. They also cited his "manly love of danger and adventure, with a natural admiration for every individual who fights the good fight in a world of reality overshadowed by violence and death."

From the 1920s until his death in 1961, "Papa" Hemingway was a larger-than-life literary figure whose everyday exploits became legendary. He was a friend of celebrities, a war correspondent, journalist, renowned big-game hunter, record-setting saltwater angler, and hard-drinking brawler whose reputation preceded him.

Though Hemingway was and remains an American icon, he was also first and foremost a human being, as these striking black-and-white photos remind.

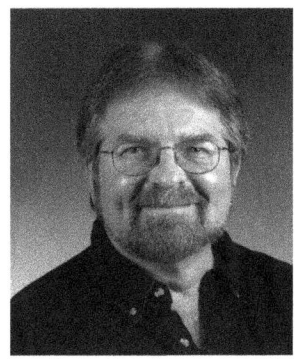

James Plath is the co-author of *Remembering Ernest Hemingway* (Ketch & Yawl Press, 1999) and former director of the Hemingway Days Writers' Workshop & Conference in Key West, Florida. A member of the Hemingway Society, he was invited twice to lecture at the Museo Ernest Hemingway, the author's former residence in Cuba. He is chair and Professor of English at Illinois Wesleyan University, where he received the university's highest teaching award in 2004.

WWW.TURNERPUBLISHING.COM

www.ingramcontent.com/pod-product-compliance
Lightning Source LLC
Chambersburg PA
CBHW052134170526
45162CB00003B/15